Snowflake Cookbook

Second Edition

Strategic and practical recipes for building governed, intelligent, AI-ready data platforms

Keith Belanger
Hamid Mahmood Qureshi
Hammad Sharif

<packt>

Snowflake Cookbook

Second Edition

Portfolio Director: Sunith Shetty
Relationship Lead: Puneet Kaur
Project Manager: Aniket Shetty
Content Engineer: Siddhant Jain
Technical Editor: Shweta Amale
Copy Editor: Siddhant Jain
Indexer: Manju Arasan
Proofreader: Siddhant Jain
Production Designer: Shankar Kalbhor
Growth Lead: Varun Nair

First published: February 2021
Second edition: June 2026

Production reference: 1140726

Published by Packt Publishing Ltd.
Grosvenor House
11 St Paul's Square
Birmingham
B3 1RB, UK.

ISBN 978-1-80638-477-8
www.packtpub.com

This book is dedicated to my wife, Jennifer.

Writing a book requires countless evenings, weekends, and moments that could have been spent together pursuing other interests and making memories. When I committed to writing this second edition, Jennifer understood the time and effort it would require and supported me throughout the journey with patience, encouragement, and understanding.

Thank you for your unwavering support, your belief in me, and for giving me the time and space needed to complete this project. This book would not have been possible without you.

— Keith Belanger

Foreword

> *It's always good to go over the recipe beforehand, so you can easily think of the next thing that needs to be done.*
>
> —*Guy Fieri, Diners, Drive-ins, & Dives*

So, you've decided to use Snowflake to build your enterprise data platform. Excellent choice!

Now what?

How do you get an account and log in? Where do you start? How do you build tables? Do you need a database and schema first? Where does the data come from (is there a data pantry)?

All very simple, reasonable questions. But wait, there's more!

Snowflake has evolved from the "data warehouse built for the cloud," to a "cloud data warehouse," then to "The Data Cloud," and now, "The AI Data Cloud."

With each of these evolutions, thanks to Snowflake's ***revolutionary*** and foundational *mutli-cluster, shared data architecture*, the capabilities, features, and functions of the product seem to just explode with every new release.

As a data architect, engineer, analyst, database administrator, CTO, CDO, or business owner, you now need to figure out which of these features your business can benefit from. And how to make them work efficiently and effectively.

That is where this book comes in. Keith is a world-renowned Snowflake Data Superhero (that means he is a legit expert) and a highly experienced architect, engineer, and consultant. With all of that knowledge and wisdom, he is giving you one of the easiest ways to familiarize yourself with Snowflake by providing this book of step-by-step recipes that guide you through all the major features and functions of Snowflake you need to know and understand so that you can build a data platform for your organization worthy of a 5-star review on YELP.

For each recipe, he guides you through the various tasks following a standard outline:

1. *Get ready* – prep steps (if needed)
2. *How to do it* – step by step instructions with all the code you need
3. *How it works* – explanation of the tools and code to build your understanding
4. *There's more* – more details, other options, more advanced things to investigate

With this approach, like a buffet line, you can skip around if you want to investigate tasks and features as you need them or are curious about them, and get a taste. Or, if you are completely new to Snowflake, read it from beginning to end to get the full picture. Then you can better determine what you will serve up for your Snowflake banquet.

The book is full of tips and tricks as well, hard-earned by Keith during all his real-world implementations. No matter what else you read, I highly recommend *Chapter 6, Performance and Cost Optimization*. While many things in Snowflake are way easier to use than legacy databases, the information in this chapter is critical to your long-term success and will ensure that you don't spend more money than you expected because of a nuance that you missed. The examples and explanations in *Chapter 6* are awesome.

While this book covers all the critical knowledge you need to begin building on Snowflake, *Chapter 11, Introduction to Snowflake Cortex,* covers the newest and hottest built-in AI features related to Snowflake Cortex. Even if your organization is not really ready to dive into data-driven AI, this chapter will help you start getting your head around the possibilities. But don't skip to the end; you need to have a handle on the basic ingredients first (from the earlier recipes) before you jump into all the AI stuff. Nobody should try to bake a soufflé before they master baking a cake first.

I know you will get great value from these recipes and enjoy dining at Café Snowflake.

So, let's get cookin'.

Kent Graziano,

The Data Warrior

Contributors

About the author

Keith Belanger is a seasoned data leader with three decades of experience helping organizations design, modernize, and optimize enterprise data platforms. Over the course of his career, he has served as a consultant, architect, practice leader, product evangelist, and executive advisor, guiding organizations through complex data transformation initiatives spanning cloud platforms, data warehousing, data governance, analytics, and artificial intelligence.

Keith is widely recognized within the data community as a Snowflake Data Superhero and is a frequent speaker at industry conferences, user groups, webinars, and community events. He regularly presents on topics such as Snowflake, data modeling, Data Vault 2.0, DataOps, cloud modernization, and the evolving role of data architecture in the age of AI.

Drawing on experience across both consulting and industry, Keith brings a practical perspective to the challenges organizations face when implementing and scaling modern data solutions. He is passionate about making complex technical concepts accessible and actionable, sharing his expertise through conference presentations, blogs, podcasts, videos, and community engagement, helping data professionals build stronger foundations and deliver greater value from their data investments.

Outside of work, Keith enjoys spending time with his family, mentoring members of the data community, and exploring emerging technologies that are shaping the future of data and analytics. He resides in New Hampshire with his wife, Jennifer. Together, they have three adult daughters, Madyson, Keiara, and Brittney, who continue to be a source of pride and inspiration in his life.

Writing a book is never a solo effort. While this second edition reflects countless hours of research, writing, testing, and revision, it has only been possible through the support and contributions of many people.

I would first like to acknowledge Hamid Mahmood Qureshi and Hammad Sharif, whose work on the first edition provided the foundation upon which this second edition was built. Their contributions helped establish the original Snowflake Cookbook and made this updated edition possible.

I would also like to thank Nick Halsey and Guy Adams at DataOps.live for their support, encouragement, and approval to undertake this project. I am especially grateful for providing access to the Snowflake account that was instrumental in developing, testing, and validating many of the examples and recipes contained throughout this book.

My sincere thanks also go to my fellow Snowflake Data Superheroes. The willingness of this community to share knowledge, challenge ideas, and support one another continues to inspire me. The relationships, discussions, and experiences I've gained through this community have played an important role in both my professional growth and the development of this book.

Throughout my nearly three decades in the data industry, I have been fortunate to work alongside many talented colleagues, mentors, customers, partners, and friends. Each of you has contributed in some way to my growth as a data professional. Whether through guidance, collaboration, encouragement, or simply sharing your expertise, you have helped shape the person I am today.

Finally, I would like to thank the Packt Publishing team, the technical reviewers, and everyone involved in bringing this second edition to life. Your professionalism, guidance, and attention to detail have been invaluable throughout this journey.

To everyone who has supported, encouraged, challenged, and inspired me over the years, thank you. This book is as much a reflection of your influence as it is my own work.

Hamid Qureshi is a senior cloud and data warehouse professional with almost two decades of total experience, having architected, designed, and led the implementation of several data warehouse and business intelligence solutions. He has extensive experience and certifications across various data analytics platforms, ranging from Teradata, Oracle, and Hadoop to modern, cloud-based tools such as Snowflake. Having worked extensively with traditional technologies, combined with his knowledge of modern platforms, he has accumulated substantial practical expertise in data warehousing and analytics in Snowflake, which he has subsequently captured in his publications.

Hammad Sharif is an experienced data architect with more than a decade of experience in the information domain, covering governance, warehousing, data lakes, streaming data, and machine learning. He has worked with a leading data warehouse vendor for a decade as part of a professional services organization, advising customers in telco, retail, life sciences, and financial industries located in Asia, Europe, and Australia during presales and post-sales implementation cycles. Hammad holds an MSc. in computer science and has published conference papers in the domains of machine learning, sensor networks, software engineering, and remote sensing.

About the reviewers

Maja Ferle is a Senior Data Architect with more than 30 years of experience in data analytics, data warehousing, data engineering, data modeling, and database administration. She holds the SnowPro Advanced: Architect, SnowPro Advanced: Data Engineer, SnowPro Specialty: Snowpark, and SnowPro Specialty: GenAI certifications. Recognized as both a Snowflake subject matter expert and a Snowflake Data Superhero, Maja has extensive experience designing and implementing modern cloud data platforms and enterprise data solutions. She is also the author of *Snowflake Data Engineering*.

Serge Gershkovich has nearly two decades of experience in data architecture and business intelligence. He currently serves as Head of Product at SqlDBM, is a Snowflake Data Superhero, and is the author of the bestselling book *Data Modeling with Snowflake*.

Table of Contents

Chapter 4: Building Data Pipelines in Snowflake 127

Chapter 5: Data Protection and Security in Snowflake 165

Chapter 6: Performance and Cost Optimization 199

Chapter 10: Extending Snowflake Capabilities 357

Chapter 11: Introduction to Snowflake Cortex 391

Chapter 12: Unlock Access to the Code Bundle and the PDF Version 423

Other Books You May Enjoy 428

Index 431

Preface

Snowflake has evolved from a modern cloud data warehouse into a comprehensive data platform that supports data engineering, analytics, data sharing, governance, machine learning, and AI-powered applications. Organizations increasingly rely on Snowflake to centralize data, build scalable pipelines, govern enterprise information, and accelerate insights while controlling costs and maintaining security.

This book provides practical, recipe-based solutions to help you build, operate, secure, and optimize modern data initiatives using Snowflake. Whether you are migrating from a traditional data warehouse, modernizing existing cloud architectures, or implementing new analytics and AI initiatives, this cookbook offers hands-on guidance based on real-world scenarios and proven practices.

The recipes in this book cover the full Snowflake journey. You will begin by learning the fundamentals of Snowflake architecture, connectivity, and administration. From there, you will explore data lifecycle management, data loading patterns, data pipelines, security, performance optimization, data sharing, Time Travel, advanced SQL techniques, extensibility, and Snowflake Cortex. Each chapter focuses on practical challenges commonly faced by data engineers, architects, administrators, analysts, and platform teams.

This second edition has been updated to reflect the modern Snowflake platform. Existing recipes have been revised to align with current Snowflake capabilities, interfaces, and best practices. New content has been added covering Dynamic Tables, governance enhancements, advanced SQL capabilities, Snowpark improvements, Cortex AI capabilities, and other platform innovations that have emerged since the first edition. The goal remains the same: to provide practical solutions that readers can immediately apply in their own Snowflake environments.

Who this book is for

This book is for data professionals who want to develop practical Snowflake skills through hands-on examples and real-world scenarios. It is particularly useful for:

- Data engineers building ingestion pipelines, transformations, and operational data workflows
- Data architects designing scalable, secure, and governed Snowflake environments

- Database administrators and platform engineers responsible for performance, security, and cost optimization
- Data analysts seeking to leverage Snowflake's analytical capabilities more effectively
- Technical leaders and consultants evaluating Snowflake best practices and implementation patterns

Readers should have a basic understanding of data warehousing concepts, SQL, and cloud computing fundamentals. Prior experience with Snowflake is helpful but not required.

What this book covers

Chapter 1, Getting Started with Snowflake, introduces the Snowflake architecture, virtual warehouses, connectivity options, and administrative fundamentals required to get started with the platform.

Chapter 2, Managing the Data Lifecycle, explores core database objects and data management techniques, including databases, schemas, tables, views, stages, and modern approaches to managing data throughout its lifecycle.

Chapter 3, Loading and Extracting Data Into and Out of Snowflake, demonstrates how to load structured and semi-structured data using a variety of techniques, including bulk loading, Snowpipe, and data unloading and extraction patterns.

Chapter 4, Building Data Pipelines in Snowflake, focuses on tasks, streams, Dynamic Tables, and other capabilities used to automate and orchestrate data processing pipelines.

Chapter 5, Data Protection and Security in Snowflake, covers role-based access control, user management, governance, data classification, masking, and techniques for securing enterprise data assets.

Chapter 6, Performance and Cost Optimization, examines warehouse sizing, query performance tuning, monitoring techniques, Query Acceleration Service, and strategies for managing Snowflake consumption efficiently.

Chapter 7, Secure Data Sharing, demonstrates how to securely share data with internal and external consumers through shares, listings, marketplaces, and reader accounts.

Chapter 8, Back to the Future with Time Travel, explores Time Travel, cloning, and recovery techniques that simplify troubleshooting and help protect against accidental data loss.

Chapter 9, Advanced SQL Techniques, introduces powerful SQL capabilities including advanced analytical functions, `QUALIFY`, user-defined data types, and other techniques that simplify complex data processing challenges.

Chapter 10, Extending Snowflake Capabilities, demonstrates how to extend Snowflake using user-defined functions, Snowpark, governance features, tagging, masking policies, and other advanced platform capabilities.

Chapter 11, Introduction to Snowflake Cortex, introduces AI and generative AI capabilities in Snowflake, including AI SQL functions, Cortex Analyst, Cortex Search, and Cortex-powered development workflows.

In writing this second edition, I wanted to share practical solutions drawn from real-world Snowflake implementations across organizations of varying sizes and industries. Every recipe is designed to solve a specific challenge that data teams commonly encounter while building and operating modern data platforms.

To get the most out of this book

To gain the maximum benefit from this cookbook, you should have a basic understanding of SQL, relational databases, data warehousing concepts, and cloud computing fundamentals. Familiarity with Snowflake is helpful but not required. Most recipes assume you have access to a Snowflake account and the ability to create databases, schemas, warehouses, and other objects required by the examples. Where specific roles or privileges are required, those prerequisites are identified within the individual recipes.

Many recipes use sample datasets provided by Snowflake, while others use downloadable assets included with the book's source code repository. You should also be comfortable executing SQL statements in Snowsight and navigating common Snowflake administrative functions. Although the recipes are organized by topic, the book follows a traditional cookbook format, allowing you to work through the chapters sequentially or jump directly to recipes that address your immediate challenges and use cases.

Download the example code files

This book includes a complete downloadable code bundle containing all the example projects and files used throughout the chapters. We recommend downloading the bundle so you can follow along smoothly and experiment with the examples.

Use the bundle as a practical starting point. Modify it, extend it, and apply what you learn by creating your own variations as you progress through the chapters.

Get the code bundle

If you bought the book directly from Packt:

1. Go to `packtpub.com`.
2. Click your **profile picture** and select **Your Orders**.
3. Find this book and click **Download Code**.

If you bought this book from Amazon or any other channel partner:

1. Go to `packtpub.com/unlock` or scan the following QR code:
2. Search for this book.
3. Sign up or log in to your free Packt account.
4. Upload your proof of purchase and download the code bundle locally.

Usage note: You're free to use and modify this code for personal learning and non-commercial projects.

Conventions used

There are a number of text conventions used throughout this book.

`CodeInText`: Indicates code words in text, database table names, folder names, filenames, file extensions, pathnames, dummy URLs, user input, and Twitter handles. For example: "We will use the `to_date` function to convert the string value into a valid date format."

A block of code is set as follows:

```
CREATE DATABASE C9_R1;
CREATE TABLE c9r1_date_test (date_id INTEGER, date_value DATE);
INSERT INTO c9r1_date_test (date_id, date_value)
Values
(1, to_date('2019-12-19','YYYY-MM-DD'));
```

Any command-line input or output is written as follows:

```
USE WAREHOUSE DEFAULT_WH;
USE DATABASE SNOWFLAKE_SAMPLE_DATA;
USE SCHEMA TPCDS_SF10TCL;
```

Bold: Indicates a new term, an important word, or words that you see on the screen. For instance, words in menus or dialog boxes appear in the text like this. For example: "In the **System Properties** window, open the **Advanced** tab and click **Environment Variables**."

> **Note**
>
> Warnings or important notes appear like this.

> **Tip**
>
> Tips and tricks appear like this.

Free benefits with your book

This book includes free benefits designed to support your learning and help you apply what you learn effectively. Activate them now for instant access (see the *How to unlock* section for instructions).

Here's a quick overview of what you can instantly unlock with your purchase:

Complete Code Bundle

Download the full source code for this book's examples and projects.

DRM-Free PDF Version

Download DRM-free PDF and ePub copies of this book.

7-Day Packt Library Access

Get 7-day unlimited access to 8,000+ books and videos. No credit card required.

Available for first-time Packt+ trial users only.

Next-Gen Reader Access

Read this book on Packt Reader with progress sync, dark mode and note-taking.

How to unlock

Scan the QR code (or go to `packtpub.com/unlock`). Search for this book by name, confirm the edition, and then follow the steps on the page.

UNLOCK NOW

Note: Have your invoice handy. Purchases made directly from the Packt website don't require an invoice.

Get in touch

Feedback from our readers is always welcome.

General feedback: If you have questions about any aspect of this book or have any general feedback, please email us at `customercare@packt.com` and mention the book's title in the subject of your message.

Errata: Although we have taken every care to ensure the accuracy of our content, mistakes do happen. If you have found a mistake in this book, we would be grateful if you reported this to us. Please visit `http://www.packt.com/submit-errata`, click **Submit Errata**, and fill in the form.

Piracy: If you come across any illegal copies of our works in any form on the internet, we would be grateful if you would provide us with the location address or website name. Please contact us at `copyright@packt.com` with a link to the material.

If you are interested in becoming an author: If there is a topic that you have expertise in and you are interested in either writing or contributing to a book, please visit `http://authors.packt.com/`.

Share your thoughts

Once you've read *Snowflake Cookbook, Second Edition* we'd love to hear your thoughts! Scan the QR code below to go straight to the Amazon review page for this book and share your feedback.

https://packt.link/r/1806384779

Your review is important to us and the tech community and will help us make sure we're delivering excellent quality content.

1

Getting Started with Snowflake

Snowflake is the AI Data Cloud, a unified platform for AI, data, and analytics. It combines the capabilities of a traditional data warehouse, data lake, and data lakehouse into a single, governed environment that spans multiple public clouds and regions.

Snowflake delivers the scalability and flexibility of the cloud while enabling you to work with data using SQL, Python, and other languages through features such as Snowpark, Streamlit, and Cortex. This makes it possible not only to analyze data but also to develop data pipelines, applications, and AI solutions directly within the platform.

In this chapter, you will learn how to set up your Snowflake environment and how to connect to your Snowflake account using both the modern Snowsight web interface and command-line tools. You'll begin by provisioning a Snowflake trial account, creating your first virtual warehouse, and executing simple queries to become familiar with the interface. You'll then explore how to connect to Snowflake programmatically using the SnowSQL client and the Snowflake JDBC driver, and finally, you'll learn how to create administrative users and understand Snowflake's built-in roles. By the end of this chapter, you'll have a fully functional Snowflake environment and a foundational understanding of how to interact with it through code.

The following recipes will be covered in this chapter:

- Creating a new Snowflake account
- Using Snowsight and creating a tailored multi-cluster virtual warehouse
- Using Snowsight and executing a query
- Using SnowSQL to connect to Snowflake
- Connecting to Snowflake with JDBC
- Creating a new account administrator user and understanding built-in roles

Let's get started!

> Note
>
> **Your purchase includes a free PDF copy + exclusive extras**
>
> Your purchase includes a DRM-free PDF copy of this book, 7-day trial to the Packt+ library (no credit card required), and additional exclusive extras. See the *Free benefits with your book* section in the *Preface* to unlock them instantly and maximize your learning.

Technical requirements

For this chapter, you will need access to a modern internet browser such as Google Chrome, Microsoft Edge, or Mozilla Firefox, along with an active internet connection to provision and connect to your Snowflake account in the cloud. You will begin by provisioning a Snowflake trial account, which provides 30 days of free access and usage credits for completing the exercises in this chapter. If you already have access to an organizational Snowflake account, you can also use that environment, provided you have the necessary administrative privileges.

Since you will be installing the SnowSQL command-line client, administrative access on your local machine will be required. In addition to SnowSQL, you should have Java 11 (or later) and Apache Maven 3.6 (or later) installed to compile and run the **Java Database Connectivity (JDBC)** connectivity examples included in this chapter. Maven automatically downloads the Snowflake JDBC driver dependency from Maven Central when the project is built, eliminating the need for manual driver installation.

If you are using a corporate Snowflake environment, authentication may be managed through your organization's **single sign-on (SSO)** or OAuth provider, depending on how access is configured.

You can download the example project and code for this book by following the instructions in the ***Download the example code files*** section in the *Preface* of this book

Creating a new Snowflake account

There are a few key decisions that you need to make when setting up a new Snowflake account through the Snowflake sign-up page at `https://signup.snowflake.com`. You'll choose your preferred Snowflake Edition and the cloud provider and region where your account will reside. These selections determine the initial configuration of your account and the location of your data within the Snowflake AI Data Cloud.

Getting ready

Before starting this process, have your contact details (name, business email address, company name, and country) ready, as you'll need them during the sign-up process. Your email address will be used to send the activation link for your Snowflake account, so ensure it is entered correctly. You don't need payment information at this stage. After the trial period ends, you can convert your account to a paid plan and continue working without losing any data or configurations.

If you're creating a Snowflake account as part of a company or enterprise, confirm whether your company already has a Snowflake Organization. If it does, you may be asked to create your new account under that organization to enable centralized governance and billing.

How to do it...

The steps for this recipe are as follows:

1. Let's start by creating a Snowflake account. Snowflake provides a simple, browser-based sign-up process for new users. The sign-up page offers a 30-day free Snowflake trial, which includes $400 worth of free usage to explore the platform and its capabilities before upgrading to a paid plan.
2. Navigate to the Snowflake trial account landing page at `https://signup.snowflake.com`. Fill out the required fields on the form, including your name, company, business email, and country, then click **Continue** at the bottom of the form to proceed.

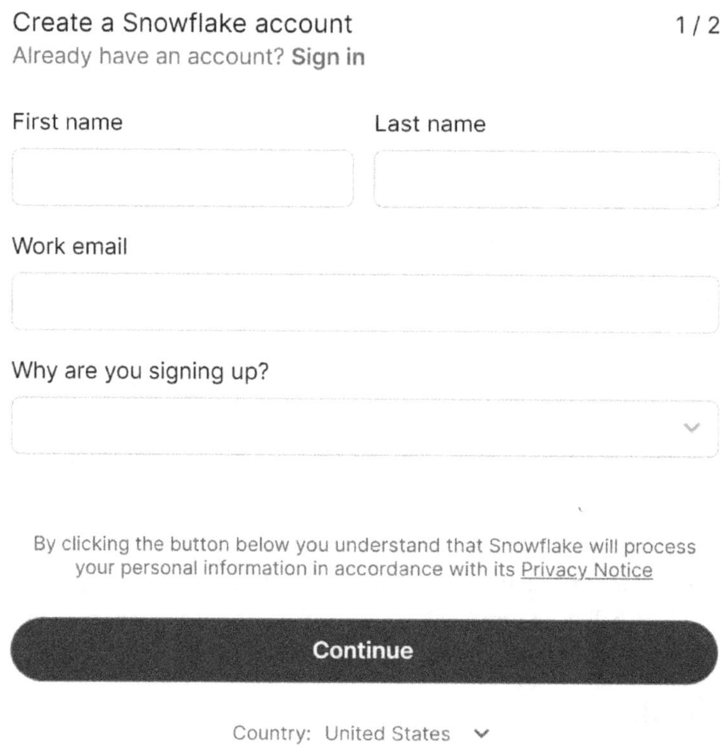

Figure 1.1 – Snowflake free trial registration form

3. On the next page, complete the form to finish setting up your account. Enter your company name and job title, then choose your Snowflake edition, cloud provider, and region:
   - **Choose your Snowflake edition:** Select from **Standard**, **Enterprise (Most popular)**, or **Business Critical**. The Enterprise edition is recommended for most users because it includes multi-cluster virtual warehouses and extended time-travel features.
   - **Choose your cloud provider**: Select the platform where your data and workloads primarily reside (**Microsoft Azure**, **Amazon Web Services**, or **Google Cloud Platform**)
   - **Region:** Pick the region closest to your users or data sources for the best performance and lowest latency.

   Check the box to accept the **Snowflake Self-Service On Demand Terms**, and then click **Get started** to begin provisioning your account.

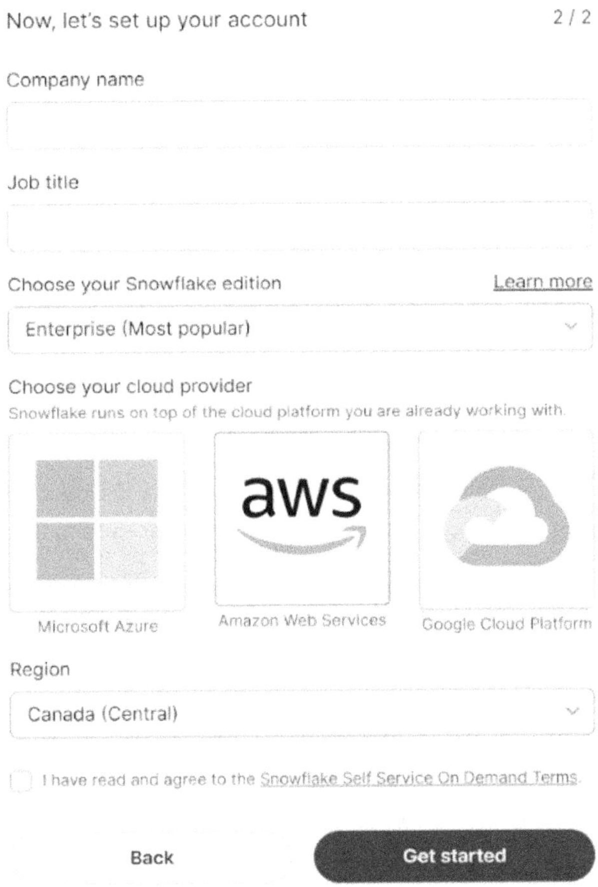

Figure 1.2 – Snowflake free trial registration form

4. You may be prompted to complete a CAPTCHA verification before continuing. Follow the on-screen instructions (for example, selecting images that match a description), then click **Next** to proceed.
5. On the next screen, Snowflake will ask how you plan to use your account. This step helps Snowflake personalize your experience but is optional. You can select one or more of the listed options, for example, **loading data, building applications, training machine learning models**, or **using Snowflake Cortex AI** and then click **Continue**, or click **Skip** to proceed without answering.
6. You'll then be asked to select your preferred programming language(s) to work in. Choose from options such as Python, Scala, Java, or SQL, or select Other to specify a different language. This step is optional and is used by Snowflake for onboarding and

personalization purposes only; it does not affect your ability to use any language later. If you don't have coding experience, you can check the I don't have coding experience option. When finished, click **Submit** or **Skip** to continue.

7. After submitting your selections, Snowflake begins provisioning your account. You'll briefly see a **Setting up your account** message, followed by a confirmation screen that reads **Check your inbox!**.
8. Snowflake sends an activation email to the address you provided. Open the email and click the **Click to Activate** button to complete your account setup. This activation link is temporary and expires after 72 hours, so be sure to activate your account promptly.
9. Once activated, you'll be redirected to your new Snowflake account, accessible through your unique login URL, which follows this pattern: `https://<account_identifier>.snowflakecomputing.com/console/login`.
10. On this initial screen, you will be prompted to enter the username and password you created during sign-up. These credentials will be used for subsequent logins to your Snowflake account.
11. The first user created during sign-up is automatically granted the ACCOUNTADMIN role, which provides full administrative privileges within the account.

How it works...

Snowflake provides a fully managed service that abstracts away the infrastructure of the underlying cloud provider. Unlike other cloud solutions that require you to deploy and manage database resources directly within AWS, Azure, or Google Cloud, Snowflake provisions your environment automatically as part of the AI Data Cloud.

Each account exists within a Snowflake Organization, which serves as the top-level account for managing multiple accounts, centralized billing, governance, and data sharing across your enterprise. When you create a trial or production account, Snowflake automatically assigns it to an organization and provisions the necessary compute and storage resources behind the scenes.

Every Snowflake account is accessible through a unique URL based on its account locator and cloud region. The general format follows this pattern: `https://<account_locator>.<cloud_region_id>.<cloud>.snowflakecomputing.com`.

Depending on the cloud platform and region in which your account is hosted, some segments may be optional. For example:

- In certain AWS regions, only the account locator is required: `https://<account_locator>.<cloud_region_id>.<cloud>.snowflakecomputing.com`
- In other regions, the cloud region and cloud provider must also be included: `https://xy12345.us-east-2.aws.snowflakecomputing.com`

This structured format ensures that your login URL uniquely identifies your Snowflake account across different cloud providers (Microsoft Azure, Amazon Web Services, or Google Cloud Platform) and geographical regions. Because Snowflake handles infrastructure management, scaling, and optimization automatically, you never need to interact with the underlying cloud provider to use your account. However, selecting the same cloud provider and region where your data and applications already reside can reduce data transfer costs and improve latency performance.

Using Snowsight and creating a tailored multi-cluster virtual warehouse

A virtual warehouse is Snowflake's compute engine. It provides the processing power required to execute SQL queries, load data, and perform transformations. Unlike traditional database systems where storage and compute are tightly coupled, Snowflake separates compute from storage. This means multiple virtual warehouses can access the same underlying data independently, allowing different workloads, such as reporting, data engineering, and data science, to run concurrently without resource contention.

Creating a standard virtual warehouse is straightforward, but configuring one for optimal scalability and performance requires a few additional steps. In this recipe, you'll use Snowsight, Snowflake's modern web interface, to create and configure a multi-cluster virtual warehouse that automatically scales up and down based on query demand. You'll also adjust parameters to handle higher concurrency while balancing cost efficiency, all within Snowsight's workspaces.

Getting ready

You should have received a link to your Snowflake account in your account activation email. Keep this link, along with your username and password, handy so you can log in to Snowsight, Snowflake's modern web interface.

To create a multi-cluster virtual warehouse, your account must be running Enterprise Edition or higher. If you attempt to configure multi-cluster settings using Standard Edition, Snowflake will return an error indicating that the feature is not available.

You will also need the SYSADMIN role or higher, as this role (and the ACCOUNTADMIN role above it) has the privileges required to create and manage virtual warehouses.

Snowsight is Snowflake's browser-based interface for managing and interacting with your account. While its layout may evolve over time, its core capabilities remain consistent. Through Snowsight, you can navigate account resources such as databases, schemas, and compute objects, create and manage virtual warehouses, write and execute SQL queries, view and analyze query results, monitor workloads and usage, and administer account-level settings.

The interface is designed around a central workspace for developing and exploring data, along with navigation elements that provide access to account resources and administrative features. Although specific icons, menu placements, and pane layouts may change as Snowflake continues to enhance the experience, the fundamental workflow—navigate, create, query, and monitor—remains the same.

How to do it...

The steps for this recipe are as follows:

1. Open Snowsight, and sign in to your Snowflake account using your account URL. You'll be taken to Snowsight, Snowflake's modern web interface for managing databases, warehouses, and queries. Snowsight replaces the legacy Classic Console and provides a more intuitive experience with navigation, query editing, and performance monitoring built directly into the browser.
2. In the left-hand navigation menu, select **Projects** > **Workspaces**.

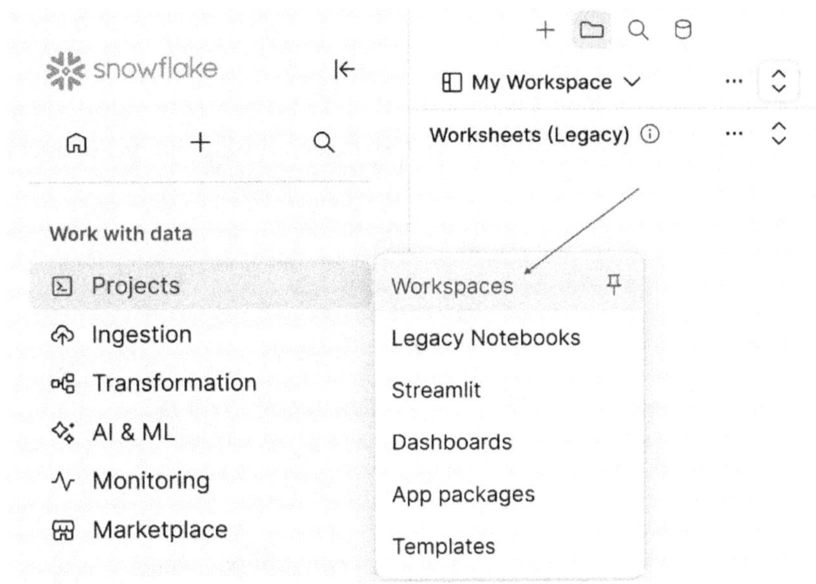

Figure 1.3 – Snowsight Projects menu

3. In the Editor pane, click **+ Add new** to add a new SQL file editor.

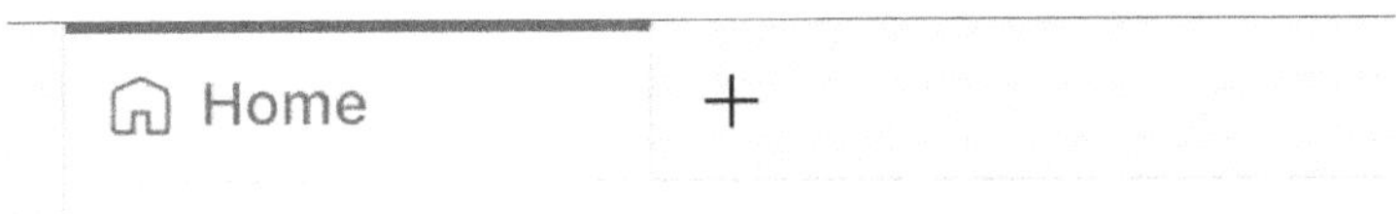

Figure 1.4 – Snowsight editor pane

4. Switch your role to SYSADMIN. You can do this in two ways:
   - From the top-right above the editor, click the current role (it may be set to ACCOUNTADMIN) and a pop-up will appear where you can select SYSADMIN.

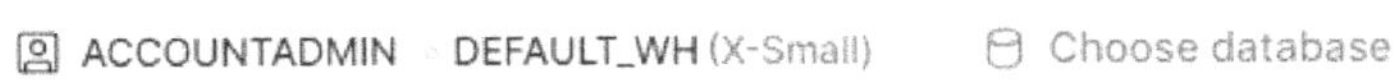

Figure 1.5 – Editor role and virtual warehouse selectors

   - Or, type the following SQL command in the SQL editor and click the blue Play button in the upper-right area above the worksheet to execute it:

```
USE ROLE SYSADMIN;
```

To verify your active role, run:

```
SELECT CURRENT_ROLE();
```

The result should display SYSADMIN, confirming that the correct role is active.

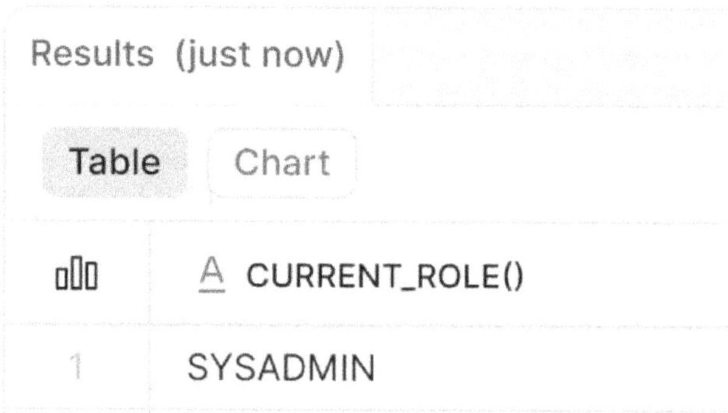

Figure 1.6 – CURRENT_ROLE results

5. Create a virtual warehouse that can auto-scale between one and three clusters, depending on the demand:

```
CREATE WAREHOUSE ELT_WH
WAREHOUSE_SIZE = XSMALL
MAX_CLUSTER_COUNT = 3
MIN_CLUSTER_COUNT = 1
SCALING_POLICY = ECONOMY
AUTO_SUSPEND = 300 -- suspend after 5 minutes (300 seconds) of inactivity
AUTO_RESUME = TRUE
INITIALLY_SUSPENDED = TRUE
COMMENT = 'Virtual warehouse for ETL
workloads. Auto scales between 1 and 3 clusters depending on the workload'
```

This command creates a warehouse named `ELT_WH` that will automatically add or remove clusters based on workload demand. It also suspends after 5 minutes of inactivity to optimize cost.

6. After the command is completed, verify that the warehouse was created successfully:

```
SHOW WAREHOUSES LIKE 'ELT_WH';
```

You should see the new warehouse listed with its current state (**SUSPENDED**) and configuration details.

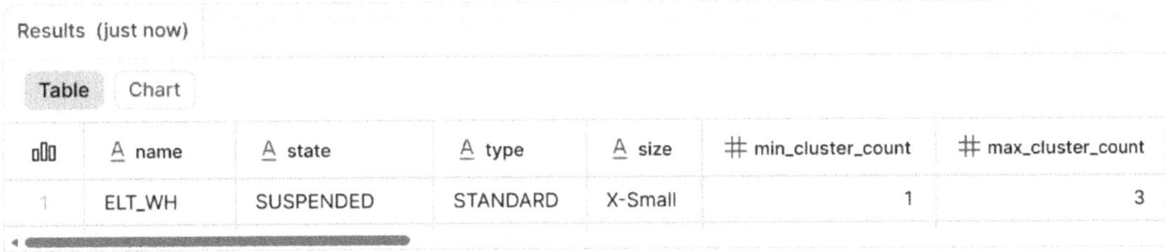

Results (just now)

Table Chart

	name	state	type	size	min_cluster_count	max_cluster_count
1	ELT_WH	SUSPENDED	STANDARD	X-Small	1	3

Figure 1.7 – Show warehouse results

How it works...

Setting `MIN_CLUSTER_COUNT` and `MAX_CLUSTER_COUNT` to different values ensures that the multi-cluster virtual warehouse starts with a number of clusters equal to `MIN_CLUSTER_COUNT` initially. If the number of concurrent queries exceeds the warehouse's capacity and queries begin to queue, Snowflake automatically adds clusters up to the value specified by `MAX_CLUSTER_COUNT`.

Setting `SCALING_POLICY` to `ECONOMY` (as opposed to `STANDARD`) ensures that additional clusters are started only when there are enough queries to keep them active for at least six minutes. This helps balance performance and cost efficiency.

Finally, the `AUTO_SUSPEND` setting ensures that the warehouse is suspended automatically after 300 seconds (or 5 minutes) of inactivity, and `AUTO_RESUME` allows it to start again automatically when new queries are submitted.

There's more...

The size of a warehouse in Snowflake determines the number of compute nodes (or clusters) that make up its capacity. Larger warehouses contain more nodes and therefore provide more compute power, which can improve performance for complex or large-scale queries.

However, bigger isn't always better. Some queries benefit from additional compute, while others may not. The best practice is to start with a smaller size and gradually increase it until you reach a point where no additional performance improvement is observed.

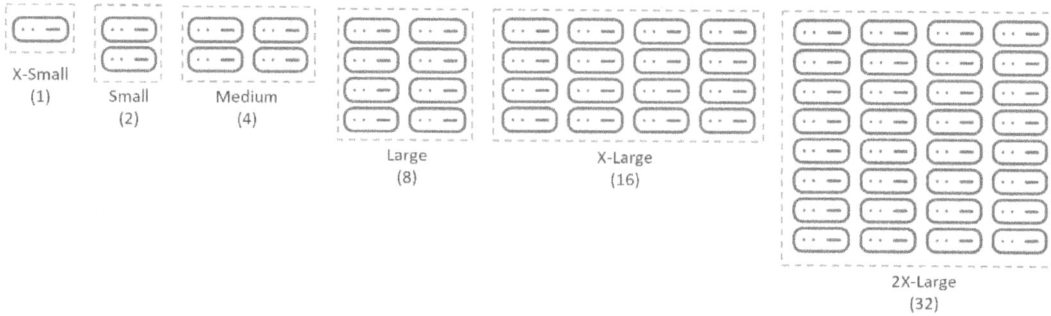

Figure 1.8 – Virtual warehouses' (relative) sizes in terms of nodes

Snowflake currently offers warehouse sizes ranging from X-SMALL to 6X-LARGE, with additional custom configurations available for specialized workloads.

Warehouse size	# Nodes
X-Small	1
Small	2
Medium	4
Large	8
X-Large	16
2X-Large	32
3X-Large	64
4X-Large	128
5X-Large	256
6X-Large	512

Table 1.1 – Virtual warehouses' (relative) sizes in terms of nodes

Virtual warehouses are the compute engines of a Snowflake account. You can create multiple warehouses within the same account, each configured with different sizes and settings to meet specific workload needs.

Warehouses can be suspended automatically when not in use and resumed on demand as soon as a new query arrives. This allows Snowflake to optimize credit consumption by ensuring compute resources are active only when needed.

This flexibility enables near-infinite scalability, you can assign different warehouses to specific workloads, teams, or users and size each one dynamically based on performance and cost requirements.

Figure 1.9 illustrates how different workload types can be supported by virtual warehouses of varying sizes and configurations. In this example, smaller warehouses are used for administrative and BI workloads, while larger and multi-cluster warehouses handle ad hoc analytics and data science use cases. Each warehouse accesses the same underlying data, enabling concurrent workloads without resource contention.

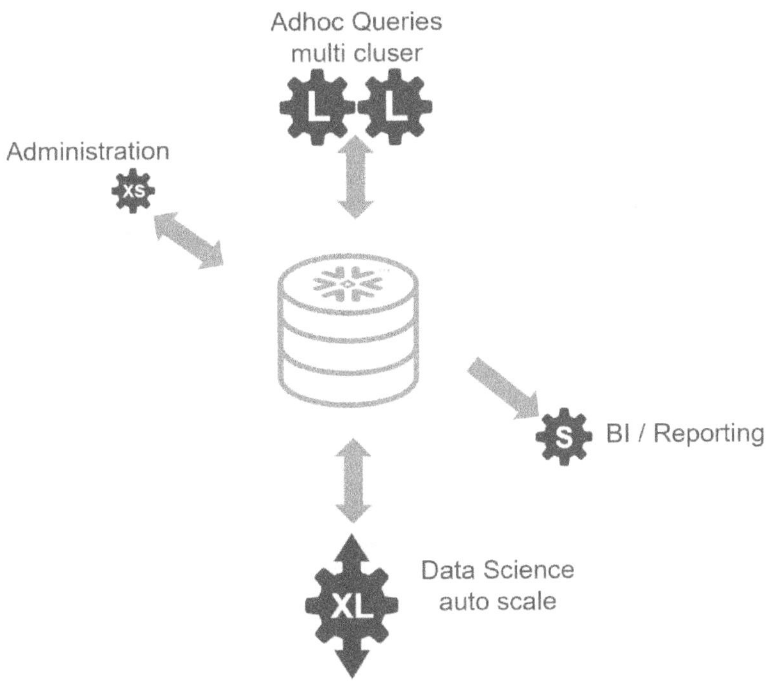

Figure 1.9 – Virtual warehouse size and uses

We'll explore warehouse management and optimization in more detail in *Chapter 6, Performance and Cost Optimization*.

All new Snowflake accounts now use Generation 2 (Standard Gen 2) warehouses by default. Gen 2 is built on faster hardware and optimized software, providing better overall performance for analytics and data-engineering workloads, especially for `DELETE`, `UPDATE`, `MERGE`, and large scan operations.

Snowpark-optimized warehouses remain a separate option, tuned for Python, machine-learning, and Snowpark workloads. You can switch between standard and Snowpark-optimized types using the `WAREHOUSE_TYPE` and `RESOURCE_CONSTRAINT` clauses.

Using Snowsight and executing a query

In this recipe, you'll learn how to connect to your Snowflake database using Snowsight, create a new SQL workspace, and execute your first query against a sample database.

Getting ready

You should already be logged in to your Snowflake account through the Snowsight interface from the previous recipe. If you've signed out, use the activation link from your welcome email to sign in with your username and password.

How to do it...

The steps for this recipe are as follows:

1. In the left-hand navigation menu, select **Projects** > **Workspaces**.

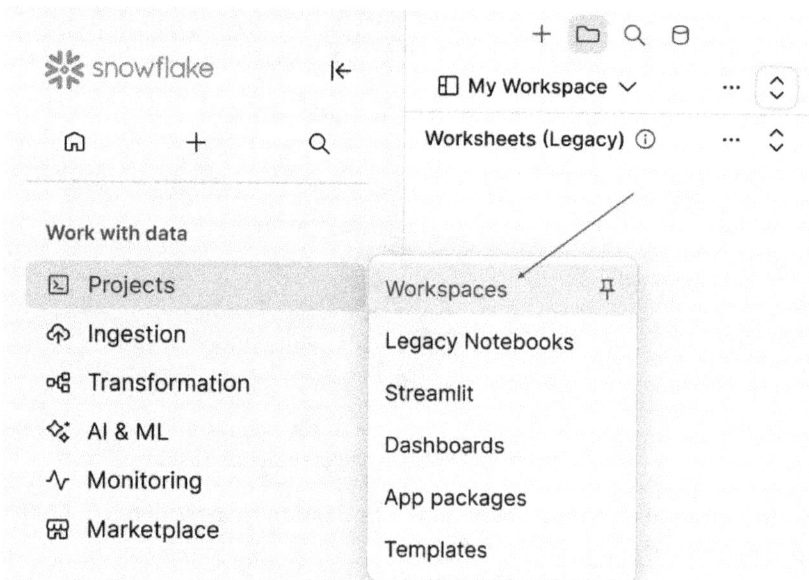

Figure 1.10 – Snowsight Projects menu

2. In the Editor pane, click **+** to add a new SQL file editor

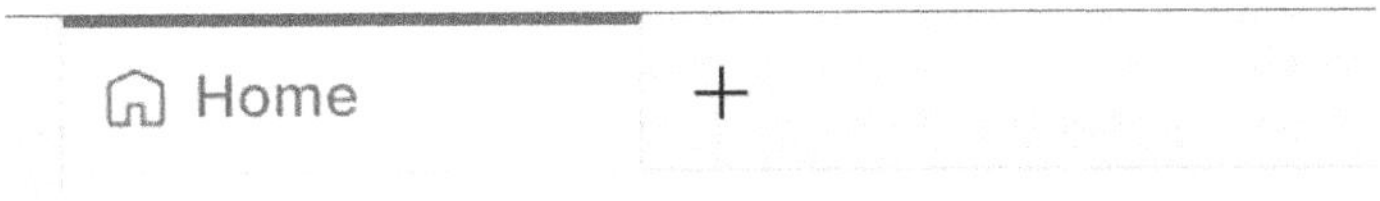

Figure 1.11 – Snowsight editor pane

3. From the top-right above the editor, click the current role (it may be set to ACCOUNTADMIN) and a pop-up will appear where you can select SYSADMIN.

Figure 1.12 – Editor role and virtual warehouse selectors

4. In the new editor, enter the following sql to create a new database.

```
CREATE DATABASE COOKBOOK;
```

You should see a success message:

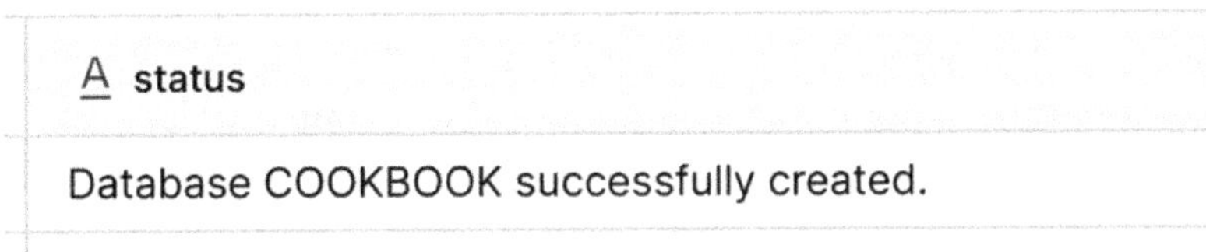

Figure 1.13 – Database created success message

5. Create a new table in this newly created database by running the following SQL statement.
If you have not explicitly selected or created a schema, Snowflake will use the current active schema. In newly created databases, this is typically the `PUBLIC` schema unless another schema has been selected using `USE SCHEMA`.

```
USE DATABASE COOKBOOK;
CREATE OR REPLACE TABLE MY_FIRST_TABLE
(
    ID STRING,
    NAME STRING
);
```

> **Note**
>
> Table **Data Definition Language** (**DDL**) in Snowflake now supports declarative DDL, allowing you to define objects based on their desired end state. We'll explore this in more detail in *Chapter 2, Managing Data Lifecycle*.

6. Query the newly created table by running a simple `SELECT` query. You will get zero rows as a result as there is no data in the table, but the query should run successfully:

```
SELECT * FROM MY_FIRST_TABLE;
```

How it works...

Snowsight is the central interface for querying and managing your Snowflake account. The options and objects you see depend on the role you have selected, and the privileges associated with that role.

Each Workspace (formerly called a Worksheet) can maintain its own context, including a specific role, virtual warehouse, database, and schema. This context determines where and how your queries run. To execute a query successfully, you must select a valid role and an active warehouse, and then choose the database and schema that contain your target tables.

You can also fully qualify object names when querying across multiple databases or schemas in a single statement, for example: `SELECT * FROM <database_name>.<schema_name>.<table_name>;`.

Using SnowSQL to connect to Snowflake

We looked at how Snowflake's Snowsight interface allows you to connect to, manage, and query data stored in Snowflake. In this recipe, you'll learn how to install Snowflake's command-line interface, Snowflake CLI, and use it to connect to your Snowflake account. You'll see how to configure connectivity and run queries directly from the terminal.

Getting ready

This recipe assumes you are using a Windows machine and have access to the Snowsight interface through a compatible web browser. Google Chrome or Microsoft Edge are recommended, as Snowflake tests Snowsight extensively against both.

Since SnowSQL is the command-line interface for Snowflake, you'll need command-line access to your operating system with administrative privileges to install the software.

Snowflake provides official SnowSQL installers for all major operating systems, including:

- Windows (installer)
- macOS (installer or Homebrew cask)
- Linux (installer or RPM package)

You can find the most up-to-date installation options in the Snowflake documentation: `https://docs.snowflake.com/en/user-guide/snowsql-install-config#installing-snowsql-on-microsoft-windows-using-the-installer`.

How to do it...

The steps for this recipe are as follows:

1. Go to the official Snowflake page for SnowSQL Download:`https://www.snowflake.com/en/developers/downloads/snowsql/`. Download the Windows installer and follow the on-screen prompts to complete the setup.

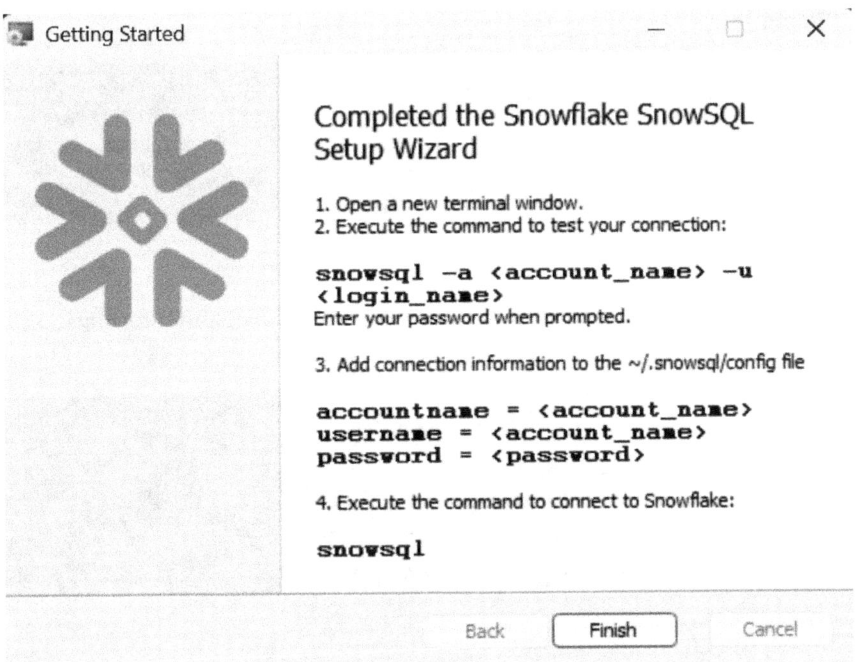

Figure 1.14 – Snowflake SnowSQL setup wizard

2. To verify the installation, open Command Prompt or PowerShell and run:

```
snowsql -v
```

This displays the installed version number, confirming that SnowSQL was installed successfully.

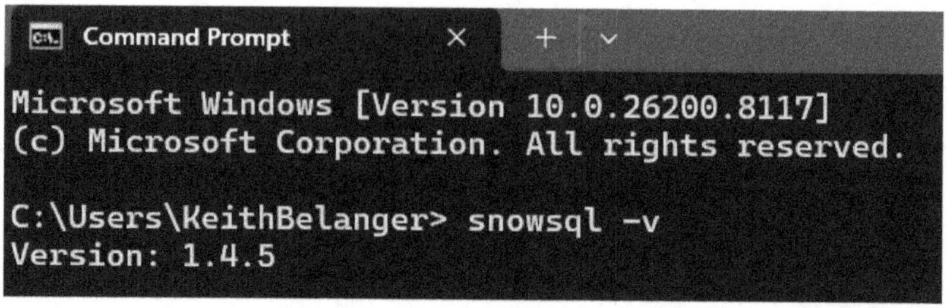

Figure 1.15 – SnowSQL version number

3. To connect to your Snowflake account, run the following command:

```
snowsql -a <account_identifier> -u <username>
```

Example:

```
snowsql -a IFZJGKM-DOL_KEITH_LAB_KRXBTD -u KBELANGER

account_identifier = IFZJGKM-DOL_KEITH_LAB_KRXBTD
username = KBELANGER
```

You'll be prompted to enter your password.

4. After successful authentication, SnowSQL displays version information and your connection prompt:

```
C:\Users\KeithBelanger>snowsql -a IFZJGKM-DOL_KEITH_LAB_KRXBTD -u KBELANGER
Password:
* SnowSQL * v1.4.5
Type SQL statements or !help
KBELANGER#DEFAULT_WH@(no database).(no schema)>
```

Note

If you're having trouble finding your account information, click your username in the lower-left corner of Snowsight as shown in *Figure 1.16*.

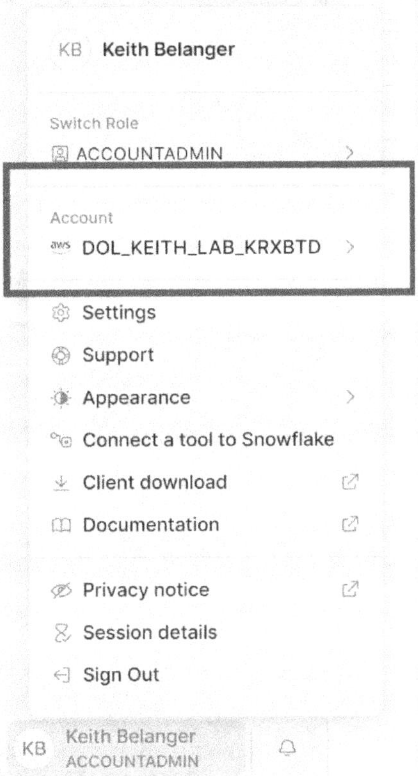

Figure 1.16 – Account information

5. You can now execute commands such as:

```
SELECT CURRENT_VERSION();

+-------------------+
| CURRENT_VERSION() |
|-------------------|
| 9.35.2            |
+-------------------+
1 Row(s) produced. Time Elapsed: 0.508s
```

```
SELECT CURRENT_ACCOUNT();

+-------------------+
| CURRENT_ACCOUNT() |
|-------------------|
| EPB34842          |
+-------------------+
1 Row(s) produced. Time Elapsed: 0.193s
```

6. Before running queries against a table, specify which warehouse, database, and schema SnowSQL should use. This ensures your queries run in the correct environment and prevents "no database/no schema" errors in the prompt.

```
USE WAREHOUSE DEFAULT_WH;
USE DATABASE SNOWFLAKE_SAMPLE_DATA;
USE SCHEMA TPCDS_SF10TCL;
```

Once your context is set, the prompt will update to reflect it, for example:

```
KBELANGER#DEFAULT_WH@SNOWFLAKE_SAMPLE_DATA.TPCDS_SF10TCL>
```

7. You can now execute queries such as:

```
SELECT COUNT(*) FROM ITEM;
+----------+
| COUNT(*) |
|----------|
|   402000 |
+----------+
```

The preceding query will produce the following output:

```
1 Row(s) produced. Time Elapsed: 0.692s
```

The query results also inform the user that only one row was returned by the database.

8. When you're finished, simply close the command window or run the following command to exit SnowSQL:

```
!exit
```

How it works...

The SnowSQL installer for Windows (and other operating systems) downloads the latest version of Snowflake's command-line client directly from Snowflake's official distribution repository. During installation, it registers the `snowsql` command so it can be run from any terminal window.

When you connect using: snowsql -a <account_identifier> -u <username> SnowSQL opens a secure, encrypted HTTPS session to the Snowflake service using the same API endpoints that Snowsight and other Snowflake clients use. After authentication succeeds, SnowSQL establishes a session that is tied to your user, role, warehouse, database, and schema contexts.

These contexts define where and how each command runs. For example, `USE WAREHOUSE` selects the compute resource that executes your queries, while `USE DATABASE` and `USE SCHEMA` determine which objects you're referencing by default.

Every command you issue through SnowSQL is sent securely over HTTPS to Snowflake's virtual warehouse service layer, processed, and then returned as formatted results in your terminal window.

There's more...

At the time of writing, SnowSQL version 1.4.x is the latest generally available release. If a newer version has been released, you can install or upgrade to it by following the instructions in the Snowflake documentation. SnowSQL is also backward compatible with older Snowflake account versions, so updating your client won't affect connectivity or query behavior.

You can always find the latest client release notes here: `https://docs.snowflake.com/en/release-notes/client-change-log-snowsql`.

Connecting to Snowflake with JDBC

The previous recipe demonstrated how to connect to Snowflake using SnowSQL, which provides command-line control for interacting with Snowflake. While SnowSQL is ideal for scripting and automation, many applications need programmatic access to Snowflake as part of their data tier. In these cases, the Java Database Connectivity (JDBC) driver offers a standard way for Java applications to connect, execute SQL, and retrieve results from a Snowflake account.

In this recipe, you'll learn how to install Snowflake's JDBC driver and use it in a simple Java application to connect to and run queries against Snowflake.

Getting ready

This recipe assumes that you have Java 8 or later installed on your system and access to the internet. The project uses Apache Maven to manage dependencies, compile code, and run the example. The Snowflake JDBC driver is defined as a Maven dependency in the project's `pom.xml`, and Maven automatically downloads the required driver from Maven Central the first time you build or run the project; no manual download is needed.

The latest version and details are available in the Snowflake documentation:`https://docs.snowflake.com/en/developer-guide/jdbc`.

Snowflake's JDBC driver is cross-platform and works on Windows, macOS, and Linux. You can develop and run the example in this recipe on any operating system that supports Java.

The example in this recipe was developed using OpenJDK 11 (Temurin build) on Windows 11, which is fully supported by the Snowflake JDBC driver. Any Java version 8 or later will work.

Check if Maven is installed

Open Command Prompt or PowerShell and type:

```
mvn -v
```

If Maven is installed, you'll see output similar to:

```
Apache Maven 3.9.11
Maven home: C:\Program Files\Apache\Maven\apache-maven-3.9.11
Java version: 11.0.25, vendor: Eclipse Adoptium, runtime: C:\Program Files\Eclipse
Adoptium\jdk-11.0.25.9-hotspot
```

If you see the above, Maven is ready to use and skip over to *How To Do It...*

If Maven is not installed, follow these steps:

1. Visit the official Apache Maven download page:`https://maven.apache.org/download.cgi`.
2. Download the latest binary zip archive (for example, apache-`maven-3.9.11-bin.zip`).
3. Extract Maven and unzip the downloaded file to a folder such as:

   ```
   C:\Program Files\Apache\Maven
   ```

4. After extraction, confirm that you can see the following folder:

```
C:\Program Files\Apache\Maven\apache-maven-3.9.11\bin
```

5. Add Maven to your PATH.
6. Press **Windows key + R**, type `sysdm.cpl`, and press **Enter**.
7. In the System Properties window, open the **Advanced** tab and click **Environment Variables**.
8. Under System variables, select **Path** > **Edit** > **New**, then paste:

```
C:\Program Files\Apache\Maven\apache-maven-3.9.11\bin
```

9. Click **OK** to save the changes and close all dialog boxes.
10. Verify the installation and open a new Command Prompt or PowerShell window and run:

```
mvn -v
```

You should see output similar to:

```
Apache Maven 3.9.11
Maven home: C:\Program Files\Apache\Maven\apache-maven-3.9.11
Java version: 11.0.25, vendor: Eclipse Adoptium
```

If the command fails, double-check that you opened a new terminal window and that the path to Maven's bin folder was entered correctly.

Check if the JDBC driver is installed

Open Command Prompt or PowerShell and type:

```
java -version
```

You'll see output similar to:

```
openjdk version "11.0.25" 2024-10-15
OpenJDK Runtime Environment Temurin-11.0.25+9 (build 11.0.25+9)
OpenJDK 64-Bit Server VM Temurin-11.0.25+9 (build 11.0.25+9, mixed mode)
```

How to do it...

The steps for this recipe are as follows:

1. Create a new Maven project (Windows).
2. Open Command Prompt (or PowerShell) and create a folder, then initialize a basic project structure (feel free to use your IDE instead):

   ```
   mvn archetype:generate -DgroupId=com.example -DartifactId=snowflake-jdbc-
   demo2 -DarchetypeArtifactId=maven-archetype-quickstart -
   DinteractiveMode=false
   ```

   This command creates a new folder named `snowflake-jdbc-demo2`, downloads the Maven quickstart archetype, and generates a standard Maven project layout, including the `pom.xml` file and the `src/main/java directory` structure.

3. When the command completes successfully and displays `BUILD SUCCESS`, navigate into the newly created project directory:

   ```
   cd snowflake-jdbc-demo2
   ```

   Confirm the structure:

   ```
   dir
   ```

   You should see:

   ```
   pom.xml
   src\
     main\java\com\example\App.java
     test\java\com\example\AppTest.java
   ```

4. Update the default `pom.xml` contents
5. Navigate to your project folder (the one Maven created):

   ```
   cd C:\projects\snowflake-jdbc-demo2
   ```

6. Open the file in Notepad or VS Code:

```
notepad pom.xml

(If you're using VS Code, you can do code pom.xml instead.)
```

Select all the existing contents in the file and delete them. Replace the entire contents of the default `pom.xml` with the following configuration.

```
<project xmlns="http://maven.apache.org/POM/4.0.0"
         xmlns:xsi="http://www.w3.org/2001/XMLSchema-instance"
         xsi:schemaLocation="http://maven.apache.org/POM/4.0.0 http://
maven.apache.org/xsd/maven-4.0.0.xsd">
  <modelVersion>4.0.0</modelVersion>
  <groupId>com.example</groupId>
  <artifactId>snowflake-jdbc-demo</artifactId>
  <version>1.0.0</version>

  <dependencies>
    <!-- Snowflake JDBC driver (use latest version) -->
    <dependency>
      <groupId>net.snowflake</groupId>
      <artifactId>snowflake-jdbc</artifactId>
      <version>3.27.1</version>
    </dependency>
  </dependencies>

  <build>
    <plugins>
      <plugin>
        <groupId>org.codehaus.mojo</groupId>
        <artifactId>exec-maven-plugin</artifactId>
        <version>3.1.0</version>
        <configuration>
          <mainClass>com.example.SnowflakeJDBCDemo</mainClass>
        </configuration>
      </plugin>
    </plugins>
  </build>
</project>
```

This version adds the Snowflake JDBC dependency and a plugin that allows you to run the Java program directly from Maven.

7. Run the following command to confirm that Maven is able to process the project:

```
cd mvn validate
```

You should see:

```
BUILD SUCCESS
```

8. From the command line, navigate to the folder where Maven created your project. For example, on Windows, this might be:

```
cd C:\Users\<YourUserName>\snowflake-jdbc-demo2
```

Replace `<YourUserName>` with your own system username or the path where you ran the Maven command.

9. Verify you're in the correct directory by running:

```
dir
```

You should see a `pom.xml` file and a `src` folder.

10. From the project root, move into the package folder where you'll create your Java file:

```
cd src/main/java/com/example
```

11. Let's create a small Java program to demonstrate how to connect to your Snowflake account using the Snowflake JDBC driver.
This program performs three core actions that mirror how most Java applications interact with Snowflake:

    1. Establishes a connection to your Snowflake account using the JDBC URL, username, password, and session parameters such as warehouse, database, and schema.
    2. Executes a SQL query against one of Snowflake's sample datasets to confirm that the connection is working.
    3. Retrieves and displays the result in the console, then cleanly closes all resources.

You can think of this as a simple "smoke test" for any Java application that will use Snowflake as its data source.

12. Create the `SnowflakeJDBCDemo.java` file:

```
notepad SnowflakeJDBCDemo.java
```

13. Paste the following code into the file. Before saving, update the placeholder values for your Snowflake account, username, password, warehouse, database, and schema.

```
package com.example;

import java.sql.Connection;
import java.sql.DriverManager;
import java.sql.ResultSet;
import java.sql.Statement;

public class SnowflakeJDBCDemo {

    public static void main(String[] args) {

        // Replace with your own Snowflake connection details
        String url = "jdbc:snowflake://
<your_account>.snowflakecomputing.com";
        String user = "<your_username>";
        String password = "<your_password>";
        String warehouse = "COMPUTE_WH";
        String database = "SNOWFLAKE_SAMPLE_DATA";
        String schema = "TPCDS_SF10TCL";

        try {
            // Build full connection URL
            String connectStr = String.format("%s?
user=%s&password=%s&warehouse=%s&db=%s&schema=%s",
                    url, user, password, warehouse, database, schema);

            // Connect to Snowflake
            Connection connection =
DriverManager.getConnection(connectStr);
            System.out.println("✅ Successfully connected to Snowflake!");
```

```
            // Create a statement and run a simple query
            Statement statement = connection.createStatement();
            ResultSet resultSet = statement.executeQuery("SELECT COUNT(*)
FROM ITEM");

            // Display the result
            while (resultSet.next()) {
                System.out.println("Total rows in ITEM table: " +
resultSet.getInt(1));
            }

            // Clean up
            resultSet.close();
            statement.close();
            connection.close();

        } catch (Exception e) {
            e.printStackTrace();
        }
    }
}
```

> **Note**
>
> In this example, the Snowflake password is stored directly in the source code for simplicity and demonstration purposes. In a production or enterprise environment, credentials should never be hardcoded. Instead, consider one of the following secure approaches:
>
> - Use environment variables or an external configuration file.
> - Use Snowflake key-pair authentication or OAuth tokens.
> - Integrate with a secrets manager, such as AWS Secrets Manager or Azure Key Vault.

14. Now test the connection by entering the following command:

```
mvn exec:java -Dexec.mainClass=com.example.SnowflakeJDBCDemo
```

If the connection is successful, you'll see output similar to:

```
Successfully connected to Snowflake!
Total rows in ITEM table: 402000
```

How it works...

When you connect to Snowflake using JDBC, your Java application communicates with Snowflake over HTTPS using the Snowflake JDBC driver. The driver acts as a translation layer between standard JDBC calls (such as creating connections, executing SQL statements, and processing result sets) and Snowflake's REST-based backend services.

In this recipe, Maven was used to manage dependencies and project structure. By declaring the Snowflake JDBC driver as a dependency in the `pom.xml` file, Maven automatically downloaded the required driver and its transitive dependencies from the Maven Central repository during the build process. This eliminates the need to manually download and manage JAR files and ensures consistent builds across environments.

The Java application establishes a connection to Snowflake using a JDBC connection string that includes your account identifier, user credentials, and optional session properties such as the warehouse, database, and schema. Once the connection is established, SQL statements are executed using standard JDBC APIs, and the results are returned as a ResultSet object that can be processed programmatically.

Under the hood, Snowflake executes these queries using the virtual warehouse specified in the session. As with queries executed through Snowsight or SnowSQL, the warehouse provides the compute resources required to process the request.

This approach enables external applications to integrate directly with Snowflake as a data platform, allowing developers to embed analytics, automate workflows, and build data-driven services using familiar Java and JDBC patterns.

There's more...

The Snowflake JDBC driver supports many configuration options that extend beyond this basic example. Once you're comfortable establishing a connection and running simple queries, you can explore:

- Key-pair authentication for secure, passwordless access
- External browser or OAuth authentication to integrate with single sign-on (SSO) solutions

- Connection pooling to optimize performance for applications that open multiple concurrent sessions
- Session parameters and timeouts to control query execution behavior and resource utilization

These options are fully documented in the official Snowflake JDBC documentation.

Creating a new account admin user and understanding built-in roles

Snowflake uses a **role-based access control** (**RBAC**) model to manage permissions and enforce security boundaries between users and objects. Every user is assigned one or more roles, and each role determines which operations that user can perform.

In this recipe, you'll create a new ACCOUNTADMIN-level user to perform administrative tasks instead of relying solely on the default built-in ACCOUNTADMIN user. The best recommended practice is to maintain at least two users with the ACCOUNTADMIN role to ensure continued administrative access if one account becomes unavailable.

Snowflake has also introduced **user-based access control** (**UBAC**), which provides finer-grained, data-level security by tailoring access dynamically to individual users. While RBAC remains the foundation for account and role management, UBAC and related advanced security features will be explored later in *Chapter 5, Data Protection and Security in Snowflake*.

How to do it...

The steps for this recipe are as follows:

1. Sign in to your Snowflake account and open Snowsight.
2. From the navigation menu, select **Projects** → **Workspaces**, and create a SQL workspace.
3. You need security administrator privileges to create and manage users. In your SQL workspace, execute the following command to ensure you're operating under the SECURITYADMIN role:

```
USE ROLE SECURITYADMIN;
```

4. Run the following SQL command to create a new user:

```
CREATE USER SECONDARY_ACCOUNT_ADMIN
  PASSWORD = 'Snowflake@123'
```

```
DEFAULT_ROLE = ACCOUNTADMIN
MUST_CHANGE_PASSWORD = TRUE;
```

The `MUST_CHANGE_PASSWORD = TRUE` parameter ensures the new user resets their password upon first login.

> Note
>
> **Note:** You can use `CREATE OR REPLACE USER` if you're rerunning this script for testing or automation purposes. However, be aware that replacing a user removes all existing grants and associations for that user, so it should be used with caution in production environments.

5. Still within your workspace, execute the following command to grant the ACCOUNTADMIN role to the new user.

```
GRANT ROLE ACCOUNTADMIN TO USER SECONDARY_ACCOUNT_ADMIN;
```

6. You can confirm that the user was created and assigned the correct role by running:

```
SHOW GRANTS TO USER SECONDARY_ACCOUNT_ADMIN;
```

7. Log out and test the new user:
   - Sign out of Snowsight
   - Log in with the newly created username
   - When prompted, create a new password

   After logging in, verify that you have access to account-level operations (for example, view warehouses or manage roles).

How it works...

Snowflake manages access control through a role hierarchy, where each role can own objects and grant privileges to other roles or users. The model follows the principle of role inheritance, meaning that when one role is granted to another, it also inherits all of that role's privileges.

In this recipe, you first switched to the SECURITYADMIN role. This is required because SECURITYADMIN manages users, roles, and grants within the account.

While the ACCOUNTADMIN role has full privileges, including those of SECURITYADMIN, it's considered a best practice to perform day-to-day security administration using the more limited SECURITYADMIN role, reserving ACCOUNTADMIN for higher-risk account-level operations.

When you executed the `CREATE USER` statement, you defined a new user profile in the account's security metadata. Assigning `DEFAULT_ROLE = ACCOUNTADMIN` means that, upon login, the user automatically operates under that role unless another is specified.

By following up with `GRANT ROLE ACCOUNTADMIN TO USER SECONDARY_ACCOUNT_ADMIN`, you explicitly gave that user the administrative capabilities associated with the role, including managing warehouses, users, integrations, and overall account configuration. It's important to remember that roles, not users, own Snowflake objects. Users perform actions through their active role. This separation allows for clean privilege management, easy role auditing, and alignment with enterprise governance standards.

There's more...

Snowflake provides five built-in system roles arranged in a hierarchy, where higher-level roles inherit the privileges of those beneath them. These roles are:

- **ACCOUNTADMIN** – Full control of the Snowflake account, including billing, security, and all account objects
- **SECURITYADMIN** – Manages roles, privileges, and access control across the account
- **USERADMIN** – Manages users and basic role assignments
- **SYSADMIN** – Manages databases, warehouses, and other core operational objects
- **PUBLIC** – A minimal-access role automatically granted to all users for shared or common objects

Because of this hierarchy, a user assigned the ACCOUNTADMIN role automatically inherits the capabilities of the other roles.

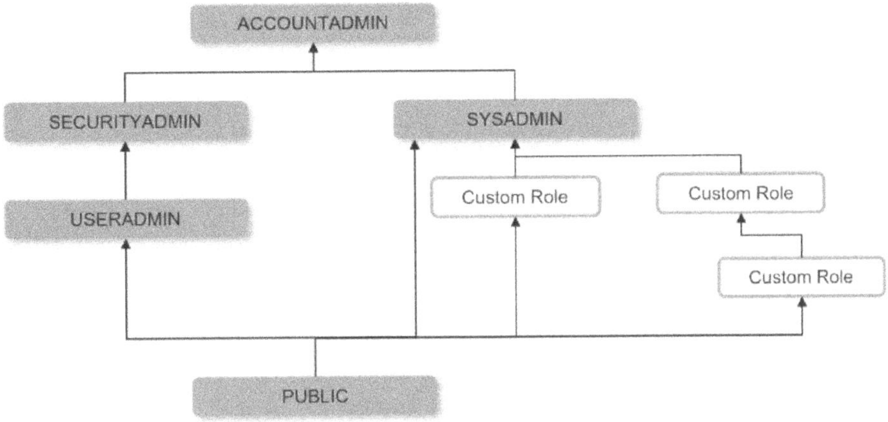

Figure 1.17 – Graphical depiction of the role hierarchy

When creating new custom roles, it's considered best practice to grant them to the SYSADMIN role.

Doing so maintains a clean and complete role hierarchy, ensuring that system administrators retain sufficient privileges to manage and operate all objects, regardless of which role originally created them.

Get this book's PDF version and more

Scan the QR code (or go to `packtpub.com/unlock`). Search for this book by name, confirm the edition, and then follow the steps on the page.

UNLOCK NOW

Note: Keep your invoice handy. Purchases made directly from Packt don't require an invoice.

2

Managing the Data Life Cycle

This chapter introduces the essential concepts involved in managing data throughout its lifecycle within Snowflake. While many of the underlying principles will feel familiar to those with traditional database experience, Snowflake's cloud-native design introduces new approaches to how data is structured and managed over time.

In the recipes that follow, you will learn how to create and manage databases and schemas, define tables using permanent, transient, and temporary storage types, and work with external stages and external tables to access data stored outside Snowflake. You will also learn how to standardize data ingestion using file formats, build views for simplified data access, and integrate Snowflake with Git for version-controlled object management.

Together, these topics provide a practical foundation for managing Snowflake objects, supporting consistent data ingestion, and maintaining reliable and repeatable data workflows across environments.

The following recipes are included in this chapter:

- Managing a database
- Managing a schema
- Managing tables
- Managing external tables and stages
- Managing views in Snowflake
- Integrating Snowflake with Git

Technical requirements

The chapter assumes that you have a Snowflake account already set up. It also requires you to have access to an Amazon S3 bucket to use to get hold of external data and use it within Snowflake.

You can download the example project and code for this book by following the instructions in the ***Download the example code files*** section in the *Preface* of this book

Managing a database

In this recipe, we will create a new database with default settings and walk through several variations on the database creation process. The recipe provides details such as how to minimize storage usage when creating databases and how to set up the replication of databases across regions and when to do so.

Getting ready

This recipe describes the various ways to create a new database in Snowflake. These steps can be run either in Snowsight or in the Snowflake CLI command-line client.

Some steps in this chapter involve configuring Time Travel settings. To extend Time Travel retention beyond 1 day, Snowflake Enterprise Edition (or higher) is required. Most Snowflake trial accounts include Enterprise-level features; however, capabilities may vary depending on your account configuration. If your account does not support extended retention, the default value of 1 day will apply.

How to do it...

The steps for this recipe are as follows:

1. The syntax for creating a new database is fairly straightforward. We are assuming that the database doesn't exist already. Run the following SQL command to create a new database named OUR_FIRST_DATABASE:

   ```
   USE ROLE SYSADMIN;

   CREATE DATABASE OUR_FIRST_DATABASE
   COMMENT = 'OUR_FIRST_DATABASE';
   ```

   The command should successfully execute with the following message:

	status
1	Database OUR_FIRST_DATABASE successfully created.

Figure 2.1 – Database successfully created

2. To verify that the database was created successfully and review its default properties, run the following command:

```
SHOW DATABASES LIKE 'OUR_FIRST_DATABASE';
```

The query should return a single row showing information about the newly created database, including the database name, owner, comments, and retention time. Notice that `RETENTION_TIME` is set to `1` and the `OPTIONS` column is blank. The retention time of 1 indicates that Time Travel is enabled for one day, which is the default setting in Standard Edition accounts. This means dropped or modified data can be recovered within that time window. The blank options column indicates that no additional properties, such as transient or replication settings, have been applied to the object.

	created_on	name	is_default	is_current	origin	owner	comment
1	2026-04-12 14:17:05	OUR_FIRST_DATABASE	N	Y		ACCOUNTADMIN	Our first data

Figure 2.2 – Information of the newly created database

3. Let's create another database for which we will set the Time Travel duration to 15 days. The retention period can be adjusted depending on your account edition.

```
CREATE DATABASE PRODUCTION_DATABASE
DATA_RETENTION_TIME_IN_DAYS = 15
COMMENT = 'Critical production database';

SHOW DATABASES LIKE 'PRODUCTION_DATABASE';
```

The output of `SHOW DATABASES` should now show `retention_time` as 15, indicating that the Time Travel duration for the database is 15 days:

	created_on	name	is_default	is_current	origin	owner	comment
1	2025-12-12 10:44:16	PRODUCTION_DATABA	N	N		ACCOUNTADMIN	Critical produ

Figure 2.3 – SHOW DATABASES output

4. While Time Travel is normally required for production databases, you would not typically need Time Travel or fail-safe protection for temporary or ELT-focused databases. Fail-safe is an additional data recovery mechanism provided by Snowflake that retains data for a fixed period after Time Travel has expired, primarily for disaster recovery scenarios. Removing Time Travel and fail-safe helps reduce storage costs. Let's see how that is done:

```
CREATE TRANSIENT DATABASE TEMPORARY_DATABASE
DATA_RETENTION_TIME_IN_DAYS = 0
COMMENT = 'Temporary database for ELT processing';
```

5. Next, verify that the database was created and confirm its retention settings:

```
SHOW DATABASES LIKE 'TEMPORARY_DATABASE';
```

The output of `SHOW DATABASES` shows `RETENTION_TIME` set to `0` and the `TRANSIENT` option enabled. This confirms that Time Travel is disabled and fail-safe storage does not apply to this database.

6. The time travel configuration can also be changed later by altering the database with `ALTER`:

```
ALTER DATABASE TEMPORARY_DATABASE
SET DATA_RETENTION_TIME_IN_DAYS = 1;

SHOW DATABASES LIKE 'TEMPORARY_DATABASE';
```

The output now shows `RETENTION_TIME` set to `1`, demonstrating that Time Travel can be re-enabled for a transient database while fail-safe protection remains disabled.

How it works...

When a database is created without explicit lifecycle settings, Snowflake applies the account-level defaults. By default, this includes one day of Time Travel and fail-safe protection, both of which incur storage costs.

For **extract, load, transform** (**ELT**) or staging workloads where data is frequently inserted, updated, or deleted, these default protections may be unnecessary. Each data change generates historical storage, increasing costs without providing meaningful recovery value. Marking a database as TRANSIENT disables fail-safe by default for objects created within it and setting `DATA_RETENTION_TIME_IN_DAYS = 0` removes Time Travel storage entirely.

Although these settings reduce recovery options, they are appropriate for temporary or reproducible datasets. Importantly, database-level settings define defaults, not hard limits. Individual tables within a transient database can still be configured with Time Travel or fail-safe if needed.

The `ALTER DATABASE` command provides flexibility for evolving requirements. In addition to retention changes, it supports renaming databases, swapping databases, and resetting properties to their defaults.

One final point to note is that creating a database automatically sets it as the current database for the session, similar to executing a `USE DATABASE` command. Subsequent DDL operations will apply to this database unless another database is explicitly selected.

There's more...

Time Travel and cloning are explored in detail in *Chapter 8*, *Back to the Future with Time Travel*. In that chapter, we will demonstrate object recovery, point-in-time querying, cloning for debugging, retention policy management, and cross-region disaster recovery.

Managing a schema

In this recipe, you will be introduced to the concept of a schema and its uses. A schema is a logical container within a database used to organize related objects such as tables, views, and functions. In Snowflake, databases and schemas together define a namespace, meaning that objects are uniquely identified by qualifying them with a database and schema name (for example, `DATABASE.SCHEMA.TABLE`).

There can be multiple schemas in a database, but each schema belongs to a single database. In practice, databases are often used to separate environments or major domains, while schemas are used to group related objects within a database, such as by application or subject area.

We will see how a schema is created and used. Apart from user-created schemas, we will also look at schemas that are automatically available with a database, including the `INFORMATION_SCHEMA` provided by Snowflake

Getting ready

The following examples can be run either via the Snowsight UI or the Snowflake CLI command-line client.

Some features demonstrated in this recipe, such as Time Travel and fail-safe storage may incur additional storage costs depending on your Snowflake edition and retention settings. If you are working in a shared or production environment, review your account configuration before making changes.

How to do it...

The steps for this recipe are as follows:

1. For this recipe, we will create a database where we will test the schema creation:

```
USE ROLE SYSADMIN;

CREATE DATABASE TESTING_SCHEMA_CREATION;
```

   You should see a message stating that a database schema was successfully created:

	status
1	Database TESTING_SCHEMA_CREATION successfully created.

Figure 2.4 – Database created successfully

2. Check whether the newly created database already has a schema in it:

```
SHOW SCHEMAS IN DATABASE TESTING_SCHEMA_CREATION;
```

   You should see two rows in the result set; this is the **INFORMATION_SCHEMA** and **PUBLIC** schema, which are the two default schemas that are automatically created with every new database:

	created_on	name	is_default	is_current	database_name
1	2026-04-12 14:23:08.700 -0700	INFORMATION_SCHEMA	N	N	TESTING_SCHEMA_CREATION
2	2026-04-12 14:22:34.964 -0700	PUBLIC	N	Y	TESTING_SCHEMA_CREATION

Figure 2.5 – Schemas of the new database

3. Now create a new schema. The syntax for creating a standard schema without any additional settings is as follows:

```
USE DATABASE TESTING_SCHEMA_CREATION;

CREATE SCHEMA A_CUSTOM_SCHEMA
COMMENT = 'Custom schema example';
```

The command executes successfully and returns a message similar to:

Schema A_CUSTOM_SCHEMA successfully created.

	status
1	Schema A_CUSTOM_SCHEMA successfully created.

Figure 2.6 – New schema successfully created

4. Let's verify that the schema has been created successfully and look at the default values that were set automatically for its various attributes.

```
SHOW SCHEMAS LIKE 'A_CUSTOM_SCHEMA' IN DATABASE TESTING_SCHEMA_CREATION;
```

The query should return one row displaying information such as the schema name, the database name in which the schema resides, and the Time Travel retention duration in days:

	created_on	name	is_default	is_current	database_name	owner	comment
1	2026-04-12 14:24:00	A_CUSTOM_SCHEMA	N	Y	TESTING_SCHEMA_CR	ACCOUNTADMIN	Custom sche

Figure 2.7 – Validating the schema

5. Let's create another schema for which we will set the Time Travel duration to be `0` days and the schema to be `TRANSIENT`. It is common to use these settings on data for which Snowflake data protection features are not required, such as temporary data:

```
USE DATABASE TESTING_SCHEMA_CREATION;

CREATE TRANSIENT SCHEMA TEMPORARY_DATA
```

```
DATA_RETENTION_TIME_IN_DAYS = 0
COMMENT = 'Schema containing temporary data used by ELT processes';
```

The schema creation should succeed with the following message:

	status
1	Schema TEMPORARY_DATA successfully created.

Figure 2.8 – New schema successfully created

6. Let's view what the schema settings are by running the `SHOW SCHEMAS` command as shown:

```
SHOW SCHEMAS LIKE 'TEMPORARY_DATA' IN DATABASE TESTING_SCHEMA_CREATION;
```

The output of `SHOW SCHEMAS` is shown here:

	urrent	database_name	owner	comment	options	retention_time
1		TESTING_SCHEMA_CR	ACCOUNTADMIN	Schema containing tem	TRANSIENT	0

Figure 2.9 – Output of SHOW SCHEMAS

The output should show `retention_time` as zero or a blank value, indicating that there is no Time Travel storage for this schema, and the **options** column should show **TRANSIENT** as the option, which essentially means that there will be no fail-safe storage for this schema.

How it works...

The standard `CREATE SCHEMA` command uses the defaults set at the database level. If you haven't changed any configuration, the created schema inherits settings such as Time Travel retention from the database. By default, Time Travel is enabled for 1 day and fail-safe protection is also enabled.

Snowflake applies these settings hierarchically. Database-level settings act as defaults for schemas, and schema-level settings act as defaults for objects such as tables created within that schema. This means that when a schema is created, it inherits the database configuration, and any tables created within that schema inherit the schema's configuration unless explicitly overridden.

For schemas that will store temporary or intermediate data, such as tables used in ELT processing, a schema can be created as a transient schema. Transient schemas do not use fail-safe storage, which reduces storage costs. Time Travel can also be set to zero to further reduce costs. By default, however, transient schemas still have a Time Travel retention of 1 day unless it is explicitly changed.

Although a schema may be configured with no Time Travel and no fail-safe, individual tables within the schema can still override these defaults and enable these features as needed.

It is also important to note that creating a new schema sets the current schema for the session. As a result, subsequent DDL commands, such as `CREATE TABLE`, will create objects in that schema unless another schema is explicitly selected using `USE SCHEMA`.

There's more...

Every database in Snowflake automatically includes a `PUBLIC` schema, along with an `INFORMATION_SCHEMA` that exposes system metadata. The information schema implements the SQL standard information schema and extends it with Snowflake-specific details, allowing you to query metadata about databases, schemas, tables, columns, and other objects. This metadata plays an important role in governance, automation, and observability across the Snowflake platform.

Beyond these system-defined schemas, Snowflake places very few restrictions on how you organize schemas within a database. How you choose to structure databases and schemas should be driven by the architectural methodology you are following and the operating model of your organization. For example, teams using dimensional modeling, Data Vault, medallion architectures, or domain-oriented approaches may organize schemas very differently, and Snowflake supports all of these patterns equally well.

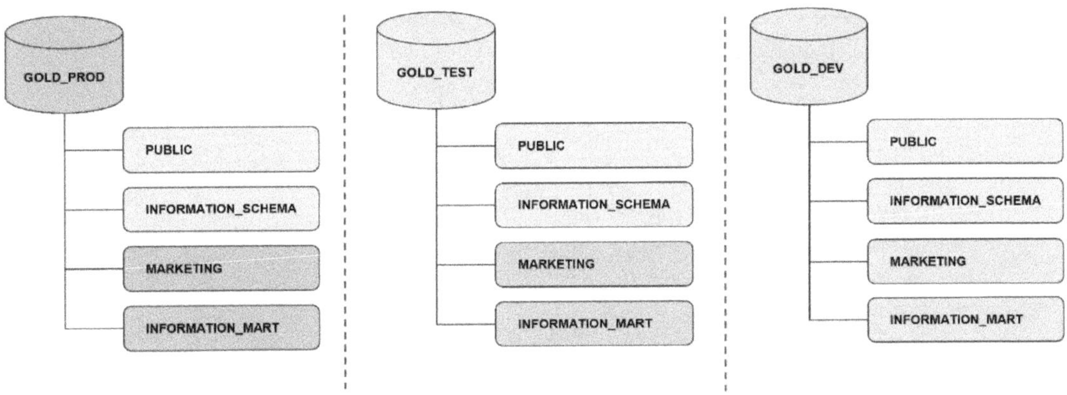

Figure 2.10 – A DEV, TEST, PROD setup using databases and schemas

A common and recommended practice is to isolate environments at the database level by creating separate databases for development, testing, and production. These databases typically share the same logical name with an environment-specific suffix, such as `GOLD_DEV`, `GOLD_TEST`, and `GOLD_PROD`. This approach simplifies access control, deployment workflows, and lifecycle management while maintaining clear separation between environments.

Within each database, schemas should be created as needed based on domain boundaries, source systems, or functional purpose rather than following a rigid, predefined structure. This flexibility allows Snowflake implementations to evolve naturally as data products, teams, and architectural strategies mature over time.

Managing tables

This recipe shows you how to create a table and insert data to explain different behaviors in storing data. You will be introduced to the different lifecycle options available in Snowflake, such as permanent, transient, and temporary tables. While the core concepts of table creation and data insertion are common across relational databases, the focus here is on Snowflake-specific capabilities, including Time Travel retention, transient behavior, cloning, and how Snowflake manages storage and metadata differently from traditional systems. We will start by creating a table and then insert some sample data to explore these Snowflake-specific behaviors.

Getting ready

The following examples can be run either in Snowsight or in the Snowflake CLI command-line client. Some steps later in this recipe use Snowsight-specific workflows and will be called out explicitly.

How to do it...

The steps for this recipe are as follows:

1. Execute the following statements to create a table named `CUSTOMER` in Snowflake:

```
USE ROLE SYSADMIN;
USE DATABASE OUR_FIRST_DATABASE;
USE SCHEMA A_CUSTOM_SCHEMA;

CREATE OR REPLACE TABLE CUSTOMER (
  CUSTOMER_ID         INT NOT NULL,
  LAST_NAME           VARCHAR(100),
  FIRST_NAME          VARCHAR(100),
  EMAIL_ADDRESS       VARCHAR(100),
```

```
    COMPANY_NAME        VARCHAR(100),
    PHONE_NUMBER        VARCHAR(100),
    ADDRESS_LINE_1      VARCHAR(150),
    ADDRESS_LINE_2      VARCHAR(150),
    CITY_NAME           VARCHAR(100),
    STATE_NAME          VARCHAR(100),
    POSTAL_CODE         VARCHAR(15),
    COUNTRY_NAME        VARCHAR(50)
);
```

The command should successfully execute, generating the following message:

	status
1	Table CUSTOMER successfully created.

Figure 2.11 – Table created successfully

2. To confirm that the table has been generated as per the specification, we can run a `DESCRIBE TABLE` statement as shown:

```
DESCRIBE TABLE CUSTOMER;
```

The `DESCRIBE TABLE` output should list all defined columns along with their data types and nullability. Confirm that `CUSTOMER_ID` is `NOT NULL` and that the table structure matches the DDL definition.

	name	type	kind	null?	default	primary key	unique key
1	CUSTOMER_ID	NUMBER(38,0)	COLUMN	N	null	N	N
2	LAST_NAME	VARCHAR(100)	COLUMN	Y	null	N	N
3	FIRST_NAME	VARCHAR(100)	COLUMN	Y	null	N	N
4	EMAIL_ADDRESS	VARCHAR(100)	COLUMN	Y	null	N	N
5	COMPANY_NAME	VARCHAR(100)	COLUMN	Y	null	N	N
6	PHONE_NUMBER	VARCHAR(100)	COLUMN	Y	null	N	N
7	ADDRESS_LINE_1	VARCHAR(150)	COLUMN	Y	null	N	N
8	ADDRESS_LINE_2	VARCHAR(150)	COLUMN	Y	null	N	N

Figure 2.12 – Output of the DESCRIBE statement

3. Let's assume there was something wrong with a data type; for example, say `ADDRESS_LINE_1` and `ADDRESS_LINE_2` were supposed to be stored as `STRING` data types.

> **Note**
>
> The `CREATE OR REPLACE` statement drops the existing table and recreates it. Any data currently stored in the table will be lost. If you are following along with your own data, ensure that the table does not contain data you need to preserve.

```
CREATE OR REPLACE TABLE CUSTOMER (
  CUSTOMER_ID         INT NOT NULL,
  LAST_NAME           VARCHAR(100),
  FIRST_NAME          VARCHAR(100),
  EMAIL_ADDRESS       VARCHAR(100),
  COMPANY_NAME        VARCHAR(100),
  PHONE_NUMBER        VARCHAR(100),
  ADDRESS_LINE_1      STRING,
  ADDRESS_LINE_2      STRING,
  CITY_NAME           VARCHAR(100),
  STATE_NAME          VARCHAR(100),
  POSTAL_CODE         VARCHAR(15),
  COUNTRY_NAME        VARCHAR(50)
);
```

4. Let's verify whether the desired change has been successfully applied. For that, we can execute the `DESCRIBE TABLE` statement as shown:

```
DESCRIBE TABLE CUSTOMER;
```

It should generate the following result in the Snowflake web UI:

	name	type	kind	null?	default	primary key	unique key
1	CUSTOMER_ID	NUMBER(38,0)	COLUMN	N	null	N	N
2	LAST_NAME	VARCHAR(100)	COLUMN	Y	null	N	N
3	FIRST_NAME	VARCHAR(100)	COLUMN	Y	null	N	N
4	EMAIL_ADDRESS	VARCHAR(100)	COLUMN	Y	null	N	N
5	COMPANY_NAME	VARCHAR(100)	COLUMN	Y	null	N	N
6	PHONE_NUMBER	VARCHAR(100)	COLUMN	Y	null	N	N
7	ADDRESS_LINE_1	VARCHAR(16777216	COLUMN	Y	null	N	N
8	ADDRESS_LINE_2	VARCHAR(16777216	COLUMN	Y	null	N	N
9	CITY_NAME	VARCHAR(100)	COLUMN	Y	null	N	N
10	STATE_NAME	VARCHAR(100)	COLUMN	Y	null	N	N

Figure 2.13 – Output of the DESCRIBE statement after the changes in the table

Please note the data types. We will discuss this in the *How it works...* section later, along with how `REPLACE` works and how it's a shorthand for a two-step process typically required for managing the life cycle of a table.

5. Now let's load the customer data from a CSV file (`CUSTOMER_SAMPLE_100.csv`). This file is available in the GitHub repository for this chapter (`Chapter02 folder`). Download the file to your local machine before proceeding with the upload steps.

> **Note**
>
> The following workflow uses the Snowsight interface and cannot be completed directly from Snowflake CLI. If you are using Snowflake CLI, you would need to first upload the file to an internal stage using the `PUT` command and then use `COPY INTO` to load the data. The graphical file upload process described below is only available in Snowsight.

   a. Opening the data loading workflow:

      1. Navigate to **Catalog** » **Database Explorer**.
      2. Select the Database `OUR_FIRST_DATABASE`.
      3. Select the Schema `A_CUSTOM_SCHEMA`.
      4. Select the Tables `CUSTOMER`.
      5. Click **Load Data** in the upper right.

b. Uploading the local file:

1. Choose **Load** from your computer.
2. Select the file `CUSTOMER_SAMPLE_100.csv` from your local machine and click **Next**.
3. Snowsight will automatically preview the file and validate that the columns align with the table definition. Review the preview and select **Load**.
4. Your data has now been successfully loaded.
5. This should be completed with the following message:

Figure 2.14 – Table loaded

6. Let's now look at scenarios where the creation of a table is based on an existing table. A common pattern in the table life cycle involves deriving a table from an existing table. This is called `CTAS` or `CREATE TABLE ... AS SELECT`. To explain the use of `CTAS`, we will have some records inserted into the `CUSTOMER` table. The dataset has 100 rows, as shown in *Figure 2.15* (showing the first six columns of the table):

	MER_ID	LAST_NAME	FIRST_NAME	EMAIL_ADDRESS	COMPANY_NAME	PHONE_NUM
1	1	SMITH	ALEX	ALEX.SMITH001@EXAMPLE.COM	NORTHWIND	555-001-10
2	2	JOHNSON	JAMIE	JAMIE.JOHNSON002@EXAMPLE.COM	CONTOSO	555-002-10
3	3	WILLIAMS	TAYLOR	TAYLOR.WILLIAMS003@EXAMPLE.COM	FABRIKAM	555-003-10
4	4	BROWN	MORGAN	MORGAN.BROWN004@EXAMPLE.COM	ADVENTUREWORKS	555-004-10
5	5	JONES	CASEY	CASEY.JONES005@EXAMPLE.COM	WOODGROVE	555-005-10
6	6	GARCIA	RILEY	RILEY.GARCIA006@EXAMPLE.COM	LITWARE	555-006-10
7	7	MILLER	JORDAN	JORDAN.MILLER007@EXAMPLE.COM	COHO	555-007-10
8	8	DAVIS	SKYLER	SKYLER.DAVIS008@EXAMPLE.COM	PROSEWARE	555-008-10

Figure 2.15 – Sample data shown for the customer table

7. The dataset will be copied into a new table that will have the same structure as the `CUSTOMER` table. The statements to be executed are as follows:

```
USE DATABASE OUR_FIRST_DATABASE;

CREATE SCHEMA IF NOT EXISTS A_CUSTOM_SCHEMA;
USE SCHEMA A_CUSTOM_SCHEMA;

CREATE OR REPLACE TABLE CUSTOMER_DEEP_COPY
AS
SELECT *
FROM CUSTOMER;
```

This should succeed with the following message:

	status
1	Table CUSTOMER_DEEP_COPY successfully created.

Figure 2.16 – Deep copy table created

What we've created is a deep copy of the `CUSTOMER` table and a new table, which has received all data from the `CUSTOMER` table and is called `CUSTOMER_DEEP_COPY`. A deep copy duplicates both the table structure and its data, whereas a shallow copy duplicates only the structure. This new table is now an independent copy that can have a life cycle of its own with no changes or side effects originating from any operations performed on the `CUSTOMER` table. A `SELECT QUERY` statement on this new table would generate the same results as shown in the previous table.

8. Now let's look at another table copying method, shallow copy. You can continue working in the same session or workspace. In certain situations, a new table is required to be created with the same structure as an existing table, but without copying the data. This is known as a shallow copy and is achieved using the `LIKE` keyword:

```
CREATE OR REPLACE TABLE
CUSTOMER_SHALLOW_COPY
LIKE CUSTOMER;
```

This should succeed with the following message:

	status
1	Table CUSTOMER_SHALLOW_COPY successfully created.

Figure 2.17 – Shallow copy table created

This creates a new table with the same structure as the `CUSTOMER` table but without copying any data. Unlike the previous example using `CREATE TABLE AS SELECT` which copied both the table structure and its data, the `LIKE` keyword copies only the metadata definition of the table. You can confirm that no data was copied by running:

```
SELECT
COUNT(*)
FROM
CUSTOMER_SHALLOW_COPY;
```

The result of the following count query is zero rows, as shown:

	# COUNT(*)
1	

Figure 2.18 – New empty table created

9. Until now, we have seen the creation of tables with permanent life – the table will exist and store data until explicitly dropped. This is the default behavior from a life cycle

perspective. There are tables that handle transitory data and so they might be required only temporarily. For such scenarios, there are temporary and transient tables. Let's create these tables by running the following SQL statements:

```
CREATE OR REPLACE TEMPORARY TABLE CUSTOMER_TEMP
AS
SELECT *
FROM CUSTOMER
WHERE TRY_TO_NUMBER(POSTAL_CODE) IS NOT NULL;

CREATE OR REPLACE TRANSIENT TABLE CUSTOMER_TRANS
AS
SELECT *
FROM CUSTOMER
WHERE TRY_TO_NUMBER(POSTAL_CODE) IS NULL;
```

10. The preceding statements create two non-permanent tables: `CUSTOMER_TEMP` and `CUSTOMER_TRANS`.

    Temporary tables exist only for the duration of the current session. If the web UI session is closed or the user logs out, the temporary table will be dropped automatically and cannot be recovered.

    Transient tables persist across sessions and remain available after logging out and back in. However, transient tables do not consume fail-safe storage. This makes them useful for intermediate datasets that need to survive across sessions but do not require long-term recovery protection. Transient tables are commonly used in ELT workflows and stateful processing scenarios where storage cost optimization is important.

How it works...

The `CREATE OR REPLACE TABLE` statement used throughout this recipe is effectively a shorthand for a two-step process that would otherwise be required when a table needs to be deleted and recreated. Without using `REPLACE`, this would typically involve executing the following statements in sequence:

```
DROP TABLE IF EXISTS CUSTOMER;
CREATE TABLE CUSTOMER ...
```

Using `CREATE OR REPLACE TABLE` simplifies this workflow by atomically dropping the existing table (if it exists) and recreating it with the new definition. The difference between deep and shallow copies can be observed by running the following command:

```
SHOW TABLES LIKE 'CUSTOMER%';
```

This returns multiple rows summarizing the tables that have been created so far, allowing you to compare their structure and contents. The output highlights that the deep copy contains both the table structure and the data from the original table, while the shallow copy contains only the table structure. Although the metadata for the deep and shallow copies is similar, the shallow copy does not contain any data rows.

	created_on	name	database_name	schema_name
1	2026-04-12 14:44:14.904 -0700	CUSTOMER	OUR_FIRST_DATABASE	A_CUSTOM_SCHEMA
2	2026-04-12 15:04:40.437 -0700	CUSTOMER_DEEP_COPY	OUR_FIRST_DATABASE	A_CUSTOM_SCHEMA
3	2026-04-12 15:05:32.849 -0700	CUSTOMER_SHALLOW_	OUR_FIRST_DATABASE	A_CUSTOM_SCHEMA

Figure 2.19 – The show tables command output showing the copies of the table

One important column to note in the output is the **KIND** column. For the tables `CUSTOMER`, `CUSTOMER_DEEP_COPY`, and `CUSTOMER_SHALLOW_COPY`, the `KIND` value is `TABLE`, indicating that they are permanent tables. Permanent tables are the default table type in Snowflake and are designed to store data until they are explicitly dropped.

(For clarity, only a subset of columns is shown in the figure.)

Temporary tables, sometimes referred to as volatile tables, exist only for the duration of the user session in which they are created. These tables are not visible to other users, and both their definition and contents are automatically dropped when the session ends.

Transient tables are also non-permanent, but unlike temporary tables, they persist beyond the lifetime of a single session and are visible to any user with the appropriate privileges. Transient tables do not consume fail-safe storage and therefore offer a lower level of data protection than permanent tables. Data stored in transient tables may be lost in the event of a system failure and should only be used for data that can be easily recreated.

Running a `SHOW TABLES` command for the `CUSTOMER_TEMP` and `CUSTOMER_TRANS` tables produces the following output:

	created_on	name	database_name	schema_name	kind
1	2026-04-12	CUSTOMER_TEMP	OUR_FIRST_DATABASE	A_CUSTOM_SCHEMA	TEMPORARY
2	2026-04-12	CUSTOMER_TRANS	OUR_FIRST_DATABASE	A_CUSTOM_SCHEMA	TRANSIENT

Figure 2.20 – The show tables command output highlighting the temporary and transient nature of tables

Please note the content for the **kind** column. It shows that the tables are transient tables. In Snowflake, transient tables are still permanent objects, but they do not include fail-safe data protection like standard tables.

There's more...

One important table capability that has intentionally not been covered in this recipe is table cloning. Cloning differs from both deep and shallow copies shown in this recipe. A deep copy physically duplicates both the structure and the data, while a shallow copy duplicates only the structure. In contrast, Snowflake's cloning functionality creates a new table using zero-copy techniques, meaning the cloned table initially shares the underlying storage with the source table without physically copying the data. Cloning is closely tied to Snowflake's Time Travel features and will be explored in detail in *Chapter 8, Back to the Future with Time Travel.*

It is also important to note that temporary tables cannot be cloned, and only permanent tables are protected by fail-safe. Transient tables do not consume fail-safe storage, and temporary tables are dropped automatically at the end of a session. Fail-safe behavior and recovery mechanisms will be discussed further in *Chapter 8, Back to the Future with Time Travel.*

In addition, Snowflake has introduced a more deterministic, declarative approach to managing table definitions. Historically, making changes to an existing table often required writing and maintaining multiple `ALTER TABLE` statements to evolve the structure over time. The `CREATE OR REPLACE TABLE CUSTOMER` statement introduced in *Step 1* illustrates this declarative approach in practice. With Snowflake's current capabilities, you can use `CREATE OR REPLACE` or `ALTER TABLE` declaratively, and Snowflake will automatically determine the necessary differences and apply the appropriate changes. This allows table definitions to be treated as desired end states rather than a sequence of imperative modification steps.

This approach simplifies schema evolution by treating definitions as a desired end state; depending on the change and object type, Snowflake can apply compatible updates without requiring you to manually author a sequence of `ALTER` statements. Deterministic table definitions are particularly valuable in automated and CI/CD-driven environments, where consistency and repeatability across development, test, and production environments are critical.

Managing external tables and stages

An important aspect of building data solutions in Snowflake is managing how data is accessed and staged before it becomes part of native database tables. In this recipe, you will create an external stage, list and inspect files stored in cloud storage, define external tables over those files, and query the staged data. This demonstrates how Snowflake can reference data stored outside the platform while maintaining metadata and query access.

Getting ready

The following examples can be run using Snowsight or the Snowflake CLI. This recipe uses a publicly accessible Amazon S3 bucket provided for demonstration purposes. No additional setup or access to your own AWS account is required.

How to do it...

The steps for this recipe are as follows:

1. Let's first create a stage. A **stage** is a logical concept or an abstraction of a filesystem location that is external or internal to Snowflake. In this case, an external stage has been used. The stage location can be managed in an object store supported by the underlying cloud platform. On AWS, this is Amazon S3, which is used in this recipe. The following statement creates a stage named `SFUSER_EXT_STAGE`. The stage should be accessible to Snowflake:

```
CREATE OR REPLACE STAGE  SFUSER_EXT_STAGE
URL='s3://snowflake-cookbook/Chapter02/r4/';
```

The response should say that a stage has been created successfully, as shown in the following figure:

	A status
1	Stage area SFUSER_EXT_STAGE successfully created.

Figure 2.21 – Stage area created

2. Let's now do a listing on the `SFUSER_EXT_STAGE` stage pointing to the `snowflake-cookbook` S3 bucket:

```
LIST@SFUSER_EXT_STAGE;
```

This statement should generate the following output in the web UI:

	name	size
1	s3://snowflake-cookbook/Chapter02/r4/csv/electronic-carc	3071481
2	s3://snowflake-cookbook/Chapter02/r4/csv/electronic-carc	3071640
3	s3://snowflake-cookbook/Chapter02/r4/parquet/userdata1	113629

Figure 2.22 – Listing the stage to the S3 bucket

We can see that there are two types of files in the preceding listing: `csv` and `parquet`. In the case of `csv`, the `electronic-card-transactions-may-2020-headless.csv` file is a header-less version of the `electronic-card-transactions-may-2020.csv` file. There is a `parquet` format file as well called `userdata1.parquet`. We shall create external tables on both files. An external table is different from usual database tables because unlike tables that point to data inside a database, external tables provide a view on top of files stored in a stage.

These are read-only tables that maintain metadata that's helpful in interpreting the contents of a file, which could be formatted as `parquet`, `csv`, and so on.

3. Let's now look at how the `parquet` file can be loaded into an external table.
   The creation of the external table requires a location from which data can be read, as well as a file format definition. In this example, we use the external stage `SFUSER_EXT_STAGE` created in the previous step as the data source. Since the file is in Parquet format, the file format is specified accordingly:

```
create or replace external table ext_tbl_userdata1
with location = @sfuser_ext_stage
file_format = (type = parquet);
```

4. Let's query the newly created external table. This would show each row of the result set as a JSON document. Within each row, you should be able to see different columns with their respective values as key-value pairs:

```
select * from ext_tbl_userdata1;
```

The following screenshot shows only some of the key-value pairs due to size constraints:

	{?} VALUE
1	{ "birthdate": "3/8/1971", "cc": "6759521864920116", "comments": "1E+02", "country": "Indonesia", "email": "ajordan
2	{ "birthdate": "1/16/1968", "cc": "", "comments": "", "country": "Canada", "email": "afreeman1@is.gd", "first_name": "Alt
3	{ "birthdate": "2/1/1960", "cc": "6767119071901597", "comments": "", "country": "Russia", "email": "emorgan2@alterv
4	{ "birthdate": "4/8/1997", "cc": "3576031598965625", "comments": "", "country": "China", "email": "driley3@gmpg.org
5	{ "birthdate": "", "cc": "5602256255204850", "comments": "", "country": "South Africa", "email": "cburns4@miitbeian.g

Figure 2.23 – Output of the query showing key-value pairs

Similarly, by pointing to a different location, the CSV file can be loaded into another external table. An `EXT_CARD_DATA` table is created with its location pointing to a different path within the stage where the CSV files are stored. The `FILE_FORMAT` specifies that the files are in CSV format, and a file filter is applied to constrain the selection to files with "headless" in their names:

```
create or replace external table ext_card_data
with location = @sfuser_ext_stage/csv
file_format = (type = csv)
pattern = '.*headless[.]csv';
```

5. Let's query the new external table to inspect how Snowflake interprets the CSV data stored in the stage:

```
select * from ext_card_data;
```

The following screenshot of the resulting records shows some of the rows generated by the query. Please note the difference here. There are no meaningful column names in this case, unlike the previous case of the Parquet file:

	{?} VALUE
1	{ "c1": "ECTA.S19A1", "c10": "Actual", "c11": "RTS total industries", "c2": "2001.03", "c3": "2462.5", "c5": "F",
2	{ "c1": "ECTA.S19A1", "c10": "Actual", "c11": "RTS total industries", "c2": "2002.03", "c3": "17177.2", "c5": "F",
3	{ "c1": "ECTA.S19A1", "c10": "Actual", "c11": "RTS total industries", "c2": "2003.03", "c3": "22530.5", "c5": "F",
4	{ "c1": "ECTA.S19A1", "c10": "Actual", "c11": "RTS total industries", "c2": "2004.03", "c3": "28005.1", "c5": "F",
5	{ "c1": "ECTA.S19A1", "c10": "Actual", "c11": "RTS total industries", "c2": "2005.03", "c3": "30629.6", "c5": "F",

Figure 2.24 – Output of the select statement

As we have observed, an external table stores data in a `VARIANT` column. Although the data may appear JSON-like when queried, especially for semi-structured formats, structured formats such as Parquet are mapped into `VARIANT` and are not stored as raw JSON. This step shows how some meaningful names can be given to the dummy or automatically created columns in the JSON document and how it can be flattened to generate column-oriented rows. The following query shows how aliases can be created for the automatically created column names. Please note that the query only selects two columns, `c3` and `c2`, and creates the `card_sum` and `period` aliases, respectively. Moreover, to use the columns effectively, casting has been carried out for each column value:

```
select top 5 value:c3::float as card_sum,
value:c2::string as period
from ext_card_data;
```

The result of the query is shown:

	# CARD_SUM	A PERIOD
1	2462.5	2001.03
2	17177.2	2002.03
3	22530.5	2003.03
4	28005.1	2004.03
5	30629.6	2005.03

Figure 2.25 – Output of the query selecting two columns

6. Now that we have loaded tables and we can see how this data can be used in queries, we can drop the tables. This would end the life of the external tables that have been created to run queries on raw data – a typical purge-on-load pattern is applicable:

```
drop table ext_card_data;
drop table ext_tbl_userdata1;
```

How it works...

The stage created in *Step 1* can be thought of as a reference to a storage location. It is treated as a read-only location that can only be accessed using the appropriate access rights. The S3 bucket in *Step 1* is a public bucket and does not need credentials to be accessed. In *Chapter 3*,

Loading and Extracting Data Into and Out of Snowflake, when we look at staging in more detail, we shall start delving into securing the staging locations.

Step 2 is dereferencing the specified S3 bucket to list all the files that are available along with the last modified dates.

In *Step 3*, when the Parquet file is loaded into the external table, the table rows have all the field names captured, as shown in *Step 4*. But in *Step 5*, when the CSV-formatted file is loaded into the external table, there are dummy column names created by Snowflake, as can be seen in *Step 6*. This is because a Parquet file has metadata stored inside the file, while a CSV file does not have that metadata embedded in it. This is a major difference and would usually require additional steps as shown in *Step 7* to generate meaningful column names, plus the casting of data types.

There's more...

In this recipe, we did not look at how data could be loaded into a stage. It is possible to load data into a stage from a local filesystem. This method will be discussed in *Chapter 3, Loading and Extracting Data Into and Out of Snowflake*.

Looking at the metadata limitations for external tables, it can be argued that Avro files are a strong choice for staging data as Avro files can specify field names and data types as well.

Please note that the last modified dates for each file in a stage can be a useful mechanism to trigger updating data in an external table and can be used for running the ELT process.

Managing views in Snowflake

This recipe will introduce you to different variations of views that are specific to Snowflake and in what scenario a variant of a view should be used. The recipe will cover simple views and materialized views and will provide guidance on when to use what type of view.

Getting ready

The following examples can be run either via the Snowflake Snowsight or the Snowflake CLI command-line client. Please make sure that you have access to the `SNOWFLAKE_SAMPLE_DATA` database in your Snowflake instance. The `SNOWFLAKE_SAMPLE_DATA` database is automatically shared by Snowflake and provides sample data for testing and benchmarking.

How to do it...

The steps for this recipe are as follows:

1. The `SNOWFLAKE_SAMPLE_DATA` database contains a number of schemas. We will make use of the schema called `TPCH_SF1000`. Within this schema, there are multiple tables,

and our view will make use of the `STORE_SALES` table to produce an output that shows the sales against order dates. Before we create our first view, let's create a database where we will create the views:

```
CREATE OR REPLACE DATABASE TEST_VIEW_CREATION;
```

2. Create the view called `DATE_WISE_PROFIT` that, as the name suggests, shows the profit against the date:

```
CREATE OR REPLACE VIEW TEST_VIEW_CREATION.PUBLIC.DATE_WISE_PROFIT
AS
SELECT
  L_COMMITDATE AS ORDER_DATE,
  SUM(L_QUANTITY) AS TOTAL_QUANTITY,
  SUM(L_EXTENDEDPRICE) AS TOTAL_PRICE
FROM SNOWFLAKE_SAMPLE_DATA.TPCH_SF1000.LINEITEM
GROUP BY L_COMMITDATE;
```

The view is successfully created with the following message:

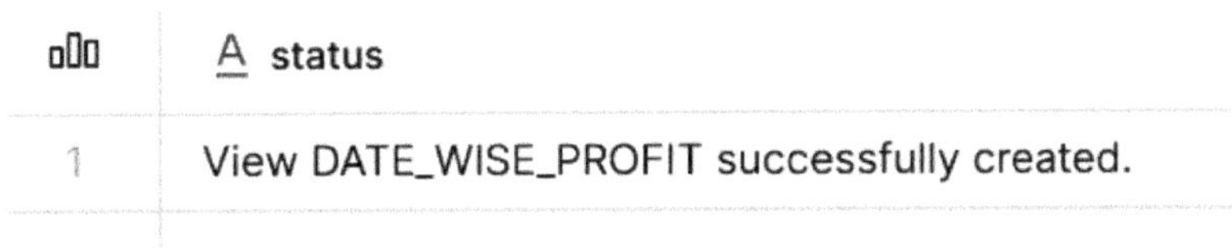

Figure 2.26 – View created successfully

3. Let's select some data from this view:

```
SELECT *
FROM TEST_VIEW_CREATION.PUBLIC.DATE_WISE_PROFIT;
```

The view will take a few minutes to execute as the underlying tables contain a large amount of data. This latency in execution can be managed by opting for a larger warehouse. An extra-small warehouse has been used in this case. After some time, you should see the result set returned as shown in *Figure 2.27*, which will be approximately 2,500 rows:

Table | Chart | 2,466 rows | 1m 9s

	ORDER_DATE	TOTAL_QUANTITY	TOTAL_PRICE
1	1995-09-07	63631154.00	95440970670.63
2	1995-08-12	63569816.00	95336901539.25
3	1995-08-26	63507122.00	95230644409.23
4	1995-09-14	63736339.00	95587215615.37

Figure 2.27 – Selecting data from the view

4. As you might have noticed, selecting data from this view took a reasonable amount of time to execute, and this time would increase if the amount of data in the table increased over time. To optimize performance, you can choose to create this view as a materialized view. Please note that creating materialized views requires at least a Snowflake Enterprise license:

```
CREATE OR REPLACE MATERIALIZED VIEW
TEST_VIEW_CREATION.PUBLIC.DATE_WISE_ORDER_FAST
AS
SELECT
  L_COMMITDATE AS ORDER_DATE,
  SUM(L_QUANTITY) AS TOTAL_QUANTITY,
  SUM(L_EXTENDEDPRICE) AS TOTAL_PRICE
FROM SNOWFLAKE_SAMPLE_DATA.TPCH_SF1000.LINEITEM
GROUP BY L_COMMITDATE;
```

It will take noticeably longer to create the materialized view compared to the immediate creation we saw in *Step 2*. In this example, the creation took approximately 1 minute and 7 seconds. This is because materialized views store the result set physically, unlike standard views, which only store the query definition and compute results at runtime when referenced.

Table | Chart | 1 row | 1m 17s

	status
1	Materialized view DATE_WISE_ORDER_FAST successfully created.

Figure 2.28 – Creating a materialized view

It will take a fair bit of time to create the view as opposed to the immediate creation that we saw in *Step 2*, mainly because materialized views store data, unlike normal views, which just store the DDL commands and fetch data on the fly when the view is referenced.

5. Let's now select from the materialized view:

```
SELECT * FROM TEST_VIEW_CREATION.PUBLIC.DATE_WISE_ORDER_FAST;
```

The results are returned almost immediately as we are selecting from a materialized view, which performs much better than a simple view.

How it works...

A standard view in Snowflake is a way to treat the result of a query as if it were a table. The query itself is part of the view definition. When data is selected from a standard view, the query in the view definition is executed and the results are presented back as a table to the user. Since the view appears as a table, it can be joined with other tables as well and used in queries in most places where tables can be used. Views are a powerful method to abstract complex logic from the users of data; that is, a reusable query with complex logic can be created as a view. As such, this takes the burden off the end users to know the logic. Views can also be used to provide access control on data, so for various departments in an organization, different views can be created, each of which provides a subset of the data.

Since a standard view executes its definition at runtime, it can take some time to execute. If there is a complex query that is commonly used, it can be created as a materialized view. A materialized view looks similar to a standard view, but it doesn't run the query in its definition at runtime. Rather, when a materialized view is created, it runs the query right away and stores the results. The advantage is that when the materialized view is queried, it does not have to execute but can retrieve the stored results immediately, providing

a performance boost. A materialized view will however incur additional maintenance and storage costs since every time the underlying table is changed, the view recalculates the results and updates the storage.

There's more...

Unlike materialized views in some traditional database platforms, such as Oracle, Snowflake materialized views are limited to a single base table and cannot be defined over joins involving multiple tables. When you need to materialize transformations that combine data from multiple tables, Dynamic Tables are generally the preferred solution because they support complex SQL transformations while automatically maintaining the derived dataset.

In addition to standard views and materialized views, Snowflake also offers additional view types such as secure views and recursive views. We will explore the application of secure views in *Chapter 7, Secure Data Sharing*.

Integrating Snowflake with Git

This recipe demonstrates how to integrate Snowflake with an existing Git repository to enable version-controlled management of Snowflake objects. By linking Snowflake to a remote Git repository, SQL artifacts such as table definitions can be tracked, reviewed, and promoted using standard Git workflows.

By the end of this recipe, you will be able to register a Git repository in Snowflake, browse its contents, and execute a version-controlled SQL file directly from Git.

This approach aligns Snowflake development with modern DataOps practices, where Git serves as the system of record and Snowflake consumes versioned definitions as part of the data lifecycle.

Getting ready

Before starting this recipe, ensure the following requirements are met:

1. You already have access to a Git repository hosted on a supported platform such as GitHub or GitLab.
2. The repository contains at least one branch.
3. SQL file has been created and committed to the repository using your standard Git tooling. In this recipe, the file contains the `CUSTOMER` table definition created in the *Managing tables* recipe earlier in this chapter.
4. You have the appropriate privileges in Snowflake to create security and integration objects such as `SECRETS`, `API INTEGRATIONS`, and `GIT REPOSITORIES`. In many organizations, these objects are created by platform or security administrators rather than individual developers.

Creating and managing Git repositories, branches, and commits is outside the scope of this recipe. For more information, refer to the official Git documentation at `https://git-scm.com/docs` and the documentation of your Git hosting provider.

How to do it...

In the following steps we will integrate Snowflake with an existing Git repository, synchronize its contents into Snowflake, and execute a version-controlled SQL artifact directly from Git. This demonstrates how Snowflake can participate in a Git-driven change management workflow, where database objects are defined declaratively and tracked over time.

The steps to complete this recipe are as follows:

1. Integration and tooling objects are typically separated from business data. We will begin by creating a dedicated database and schema to store Git-related objects:

```
CREATE OR REPLACE DATABASE DATAOPS;
CREATE OR REPLACE SCHEMA DATAOPS.GIT;

USE DATABASE DATAOPS;
USE SCHEMA GIT;
```

2. If the Git repository is private, Snowflake must authenticate securely when accessing it. Snowflake uses secrets to store credentials such as personal access tokens, ensuring credentials are not embedded directly in SQL code.

```
CREATE OR REPLACE SECRET GIT_CREDENTIAL_SECRET
  TYPE = PASSWORD
  USERNAME = '<GIT_USERNAME>'
  PASSWORD = '<PERSONAL_ACCESS_TOKEN>';
```

If the repository is public, this step can be skipped.

	A status
1	Secret GIT_CREDENTIAL_SECRET successfully created.

Figure 2.29 – GIT_CREDENTIAL_SECRET response

3. Snowflake connects to Git repositories over HTTPS using an API. The API integration defines which external endpoints Snowflake is allowed to access and which authentication mechanisms it can use.

```
CREATE OR REPLACE API INTEGRATION GIT_API_INTEGRATION
  API_PROVIDER = GIT_HTTPS_API
  API_ALLOWED_PREFIXES = ('https://github.com/<ORG_OR_USER>/')
  ALLOWED_AUTHENTICATION_SECRETS = (GIT_CREDENTIAL_SECRET)
  ENABLED = TRUE;
```

The allowed prefixes should be restricted to the Git provider and organization hosting the repository.

	status
1	Integration GIT_API_INTEGRATION successfully created.

Figure 2.30 – GIT_API_INTEGRATION response

4. Next, we will create a Git repository object in Snowflake. This registers the remote repository and creates a Git repository clone inside Snowflake that mirrors the repository structure, including branches and commit history.

```
CREATE OR REPLACE GIT REPOSITORY COOKBOOK_REPO
  API_INTEGRATION = GIT_API_INTEGRATION
  ORIGIN = 'https://github.com/<ORG_OR_USER>/<REPO_NAME>.git';
```

	status
1	Git Repository COOKBOOK_REPO was successfully created.

Figure 2.31 – REPOSITORY COOKBOOK_REPO response

5. At this point, the Git repository has been registered in Snowflake, but Snowflake has not yet synchronized any files. Fetching synchronizes the remote repository into the Git repository clone in Snowflake.
   Before running the fetch, ensure the SQL file containing the `CUSTOMER` table definition has already been committed to the branch you intend to use. In this recipe, we assume a file named `CUSTOMER.sql` exists in the repository. This file should contain a table definition statement (for example, a `CREATE OR ALTER TABLE` statement) that defines the `CUSTOMER` table structure created earlier in the Managing tables recipe.

   Run the following command to fetch the latest repository contents:

```
ALTER GIT REPOSITORY COOKBOOK_REPO FETCH
```

	scope	name	result
1	Branch	cookbook	FAST_FORWARD

Figure 2.32 – Fetching the latest contents from the Git repository clone in Snowflake

After fetching, verify which branches Snowflake can see from the repository:

```
SHOW GIT BRANCHES IN GIT REPOSITORY COOKBOOK_REPO;
```

	name	path	checkouts	commit_hash
1	cookbook	/branches/cookbook		28574148bd08050d011bc5f1e778dcdf34
2	main	/branches/main		58b594800354f7e0e26293a03a6a02765

Figure 2.33 – Listing available Git branches in the Snowflake repository clone

This output confirms the branch names you can reference in repository paths (for example, **main**).

6. After fetching the repository contents, list the files available in the branch you intend to use. In Snowflake, files in a Git repository clone are referenced by branch name, followed by the directory path as it exists in the repository.
   To list the contents of a branch, use the following pattern:

   ```
   LS @COOKBOOK_REPO/branches/<BRANCH_NAME>/;
   ```

   Replace <BRANCH_NAME> with the name of the branch that contains your SQL file (for example, `main`, `dev`, `int`, or `cookbook`).

   If your SQL files are stored in a subdirectory, include the directory path as well:

	name	size	md5	sha1
1	cookbook_repo/branches/cookbook/CUSTOMER.sql	458	null	b4e6f75c4a57b460c3db1d0836d
2	cookbook_repo/branches/cookbook/README.md	69	null	3f4bbc4837ffec764f308ca4a6ac7

Figure 2.34 – Viewing files available in the cookbook branch of the repository

   Confirm that the SQL file containing the `CUSTOMER` table definition (for example, `CUSTOMER.sql`) appears in the output before proceeding.

7. Now execute the SQL file directly from the Git repository clone in Snowflake. This demonstrates how Snowflake can apply version-controlled object definitions.
   Example using the recommended folder structure:

   ```
   EXECUTE IMMEDIATE FROM
     @COOKBOOK_REPO/branches/<BRANCH NAME>/CUSTOMER.sql;
   ```

	status
1	Table CUSTOMER successfully created.

Figure 2.35 – Executing a SQL file directly from the Git repository clone in Snowflake

How it works...

When a Git repository is integrated with Snowflake, Snowflake creates a Git repository clone that mirrors the remote repository. This clone contains the full repository structure, including branches, tags, and commit history. Snowflake does not automatically synchronize repository contents; instead, changes are pulled explicitly using a fetch operation. This ensures that updates are applied in a controlled and repeatable manner.

The Git repository clone behaves similarly to a Snowflake stage. Files stored in the repository can be browsed using standard listing commands and referenced by their branch name and path. Snowflake does not impose any required directory structure on the repository; paths reflect the layout defined in the remote Git repository.

By executing SQL directly from the Git repository clone using `EXECUTE IMMEDIATE FROM`, Snowflake applies database changes based on version-controlled definitions rather than ad hoc statements executed from worksheets. This establishes Git as the authoritative source for Snowflake object definitions, while Snowflake acts as the execution engine that applies the declared end state.

This pattern aligns with a deterministic approach to change management. Instead of writing and maintaining incremental `ALTER` statements, objects such as tables can be created or evolved using declarative SQL stored in Git. Snowflake determines the necessary changes at execution time, allowing schema evolution while preserving data when supported by the object type.

Together, Git integration and deterministic SQL provide a strong foundation for managing the Snowflake object lifecycle, enabling teams to adopt modern DataOps practices while maintaining consistency across environments.

There's more...

Snowflake's Git integration supports more than the repository synchronization and SQL execution demonstrated in this recipe. In addition to fetching repository contents and executing files, Snowflake provides SQL commands and Snowsight interfaces for performing common repository operations such as viewing branches, browsing files, and selecting specific versions of repository content.

Git integration in Snowflake also extends beyond SQL-based workflows. The following Snowflake features provide their own interfaces for working with Git repositories and performing Git operations:

- Workspaces
- Streamlit apps
- Snowflake notebooks

These capabilities allow teams to integrate Git into Snowflake in ways that align with their preferred development and operational workflows, ranging from read-only execution to interactive, collaborative development experiences.

Get this book's PDF version and more

Scan the QR code (or go to `packtpub.com/unlock`). Search for this book by name, confirm the edition, and then follow the steps on the page.

UNLOCK NOW

Note: Keep your invoice handy. Purchases made directly from Packt don't require an invoice.

3

Loading and Extracting Data Into and Out of Snowflake

Getting data into and out of Snowflake is one of the most critical aspects of building a reliable analytics platform. While Snowflake simplifies many traditional data warehousing challenges, designing ingestion patterns that are scalable, repeatable, and operationally sound still requires thoughtful implementation. This chapter focuses on the foundational mechanisms Snowflake provides for ingesting and extracting data, ranging from batch-based file loading to near real-time, event-driven ingestion, and sets the stage for building ingestion pipelines that can support modern analytics, data products, and AI-ready architecture.

The following recipes are included in this chapter:

- Preparing stage for data loading
- Loading delimited bulk data into Snowflake from cloud storage
- Loading delimited bulk data into Snowflake from your local machine
- Loading Parquet files into Snowflake
- Transforming JSON data into a relational tables in Snwoflake
- Processing newline-delimited JSON (NDJSON) into a Snowflake table
- Processing near real-time data into Snowflake using Snowpipe
- Extracting data from Snowflake into internal and external stages
- Building data ingestion pipelines with Snowflake Openflow

Technical requirements

This chapter requires access to a modern web browser (such as Chrome, Edge, or Firefox) and an active internet connection to access your Snowflake account in the cloud. Throughout the chapter, Snowflake's web interface (Snowsight) is used to create and manage database objects, stages, and ingestion processes.

Several recipes demonstrate loading data from a local machine using internal stages. For these recipes, the Snowflake CLI command-line client must be installed on your system. Snowflake CLI is used to upload files from a local filesystem into Snowflake and to execute SQL commands directly against your Snowflake account.

To demonstrate loading data from external sources, some recipes require access to cloud storage services such as Amazon S3, Azure Blob Storage, or Google Cloud Storage. These services are used as external stages for bulk and near real-time data ingestion.

For recipes that demonstrate near real-time ingestion using Snowpipe, access to cloud events or messaging services is required so that Snowflake can automatically detect newly arrived files. Examples in this chapter use services provided by AWS and Azure.

The final recipe in this chapter introduces Openflow, Snowflake's managed ingestion orchestration framework. This recipe requires access to Openflow in your Snowflake account and a PostgreSQL database to act as a source system. PostgreSQL may be installed locally or hosted in a virtual machine or cloud environment, provided it is reachable over the network from Openflow.

You can download the example project and code for this book by following the instructions in the ***Download the example code files*** section in the *Preface* of this book.

Preparing stage for data loading

Before data can be loaded into Snowflake, access to the source data must be established in a secure and governed way. Snowflake uses the concept of stages to abstract where data is located and how it can be accessed, whether the data resides internally within Snowflake or externally in cloud object storage. Preparing stages correctly is a foundational step, as every bulk load, near real-time ingestion, or orchestrated pipeline depends on this configuration.

In this recipe, you will learn how to create and configure both internal and external stages, with a focus on securely accessing private cloud storage locations such as Amazon S3. You will also see how stages enable Snowflake to separate storage access from data loading logic, providing flexibility, security, and reusability across ingestion workflows.

Getting ready

Before starting this recipe, you should have access to a private cloud storage location that will be used as a data source for Snowflake ingestion. In this example, an Amazon S3 bucket is used, but the same concepts apply to Azure Blob Storage and Google Cloud Storage. If you have not already done so, create an S3 bucket in your AWS account and have the bucket name available, as it will be referenced when configuring access policies and integrations.

You should have sufficient privileges in your cloud environment to configure secure access for Snowflake. For AWS-based examples, this includes the ability to create and manage AWS **Identity and Access Management** (**IAM**) roles and policies. This recipe assumes you are familiar with managing AWS accounts and S3 storage and does not cover detailed AWS configuration steps.

You should also know the AWS region in which your Snowflake account is deployed, as Snowflake requires region alignment when accessing external cloud storage.

Within Snowflake, you will need privileges to create storage integrations and stages. In a lab or demonstration environment, this typically requires access to a high-privilege role such as ACCOUNTADMIN. In production environments, these privileges are often delegated to a dedicated platform or security role.

How to do it...

Let's go through the steps required to set up a private or restricted S3 bucket for use with Snowflake:

1. Before configuring access, identify the cloud region in which your Snowflake account is deployed. The easiest way to determine this is by examining the URL used to access Snowsight. For example, if your Snowflake URL contains (`ap-southeast-2.snowflakecomputing.com`) then your Snowflake account is deployed in the ap-southeast-2 region. This region must be enabled for AWS **Security Token Service** (**STS**).
2. Let's verify that the AWS STS regional endpoint is enabled. STS is enabled by default in all AWS accounts and does not incur additional charges. However, Snowflake requires access to the STS endpoint in the same region as your Snowflake account.
   To confirm the STS endpoint settings, log in to the AWS Management Console and navigate to **IAM**. Under Account settings, verify that the STS endpoint for your Snowflake region is enabled. In most modern AWS accounts, this endpoint is already active and no changes are required.

This step ensures that Snowflake can assume the IAM role securely using temporary credentials.

3. In IAM, create a new policy that grants Snowflake access to the S3 bucket you intend to use. At a minimum, Snowflake requires permission to list the bucket and read objects. If the bucket will also be used for unloading data, write permissions are also required. Create the policy using the JSON editor and replace `<bucket>` with your bucket name:

```
{
  "Version": "2012-10-17",
  "Statement": [
    {
      "Effect": "Allow",
      "Action": [
        "s3:GetObject",
        "s3:GetObjectVersion",
        "s3:PutObject",
        "s3:DeleteObject",
        "s3:DeleteObjectVersion"
      ],
      "Resource": "arn:aws:s3:::<bucket>/*"
    },
    {
      "Effect": "Allow",
      "Action": "s3:ListBucket",
      "Resource": "arn:aws:s3:::<bucket>"
    }
  ]
}
```

4. Scroll to the bottom of the policy creation page and click Review policy. The resulting screen will show that the policy allows list and read access on S3 buckets, as shown in the following *Figure 3.1*.

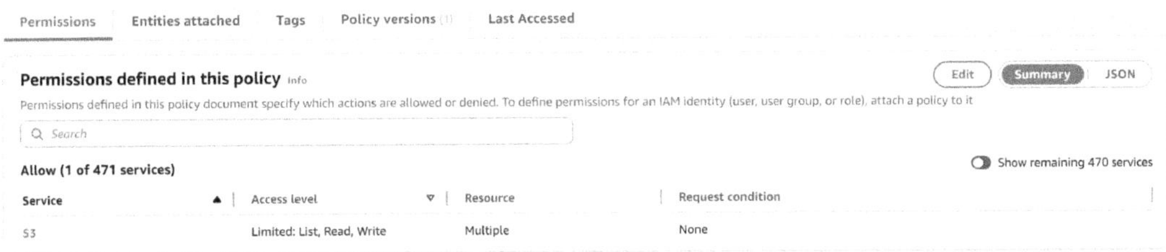

Figure 3.1 – Review policy page showing the allowed services

5. On the review screen, provide a name for the policy, for example, `snowflake_s3_access`, and click **Create policy**.
6. Now click on **Roles** in the left-hand navigation pane. From the Roles page, choose **Create role** and, when prompted, select **Another AWS account** as the trusted entity type. For the **Account ID**, temporarily enter your own AWS account ID. When prompted for an external ID, enter a placeholder value (for example, `snowflake_external_id_placeholder`). These values are used only to complete the role creation process and will be replaced later in this recipe when the trust relationship is updated using the values from the storage integration (see *Step 12*). Click **Next** to proceed to the permissions step.
7. Now search for the policy that we created in the previous steps, that is, the policy called `snowflake_s3_access` (or the name that you assigned in *step 5*). Check the checkbox against the policy and click **Next** to proceed to the review page.

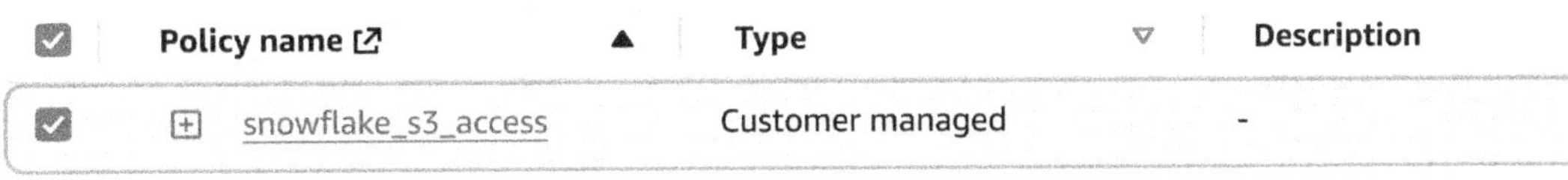

Figure 3.2 – Checking a policy to grant permissions

8. Give the role a name such as `Role_For_Snowflake` and click **Create Role**:

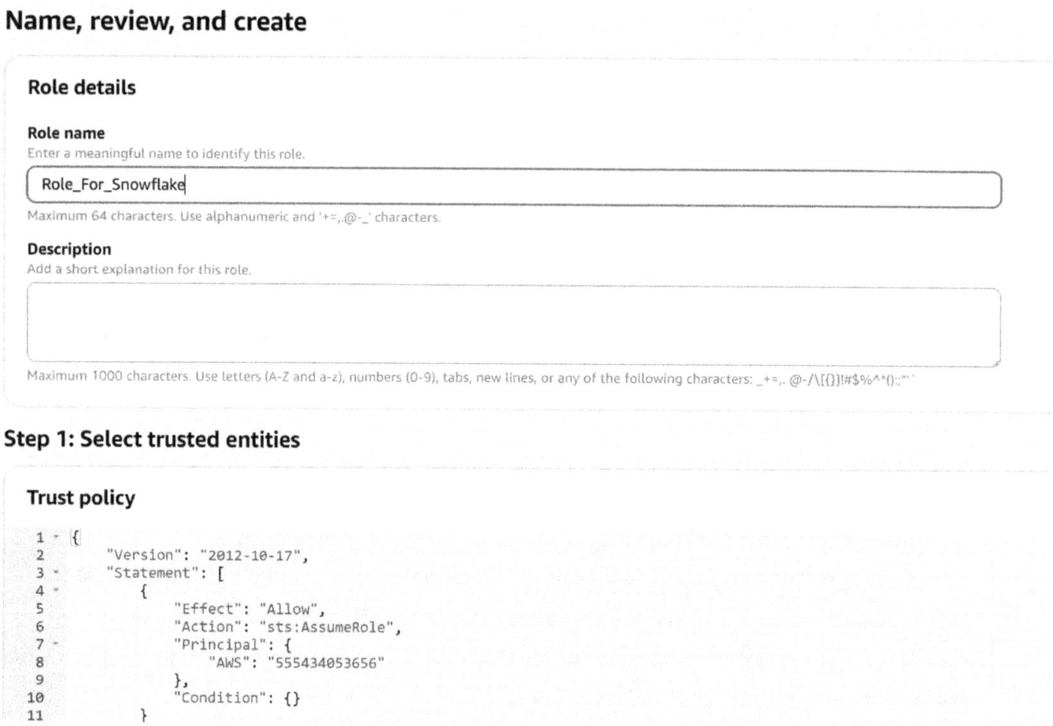

Figure 3.3 – Review page

9. Once the role is created, click on it and copy its ARN value. We will use the ARN to create the integration between Snowflake and the cloud storage.

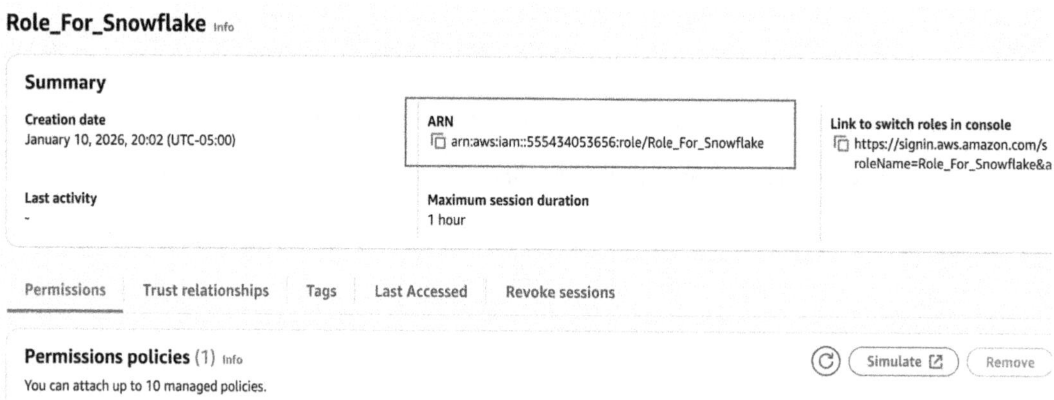

Figure 3.4 – Role page of a created role

10. Log in to Snowflake and switch to a role with privileges to create storage integrations. In many environments, this is the ACCOUNTADMIN role, although any role granted the `CREATE INTEGRATION` privilege can be used.

```
CREATE STORAGE INTEGRATION S3_INTEGRATION
  TYPE = EXTERNAL_STAGE
  STORAGE_PROVIDER = S3
  ENABLED = TRUE
  STORAGE_AWS_ROLE_ARN =
'<arn:aws:iam::123456789123:role/Role_For_Snowflake>'
  STORAGE_ALLOWED_LOCATIONS = ('s3://<bucket>');
```

Please replace the following values:

- `arn:aws:iam::123456789123:role/Role_For_Snowflake` with the IAM Role ARN created in *Step 9*
- `<bucket>` with the name of your existing S3 bucket

This command registers the IAM role with Snowflake and restricts access to the specified S3 location.

11. Now run a describe statement on the storage integration object that we just created and note down the values for `STORAGE_AWS_IAM_USER_ARN` and `STORAGE_AWS_EXTERNAL_ID`.

```
DESC INTEGRATION S3_INTEGRATION;
```

You can see the output for the describe statement in *Figure 3.5*.

	property	property_type	property_value	property_default
1	ENABLED	Boolean	true	false
2	STORAGE_PROVIDER	String	S3	
3	STORAGE_ALLOWED_LOCATIONS	List	s3://cookbook-raw/	[]
4	STORAGE_BLOCKED_LOCATIONS	List		[]
5	STORAGE_AWS_IAM_USER_ARN	String	arn:aws:iam::912178297543:user/87fa1000-	
6	STORAGE_AWS_ROLE_ARN	String	arn:aws:iam::555434053656:role/Role_For_Si	
7	STORAGE_AWS_EXTERNAL_ID	String	EPB34842_SFCRole=2_XpEey+wDseLTuBEFS	
8	USE_PRIVATELINK_ENDPOINT	Boolean	false	false
9	COMMENT	String		

Figure 3.5 – Output of the DESC statement

12. Now, return to the AWS console, select **IAM**, and click **Roles** from the navigation bar. Select the role that we created earlier, that is, `Role_For_Snowflake`. Click the **Trust relationships** tab and click **edit trust relationship**:

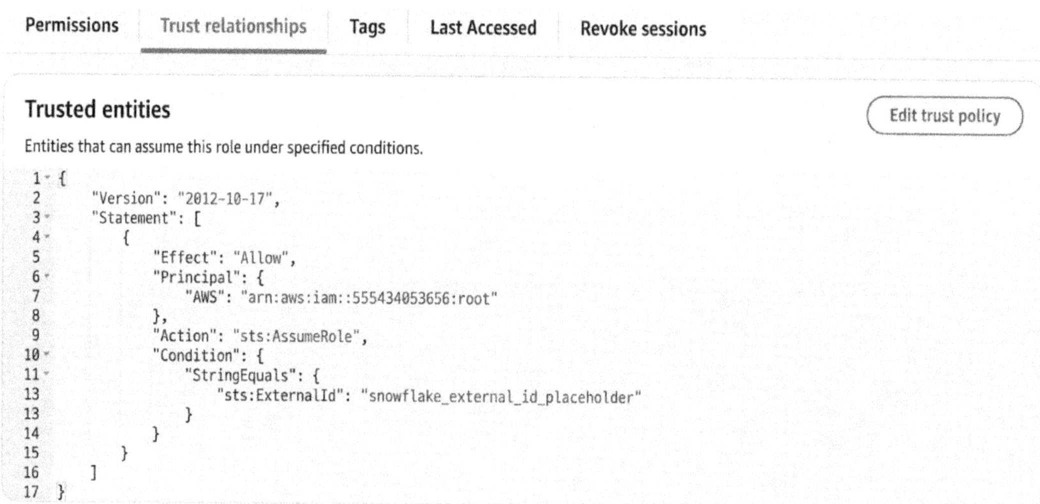

Figure 3.6 – Trust relationships tab

In the policy document, replace the text with the text shown in the following code block and replace the highlighted values with the values you copied in the previous step, and click **Update Policy**.

```
{
  "Version": "2012-10-17",
  "Statement": [
    {
      "Effect": "Allow",
      "Principal": {
        "AWS": "<STORAGE_AWS_IAM_USER_ARN>"
      },
      "Action": "sts:AssumeRole",
      "Condition": {
        "StringEquals": {
          "sts:ExternalId": "<STORAGE_AWS_EXTERNAL_ID>"
        }
      }
    }
  ]
}
```

13. We will now go back to Snowflake and grant the integration object to the SYSADMIN role so that the system admin can use the integration object in the definition of other external stages. This step must be run as ACCOUNTADMIN or by the role that created the storage integration:

```
GRANT USAGE ON INTEGRATION S3_INTEGRATION TO ROLE
SYSADMIN;
```

14. Now, let's create an external stage that uses the storage integration object we created earlier. We will try and list the files in the stage, and if we do not get any issues, it means that the configuration is correctly set up. Please ensure that you replace <BUCKET_NAME> with your desired S3 bucket name in the following code segment.
15. To keep this recipe self-contained, create and select a database and schema before creating the stage:

```
USE ROLE SYSADMIN;

CREATE DATABASE IF NOT EXISTS STAGE_EX;
```

```
USE DATABASE STAGE_EX;

CREATE SCHEMA IF NOT EXISTS EXTERNAL_STAGE;
USE SCHEMA EXTERNAL_STAGE;

CREATE STAGE S3_RESTRICTED_STAGE
 STORAGE_INTEGRATION = S3_INTEGRATION
 URL = 's3://<BUCKET_NAME>';
```

16. Let's try running `LIST` on the stage we just created:

    ```
    LIST @S3_RESTRICTED_STAGE;
    ```

    If the configuration is correct, the command will complete without authorization errors. If files are present in the referenced S3 bucket or prefix, they will be listed in the result. If no files are present, the command may return no rows, which is expected behavior and still indicates that the stage has been configured successfully.

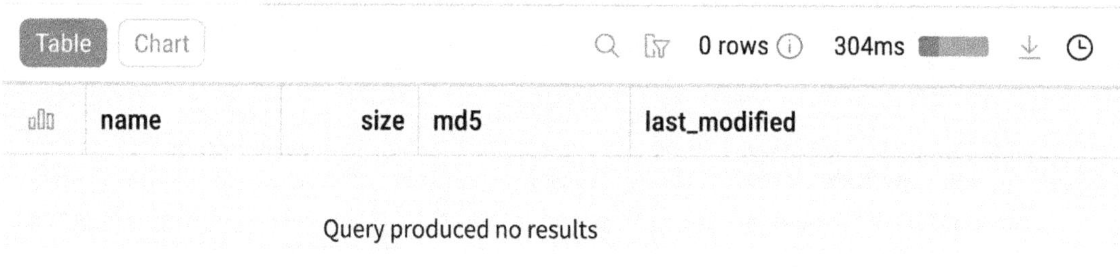

Figure 3.7 – Output of LIST

At this point, the required configuration is complete and Snowflake can securely access the S3 bucket using role-based authorization.

How it works...

The secure access configured in this recipe is based on role assumption rather than static credentials. When Snowflake needs to access data stored in a private Amazon S3 bucket through an external stage, it does not use embedded access keys or long-lived users. Instead, Snowflake temporarily assumes an AWS IAM role that you explicitly authorize.

As shown in *Figure 3.8*, the process begins within Snowflake, where a storage integration is created (4). This integration defines how Snowflake is allowed to authenticate with AWS and which S3 locations it is permitted to access. As part of this process, Snowflake generates an AWS IAM principal (1) along with an external ID, which are used to establish a secure trust relationship.

On the AWS side, an IAM role (2) is configured with a policy (3) that grants access to the required S3 bucket or prefix. A trust relationship (5) is then established that allows Snowflake's generated IAM principal to assume this role, provided the correct external ID is supplied. This ensures that only Snowflake, and only for explicitly allowed locations, can assume the role and access the data.

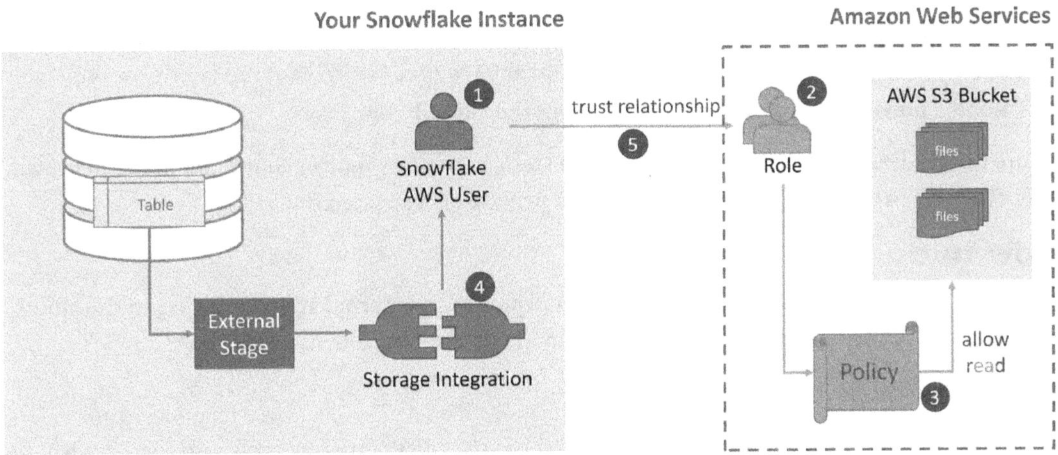

Figure 3.8 – Configuring Snowflake access to private S3 buckets

When a command such as `LIST`, `COPY INTO`, or a Snowpipe load is executed against the external stage, Snowflake temporarily assumes the IAM role using AWS STS. AWS issues short-lived credentials for the role, which Snowflake uses to access the S3 bucket for the duration of the operation. Once the operation completes, the credentials expire automatically.

This approach provides strong security guarantees by eliminating the need for static credentials, enforcing least-privilege access, and ensuring that storage access is tightly scoped and auditable. The same pattern is reused across Snowflake features that interact with cloud storage, including Snowpipe, data unloading, and orchestrated ingestion pipelines.

Loading delimited bulk data into Snowflake from cloud storage

Bulk file loading from cloud object storage remains one of the most common ingestion patterns in Snowflake. Whether data arrives periodically as batch extracts or is delivered by upstream systems, Snowflake provides a simple and scalable mechanism for loading delimited files using external stages and the `COPY INTO` command.

In this recipe, you will load a delimited text file stored in cloud storage into a Snowflake table. The recipe demonstrates how file formats, external stages, and the `COPY INTO` command work together to support repeatable, production-ready bulk ingestion.

Getting ready

As we will be loading a file from cloud storage into Snowflake, you should have a cloud storage bucket already created and at least one delimited file uploaded to a known path within the bucket (for example, `s3://cookbook-raw/chapter03/r2/cc_info.csv`). To save time, you can download a previously created sample file from the GitHub repository.

Before proceeding with this recipe, follow the steps in the *Configuring Snowflake access to private S3 buckets* recipe to set up access when using a private or restricted bucket.

How to do it...

In order to load a file from cloud storage, we will create an external stage pointing to the cloud storage and use the `COPY INTO` command to load the external file into Snowflake.

The steps are as follows:

1. Let's first create and set the database where we will create our table and load it with some sample data:

```
CREATE OR REPLACE DATABASE C3_R2;
USE DATABASE C3_R2;
```

2. Now that we have a database created, let's create a new table named `CREDIT_CARDS`. We will load the sample data into this table:

```
CREATE OR REPLACE TABLE CREDIT_CARDS
(
  CUSTOMER_NAME STRING,
  CREDIT_CARD   STRING,
  TYPE          STRING,
  CCV           STRING,
  EXP_DATE      STRING
);
```

3. Before loading the data, we must define how Snowflake should interpret the structure of the files stored in cloud storage. This is done using a file format object. The file format describes how the data is organized, including how fields are separated, whether a header row is present, and how values are enclosed.

In this example, the source file is a standard CSV file. The first row of the file contains column headers rather than data, so the header row must be skipped during loading. Additionally, some fields may be enclosed in double quotes, which Snowflake must handle correctly when parsing the file.

Create a named file format so that this definition can be reused across multiple stages and load operations:

```
CREATE OR REPLACE FILE FORMAT GEN_CSV
TYPE = CSV
SKIP_HEADER = 1
FIELD_OPTIONALLY_ENCLOSED_BY = '"';
```

4. To simplify this recipe, the sample data has already been uploaded to a cloud storage location. In practice, this data would typically reside in a private bucket secured using a storage integration, as described in the first recipe, *Preparing stages for data loading*. For this step, we will focus on creating the external stage that references the storage location, regardless of whether the bucket is public or restricted.
An external stage in Snowflake provides a logical reference to files stored in external cloud storage, such as Amazon S3. The stage does not store data itself; instead, it defines where the files are located and how Snowflake should interpret them using a file format.

5. Create the external stage using one of the following approaches, depending on how you are accessing the data. If you are using the public sample data provided with this book, you can create the stage directly without a storage integration:

```
CREATE OR REPLACE STAGE C3_R2_STAGE
 URL = 's3://cookbook-raw/chapter03/r2/'
 FILE_FORMAT = GEN_CSV;
```

This option uses a publicly accessible S3 bucket and does not require a storage integration. Alternatively, if you are using your own S3 bucket and have created a storage integration in the previous recipe, create the stage as follows:

```
CREATE OR REPLACE STAGE C3_R2_STAGE
  URL = 's3://<BUCKET_NAME>/<PATH>/'
  STORAGE_INTEGRATION = <STORAGE_INTEGRATION_NAME>
  FILE_FORMAT = GEN_CSV;
```

In this case, replace <BUCKET_NAME>, <PATH>, and <STORAGE_INTEGRATION_NAME> with values appropriate for your environment.

> **Note**
>
> Cloud storage buckets should not be publicly accessible in production environments. Public access is used here only to simplify the example and avoid additional configuration steps.

6. In this example, the stage is created using a fully qualified path within the bucket. Alternatively, you could define the stage at the bucket root and specify subdirectories later when running the `COPY INTO` command. Both approaches are supported, and the choice typically depends on how you organize data within your storage hierarchy. When accessing private or restricted cloud storage, the stage must reference a storage integration, which provides Snowflake with the required permissions to access the specified bucket or path. Let's try and list the files in the stage so that we can be sure that we are able to access the data in the S3 bucket:

```
LIST @C3_R2_STAGE;
```

You should see the list of files in the bucket, which indicates that Snowflake is able to access the data:

	name	size	md5
1	s3://cookbook-raw/chapter03/r2/cc_info.c	64973	a48d9bd1ca9542c8464a09516b67991d

Figure 3.9 – List of files in the bucket

7. Now that the data is accessible through the external stage, the files can be loaded into the target table using the `COPY INTO` command. This command instructs Snowflake to read the files referenced by the stage, apply the file format rules, and insert the parsed data into the table.

```
COPY INTO CREDIT_CARDS
FROM @C3_R2_STAGE;
```

8. When the command completes, Snowflake returns a load status result showing how many files were processed, how many rows were loaded, and whether any errors occurred. If you are using the sample file provided with this book, the output should indicate that 1,000 rows were successfully loaded into the table.

> **Note**
>
> By default, `COPY INTO` is idempotent and tracks which files have already been loaded. If you run the command again without changing the files or load options, Snowflake will not reload the same data unless explicitly instructed to do so.

9. After the load operation completes, verify that the data has been inserted into the table by querying the row count. The query should return the total number of rows loaded into the table.

```
SELECT COUNT(*) FROM CREDIT_CARDS;
```

How it works...

Snowflake supports multiple approaches for loading data from cloud storage, but the recommended and most commonly used method is through the use of external stages. As illustrated in *Figure 3.10*, an external stage acts as a logical reference inside Snowflake that points to data stored in external cloud storage, such as Amazon S3. The key distinction is that an external stage does not store any data itself; instead, it exposes the files that already exist in cloud storage so they can be accessed securely and consistently.

An alternative approach is to reference cloud storage locations directly within the `COPY INTO` command. While this method is supported, using external stages is generally preferred because it separates storage location, security configuration, and file format definitions from the load logic itself. This separation improves reuse, readability, and maintainability of ingestion workflows.

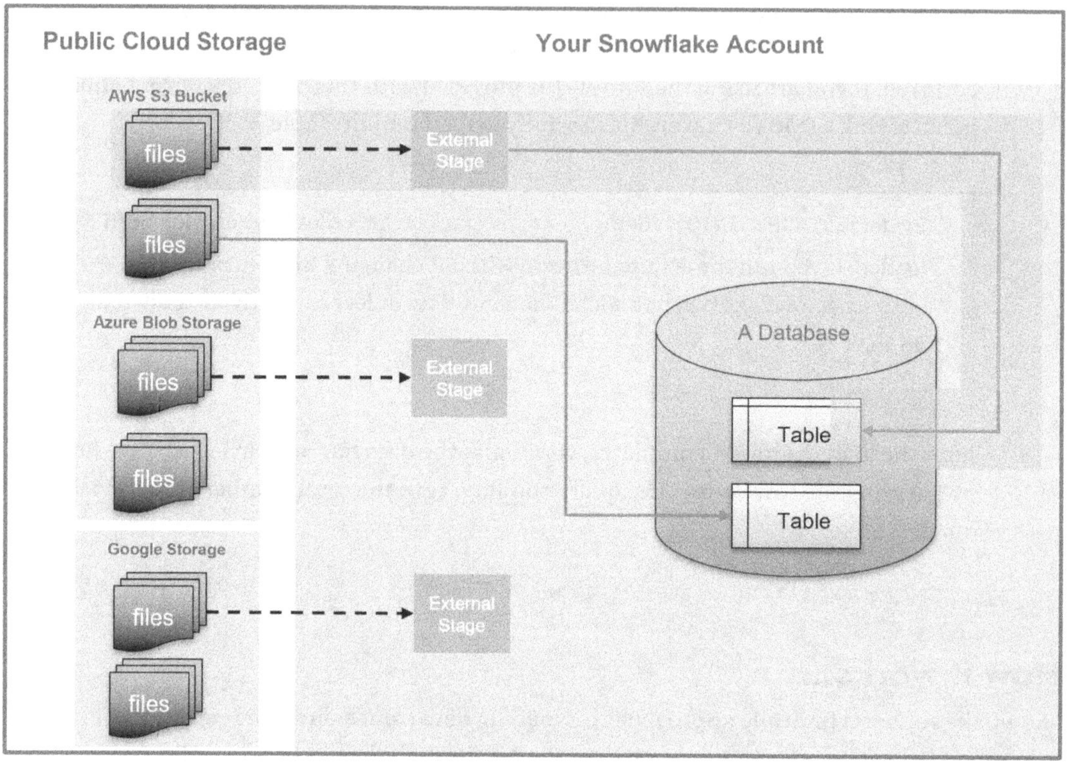

Figure 3.10 – Loading from cloud storage via external stages

In this recipe, a named file format is first created to describe how Snowflake should interpret the structure of the delimited files, including field separators and header rows. Next, an external stage is defined to reference a specific location in cloud storage and associate it with the file format. When working with private or restricted buckets, the stage also references a storage integration, which allows Snowflake to securely access the storage location using role-based authorization.

Before loading data, the contents of the external stage are listed to validate that Snowflake can successfully access the files. Once access is confirmed, the `COPY INTO` command is executed to read the files from the stage, apply the file format rules, and load the parsed data into the target table. Snowflake manages the compute resources required for this operation and returns detailed load results indicating success or failure.

This pattern of combining file formats, external stages, and the `COPY INTO` command, forms the foundation for batch-based data ingestion in Snowflake and is reused across a wide range of ingestion scenarios, regardless of the underlying cloud provider.

Loading delimited bulk data into Snowflake from your local machine

In some scenarios, data originates outside of cloud storage and must be loaded directly from an on-premises system or a local workstation. This recipe demonstrates how to load delimited files from a local machine into Snowflake using Snowflake CLI and internal stages. The local system may be a server running within your network or a personal workstation containing files that need to be ingested.

Getting ready

Since we will be loading a file from your local system into Snowflake, you will first need to have a file available locally. To save time, you can download a sample file from the book's GitHub repository.

Because the data is being loaded from a local machine, a command-line tool is required to upload the file into Snowflake. In this recipe, we will use the Snowflake CLI to copy the file into an internal stage. Ensure that the Snowflake CLI is installed and configured on your system, and that you can successfully connect to your Snowflake account before proceeding.

How to do it...

This recipe begins by creating a database, table, and file format. An internal stage is then created, after which the Snowflake CLI is used to upload the file from the local machine into the stage. Finally, the data is loaded from the stage into the target table.

The steps for this recipe are as follows:

1. Let's begin by creating a database that will be used to store the table and load the sample data:

```
CREATE DATABASE IF NOT EXISTS C4_LD_EX;

USE DATABASE C4_LD_EX;
```

2. Create a table called `CUSTOMER`. We will load the sample data into this table:

```
CREATE OR REPLACE TABLE CUSTOMER
(
  FNAME          STRING,
  LNAME          STRING,
  EMAIL          STRING,
  DATE_OF_BIRTH  DATE,
```

```
    CITY            STRING,
    COUNTRY         STRING
);
```

3. Before loading the file, define a named file format that describes how Snowflake should interpret the data. In this example, the file is pipe-delimited (|), includes a header row, and contains dates formatted as YYYY-MM-DD:

```
CREATE OR REPLACE FILE FORMAT PIPE_DELIM
  TYPE = CSV
  FIELD_DELIMITER = '|'
  FIELD_OPTIONALLY_ENCLOSED_BY = '"'
  SKIP_HEADER = 1
  DATE_FORMAT = 'YYYY-MM-DD';
```

   Using a named file format allows the same parsing rules to be reused across stages and load operations.

4. Let's create an internal named stage that will be used to temporarily store the file before loading it into the target table. The stage is associated with the file format created in the previous step so that Snowflake knows how to interpret any files uploaded to this stage.

```
CREATE OR REPLACE STAGE CUSTOMER_STAGE
  FILE_FORMAT = PIPE_DELIM;
```

   By associating the file format with the stage, the parsing rules do not need to be repeated when loading the data. If a named file format had not been created, the file format options could instead be specified directly in the `CREATE STAGE` or `COPY INTO` statement.

5. Now that the internal stage has been created, upload the file from the local system into the stage. Because the file resides on a local filesystem, this step must be executed using the Snowflake CLI, which runs from your operating system command line and allows you to interact with Snowflake resources.
6. Ensure that your Snowflake CLI connection is configured with the correct database and schema, as internal named stages are schema-scoped.
7. Next, use the Snowflake CLI to upload the file into the internal stage:

```
snow stage copy file://customers.csv @CUSTOMER_STAGE;
```

In this example, the `file://customers.csv` path assumes that the Snowflake CLI is being run from the directory containing the file. If the file is located in a different directory, provide the full file path instead.

During this operation, Snowflake automatically compresses and encrypts the file as it is transferred into the internal stage.

8. Verify that the file has been uploaded successfully by listing the contents of the stage:

```
LIST @CUSTOMER_STAGE;
```

The output should show the uploaded file, such as customers.csv, along with additional metadata about the file.

9. Now that the file has been uploaded to a Snowflake internal stage, the data can be loaded into the target table using the `COPY INTO` command. At this point, the data is no longer on the local filesystem, so the load operation can be executed either from the Snowflake CLI or from the Snowflake web interface (Snowsight).

```
COPY INTO CUSTOMER
FROM @CUSTOMER_STAGE;
```

If the operation is successful, Snowflake will return a status message indicating how many rows were loaded. When using the sample file provided with this book, 200 rows should be loaded into the `CUSTOMER` table.

10. Verify that the data has been loaded into the target table by querying the table. If the load was successful and you are using the sample file provided with this book, the table should contain 200 rows.

```
SELECT * FROM CUSTOMER;
```

11. Once the data has been successfully loaded into the target table, it is generally no longer necessary to retain the files in the internal stage. To minimize storage usage, you can remove any files that remain in the stage:

```
REMOVE @CUSTOMER_STAGE;
```

How it works...

Snowflake provides three types of stages for loading data from on-premises systems: internal named stages, user stages, and table stages. In this recipe, we used an internal named stage, which is a reusable, schema-scoped staging location managed entirely within Snowflake.

The overall process involves transferring a file from a local system into an internal stage and then loading that data into a target table within Snowflake.

Before creating the stage, we first defined a file format that describes the structure of the incoming data. In this case, the file format specifies a delimited file with a header row, fields enclosed in double quotes, and a standardized date format (YYYY-MM-DD). Defining a named file format allows this configuration to be reused across multiple stages and load operations, making it easier to manage and standardize ingestion logic.

Next, we created an internal named stage and associated it with the file format. Because the source file resides on a local filesystem, the data transfer into Snowflake must be initiated using a client that has access to that filesystem. The Snowflake web interface (Snowsight) cannot directly access local files, so we used the Snowflake CLI command-line client to upload the file into the internal stage using the snow stage copy command.

When files are uploaded to an internal stage, Snowflake automatically compresses and encrypts them as part of the transfer process. Once the file is available in the internal stage, loading the data into the target table is handled using a standard `COPY INTO` command.

After the data has been successfully loaded, the staged files are no longer required for most use cases. Removing files from the internal stage helps reduce unnecessary storage usage, which is why the recipe concludes with a cleanup step.

Loading Parquet files into Snowflake

This recipe demonstrates how to load Parquet-formatted data stored in cloud object storage into Snowflake. We will use an external stage created on top of an Amazon S3 bucket and load the Parquet data into a relational Snowflake table by extracting fields from the semi-structured data.

Getting ready

To complete this recipe, you need access to a cloud storage location containing Parquet files. To save time, you can download a sample Parquet file to from the book's GitHub repository.

If your data resides in a private or restricted S3 bucket, ensure that access has been configured as described in the *Preparing stage for data loading* recipe earlier in this chapter.

How to do it...

We will start by creating a database and a target table, followed by defining a Parquet file format and an external stage. The Parquet data will then be queried and transformed into relational columns.

The steps for this recipe are as follows:

1. Let's first create and set the database where we will create our table and load it with some sample data.

```
CREATE DATABASE C3_R4;
USE C3_R4;
```

2. Create a new table called `TRANSACTIONS`. We will load the sample data into this table.

```
CREATE OR REPLACE TABLE TRANSACTIONS
(
    TRANSACTION_DATE DATE,
    CUSTOMER_ID NUMBER(38,0),
    TRANSACTION_ID NUMBER(38,0),
    AMOUNT NUMBER(38,0)
);
```

3. Define a named file format that describes how Snowflake should interpret the incoming Parquet files. Creating a named file format allows the same configuration to be reused across multiple stages and load operations.
In this example, the file format specifies that the source data is in Parquet format, enables automatic compression detection, and defines string values that should be interpreted as `NULL`. Specifically, if the value `MISSING` or an empty string is encountered in the data, it will be converted to `NULL` during ingestion.

```
CREATE OR REPLACE FILE FORMAT GEN_PARQ
TYPE = PARQUET
COMPRESSION = AUTO
NULL_IF = ('MISSING','');
```

4. To simplify this recipe, the sample Parquet files have already been uploaded to a public Amazon S3 bucket named `snowflake-cookbook`. In real-world scenarios, data should typically reside in private or restricted buckets; access to such buckets was covered earlier in this chapter when configuring storage integrations.

Create an external stage that points to the location containing the Parquet files and associate it with the file format defined in the previous step:

```
CREATE OR REPLACE STAGE C3_R4_STAGE
url='s3://snowflake-cookbook/Chapter03/r4'
FILE_FORMAT = GEN_PARQ;
```

> **Note**
>
> For simplicity, this example uses a public bucket. Storing data in public cloud storage is generally not recommended for production workloads.

5. Before loading the data, verify that Snowflake can access the Parquet files in the external stage by listing the stage contents:

```
LIST @C3_R4_STAGE;
```

If the stage has been configured correctly, Snowflake will return a list of Parquet files available at the specified location in the S3 bucket. Successfully listing the files confirms that Snowflake has read access to the storage location.

	name	size	md5
1	s3://snowflake-cookbook/Chapter03/r4/transactions.parquet	3929	aac8101db9d3de72231fb9f2dac28a5f

Figure 3.11 – List of files in the bucket

6. Now that the data is accessible through the external stage, preview the contents of the Parquet files by querying the stage directly:

```
SELECT $1 FROM @C3_R4_STAGE;
```

When Parquet data is queried from a stage, Snowflake returns each record as a single semi-structured value represented using the `VARIANT` data type. The output is displayed in a JSON-like format, allowing you to inspect the structure and field names before loading the data into a relational table.

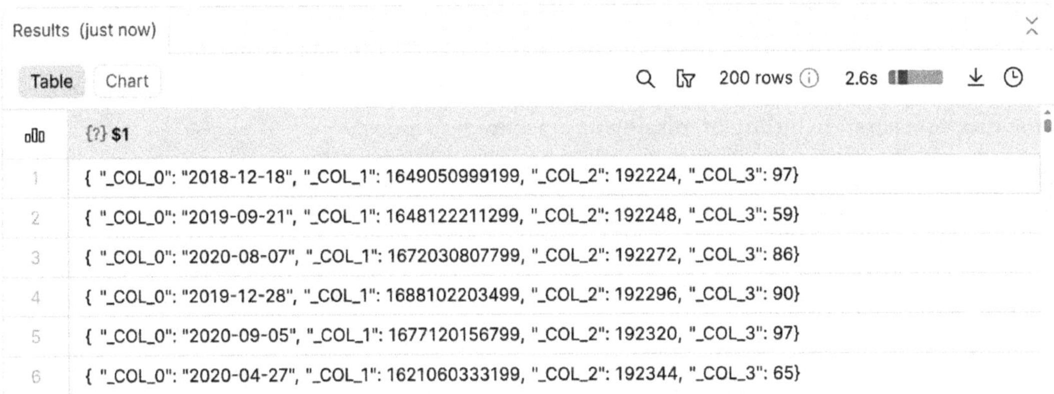

Figure 3.12 – Previewing the data in the stage

7. Each Parquet record is exposed as a single VARIANT value when queried from the external stage. Individual fields within that record can be accessed using path notation and explicitly cast to the appropriate relational data types.
   In this example, the fields are accessed using the syntax $1:<field_name> and cast using the :: operator before being inserted into the target table:

```
INSERT INTO TRANSACTIONS
SELECT
    $1:_COL_0::DATE,
    $1:_COL_1::NUMBER,
    $1:_COL_2::NUMBER,
    $1:_COL_3::NUMBER
FROM @C3_R4_STAGE;
```

   If the operation is successful and you are using the sample files provided with this book, 200 rows should be inserted into the TRANSACTIONS table.

8. Verify that the Parquet data has been loaded into the target table. If you are using the sample files provided with this book, the table should contain 200 rows.

```
USE C3_R4;
SELECT * FROM TRANSACTIONS;
```

How it works...

In this recipe, we defined a named file format GEN_PARQ using the CREATE FILE FORMAT statement to describe how Snowflake should interpret the incoming Parquet files. The TYPE =

`PARQUET` setting indicates that the source data is stored in Parquet format, while `COMPRESSION = AUTO` instructs Snowflake to automatically detect any compression applied to the files. The `NULL_IF` option specifies string values that should be converted to `NULL` during ingestion, ensuring consistent handling of missing or placeholder values.

When Parquet data is accessed through an external stage, Snowflake exposes each record as semi-structured data represented using the `VARIANT` data type. Although Parquet is a strongly typed, columnar format, Snowflake presents the data in a JSON-like structure to provide a unified approach for working with semi-structured data formats.

Because each record is returned as a single `VARIANT` column, it can be referenced using the `$1` notation when querying the stage. Individual fields within the Parquet record are accessed using path expressions such as `$1:_COL_0` and explicitly cast to relational data types using the `::` operator.

Once the required fields have been extracted and converted to the appropriate data types, the transformed data is inserted into the target relational table using a standard `INSERT` statement, completing the transition from Parquet files in cloud storage to structured data in Snowflake.

Transforming JSON data into relational tables in Snowflake

This recipe demonstrates how to load JSON semi-structured data into Snowflake and transform it into a relational representation that can be queried and processed using standard SQL. You will learn how Snowflake stores JSON data using the `VARIANT` data type and how functions such as `FLATTEN` can be used to convert nested arrays into rows.

Getting ready

This recipe builds on concepts introduced earlier in this chapter, in the recipe *Loading delimited bulk data into Snowflake from cloud storage*. To keep the focus on JSON processing, the steps for creating file formats and external stages are not repeated here. Please refer to that recipe for detailed setup instructions.

A sample JSON file has been made available in a public cloud storage bucket. The JSON document contains two top-level fields, `data_set` and `extract_date`, along with an array of objects named `credit_cards`. The objective of this recipe is to transform the following nested JSON structure into a relational format.

```
{
    "data_set":"credit_cards",
    "extract_date":"2019-10-26",
    "credit_cards": [
        {
            "CreditCardNo": "527147 8139869068",
            "CreditCardHolder": "Alfreda Y. Meyers",
            "CardPin": "1634",
            "CardCVV": "929",
            "CardExpiry": "03/20"
        },
        {
            "CreditCardNo": "57705658951575987",
            "CreditCardHolder": "Libby I. Delaney",
            "CardPin": "7235",
            "CardCVV": "596",
            "CardExpiry": "03/20"
        },
        {
            "CreditCardNo": "6473 9323 3107 7122",
            "CreditCardHolder": "Libby T. Ray",
```


Figure 3.13 – Sample JSON data

The JSON sample file can be found in the book's GitHub repository.

Please download and familiarize yourself with the JSON structure. Also, if you like, you can download it and use it in your own cloud storage buckets for testing purposes.

How to do it...

We will load a JSON document into Snowflake, store it as semi-structured data using the `VARIANT` data type, and then transform that data into a relational representation suitable for downstream processing.

The steps for this recipe are as follows:

1. Begin by creating a dedicated database. This database will contain the staging table used to store the raw JSON data and the queries used to transform it.

    ```
    CREATE DATABASE JSON_EX;
    ```

2. Rather than repeating the full setup for cloud storage access, this recipe uses a sample JSON file hosted in a public Amazon S3 bucket. In production scenarios, this data would typically reside in a private bucket secured using a storage integration.

Create an external stage that points to the location containing the JSON file and specify the file format as JSON:

```
CREATE OR REPLACE STAGE JSON_STG url='s3://snowflake-cookbook/Chapter03/r5'
FILE_FORMAT = (TYPE = JSON);
```

3. Before attempting to load or process the data, verify that Snowflake can access the file by listing the contents of the stage.

```
LIST @JSON_STG;
```

If the configuration is correct, Snowflake will return the name of the JSON file in the bucket. Successfully listing the file confirms that the stage is accessible and ready for use.

	name	size	md5
1	s3://snowflake-cookbook/Chapter03/r5/json_sample.json	33395	2b050d44a704dc06119d2dd2a934f4fa

Figure 3.14 – List of files in the bucket

4. Before loading the JSON into a table, it is useful to validate that the file can be parsed correctly. This step helps catch malformed JSON early in the process.

```
SELECT  PARSE_JSON($1)
FROM @JSON_STG;
```

The query should return a single row containing the full JSON document. Any parsing errors at this stage indicate issues with the source file.

	PARSE_JSON($1)
1	{ "credit_cards": [{ "CardCVV": "929", "CardExpiry": "03/20", "CardPin": "1634", "CreditCardHolder": "Alfreda Y. Meyers", "CreditCardNo": "527147 8139869068" },

Figure 3.15 – Parsing and validating the JSON data

5. Let's create a table to store the JSON document exactly as it is received. The table contains a single column of type `VARIANT`, which is Snowflake's universal data type for semi-structured data.

```
CREATE OR REPLACE TABLE CREDIT_CARD_TEMP
(
```

```
    MY_JSON_DATA VARIANT
);
```

This approach preserves the original JSON structure and allows flexible downstream transformations without requiring a predefined schema.

6. Use the `COPY INTO` command to load the JSON document from the external stage into the staging table.

```
COPY INTO CREDIT_CARD_TEMP
FROM @JSON_STG;
```

At this point, the entire JSON document is stored as a single `VARIANT` value in the table.

7. Once the data is loaded, access fields that exist at the top level of the JSON structure using path notation.

```
SELECT
    MY_JSON_DATA:data_set,
    MY_JSON_DATA:extract_date
FROM CREDIT_CARD_TEMP;
```

This confirms that individual fields within the JSON document can be queried directly.

8. The JSON document also contains an array named `credit_cards`. Selecting this array directly returns the entire array as a single semi-structured value:

```
SELECT MY_JSON_DATA:credit_cards FROM
CREDIT_CARD_TEMP;
```

9. While it is possible to access individual array elements using positional notation, this approach is not practical for relational processing.

```
SELECT
    MY_JSON_DATA:credit_cards[0].CreditCardNo,
    MY_JSON_DATA:credit_cards[0].CreditCardHolder
FROM CREDIT_CARD_TEMP;
```

This query returns only a single element from the array.

10. To convert the `credit_cards` array into a relational structure, use the `FLATTEN` function. This function expands each element in the array into its own row.

```
SELECT
    MY_JSON_DATA:extract_date,
    value:CreditCardNo::STRING,
    value:CreditCardHolder::STRING,
    value:CardPin::INTEGER,
    value:CardCVV::STRING,
    value:CardExpiry::STRING
FROM CREDIT_CARD_TEMP,
     LATERAL FLATTEN(INPUT => MY_JSON_DATA:credit_cards);
```

Each object in the `credit_cards` array is converted into a separate row, producing 200 rows when using the sample file. The output is as follows:

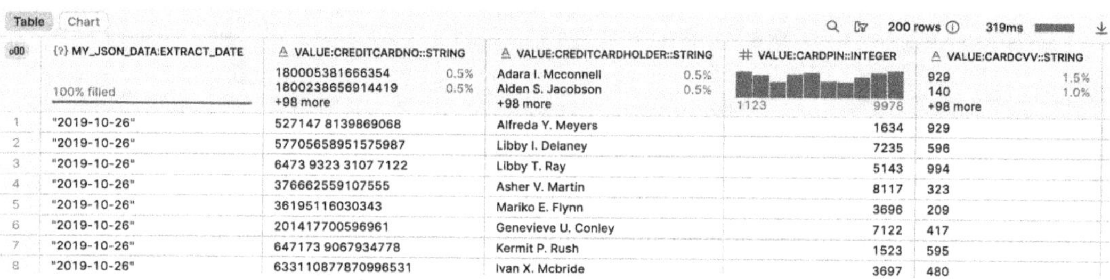

Figure 3.16 – Relation view using the flatten function

The data is now converted to a relational format and can be used for further processing just like an ordinary table.

How it works...

When the external stage was created for this recipe, the file format was defined as JSON, which instructed Snowflake to expect JSON-formatted input. When the data was loaded from the stage, it was stored in a table with a single column of type `VARIANT`. The `VARIANT` data type is Snowflake's universal container for semi-structured data and is capable of storing hierarchical structures such as objects and arrays without requiring a predefined schema.

Once the JSON document is stored in the table, individual fields can be accessed using path expressions such as `MY_JSON_DATA:<field_name>`. This approach works well for fields located at the top level of the JSON structure, such as `data_set` and `extract_date`.

However, the `credit_cards` element in the JSON document is an array of objects. Accessing the array directly returns the entire array as a single semi-structured value, which is not suitable for relational processing. While it is technically possible to reference individual array elements using positional notation, this method does not scale and is not practical when working with variable-length arrays.

To convert the array into a relational form, the `FLATTEN` function is used. `FLATTEN` expands each element in the JSON array into a separate row, effectively transforming the hierarchical structure into a tabular representation. Fields within each array element are then accessed through the value object returned by `FLATTEN` and cast to appropriate relational data types.

In this recipe, applying `FLATTEN` to the `credit_cards` array produces one row per credit card, resulting in 200 rows, which corresponds to the number of elements in the array. This transformation enables semi-structured JSON data to be queried, joined, and processed using standard SQL, just like any other relational dataset in Snowflake.

Processing newline-delimited JSON (NDJSON) into a Snowflake table

This recipe demonstrates how to process **newline-delimited JSON** (**NDJSON**) data in Snowflake and transform it into a relational format. In NDJSON, each line in the file is a valid JSON object, allowing records to be processed independently rather than as part of a single JSON document. This format is commonly used for log data, event streams, and incremental data ingestion.

For more information on the NDJSON format, see: `http://ndjson.org/`.

Getting ready

This recipe builds on earlier recipes that introduced external stages and JSON file formats. To keep the focus on NDJSON processing, those foundational steps are not repeated in detail here.

A sample NDJSON file has been made available in a public cloud storage bucket. Each line in the file represents a single JSON object containing credit card–related data. The NDJSON sample file can be found in the book's GitHub repository.

You may download the file and place it in your own cloud storage bucket if you prefer to experiment further.

How to do it...

In this recipe, we will read an NDJSON file from cloud storage, parse each JSON record, and transform the data into relational columns that can be stored in a Snowflake table.

The steps for this recipe are as follows:

1. To isolate the objects used in this recipe, begin by creating a dedicated database:

```
CREATE DATABASE NDJSON_EX;
```

2. The sample NDJSON file has been uploaded to a public Amazon S3 bucket for convenience. In production environments, NDJSON files are typically stored in private buckets and accessed using a storage integration.
Create an external stage that points to the NDJSON file location and specify a JSON file format. The `STRIP_OUTER_ARRAY = TRUE` option ensures that Snowflake can process the file correctly if the data is wrapped in square brackets:

```
CREATE OR REPLACE STAGE NDJSON_STG
URL = 's3://snowflake-cookbook/Chapter03/r6'
FILE_FORMAT = (TYPE = JSON, STRIP_OUTER_ARRAY = TRUE);
```

3. Let's confirm that Snowflake can access the file by listing the contents of the stage:

```
LIST @NDJSON_STG;
```

A successful listing indicates that the stage is correctly configured and accessible.

	name	size	md5
1	s3:///snowflake-cookbook/Chapter03/r6/ndjson_sample.json	14834	b681bffd8a60752d9446d6ea02d172c8

Figure 3.17 – List of files in the bucket

4. Before transforming the data, validate that each line of the NDJSON file can be parsed correctly. Because NDJSON contains one JSON object per line, parsing the file returns one row per JSON record:

```
SELECT  PARSE_JSON($1)
FROM @NDJSON_STG;
```

You should see multiple rows returned, each representing a single JSON object from the file.

	{?} PARSE_JSON($1)
1	{ "CardCVV": "979", "CardExpiry": "10/2020", "CardPin": "6609", "CreditCardHolder": "Price M. Cochran", "CreditCardNo": "36526505572729"}
2	{ "CardCVV": "197", "CardExpiry": "09/2019", "CardPin": "6954", "CreditCardHolder": "Daquan I. Sullivan", "CreditCardNo": "646 22682 40124 108"}
3	{ "CardCVV": "647", "CardExpiry": "11/2020", "CardPin": "8186", "CreditCardHolder": "Violet Y. Perkins", "CreditCardNo": "36118819196153"}
4	{ "CardCVV": "316", "CardExpiry": "09/2019", "CardPin": "8710", "CreditCardHolder": "Kerry L. Sandoval", "CreditCardNo": "512 62701 88375 080"}
5	{ "CardCVV": "689", "CardExpiry": "12/2019", "CardPin": "4151", "CreditCardHolder": "Nina E. Osborne", "CreditCardNo": "2014 717935 06122"}
6	{ "CardCVV": "220", "CardExpiry": "06/2020", "CardPin": "5743", "CreditCardHolder": "Hilda G. Walsh", "CreditCardNo": "3731 610897 26185"}

Figure 3.18 – Parsing and validating the JSON data

5. Let's now parse and convert each JSON record and apply appropriate data types. This step transforms the semi-structured NDJSON data into a relational shape.

```
SELECT
    PARSE_JSON($1):CreditCardNo::STRING     AS CreditCardNo,
    PARSE_JSON($1):CreditCardHolder::STRING AS CreditCardHolder,
    PARSE_JSON($1):CardPin::INTEGER         AS CardPin,
    PARSE_JSON($1):CardExpiry::STRING       AS CardExpiry,
    PARSE_JSON($1):CardCVV::STRING          AS CardCVV
FROM @NDJSON_STG;
```

Each row in the result set corresponds to one JSON object from the NDJSON file.

	A CREDITCARDNO	A CREDITCARDHOLDER	# CARDPIN	A CARDEXPIRY	A CARDCVV
	180 00852 86370 656 1.0% 1800809904943010 1.0% +98 more	Aiko V. Hood 1.0% Alexa X. Gay 1.0% +98 more	1454 9827	03/2020 8.0% 11/2020 8.0% +22 more	285 368 +92 more
1	36526505572729	Price M. Cochran	6609	10/2020	979
2	646 22682 40124 108	Daquan I. Sullivan	6954	09/2019	197
3	36118819196153	Violet Y. Perkins	8186	11/2020	647
4	512 62701 88375 080	Kerry L. Sandoval	8710	09/2019	316

Figure 3.19 – Converting the fields into relational format

6. Once the transformation logic has been validated, create a relational table and load the parsed data into it.

```
CREATE OR REPLACE TABLE CREDIT_CARD_DATA AS
SELECT
    PARSE_JSON($1):CreditCardNo::STRING     AS CreditCardNo,
    PARSE_JSON($1):CreditCardHolder::STRING AS CreditCardHolder,
    PARSE_JSON($1):CardPin::INTEGER         AS CardPin,
    PARSE_JSON($1):CardExpiry::STRING       AS CardExpiry,
```

```
    PARSE_JSON($1):CardCVV::STRING          AS CardCVV
FROM @NDJSON_STG;
```

7. Verify that the data has been loaded successfully. The query should return rows from the table containing the loaded data.

```
SELECT * FROM CREDIT_CARD_DATA;
```

How it works...

NDJSON is a variation of JSON in which each line in the file represents a complete and independent JSON object. This structure makes NDJSON particularly well suited for incremental ingestion, event data, and streaming-style workloads.

When the external stage was created, the file format was defined as JSON, instructing Snowflake to treat each line as JSON input. The optional `STRIP_OUTER_ARRAY` setting ensures compatibility with files that may include enclosing square brackets.

When querying the staged file, the `$1` notation is used to reference the single column exposed by the staged data. The `PARSE_JSON` function converts the raw string value into a `VARIANT`, enabling JSON path expressions to be applied. Individual fields are then accessed using the `:<field_name>` syntax and cast to relational data types using the `::` operator.

Unlike the previous recipe, which required the use of `FLATTEN` to expand JSON arrays, NDJSON already represents each record as a separate row. This allows each JSON object to be transformed directly into a relational row, making NDJSON a natural fit for batch ingestion and near–real-time processing patterns.

Processing near-real-time data into a Snowflake table using Snowpipe

This recipe walks through configuring Snowpipe to enable near real-time ingestion of data files as they arrive in cloud storage. Snowpipe allows Snowflake to automatically load data without manual `COPY` commands by reacting to file arrival events.

Getting ready

Since this recipe involves configuring Snowpipe with Amazon S3, you must have the appropriate privileges to configure event notifications on the target S3 bucket. If you do not have sufficient access, you will need to work with your AWS administrator to complete the required configuration. In addition, a Snowflake storage integration must already be in place to allow Snowflake to securely access the bucket, as described in the *Preparing stage for data loading* recipe earlier in this chapter.

If you would like to download and use your own S3 bucket for testing, sample files for this recipe are available in the book's GitHub repository.

How to do it...

The following steps create a target table, an external stage, a Snowpipe, and finally configure automatic ingestion using AWS S3 event notifications.

1. Start by creating a dedicated database to isolate the objects used in this recipe.

```
CREATE OR REPLACE DATABASE SP_EX;
USE SP_EX;
```

2. Create the table that Snowpipe will load data into as new files arrive.

```
CREATE OR REPLACE TABLE TRANSACTIONS
(
  TRANSACTION_DATE DATE,
  CUSTOMER_ID NUMBER,
  TRANSACTION_ID NUMBER,
  AMOUNT NUMBER
);
```

   This table structure must align with the structure of the incoming files.

3. Create an external stage that points to the S3 bucket where new files will be delivered. This stage uses a storage integration configured earlier to allow Snowflake secure access to the bucket.
   Replace `<bucket>` with your actual bucket name:

```
CREATE OR REPLACE STAGE SP_TRX_STAGE
url='s3://<bucket>'
STORAGE_INTEGRATION = S3_INTEGRATION;
```

4. Run `LIST` on the stage to ensure that you can successfully read the associated S3 bucket. The `LIST` command should not result in any errors:

```
LIST @SP_TRX_STAGE;
```

5. Create a Snowpipe that uses a `COPY` statement internally. The `AUTO_INGEST = TRUE` setting instructs Snowflake to load files automatically when events are received from AWS:

```
CREATE OR REPLACE PIPE TX_LD_PIPE
AUTO_INGEST = TRUE
AS
COPY INTO TRANSACTIONS
FROM @SP_TRX_STAGE
FILE_FORMAT = (TYPE = CSV SKIP_HEADER = 1);
```

   At this point, the Snowpipe exists but will not ingest data yet.

6. Snowpipe relies on cloud events to trigger ingestion. Each pipe exposes a notification channel that AWS must publish events to.
   Retrieve the ARN by running:

```
SHOW PIPES LIKE '%TX_LD_PIPE%';
```

   The output for this command is as follows:

Figure 3.20 – Output of the SHOW PIPES command

   Copy the full value from the `notification_channel` column. This ARN will be used in the AWS configuration.

7. Log in to the AWS Management Console and navigate to the Amazon S3 service. Select the S3 bucket associated with the Snowpipe and open the **Properties** tab. Scroll to the **Event notifications** section and choose **Create event notification**.

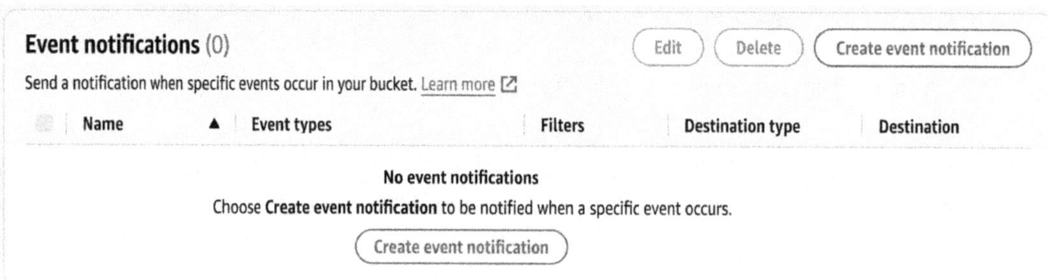

Figure 3.21 – Events screen

8. In the **Event notification** configuration screen, provide a name for the event (for example, `Trigger Snowpipe`). Under **Event types**, select **All object create events**. This ensures that an event is generated every time a new file is added to the bucket.

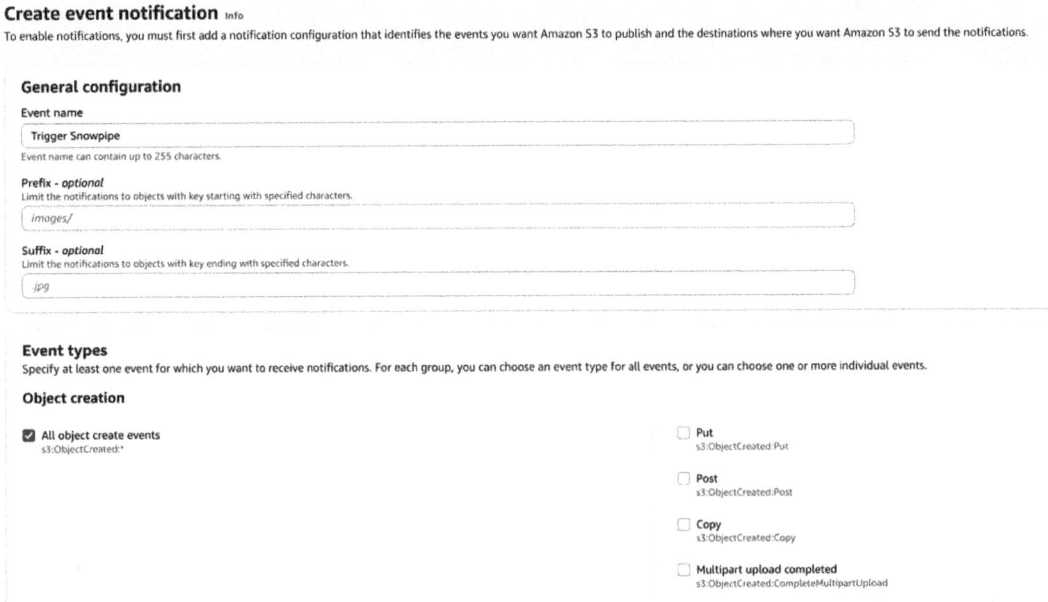

Figure 3.22 – Create event notification window

9. In the **Destination** section, select **SQS queue**, choose **Specify SQS queue ARN**, and paste the ARN value copied from the `notification_channel` column in *Step 7*. Save the event notification once the configuration is complete.

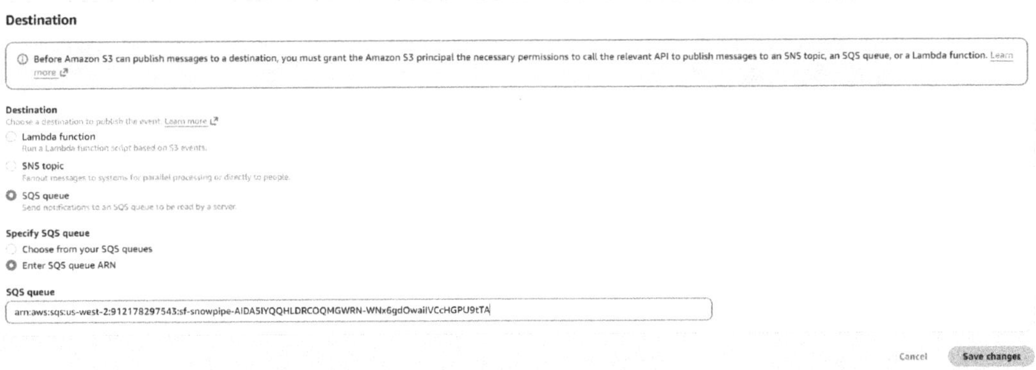

Figure 3.23 – Create event notification window

10. Upload one or more data files into the configured S3 bucket. After a short delay, Snowflake will automatically ingest the new files using Snowpipe.
11. Verify that the data has been successfully loaded by querying the target table in Snowflake.

```
SELECT COUNT(*) FROM TRANSACTIONS;
```

How it works...

Snowpipe is a continuous data ingestion service that builds upon the same `COPY` command used for bulk data loading. When a Snowpipe is created, it defines both the source location and the transformation logic required to load incoming data into a target table.

There are two ways to trigger a Snowpipe. The first method is to invoke it manually through Snowflake's REST API. The second method, which is demonstrated in this recipe, relies on cloud storage event notifications. In this approach, the cloud storage platform generates an event whenever a new object is created in the bucket. That event is delivered to the notification channel associated with the Snowpipe, which then automatically initiates the data load.

By using event-based triggering, Snowpipe enables near real-time ingestion of data as it arrives in cloud storage, without the need for polling or scheduled batch jobs.

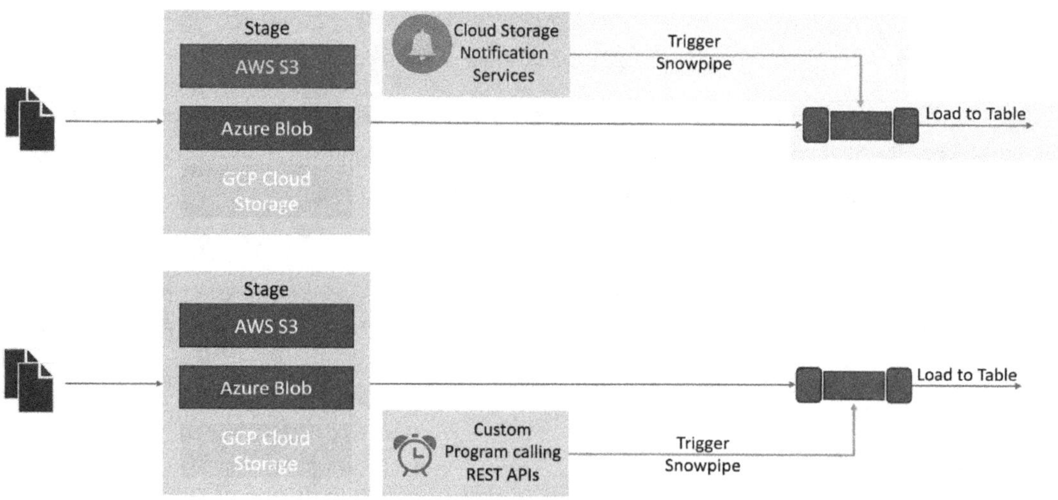

Figure 3.24 – The two methods to trigger Snowpipe

By using event-based triggering, Snowpipe enables near real-time ingestion of data as it arrives in cloud storage, without the need for polling or scheduled batch jobs.

Extracting data from Snowflake into internal and external stages

This recipe walks through the process of extracting data from Snowflake tables. We will first extract data into an internal stage and download it to a local system. We will then demonstrate how to extract data to an external stage backed by Amazon S3, resulting in data being written directly to cloud storage. Together, these approaches cover the most common Snowflake data export patterns.

Getting ready

You should already have at least one table populated with data. This can be a table created as part of this chapter or any other table available in your Snowflake environment.

Because this recipe demonstrates exporting data to both internal and external stages, ensure that you have completed the Preparing stage for data loading recipe and that the storage integration you created has both read and write permissions enabled. Without write access, Snowflake will not be able to unload data into your S3 bucket.

We will also use Snowflake CLI to download files from an internal stage to the local filesystem. Make sure Snowflake CLI is installed and that you can successfully connect to your Snowflake account. Not all steps require Snowflake CLI, and the recipe will explicitly call out when Snowflake CLI is required.

How to do it…

The steps for this recipe are as follows:

1. Start by creating and using a database that will be used to define the stage objects for exporting data:

```
CREATE DATABASE EXPORT_EX;
USE DATABASE EXPORT_EX;
```

2. Create an internal stage that defines the file format to be used when exporting data. For simplicity, we will export data in CSV format and apply `GZIP` compression:

```
CREATE OR REPLACE STAGE EXPORT_INTERNAL_STG
FILE_FORMAT = (TYPE = CSV COMPRESSION=GZIP);
```

3. Extract data from a table into the internal stage using the `COPY INTO` command. When exporting data, the direction of the `COPY` operation is reversed, and data is copied from a table into a stage.
   In this example, we use the `CUSTOMER` table from the Snowflake sample data set. You may replace this with any table available in your environment:

```
COPY INTO @EXPORT_INTERNAL_STG/customer.csv.gz
FROM SNOWFLAKE_SAMPLE_DATA.TPCH_SF1.CUSTOMER;
```

4. Let's verify that the data has been successfully unloaded by listing the contents of the stage:

```
LIST @EXPORT_INTERNAL_STG;
```

   You should see a number of files that have been extracted; Snowflake automatically splits large data into multiple files:

	name	size
1	export_internal_stg/customer.csv.gz_0_0_0.csv.gz	2722752
2	export_internal_stg/customer.csv.gz_0_1_0.csv.gz	1814064
3	export_internal_stg/customer.csv.gz_0_3_0.csv.gz	4539760

Figure 3.25 – Listing files in the stage and checking the data

5. Download the exported files from the internal stage to your local machine. This step must be executed using the Snowflake CLI, as it requires access to the local filesystem. Replace the destination path with a directory appropriate for your system:

```
snow stage copy @EXPORT_INTERNAL_STG file://C:/Downloads/;
```

6. Now create an external stage that points to your S3 bucket. Ensure that the storage integration created earlier is specified so Snowflake has permission to write to the bucket. In this example, we will export data in Parquet format with automatic compression.

Replace `<bucket>` with the name of your S3 bucket.

```
CREATE OR REPLACE STAGE EXPORT_EXTERNAL_STG
URL = 's3://<bucket>'
STORAGE_INTEGRATION = S3_INTEGRATION
FILE_FORMAT = (TYPE = PARQUET COMPRESSION = AUTO);
```

7. Extract data into the external stage. This time, rather than exporting an entire table, we will export the results of a query and write the output as a Parquet file.

```
COPY INTO @EXPORT_EXTERNAL_STG/customer.parquet
FROM (SELECT * FROM
SNOWFLAKE_SAMPLE_DATA.TPCH_SF1.CUSTOMER SAMPLE (10));
```

8. If you navigate to your S3 bucket, you will see the exported Parquet files written directly to cloud storage.

Name	Type
customer.parquet_0_0_0.snappy.parquet	parquet
customer.parquet_0_2_0.snappy.parquet	parquet
customer.parquet_0_3_0.snappy.parquet	parquet

Figure 3.26 – Data unloaded into your S3 bucket

How it works...

Extracting data from Snowflake uses the same `COPY INTO` command that is used for loading data, with the direction of data movement reversed. When exporting, Snowflake copies data from a table or query result set into a stage rather than loading it from a stage into a table.

Data can be extracted to either an internal stage or an external stage. Internal stages store files within Snowflake-managed storage and are commonly used when data needs to be downloaded to a local system. In such cases, the `GET` command, executed through Snowflake CLI, is required to retrieve files from the stage.

External stages, on the other hand, allow Snowflake to write data directly to cloud storage platforms such as Amazon S3. When exporting to an external stage, Snowflake writes the data directly to the configured bucket using the permissions defined by the storage integration.

Finally, it is worth noting that Snowflake allows data extraction not only from tables but also from views or the results of arbitrary `SELECT` queries, providing flexibility in how data is shaped and exported.

Building data ingestion pipelines with Snowflake Openflow

In the previous recipes, we focused primarily on file-based ingestion patterns, including staged files, semi-structured data, and event-driven loading using Snowpipe. While these approaches are effective for many use cases, modern data platforms often need to ingest data directly from operational systems in a reliable, repeatable, and continuously managed way. In this recipe, we introduce Openflow, Snowflake's orchestration framework for building data ingestion pipelines, and demonstrate how it can be used to ingest data directly from a relational source system into Snowflake without relying on file drops or custom code.

Getting ready

This recipe demonstrates how to use Openflow to ingest data from a relational source system into Snowflake using **change data capture** (**CDC**). To follow along, you will need access to a PostgreSQL database running on **Amazon Relational Database Service** (**Amazon RDS**) that can be reached from the environment where Openflow is running. PostgreSQL is used in this recipe because it is a widely adopted open-source relational database and represents a common operational data source for analytics ingestion.

To make the examples in this chapter easier to follow, we will assume the following logical configuration for the source database throughout the recipe:

- The PostgreSQL database name is `cookbook`
- A dedicated replication user named `Openflowuser` is used
- The password for this user is `password`

These values are used purely for clarity and consistency in the examples and should not be considered production guidance.

Before configuring anything in Snowflake or Openflow, the Amazon RDS PostgreSQL environment must be prepared to support logical replication. Openflow relies on PostgreSQL's native logical replication framework to capture and stream changes, so several database and infrastructure prerequisites must be met in advance.

The following prerequisites focus on configuring Amazon RDS, database settings, access, and connectivity to ensure the system is ready for integration:

1. Openflow supports PostgreSQL version 11 or later. Ensure that your Amazon RDS PostgreSQL instance is running a supported version and is sized appropriately to handle logical replication workloads. Because logical replication relies on replication slots, **write-ahead log** (**WAL**) files may be retained for longer periods if replication is interrupted, which can increase disk usage. Adequate storage allocation and monitoring should be in place.
2. On Amazon RDS, logical replication must be explicitly enabled through a database parameter group. The parameter group associated with the PostgreSQL instance hosting the **cookbook** database must be configured to support logical replication. At a minimum, logical replication must be enabled, and WAL settings must allow logical decoding. Because these settings include static parameters, applying the updated parameter group requires a database reboot.
3. The source PostgreSQL database must be configured to expose changes in a way that Openflow can consume. Logical replication requires the use of publications that define which tables are included in change capture. Any tables that will be replicated must have primary keys defined so that changes can be uniquely identified, and tables must use the default replica identity so primary key values are included in the WAL stream. For newer PostgreSQL versions, publications should be configured to correctly handle partitioned tables if they are present.
4. A dedicated database user must be created for Openflow. In this recipe, that user is **Openflowuser**. This user must be granted permission to perform logical replication and must have read access to all tables included in the publication. When using Amazon RDS, the user must also be granted the appropriate RDS-managed replication role to allow access to replication features. This account is used exclusively by Openflow to read changes from the PostgreSQL transaction log.
5. Openflow must be able to establish a direct network connection to the Amazon RDS PostgreSQL instance. The RDS security group must allow inbound connections on the PostgreSQL port, and network routing must exist between the Openflow runtime environment and the RDS subnets. If **virtual private cloud** (**VPC**) peering or shared networking is used, DNS resolution for the RDS endpoint must also be available across the network boundary.
6. If encrypted connections are required by your organization's security policies, ensure that the RDS PostgreSQL instance is configured to accept **transport layer security**

(**TLS**) connections and that the necessary SSL certificates are available to clients. This is typically handled as part of standard RDS configuration.

7. At this point, the Amazon RDS PostgreSQL environment is fully prepared for use with Openflow. The next section will focus on configuring Snowflake and defining the Openflow connection using this prepared source system.
8. To interact with an Amazon RDS PostgreSQL environment, you will need a PostgreSQL administration tool. In this recipe, pgAdmin is used because it is a widely available and commonly used PostgreSQL management interface.
9. pgAdmin can be downloaded from the official site: `https://www.pgadmin.org/download/`.
10. Install pgAdmin on your local machine or on a jump host that has network access to the Amazon RDS PostgreSQL instance. Once installed, use the RDS endpoint, port, and credentials from your Amazon RDS PostgreSQL environment to register the PostgreSQL server in pgAdmin. This tool will be used throughout the recipe to create and manage the database structures and data required for the recipe.

To support this recipe, sample PostgreSQL DDL and data scripts are provided in the book's GitHub repository. These scripts define the database structures used throughout the recipe and are referenced in the next section. You do not need to run them yet; they will be executed as part of the steps in the *How to do it...* section.

How to do it...

In this recipe, we will create an Openflow pipeline that ingests data from a PostgreSQL source system into Snowflake. We begin by preparing the PostgreSQL source database, including creating the required database objects and loading sample data. Once the source system is ready, we will move on to configuring the target environment in Snowflake, define the Openflow connection and ingestion pipeline, and finally validate that data has been successfully loaded and changes are captured.

The steps for this recipe are as follows:

1. Using pgAdmin, connect to your Amazon RDS PostgreSQL instance. Create a new database named `cookbook`. This database will act as the operational source system for this recipe.

```
CREATE DATABASE cookbook;
```

2. Once the database is created, connect to the cookbook database and create a dedicated schema to hold the source tables used in this recipe.

```
CREATE SCHEMA IF NOT EXISTS crm;
SET search_path TO crm;
```

3. Now create the PostgreSQL source tables that will be used for ingestion. These tables represent a simple operational data model commonly found in transactional systems and provide a clear structure for demonstrating change data capture.

```
CREATE TABLE customers (
    customer_id     INTEGER PRIMARY KEY,
    first_name      VARCHAR(50),
    last_name       VARCHAR(50),
    email           VARCHAR(100),
    created_at      TIMESTAMP DEFAULT CURRENT_TIMESTAMP
);

CREATE TABLE products (
    product_id      INTEGER PRIMARY KEY,
    product_name    VARCHAR(100),
    price           NUMERIC(10,2),
    created_at      TIMESTAMP DEFAULT CURRENT_TIMESTAMP
);

CREATE TABLE orders (
    order_id        INTEGER PRIMARY KEY,
    customer_id     INTEGER NOT NULL,
    order_date      TIMESTAMP DEFAULT CURRENT_TIMESTAMP,
    status          VARCHAR(25),
    CONSTRAINT fk_orders_customer
        FOREIGN KEY (customer_id)
        REFERENCES customers(customer_id)
);

CREATE TABLE order_items (
    order_item_id   INTEGER PRIMARY KEY,
    order_id        INTEGER NOT NULL,
    product_id      INTEGER NOT NULL,
    quantity        INTEGER,
```

```
    unit_price      NUMERIC(10,2),
    CONSTRAINT fk_items_order
        FOREIGN KEY (order_id)
        REFERENCES orders(order_id),
    CONSTRAINT fk_items_product
        FOREIGN KEY (product_id)
        REFERENCES products(product_id)
);
```

4. With the tables now created, insert some sample data to validate ingestion and demonstrate change capture.

```
INSERT INTO customers VALUES
(1, 'Jane', 'Doe', 'jane.doe@example.com', CURRENT_TIMESTAMP),
(2, 'John', 'Smith', 'john.smith@example.com', CURRENT_TIMESTAMP);

INSERT INTO products VALUES
(100, 'Snowflake T-Shirt', 25.00, CURRENT_TIMESTAMP),
(200, 'DataOps Mug', 15.00, CURRENT_TIMESTAMP);

INSERT INTO orders VALUES
(1000, 1, CURRENT_TIMESTAMP, 'NEW'),
(1001, 2, CURRENT_TIMESTAMP, 'NEW');

INSERT INTO order_items VALUES
(1, 1000, 100, 2, 25.00),
(2, 1001, 200, 1, 15.00);
```

5. Verify that the source tables contain data and are accessible. This helps confirm that the database objects were created successfully and that the sample data is available for ingestion.

```
SELECT * FROM customers;
SELECT * FROM products;
SELECT * FROM orders;
SELECT * FROM order_items;
```

6. Let's enable logical replication on PostgreSQL. This is done by creating a publication, which defines the tables whose changes will be captured, and a replication slot, which

ensures those changes are retained in the PostgreSQL WAL until they are consumed by Openflow.

Create a publication and replication slot by entering the code below; you can also edit it to be only for certain tables.

```
CREATE PUBLICATION Openflow_pub FOR ALL TABLES;
```

7. Confirm that the expected tables are included in the publication, query the PostgreSQL catalog:

```
SELECT * FROM pg_publication_tables;
```

8. Create the logical replication slot using the `pgoutput` plugin. This replication slot will be used by Openflow to read changes from the WAL.

```
SELECT pg_create_logical_replication_slot(
  'Openflow_pgoutput_slot',
  'pgoutput'
);
```

At this point, the PostgreSQL source system is fully configured to expose data changes through logical replication. The publication defines what data is captured, and the replication slot ensures changes are retained until they are consumed by Openflow.

9. Log in to your Snowflake account and set your role to ACCOUNTADMIN. Begin by creating the Snowflake database that will act as the landing zone for data ingested from PostgreSQL. Let's call it `OPENFLOW_EX`.

```
CREATE DATABASE OPENFLOW_EX;
USE DATABASE OPENFLOW_EX;
```

10. Next, create a schema within this database to hold the network rules for Openflow.

```
CREATE SCHEMA IF NOT EXISTS NETWORK;
USE SCHEMA NETWORK;
```

At this stage, no tables are created in Snowflake. Openflow will create and manage the target tables automatically based on the PostgreSQL source schema when the ingestion pipeline is defined and executed.

The Snowflake target environment is now ready to receive data from Openflow.

11. Begin by creating a dedicated role for Openflow. Using a purpose-built role avoids permission issues and is recommended over using ACCOUNTADMIN for ongoing operations.

```
CREATE ROLE IF NOT EXISTS OPENFLOW_ROLE;
```

12. Grant the role access to the target database and schema that will be used for ingestion.

```
GRANT USAGE ON DATABASE OPENFLOW_EX TO ROLE OPENFLOW_ROLE;
```

13. Grant the Openflow role permission to use an existing warehouse in your environment.

```
GRANT USAGE ON WAREHOUSE <existing_warehouse> TO ROLE OPENFLOW_ROLE;
```

Replace <existing_warehouse> with the name of a warehouse that already exists in your Snowflake account.

14. Grant the `OPENFLOW` role to the Snowflake user that will be used to configure and run Openflow.

```
GRANT ROLE OPENFLOW_ROLE TO USER <Openflow_user>;
USE ROLE OPENFLOW_ROLE;
```

Replace <Openflow_user> with the Snowflake user that will be used for Openflow configuration.

15. With Openflow being deployed using **Snowpark Container Services** (**SPCS**), an external access integration is required to allow outbound network access from Snowflake to the PostgreSQL source system in AWS.
16. Create a network rule that allows access to the Amazon RDS PostgreSQL endpoint.

```
CREATE OR REPLACE NETWORK RULE postgres_rds_rule
  MODE = EGRESS
  TYPE = HOST_PORT
  VALUE_LIST = ('<rds-endpoint>:5432');
```

Replace the placeholder <rds-endpoint> with the endpoint and port of your PostgreSQL instance.

17. Next, create the external access integration and associate it with the network rule.

```
CREATE OR REPLACE EXTERNAL ACCESS INTEGRATION postgres_ext_access
ALLOWED_NETWORK_RULES = (postgres_rds_rule)
ENABLED = TRUE;
```

18. Grant usage on the external access integration to the role used by Openflow.

```
GRANT USAGE ON INTEGRATION postgres_ext_access TO ROLE OPENFLOW_ROLE;
```

> **Note**
>
> This external access integration will be selected when creating the Openflow runtime and enables secure outbound connectivity from Snowflake to the PostgreSQL source system.

19. Now, let's launch Openflow by navigating to **Ingestion** -> **Openflow**, and then click **Launch Openflow** in the upper right corner.

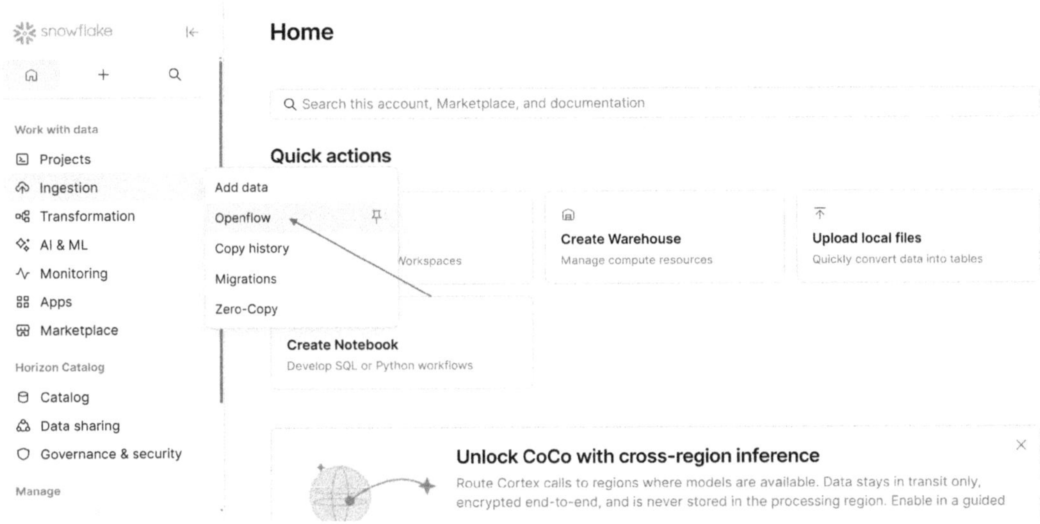

Figure 3.27 – Launch Openflow

20. When Openflow starts for the first time, you will be prompted to create a new deployment. Select **Snowflake** as the deployment location and provide a name that reflects the purpose of this recipe, such as `postgres_Openflow`. For simplicity, assign

the Usage, Operate, and Monitor roles to ACCOUNTADMIN. The deployment creation can take 15-20 minutes to complete.

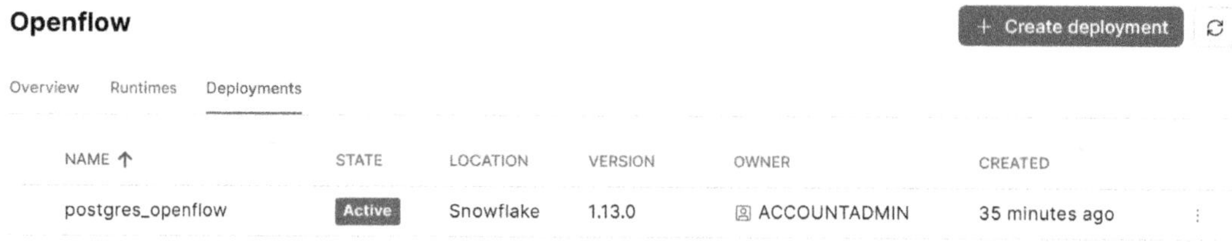

Figure 3.28 – Openflow Deployments

> **Note**
>
> For this recipe, ACCOUNTADMIN is used for the Openflow deployment roles to simplify setup and avoid permission-related issues during initial configuration. In production environments, these roles should be assigned to dedicated roles that follow the principle of least privilege and align with your organization's security standards.

21. Navigate to the Runtime section in Openflow and click **+ Create Runtime**. Select the deployment created earlier, provide `postgresql` as the runtime name, and set the Snowflake usage role to ACCOUNTADMIN. For the external access integration, select `postgres_ext_access`, which was created in the previous step. Once the configuration is complete, click **Create**. Runtime provisioning typically takes 5 to 10 minutes to complete.

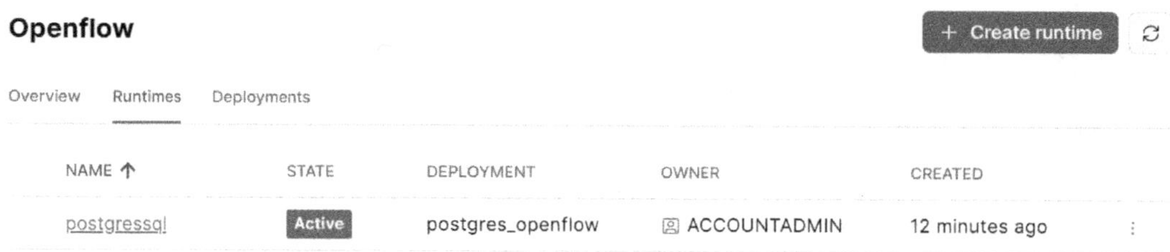

Figure 3.29 – Openflow runtimes

22. Navigate to the **Overview** section in Openflow, and select **View more connectors**. Locate the **PostgreSQL** connector in the list of available connectors and click **Install**. When prompted, select the **postgresql** runtime created earlier and choose **Add**. When asked, select **Allow** to grant the connector access to your Snowflake account.

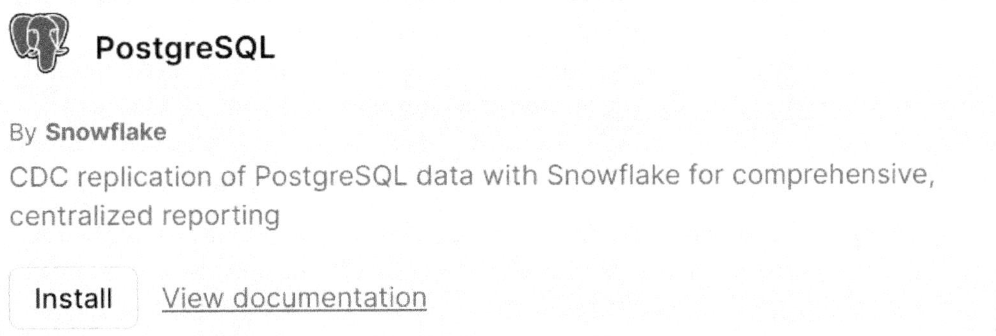

Figure 3.30 – PostgreSQL connector

23. Once in, you will want to right-click the PostgreSQL process group and select **Parameters**.

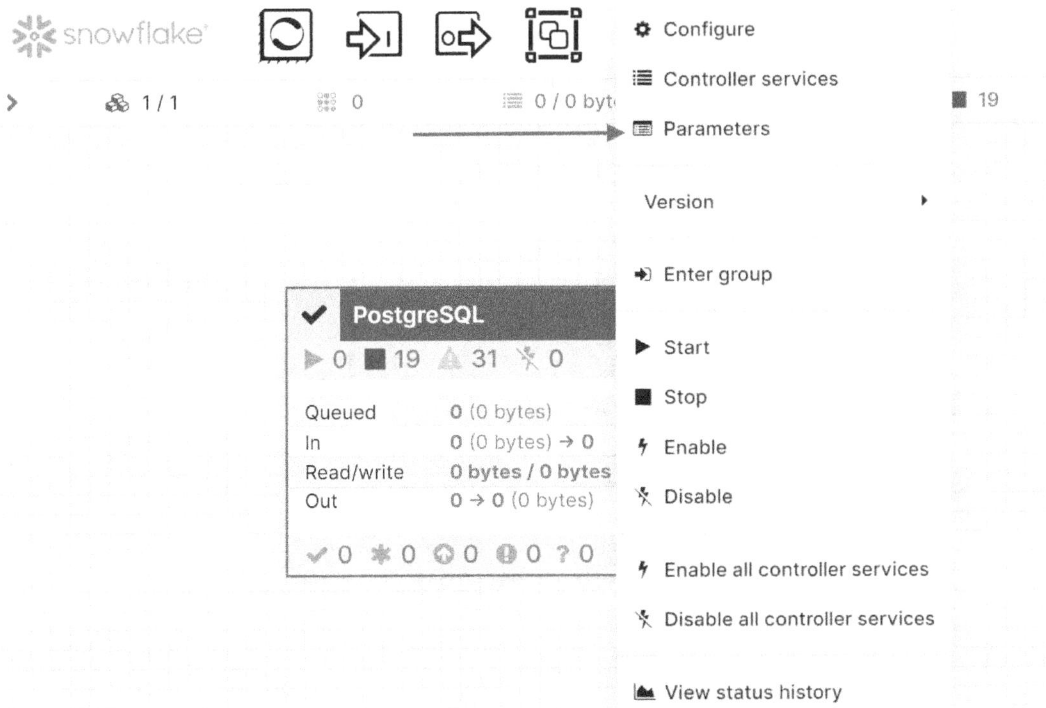

Figure 3.31 – Openflow process group parameters

24. Once you are in the **Parameters** view, the configuration is organized into three sections: **Destination**, **Ingestion**, and **Source**. Begin by locating the **Destination** section, selecting the three-dot menu, and choosing **Edit**.
    For this recipe, the connector is deployed using SPCS. When using SPCS, one important parameter to note is the Snowflake Authentication Strategy. Set this value to `SNOWFLAKE_SESSION_TOKEN`. This authentication method allows the connector to use the existing Snowflake session and does not require key-pair authentication.

    Configure the remaining destination parameters using the values established earlier in the tutorial. Set the destination database to `OPENFLOW_EX`, provide your Snowflake account identifier, and set the Snowflake role to ACCOUNTADMIN. Select an existing Snowflake warehouse from your account to be used for processing. Then select **Apply**.

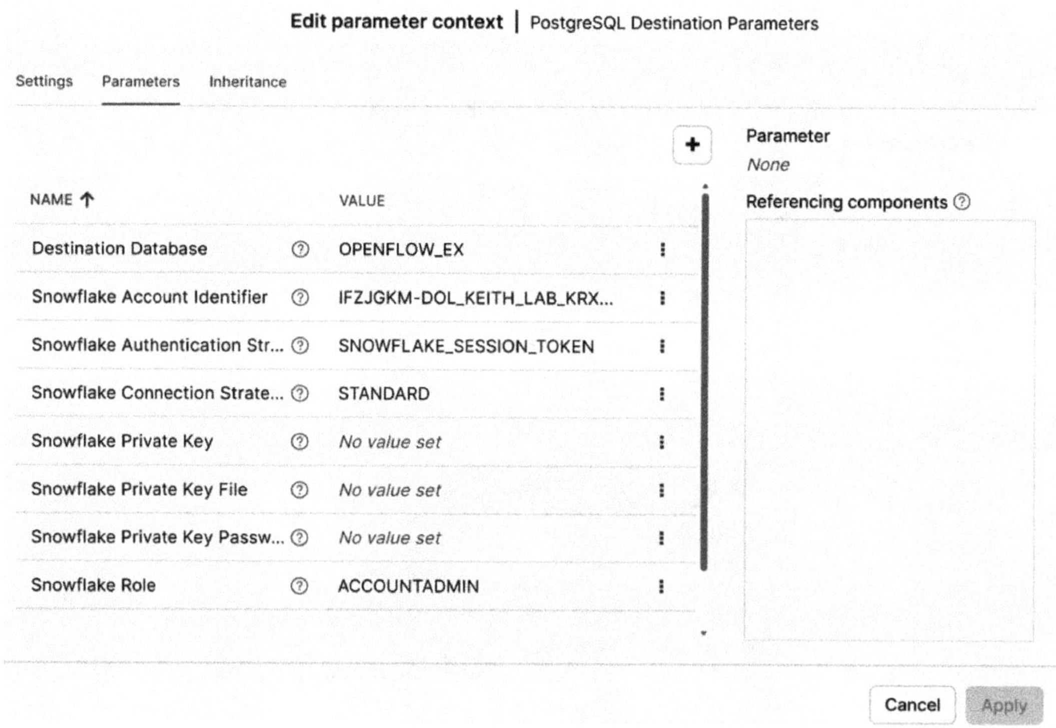

Figure 3.32 – Connector Destination Parameters

25. Next, configure the **Ingestion** parameters. This section controls which data is ingested and how frequently changes are merged into the target tables in Snowflake.
    For this recipe, ingestion is configured using a regular expression to select the source tables. Enter the expression `crm\..*` into the **Include Table Regex** to capture all tables within the `crm` schema in our source database. If you want to ingest tables from multiple schemas or specify individual tables, you can provide a comma-separated list of expressions.

    The ingestion parameters also define how often the Snowflake warehouse merges captured changes into the final tables. Use the default merge interval for this recipe.

    Once these settings are set just click **Apply**.

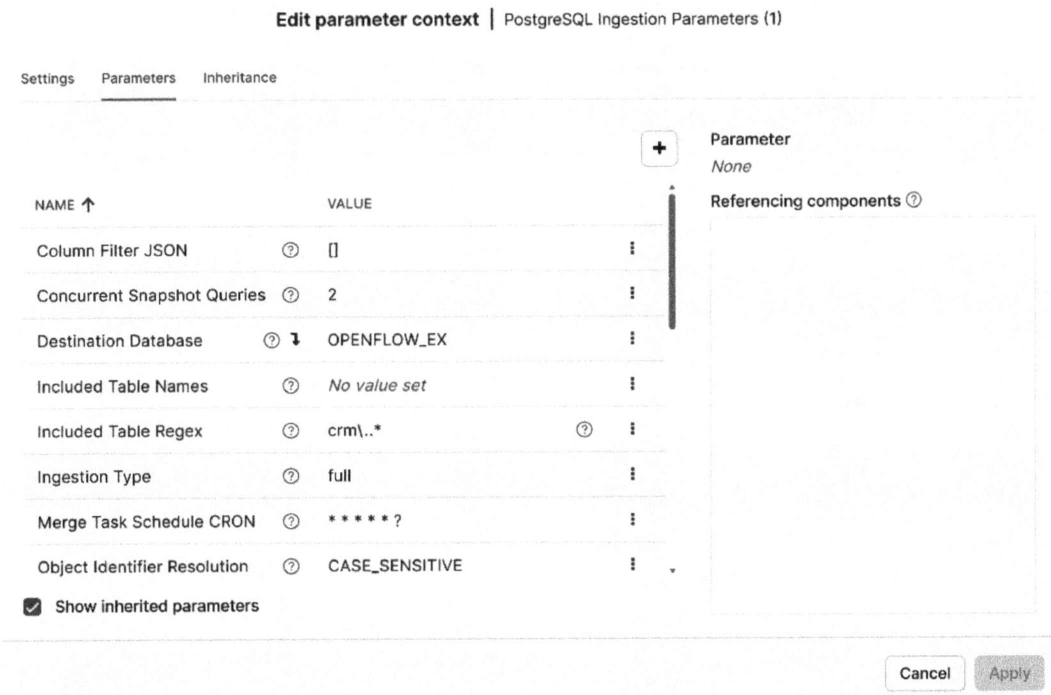

Figure 3.33 – Connector Ingestion Parameters

26. Next, navigate to the final **Source** parameters, which define how the connector connects to the PostgreSQL source system. Begin by editing the **Connection URL**. The JDBC connection string should use the following format:

27. `jdbc:postgresql://<database_endpoint>:5432/<database_name>`.

    For this recipe, the database endpoint and database name correspond to the Amazon RDS PostgreSQL instance and the `cookbook` database created earlier.

    Within the **Source** parameters, you must also provide the PostgreSQL JDBC driver and authentication details. Upload the PostgreSQL JDBC driver that was downloaded during the *Getting ready* section, then specify the PostgreSQL username and password that were used when creating the Amazon RDS database.

    Finally, configure the logical replication settings by providing the publication name and replication slot created earlier in PostgreSQL. Set the publication name to `Openflow_pub` and the replication slot name to `Openflow_pgoutput_slot`.

    Once these values are set, click **Apply**.

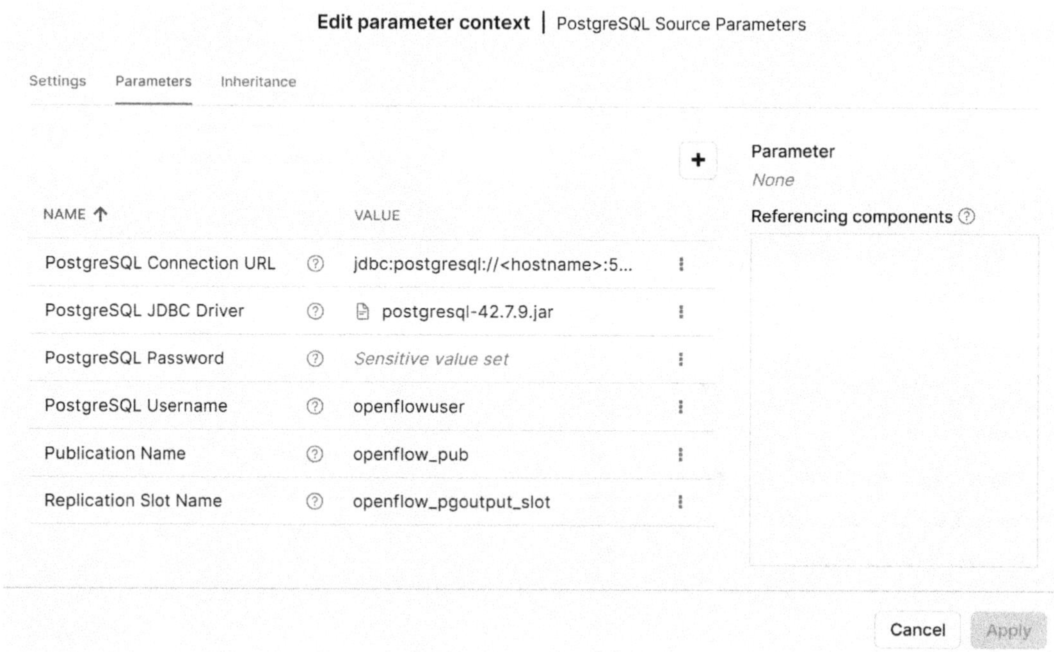

Figure 3.34 – Connector source parameters

28. Next, select **Back to Process Group** in the upper-left corner to return to the main process group view. You should now be back on the runtime's main screen, with the PostgreSQL process group displayed.

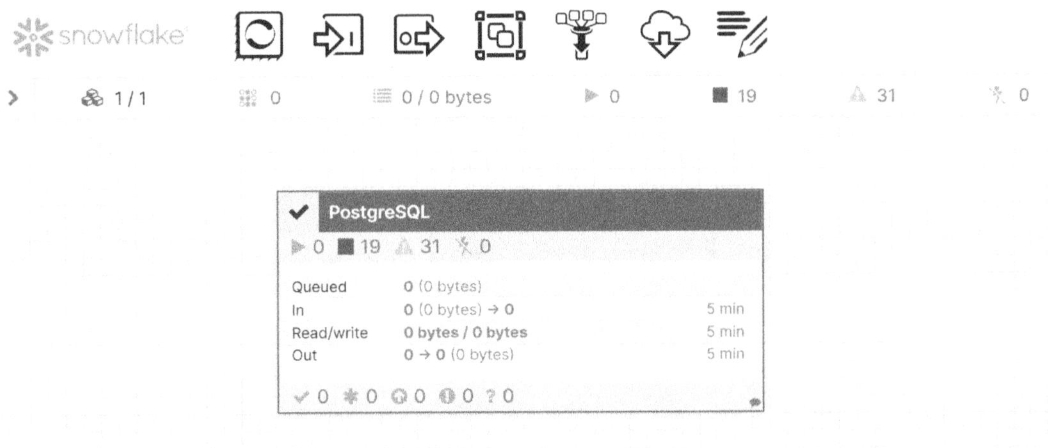

Figure 3.35 – Openflow Runtime – Postgres Process Group

29. Next, enable and start the controller services. Right-click the PostgreSQL process group and select **Enable All Controller Services**, then right-click the process group again and click **Start**.

    Starting the process group initiates the replication process. Openflow will create the corresponding data structures in Snowflake and begin ingesting data from the Amazon RDS PostgreSQL source system into Snowflake.

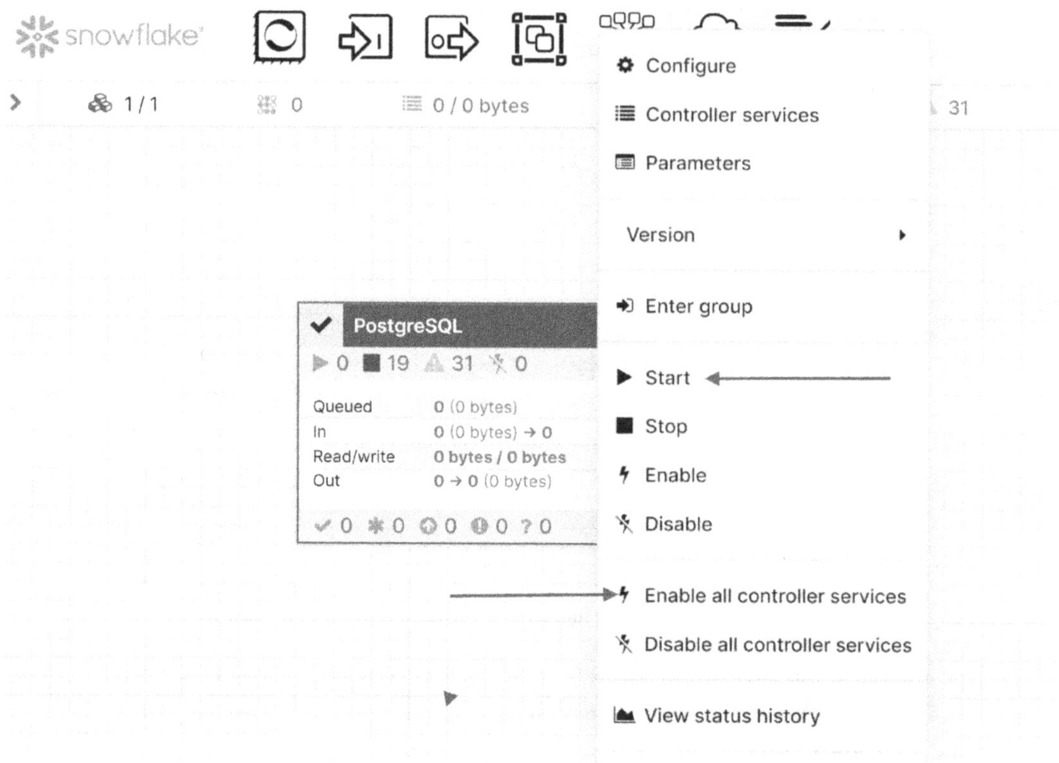

Figure 3.36 – Initiate PostgreSQL process group

30. After a few moments you should start to see values in the **Read/Write** as Openflow brings the data over to Snowflake.

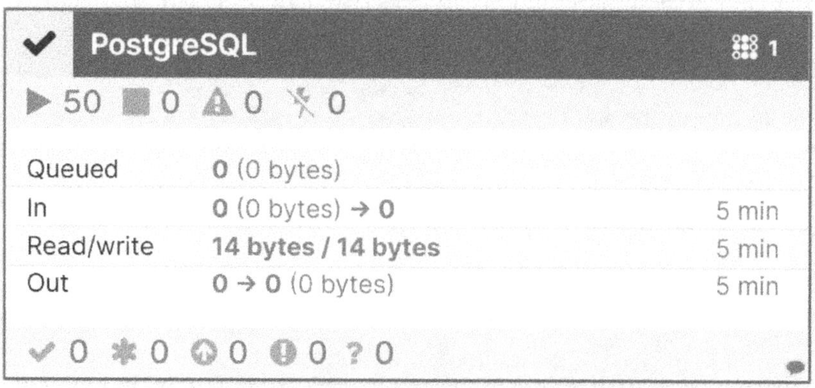

Figure 3.37 – PostgreSQL Process Group Read/write

31. With the Openflow pipeline running, the final step is to verify that data from PostgreSQL has been successfully ingested into Snowflake.

```
USE DATABASE OPENFLOW_EX;
SHOW SCHEMAS;
```

The result should include a CRM schema created by OpenFlow, as shown in *Figure 3.38*.

name	is_default	is_current	database_name	owner
INFORMATION_SCHEMA	N	N	OPENFLOW_EX	
NETWORK	N	N	OPENFLOW_EX	ACCOUNTADMIN
PUBLIC	N	Y	OPENFLOW_EX	ACCOUNTADMIN
crm	N	N	OPENFLOW_EX	ACCOUNTADMIN

Figure 3.38 – PostgreSQL source schema in Snowflake

32. Next, in SnowSight, navigate to the **Catalog** and locate the `OPENFLOW_EX` database. Expand the database and you should now see a `crm` schema that was created automatically by Openflow.
Within the `crm` schema, the tables corresponding to the PostgreSQL source tables should be present. Open one or more of these tables to verify that the data is visible. In addition to the original source columns, you will notice additional metadata columns added by Openflow, which are used to track change data capture and manage ongoing updates.

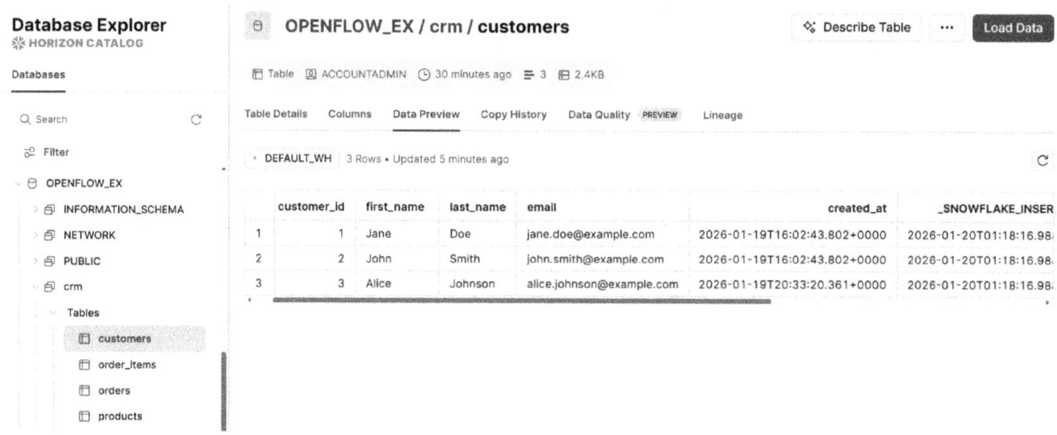

Figure 3.39 – PostgreSQL replicated schema/tables

33. At this point, you can insert, update, or delete data in the PostgreSQL source system, and those changes will be captured by Openflow and propagated into Snowflake automatically.

How it works...

In this recipe, OpenFlow is used to continuously ingest data from a PostgreSQL source system into Snowflake by leveraging PostgreSQL's native logical replication capabilities and Snowflake's Openflow capabilities.

On the PostgreSQL side, logical replication is enabled by configuring the database to emit change data into WAL. A publication defines which tables are eligible for replication, and a replication slot ensures that changes are retained until they are consumed. Together, these objects allow Openflow to read inserts, updates, and deletes from PostgreSQL without requiring triggers, extensions, or application-level changes.

Openflow connects to PostgreSQL using standard JDBC connectivity and the `pgoutput` replication protocol. When the connector starts, it first inspects the source schemas and tables selected in the ingestion configuration. During the initial run, Openflow performs a snapshot of the source tables and creates corresponding target tables in Snowflake. These tables are created automatically, preserving the source structure while also adding metadata columns used to manage change data capture and processing state.

As changes occur in PostgreSQL, they are written to the WAL and made available through the replication slot. Openflow continuously reads these changes and stages them internally. Based on the configured ingestion cadence, Openflow then merges those changes into the target tables in Snowflake, applying inserts, updates, and deletes in the correct order to maintain consistency.

When deployed on SPCS, Openflow runs entirely within Snowflake's execution environment. Outbound connectivity to PostgreSQL is tightly controlled using network rules and an external access integration, ensuring that only approved destinations can be reached. Authentication to Snowflake is handled using a session token, allowing the runtime to operate securely without managing key pairs.

The result is a fully managed, continuous ingestion pipeline that keeps Snowflake synchronized with the PostgreSQL source system. Once configured, no additional manual intervention is required. Any changes made in PostgreSQL are automatically detected, processed, and reflected in Snowflake, providing a reliable foundation for analytics and downstream data products.

There's more...

This recipe demonstrates one common pattern for ingesting data from PostgreSQL into Snowflake using Openflow, but Openflow supports a wide range of connection types and parameter configurations that enable different ingestion strategies.

Beyond PostgreSQL, Openflow provides connectors for other relational databases, event streams, and file-based sources, each with configuration options tailored to the characteristics of the source system. Within a given connector, parameters can be used to control how tables are selected, how frequently changes are merged, how schemas are mapped, and how change data capture is handled for inserts, updates, and deletes.

Ingestion behavior can also be adjusted to support different use cases. For example, pipelines can be configured for near–real-time ingestion or for batch-oriented merges, depending on workload and cost considerations. Table level filtering, schema-level selection, and regular expression based inclusion rules allow teams to precisely control which data is ingested and when.

Openflow also provides flexibility in how it is deployed and secured. Authentication strategies, runtime environments, and external access configurations can be adapted to meet enterprise security and networking requirements, while still maintaining a Snowflake-native operational model.

Together, these capabilities allow OpenFlow to support a wide variety of ingestion patterns, from simple operational replication to more complex, production-grade data integration architectures. You are encouraged to explore the available connectors and parameter options to tailor Openflow pipelines to their specific source systems and business needs.

4

Building Data Pipelines in Snowflake

Snowflake, like other data platforms, provides tools and abstractions that enable developers and users to build data pipelines for data processing and analytics. However, as a cloud-native platform, Snowflake approaches pipeline orchestration differently from traditional data platforms. In a typical data pipeline, there are mechanisms to execute code, sequence processing steps, define dependencies, and react to changes in both data and environment. Snowflake structures these pipelines primarily through the concepts of tasks and streams.

A task represents a unit of data processing logic that can be scheduled or triggered as part of a larger pipeline. Tasks can be chained together to form directed execution flows, enabling complex, multi-step data transformations. Streams complement tasks by capturing table-level data changes, allowing pipelines to process only new or modified data rather than reprocessing entire datasets. Together, tasks and streams provide a powerful foundation for building efficient, incremental data pipelines.

This chapter focuses on setting up pipelines using tasks and streams, applying common transformation techniques, and handling execution failures and operational context. By the end of this chapter, you will understand how to create and manage tasks and streams, how to combine them to support complex data processing scenarios, and how these foundational constructs fit into Snowflake's broader data pipeline capabilities.

The following recipes will be covered in this chapter:

- Creating and scheduling a task
- Connecting pipelines through a task tree
- Querying and viewing the task history

- Exploring the concept of streams to capture table-level changes
- Combining the concept of streams and tasks to build pipelines that process changed data on a schedule
- Converting data types and Snowflake's failure management
- Managing context using different utility functions
- Using Dynamic Tables for data lifecycle automation

Technical requirements

This chapter assumes that you have a Snowflake account already set up. You can download the example project and code for this book by following the instructions in the ***Download the example code files*** section in the *Preface* of this book.

Creating and scheduling a task

In this recipe, we will create a new task that runs a set of steps for processing data and configure the task to execute on a defined schedule.

Getting ready

Ensure that you have access to a Snowflake account with privileges to create databases, tables, and tasks. This recipe uses the `COMPUTE_WH` warehouse in the examples. The SQL statements in this recipe can be executed either in Snowsight or by using the Snowflake CLI.

When working with tasks, ensure that the role owning the task has usage privileges on the warehouse, as tasks do not use secondary roles during execution. For example:

```
GRANT USAGE ON WAREHOUSE COMPUTE_WH TO ROLE SYSADMIN;
```

How to do it...

To demonstrate the concept of a task, we will first create an aggregation query that we assume is being used in a report. We assume that the query takes a long time to run, so we will store the results in a physical table and refresh it periodically using a scheduled task. While Snowflake now supports additional capabilities such as serverless tasks, event-based triggers, and Dynamic Tables, this example focuses on a simple scheduled task to illustrate the core concepts.

1. To simplify the process for you, we have used the sample data provided by Snowflake and created an aggregation query on top of that.

> **Note**
>
> Sample data is included with your Snowflake instance and can be found under the `SNOWFLAKE_SAMPLE_DATA` database.

We will use a fictitious query on the sample data, as follows:

```
SELECT C.C_NAME,SUM(L_EXTENDEDPRICE),SUM(L_TAX)

FROM SNOWFLAKE_SAMPLE_DATA.TPCH_SF1.CUSTOMER C

INNER JOIN SNOWFLAKE_SAMPLE_DATA.TPCH_SF1.ORDERS O
ON O.O_CUSTKEY = C.C_CUSTKEY

INNER JOIN SNOWFLAKE_SAMPLE_DATA.TPCH_SF1.LINEITEM LI
ON LI.L_ORDERKEY = O.O_ORDERKEY

GROUP BY C.C_NAME;
```

A sample output of the preceding query is as follows:

Row	C_NAME	SUM(L_EXTENDEDPRICE)	SUM(L_TAX)
1	Customer#000052858	2593511.11	2.55
2	Customer#000090793	2525706.08	2.57
3	Customer#000132863	1643014.32	1.78

Figure 4.1 – Sample output

2. We will now create a target table where the results of this query will be saved. In addition to the columns produced by the preceding query, we will also add a `REPORTING_TIME` column. We will insert the current timestamp into this column every time we insert data:

```
USE ROLE SYSADMIN;

CREATE DATABASE task_demo;
USE DATABASE task_demo;
CREATE TABLE ordering_customers
```

```
(
  Reporting_Time TIMESTAMP,
  Customer_Name STRING,
  Revenue NUMBER(16,2),
  Tax NUMBER(16,2)
);
```

3. Now, let's create a task using the preceding SQL statement to insert data into the `ordering_customers` table. We will configure the task to run every 30 minutes:

```
CREATE TASK refresh_ordering_customers
  WAREHOUSE = COMPUTE_WH
  SCHEDULE = '30 MINUTE'
  COMMENT = 'Update Ordering_Customers Table with latest
   data'
AS
  INSERT INTO ordering_customers
  SELECT CURRENT_TIMESTAMP, C.C_NAME,
         SUM(L_EXTENDEDPRICE), SUM(L_TAX)
  FROM SNOWFLAKE_SAMPLE_DATA.TPCH_SF1.CUSTOMER C
  INNER JOIN SNOWFLAKE_SAMPLE_DATA.TPCH_SF1.ORDERS O
  ON O.O_CUSTKEY = C.C_CUSTKEY
  INNER JOIN SNOWFLAKE_SAMPLE_DATA.TPCH_SF1.LINEITEM LI
  ON LI.L_ORDERKEY = O.O_ORDERKEY
  GROUP BY CURRENT_TIMESTAMP, C.C_NAME;
```

4. Let's validate that the task has been created correctly by running the `DESC` command:

```
DESC TASK refresh_ordering_customers;
```

The output from the preceding code is shown as follows and has been split onto multiple lines for visibility. Note that by default, a new task is created in a suspended state:

created_on	name	id	databas... ↓	schema_name	owner
2021-02-15 02:15:0...	REFRESH_ORDERING_CUSTOME...	019a4e07-5...	TASK_DEMO	PUBLIC	SYSADMIN

comment	warehouse	schedule	predecessors	state	definition ↓	condition
Update Ordering_...	COMPUTE_...	30 MINUTE	NULL	suspended	INSERT INTO ordering_custome...	NULL

Figure 4.2 – DESC command output

5. Run the following statements as ACCOUNTADMIN to grant task execution privileges to the SYSADMIN role:

```
USE ROLE ACCOUNTADMIN;
GRANT EXECUTE TASK ON ACCOUNT TO ROLE SYSADMIN;
```

6. We must now set the task status to `RESUME` so that it can start executing on schedule. The task must be resumed by the role that owns it. In this example, since the task was created using the SYSADMIN role, the same role should be used to resume it:

```
ALTER TASK refresh_ordering_customers RESUME;
```

You can validate that the task has been resumed successfully by describing the task:

```
DESC TASK refresh_ordering_customers;
```

Here is the output of the preceding code:

comment	warehouse	schedule	predecessors	state	definition	condition
Update Orde...	COMPUTE_...	30 MINUTE	NULL	started	INSERT INT...	NULL

Figure 4.3 – Output of the describe command

As the state of the task is set to `started`, it means the task is now scheduled and should execute in the next 30 minutes.

7. Let's keep an eye on the task execution to validate that it runs successfully. To do that, we need to query `task_history`, as follows:

```
SELECT name, state,
        completed_time, scheduled_time,
        error_code, error_message

FROM TABLE(information_schema.task_history())
WHERE name = 'REFRESH_ORDERING_CUSTOMERS';
```

The output from the query is as follows:

NAME	STATE	COMPLETED_T	SCHEDULED_TIME	ERROR_CODE	ERROR_MESSAGE
REFRESH_ORDERING_CU	SCHEDULED	null	2026-06-08 16:51:27.794 -	null	null

Figure 4.4 – Output of task_history

As evident from the output, the task has not been executed yet, and the scheduled execution time is displayed. To speed up testing, you can either reduce the schedule interval (for example, to 10 minutes) or manually trigger the task using the following command:

```
EXECUTE TASK REFRESH_ORDERING_CUSTOMERS;
```

8. After the task has executed, either based on the schedule or by manually triggering it, re-run the preceding query. As expected, the task should have executed successfully, as shown in the following output, and the next instance is scheduled for execution:

NAME	STATE	COMPLETED_TIME	SCHEDULED_TIME	ERROR_CODE
REFRESH_ORDERING_CUSTOMERS	SCHEDULED	null	2026-06-08 17:21:27.794 -0700	null
REFRESH_ORDERING_CUSTOMERS	SUCCEEDED	2026-06-08 16:51:30.99	2026-06-08 16:51:27.794 -0700	null

Figure 4.5 – New task scheduled

9. Let's validate that the task executed successfully by querying the `ORDERING_CUSTOMERS` table:

```
SELECT * FROM ordering_customers;
```

As shown below, the query returned around 100,000 records, which indicates that the task was executed successfully.

✔ Query ID SQL 867ms 99,996 rows

Filter result... Copy Columns ▾

Row	REPORTING_TIME	CUSTOMER_NAME	REVENUE	TAX
1	2021-02-15 02:48:50.740	Customer#000009883	1501315.56	1.73
2	2021-02-15 02:48:50.740	Customer#000061001	966905.86	1.34
3	2021-02-15 02:48:50.740	Customer#000073957	1577889.21	1.22
4	2021-02-15 02:48:50.740	Customer#000036964	1988282.69	2.26

Figure 4.6 – Validating the task

How it works...

Tasks in Snowflake enable the scheduled execution of SQL statements and are commonly used to process recurring workloads such as aggregations, transformations, and data preparation for reporting. When creating a task, a virtual warehouse is typically specified to provide the compute resources required during execution, although Snowflake also supports serverless tasks that do not require an explicitly defined warehouse.

Tasks are created in a suspended state by default and must be explicitly resumed before they will execute on a schedule. A task can be resumed by the role that owns the task (typically the role that created it).

To execute successfully, the task owner role must also have the required privileges, including `EXECUTE TASK` and access to the underlying objects and warehouse. Once resumed, Snowflake automatically executes the task based on the defined schedule, and execution details can be inspected using the `TASK_HISTORY` table function.

Connecting pipelines through a task tree

In this recipe, we will connect multiple tasks together in a tree to create a data pipeline with multiple processing steps. Each task can depend on the successful completion of another task, allowing the pipeline to execute in sequence.

Getting ready

Ensure that you have access to a Snowflake account with privileges to create databases, tables, and tasks. This recipe uses the `COMPUTE_WH` warehouse in the examples. The SQL statements in this recipe can be executed either in Snowsight or by using the Snowflake CLI.

How to do it...

To demonstrate the concept of a parent-child **task tree**, we will first create an aggregation query that we assume is being used in a report. We are assuming that the query takes a long time to run; therefore, we are going to save the results of the query to a physical table and then refresh it periodically through a scheduled task. The steps are as follows:

1. To simplify the process, we have used the sample data provided by Snowflake and created an aggregation query on top of that. (Please note that sample data is included with your Snowflake instance and can be found under the `SNOWFLAKE_SAMPLE_DATA` database.) We will be using a fictitious query on the sample data, as shown:

```
SELECT C.C_NAME,SUM(L_EXTENDEDPRICE),SUM(L_TAX)
```

```
FROM SNOWFLAKE_SAMPLE_DATA.TPCH_SF1.CUSTOMER C

INNER JOIN SNOWFLAKE_SAMPLE_DATA.TPCH_SF1.ORDERS O
ON O.O_CUSTKEY = C.C_CUSTKEY

INNER JOIN SNOWFLAKE_SAMPLE_DATA.TPCH_SF1.LINEITEM LI
ON LI.L_ORDERKEY = O.O_ORDERKEY

GROUP BY C.C_NAME;
```

A sample of the output of the preceding query is as follows:

Row	C_NAME	SUM(L_EXTENDEDPRICE)	SUM(L_TAX)
1	Customer#000052858	2593511.11	2.55
2	Customer#000090793	2525706.08	2.57
3	Customer#000132863	1643014.32	1.78

Figure 4.7 – Sample data provided by Snowflake

2. We will now create a target table where we will store the results of this query. Persisting the aggregated results in a table allows the report to read precomputed data rather than rerunning the full query each time. We will also create a dedicated database for this example:

```
CREATE DATABASE TASK_TREE_DEMO;

USE DATABASE TASK_TREE_DEMO;

CREATE TABLE ORDERING_CUSTOMERS
(
  CUSTOMER_NAME STRING,
  REVENUE NUMBER(16,2),
  TAX NUMBER(16,2)
);
```

3. We will create an initialization task to clean up the table before we insert new data into the table:

```
USE DATABASE TASK_TREE_DEMO;

CREATE TASK CLEAR_ORDERING_CUSTOMERS
 WAREHOUSE = COMPUTE_WH
 COMMENT = 'Delete from ORDERING_CUSTOMERS'
AS
 DELETE FROM ORDERING_CUSTOMERS;
```

4. We will now create a task using the SQL statement in *step 1* to insert data into the `ordering_customers` table:

```
CREATE TASK INSERT_ORDERING_CUSTOMERS
  WAREHOUSE = COMPUTE_WH
  COMMENT = 'Insert into ORDERING_CUSTOMERS the latest data'
AS
  INSERT INTO ORDERING_CUSTOMERS
  SELECT C.C_NAME, SUM(L_EXTENDEDPRICE), SUM(L_TAX)
  FROM SNOWFLAKE_SAMPLE_DATA.TPCH_SF1.CUSTOMER C
  INNER JOIN SNOWFLAKE_SAMPLE_DATA.TPCH_SF1.ORDERS O
    ON O.O_CUSTKEY = C.C_CUSTKEY
  INNER JOIN SNOWFLAKE_SAMPLE_DATA.TPCH_SF1.LINEITEM LI
    ON LI.L_ORDERKEY = O.O_ORDERKEY
  GROUP BY C.C_NAME;
```

5. So far, we have created two tasks, one to delete the data and one to insert the data. Now, we will connect the two together to create a small pipeline. We will make the insert task run after the clear task:

```
ALTER TASK INSERT_ORDERING_CUSTOMERS
ADD AFTER CLEAR_ORDERING_CUSTOMERS;
```

6. Let's run a `DESC` command on the task to validate that the tasks have been connected:

```
DESC TASK INSERT_ORDERING_CUSTOMERS;
```

The output shows that the `clear_ordering_customers` task has been set as a predecessor to the `INSERT` task:

schedule	predecessors	state	definition	condition
NULL	TASK_DEMO.PUBLIC.CLEAR_ORDERING_CUSTOMERS	suspended	INSERT INT...	NULL

Figure 4.8 – Output of the describe command

7. Let's now schedule our `clear_ordering_customers` task to execute on a schedule. We will set it to run for 10 minutes for demonstration purposes:

```
ALTER TASK CLEAR_ORDERING_CUSTOMERS
SET SCHEDULE = '10 MINUTE';
```

The statement should run successfully.

8. If you are running your code through a role other than ACCOUNTADMIN, you must grant that role the privilege to execute the task:

```
GRANT EXECUTE TASK ON ACCOUNT TO ROLE SYSADMIN;
```

9. Let's now set the tasks to `RESUME`, since tasks are created in a suspended state by default and will not execute until resumed. The tasks must be resumed by the role that owns them. In this example, since the tasks were created using the SYSADMIN role, the same role should be used to resume them.

> **Note**
>
> Child tasks must be resumed before resuming the parent tasks.

```
ALTER TASK insert_ordering_customers RESUME;
ALTER TASK clear_ordering_customers RESUME;
```

Both statements should complete successfully.

10. We will now keep an eye on the task execution to validate that it runs successfully. To do that, we need to query `task_history` as follows:

```
SELECT name, state,
        completed_time, scheduled_time,
        error_code, error_message
FROM TABLE(information_schema.task_history())
WHERE name IN
```

```
('CLEAR_ORDERING_CUSTOMERS','INSERT_ORDERING_CUSTOMERS
');
```

Immediately after the creation of the task, the output from the preceding command will show only the root task (that is, the task we scheduled):

NAME	STATE	COMPLETED_TIME	SCHEDULED_TIME	ERROR_CODE	ERROR_MESSAGE
CLEAR_ORDERING_CUST(	SCHEDULED	null	2026-06-08 17:14:37.154 -	null	null

Figure 4.9 – Output showing the root task

As evident from the output, the task has not been executed yet, and the scheduled execution time is displayed. Let's check the status in another 10 minutes; by then, the task and its child tasks should have been executed.

11. After 10 minutes, re-run the preceding query. As expected, the tasks are executed successfully, as shown in the output, and the next instance is scheduled for execution. Notice that only the root task appears in the scheduled state; however, when the execution occurs, all child tasks get executed as well:

Row	NAME	STATE	COMPLETED_TIME	SCHEDULED_TIME	ERROR_CODE	ERROR_MESSAGE
1	CLEAR_ORDERING_CUSTOMERS	SCHEDULED	NULL	2021-02-15 03:47:53.14...	NULL	NULL
2	INSERT_ORDERING_CUSTOMERS	SUCCEEDED	2021-02-15 03:38:19.6...	2021-02-15 03:38:09.9...	NULL	NULL
3	CLEAR_ORDERING_CUSTOMERS	SUCCEEDED	2021-02-15 03:38:09.9...	2021-02-15 03:37:53.14...	NULL	NULL

Figure 4.10 – Output showing the new root task

12. Let's validate that the tasks executed successfully by querying data from the `ORDERING_CUSTOMERS` table:

```
SELECT * FROM ordering_customers;
```

As shown, the query returned around 100,000 records, which indicates that the task executed successfully:

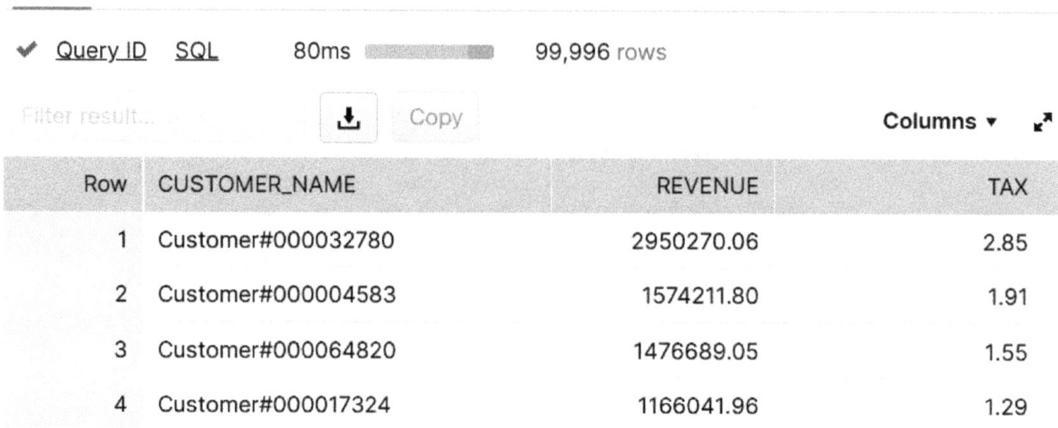

Row	CUSTOMER_NAME	REVENUE	TAX
1	Customer#000032780	2950270.06	2.85
2	Customer#000004583	1574211.80	1.91
3	Customer#000064820	1476689.05	1.55
4	Customer#000017324	1166041.96	1.29

Figure 4.11 – Validating the tasks

How it works...

Snowflake allows multiple tasks to be connected in a parent-child relationship, enabling multi-step pipelines to be built directly within the platform. A child task can be configured to run only after its predecessor completes successfully by using the AFTER clause.

This allows larger workflows to be broken into smaller, manageable steps such as clearing staging data, loading refreshed results, or applying downstream transformations. The root task is typically scheduled, while dependent child tasks run automatically when upstream tasks complete.

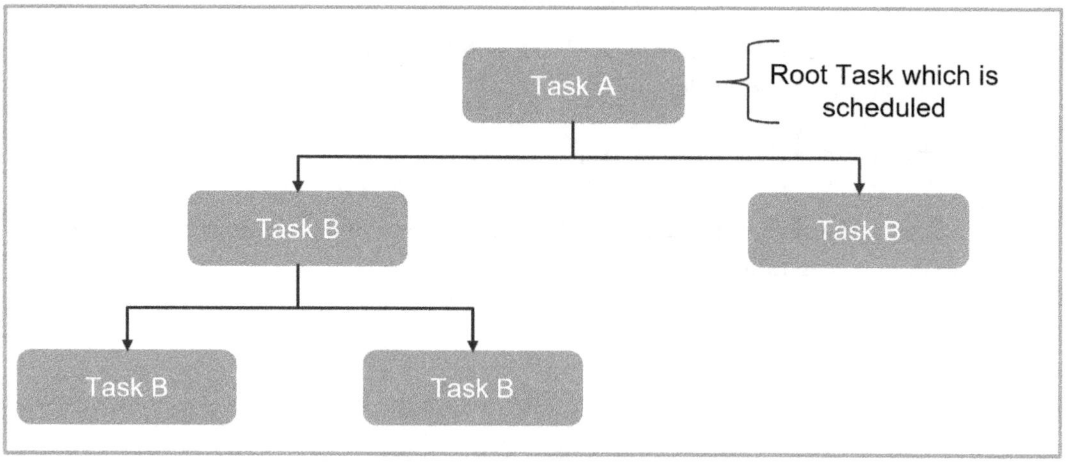

Figure 4.12 – Task tree in Snowflake

For a given task, a predecessor can be set up by specifying the `AFTER` configuration for the task. The task specified in the `AFTER` configuration becomes the parent of the task. Through this, a hierarchy of tasks is maintained. The predecessor task must complete before the child tasks can execute.

Querying and viewing task history

In this recipe, we will explore techniques that can be used to view the history of task execution using the `TASK_HISTORY` table function.

Getting ready

The following steps describe the various ways to view and analyze the history of the execution of a single task as well as a series of tasks. Note that these steps can be run either in Snowsight or the Snowflake CLI command-line client. To proceed with this recipe, ensure that you have already created and executed a few tasks; otherwise, no results will be returned.

How to do it...

To perform this recipe, follow these steps:

1. We will use the `task_history` table function, which can be used to query the history of task execution. The function takes several parameters, but all of them are optional, so to start with, we will run a query without any parameters. This will return the execution history of all the tasks:

```
USE ROLE SYSADMIN;
USE DATABASE TASK_TREE_DEMO;

SELECT *
FROM TABLE(INFORMATION_SCHEMA.TASK_HISTORY())
ORDER BY SCHEDULED_TIME;
```

A sample of the output of the preceding query is shown as follows. Please note the output is split over two rows due to lack of space:

	QUERY_ID	NAME	DATABASE_NAM	SCHEMA_NAM	QUERY_TEX	CONDITION_TEX	STATE
1	01c4de95-0209-3b26-	PROCESS_FINDINGS_TASK	null	null			SUCCEEDED
2	01c4deb6-0209-3ec4-	IS_CLASSIFICATION_USER_CHECKER_TASK	null	null			SUCCEEDED
3	01c4def2-0209-42eb-	IS_CLASSIFICATION_USER_CHECKER_TASK	null	null			SUCCEEDED

Figure 4.13 – Sample output of the preceding query

2. We will now query the view to return the task history between two timestamps. In this case, the query is for a 10-minute interval. The `TASK_HISTORY` function can return data for up to seven days in the past, so ensure your timestamps fall within that range. Please adjust the timestamps as needed before running this query:

```
 SELECT * FROM
TABLE(information_schema.task_history(
    scheduled_time_range_start=>to_timestamp_ltz
    ('2020-08-13 14:00:00.000 -0700'),
    scheduled_time_range_end=>to_timestamp_ltz('2020-
08-13 14:10:00.000 -0700')
))
ORDER BY SCHEDULED_TIME;
```

The output is shown as follows and has the task executions only from the given 10-minute interval between the two timestamps:

QUERY_ID	NAME	DATABASE_NAN	SCHEMA_NAME	QUERY_TEXT	CONDITION_TE)	STATE	ERROR_CODE
019a4e5a-0...	CLEAR_ORDERING_CUSTOMERS	TASK_DEMO	PUBLIC	DELETE FRO...	NULL	SUCCEEDED	NULL
019a4e5a-0...	INSERT_ORDERING_CUSTOMERS	TASK_DEMO	PUBLIC	INSERT INT...	NULL	SUCCEEDED	NULL

Figure 4.14 – Querying the view to return the task history between two timestamps

3. The third way to query and limit data from this view is to use the `RESULT_LIMIT` parameter. We will run a query without providing any other parameters but will supply the `RESULT_LIMIT` parameter to reduce the number of rows returned. In this instance, we will limit the results to 5:

```
SELECT * FROM
TABLE(information_schema.task_history(
      result_limit => 5
))
ORDER BY SCHEDULED_TIME;
```

The output is shown as follows and as expected, shows the last five steps executed. It is worth noting that if the result set before applying the limit is more than 5, the result set is executed by the latest execution and then the limit of 5 is applied, so you always see the latest information first after the application of the result limit:

QUERY_ID	NAME	DATABASE_NAM	SCHEMA_NAME	QUERY_TEXT	CONDITION_TE)	STATE
019a4e5a-0...	CLEAR_ORDERING_CUSTOMERS	TASK_DEMO	PUBLIC	DELETE FRO...	NULL	SUCCEEDED
019a4e5a-0...	INSERT_ORDERING_CUSTOMERS	TASK_DEMO	PUBLIC	INSERT INT...	NULL	SUCCEEDED
019a4e64-0...	CLEAR_ORDERING_CUSTOMERS	TASK_DEMO	PUBLIC	DELETE FRO...	NULL	SUCCEEDED
019a4e64-0...	INSERT_ORDERING_CUSTOMERS	TASK_DEMO	PUBLIC	INSERT INT...	NULL	SUCCEEDED
NULL	CLEAR_ORDERING_CUSTOMERS	TASK_DEMO	PUBLIC	DELETE FRO...	NULL	SCHEDULED

Figure 4.15 – Querying and limiting the data from the view

4. Now, we will query the `TASK_HISTORY` based on the task name itself. This can be performed by using the `TASK_NAME` parameter. Let's see how that is done:

```
SELECT * FROM
TABLE(information_schema.task_history(
        task_name => 'CLEAR_ORDERING_CUSTOMERS'
))
ORDER BY SCHEDULED_TIME;
```

Several results are returned; however, note that the results are filtered on the provided name and only history related to the task used in the filter is showing:

Row	QUERY_ID	NAME	DATABASE_NAM	SCHEMA_NAME	QUERY_TEXT	CONDITION_TE)	STATE
1	019a4e41-0...	CLEAR_ORDERING_CUSTOMERS	TASK_DEMO	PUBLIC	DELETE FRO...	NULL	SUCCEEDED
2	NULL	CLEAR_ORDERING_CUSTOMERS	TASK_DEMO	PUBLIC	DELETE FRO...	NULL	FAILED
3	019a4e50-0...	CLEAR_ORDERING_CUSTOMERS	TASK_DEMO	PUBLIC	DELETE FRO...	NULL	SUCCEEDED
4	019a4e5a-0...	CLEAR_ORDERING_CUSTOMERS	TASK_DEMO	PUBLIC	DELETE FRO...	NULL	SUCCEEDED
5	019a4e64-0...	CLEAR_ORDERING_CUSTOMERS	TASK_DEMO	PUBLIC	DELETE FRO...	NULL	SUCCEEDED
6	NULL	CLEAR_ORDERING_CUSTOMERS	TASK_DEMO	PUBLIC	DELETE FRO...	NULL	SCHEDULED

Figure 4.16 – Querying the TASK_HISTORY view based on the task name

5. Finally, all the parameters that we have used can be combined into a single query as well to narrow down our results:

```
SELECT * FROM
TABLE(information_schema.task_history(
        task_name => 'CLEAR_ORDERING_CUSTOMERS',
        result_limit => 2
))
ORDER BY SCHEDULED_TIME;
```

The output is shown only for the provided task, and only the last two rows are shown:

Row	QUERY_ID	NAME	DATABASE_NA	SCHEMA_NAME	QUERY_TEXT	CONDIT... ↓	STATE
1	019a4e64-0...	CLEAR_ORD...	TASK_DEMO	PUBLIC	DELETE FRO...	NULL	SUCCEEDED
2	NULL	CLEAR_ORD...	TASK_DEMO	PUBLIC	DELETE FRO...	NULL	SCHEDULED

Figure 4.17 – Combining all parameters into a single query

How it works...

`TASK_HISTORY` is a table function used to query the execution history of Snowflake tasks. The function can return task history from the previous seven days, with optional parameters available to refine the result set.

In this recipe, we explored several common usage patterns: retrieving recent task executions, filtering history between specific timestamps, limiting the number of rows returned, and querying history for a specific task. These filters can also be combined, making the function useful for troubleshooting failed tasks, validating schedules, and monitoring pipeline activity.

Exploring the concept of streams to capture table-level changes

In this recipe, we will explore the concept of streams, configure a stream on a table, and capture the changes that occur at the table level. Streams are Snowflake's way of performing change data capture on Snowflake tables and can be useful in data pipeline implementation.

Getting ready

The steps for this recipe can be run either in Snowsight or the Snowflake CLI command-line client.

How to do it...

The steps for this recipe are as follows:

1. Let's start by creating a database and a staging table on which we will create our stream object. We create a staging table to simulate data arriving from outside Snowflake and being processed further through a stream object:

```
CREATE DATABASE STREAMS_DEMO;

USE DATABASE STREAMS_DEMO;
```

```
CREATE TABLE CUSTOMER_STAGING
(
  ID INTEGER,
  NAME STRING,
  STATE STRING,
  COUNTRY STRING
);
```

2. The process of creating a stream is quite straightforward with a simple command such as the following:

   ```
   CREATE STREAM customer_changes ON TABLE customer_staging;
   ```

3. Let's describe the stream to see what has been created:

   ```
   DESC STREAM customer_changes;
   ```

   Notice the mode of the stream is set to `DEFAULT`, which indicates it will track inserts, updates, and deletes that are performed on the table:

created_on	name	database_name	schema_name	owner	comment	table_name
2026-06-08 17:49:41	CUSTOMER_CHANGES	STREAM_DEMO	PUBLIC	ACCOUNTADMIN		STREAM_DEMO.PUBLI

Figure 4.18 – The created stream

4. Let's insert some data into the staging table to simulate data arriving into Snowflake:

   ```
   INSERT INTO customer_staging VALUES (1,'Jane
   Doe','NSW','AU');
   INSERT INTO customer_staging VALUES
   (2,'Alpha','VIC','AU');
   ```

5. Validate that the data is indeed inserted into the staging table by selecting it from the table:

   ```
   SELECT * FROM customer_staging;
   ```

   As expected, two rows are present in the staging table:

Row	ID	NAME	STATE	COUNTRY
1	1	Jane Doe	NSW	AU
2	2	Alpha	VIC	AU

Figure 4.19 – Validating whether the data is inserted into the table

6. Now, let's view how the changed data has been captured through the stream. We can query the stream object directly, as shown in the following statement:

```
SELECT * FROM customer_changes;
```

7. The following output shows the rows recorded by the stream. Notice that both rows contain `INSERT` in the `METADATA$ACTION` column.

Row	ID	NAME	STATE	COUNTRY	METADATA$ACT	METADATA$ISUP	METADATA$ROW
1	1	Jane Doe	NSW	AU	INSERT	FALSE	546c1da8c5e...
2	2	Alpha	VIC	AU	INSERT	FALSE	562a8a2d053...

Figure 4.20 – Viewing the changing data

8. Now that we have our stream set up successfully, we can process the data from the stream into another table. You would normally do this as part of a data pipeline. Create a table first in which we will insert the recorded data:

```
CREATE TABLE customer
(
  ID INTEGER,
  Name STRING,
  State STRING,
  Country STRING
);
```

9. Retrieving data from a stream and inserting it into another table is as simple as performing a query on the stream itself. As shown, the query selects the required columns from the stream and inserts them into the customer table. Do note that we

have used a WHERE clause on metadata$action equal to INSERT. This is to ensure that we only process new data:

```
INSERT INTO customer
SELECT ID,Name,State,Country
FROM customer_changes
WHERE metadata$action = 'INSERT';
```

10. Let's select the data from the customer table to validate that the correct data appears there:

```
SELECT * FROM customer;
```

As expected, the two rows that were originally inserted into the staging table appear here:

Row	ID	NAME	STATE	COUNTRY
1	1	Jane Doe	NSW	AU
2	2	Alpha	VIC	AU

Figure 4.21 – Validating the data from the customer table

11. Let's find out what happens to the stream after data has been processed from it. If we perform SELECT now, there will be zero rows returned since that data has already been processed:

```
SELECT * FROM customer_changes;
```

The output shows zero rows returned:

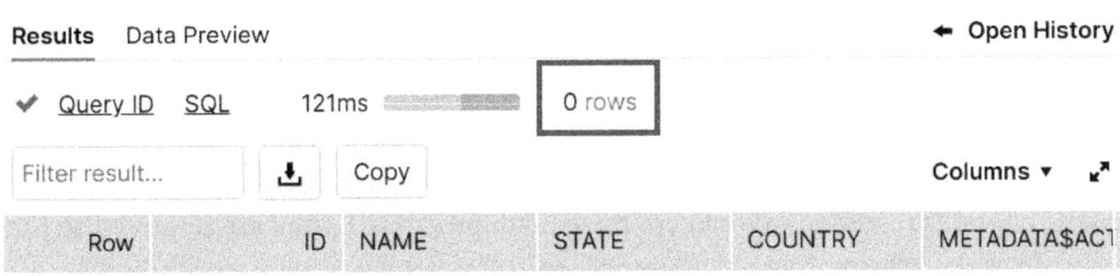

Figure 4.22 – Zero rows returned

12. Let's update a row in the staging table. We are then going to see in the stream how that update appears:

```
UPDATE customer_staging SET name = 'John Smith' WHERE
ID = 1;
```

This operation will show the following output:

number of rows updated	number of multi-joined rows updated
1	0

Figure 4.23 – Updated row in the staging table

13. Select the data from the stream:

```
SELECT * FROM customer_changes;
```

You will see two records appear in the result set, as shown:

ID	NAME	STATE	COUNTRY	METADATA$ACTION	METADATA$ISU	METADATA$RO
1	John Smith	NSW	AU	INSERT	TRUE	546c1da8c5...
1	Jane Doe	NSW	AU	DELETE	TRUE	546c1da8c5...

Figure 4.24 – Selecting the data from the stream

An update operation is essentially captured as `DELETE` followed by `INSERT`. Therefore, you will see both `INSERT` and DELETE appear in the result. If you are processing the stream for deletes as well, you will need additional logic in the consuming code to process `DELETE` correctly.

How it works...

This recipe demonstrates how streams function, which is a mechanism in Snowflake to capture changed data. A stream is created for a table and monitors any changes performed on that table. This includes all the inserts, updates, and deletes performed on the table. Streams can be queried just like tables, allowing the user to select and transform the data recorded in a stream. Once the changes recorded in a stream have been processed, they are removed so that the next processing of the stream doesn't encounter records that are already processed.

Combining the concepts of streams and tasks to build pipelines that process changed data on a schedule

In this recipe, we will combine the concept of streams and tasks, and set up a scheduled Snowflake data pipeline that processes only changed data into a target table.

Getting ready

The steps for this recipe can be run either in Snowsight or the Snowflake CLI command-line client.

How to do it...

The following steps describe how to set up a stream to track and process changes that occur on table data. The steps are as follows:

1. Let's start by creating a database and a staging table on which we will create our stream object. We will create a staging table to simulate data arriving from outside Snowflake and process it further through a stream object:

```
CREATE DATABASE stream_demo;
USE DATABASE stream_demo;
CREATE TABLE customer_staging
(
  ID INTEGER,
  Name STRING,
  State STRING,
  Country STRING
);
```

2. Next, create a stream on the table that captures only the inserts. The insert-only mode is achieved by setting `APPEND_ONLY` to `TRUE`:

```
CREATE STREAM customer_changes ON TABLE
customer_staging APPEND_ONLY = TRUE;
```

3. Let's describe the stream to see what has been created:

```
DESC STREAM customer_changes;
```

As shown in the following output, notice that the mode of the stream is set to APPEND_ONLY, which indicates it will only track inserts:

name	database_name	schema_name	owner	comment	table_name	type	stale	mode
CUSTOMER_...	STREAM_DE...	PUBLIC	SYSADMIN		STREAM_DE...	DELTA	false	APPEND_ONLY

Figure 4.25 – The created stream

4. Now that we have created a staging table and a stream on top of it, let's create the actual table into which all the new customer data will be processed:

```
CREATE TABLE customer
(
  ID INTEGER,
  Name STRING,
  State STRING,
  Country STRING
);
```

5. Let's now create a task that we will use to insert any new data that appears in the stream:

```
USE ROLE SYSADMIN;

CREATE TASK process_new_customers
  WAREHOUSE = COMPUTE_WH
  COMMENT = 'Process new data into customer'
AS
  INSERT INTO customer
SELECT ID,Name,State,Country
FROM customer_changes
WHERE metadata$action = 'INSERT';
```

6. Let's schedule this task to run every 5 minutes. We assume that new customer data is being inserted into the staging table continuously and that we need to process it every 5 minutes. Since the task was created using the SYSADMIN role, use the same role to alter and resume the task. Also ensure that the task owner role has the `EXECUTE TASK`

privilege granted; otherwise, the task may be resumed but fail when Snowflake attempts to execute it:

```
USE ROLE SYSADMIN;

GRANT EXECUTE TASK ON ACCOUNT TO ROLE SYSADMIN;

ALTER TASK PROCESS_NEW_CUSTOMERS
SET SCHEDULE = '5 MINUTE';

ALTER TASK PROCESS_NEW_CUSTOMERS RESUME;
```

7. Let's check that the target table, that is, `customer`, is empty:

```
SELECT * FROM customer;
```

As expected, no rows are present in the **customer** table:

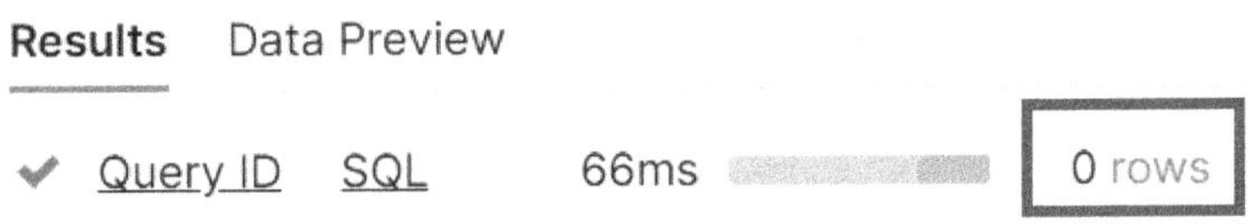

Figure 4.26 – Customer table is empty

8. We will now insert some data into the staging table (effectively simulating data that has arrived into Snowflake from an external source):

```
INSERT INTO customer_staging VALUES (1,'Jane
Doe','NSW','AU');
INSERT INTO customer_staging VALUES
(2,'Alpha','VIC','AU');
```

9. Now, let's view how the changing data has been captured through the stream. We can view the data by adding `SELECT` from the stream object itself:

```
SELECT * FROM customer_changes;
```

The following output shows the data that has been recorded by the stream. Notice both rows have been recorded with an action code of `INSERT`:

ID	NAME	STATE	COUNTRY	METADATA$ACTI	METADATA$ISUP	METADATA$ROW
2	Alpha	VIC	AU	INSERT	FALSE	c9801d993af...
1	Jane Doe	NSW	AU	INSERT	FALSE	49e84564a18...

Figure 4.27 – Viewing the changing data

10. Retrieving data from a stream and inserting it into another table is as simple as performing a query on the stream itself. As shown, the query selects the required columns from the stream and inserts them into the `customer` table. We use a `WHERE` clause on `metadata$action` set to `INSERT` to ensure that we only process new data:

```
INSERT INTO customer
SELECT ID,Name,State,Country
FROM customer_changes
WHERE metadata$action = 'INSERT';
```

11. Let's select the data from the `customer` table to validate that the correct data appears there:

```
SELECT * FROM customer;
```

As expected, the two rows that were originally inserted into the staging table appear here:

ID	NAME	STATE	COUNTRY
2	Alpha	VIC	AU
1	Jane Doe	NSW	AU

Figure 4.28 – Two rows inserted into the staging table

12. We will now insert some more data into the staging table and let it be processed by the scheduled task:

```
INSERT INTO customer_staging VALUES
(3,'Mike','ACT','AU');
INSERT INTO customer_staging VALUES
(4,'Tango','NT','AU');
```

13. Now, we wait for our scheduled task to run, which will process this staging data into the target table. You can also keep an eye on the execution and the next scheduled time by running the following query. Once the scheduled task has executed, the results will look as follows:

    ```
    SELECT * FROM
    TABLE(information_schema.task_history(
            task_name => 'PROCESS_NEW_CUSTOMERS'
    ))
    ORDER BY SCHEDULED_TIME DESC;
    ```

    Once the task has successfully executed, you will see output similar to the following. The task that has run successfully will have a `QUERY_ID` value assigned and a `STATE` value of `SUCCEEDED`:

QUER	NAME	DATABASE_NAME	SCHEMA_N	QUERY_TEXT	CONDITION_TEXT	STATE
null	PROCESS_NEW_CUSTOI	STREAM_DEMO	PUBLIC	INSERT INTO CUSTOMER SEL	null	SCHEDULED
01c4ec64-0209-46	PROCESS_NEW_CUSTOI	STREAM_DEMO	PUBLIC	INSERT INTO CUSTOMER SEL	null	SUCCEEDED

Figure 4.29 – Processing the staging data into the target table

14. Once the task has been successfully executed, select the data from the target table to validate that the rows in the staging table have been inserted into the target table:

    ```
    SELECT * FROM customer;
    ```

    You will see two additional records appear in the result set, indicating that the data from the staging table was processed through a combination of tasks and streams and inserted into the target table:

ID	NAME	STATE ↓	COUNTRY
4	Tango	NT	AU
2	Alpha	VIC	AU
1	Jane Doe	NSW	AU
3	Mike	ACT	AU

Figure 4.30 – Validating the rows in the staging table

How it works...

This recipe demonstrates combining change data capture through streams and the concept of tasks to automate the processing when changes are detected. We started by setting up a stream that captures only inserts into a staging table. The intent is that in a real-world scenario, data from external sources or data via Snowpipe may be inserted into a similar staging table. We next created a stream on top of the staging table that keeps track of the rows that are being inserted into the table. Since this is just a staging table, we would like to take data from here and insert it into an actual table, which we have referred to as the target table. A task is created that uses SQL to read new data from the stream and insert it into the target table. The task is then scheduled to run every five minutes. Any new rows that are recorded in the stream are processed and inserted into the target table.

While this pattern provides explicit control over incremental processing using streams and tasks, Snowflake also supports more declarative approaches to incremental data processing, which are explored later in this chapter.

Converting data types and Snowflake's failure management

SQL queries frequently need to convert between data types, and this recipe provides examples of such conversions. Something that comes with conversion is failure, for example, data type mismatches. Snowflake provides a novel as well as a very structured way of handling such scenarios, and mechanisms for recovery. This allows Snowflake users to build high-quality data processing pipelines that minimize failures and, when they do occur, know how to handle them, how to recover, and how to keep the system stable. Let's now look at Snowflake's unique approach for minimizing errors during query execution by using `TRY_` versions of different conversion functions.

Getting ready

Ensure that you have access to a Snowflake account and privileges to execute SQL statements. The examples in this recipe can be run either in Snowsight or by using the Snowflake CLI.

How to do it...

The following steps walk you through various data type conversion scenarios:

1. Let's start with the common scenario of converting a number stored as a string into a numeric value. We will explore the example of converting to a `NUMBER` type. The `TO_NUMBER` function takes the input string as a required parameter and can optionally

also take in the precision and scale. If the scale is not specified, it defaults to zero. The following query demonstrates the use of the conversion:

```
SELECT '100.2' AS input,
        TO_NUMBER(input),
        TO_NUMBER(input, 12, 2);
```

As shown in the following output, in the first conversion, we did not specify any scale, therefore `100.2` was converted to `100`; the decimal part was dropped. In the second case, the scale was 2, therefore the result is `100.20`:

A INPUT	# TO_NUMBER(INPUT)	# TO_NUMBER(INPUT, 12, 2)
100.2	100	100.20

Figure 4.31 – Converting data from a string to a numeric value

2. The `TO_NUMBER` function works great until it encounters a non-numeric value. If it encounters a non-numeric input, the data type conversion will fail (and the query will fail as well):

```
SELECT 'not a number' AS input,
        TO_NUMBER(input);
```

As shown in the following output, the query failed with a not recognized error:

Figure 4.32 – Failed query message

3. In order to ensure that any data type conversion errors are handled gracefully, Snowflake has type conversion functions that have a `TRY_` prefix at the start. Let's use one of these functions on a non-numeric input:

```
SELECT 'not a number' AS input,
        TRY_TO_NUMBER(input);
```

As the output shows, the type conversion does not fail anymore but rather returns with a NULL value. This ensures that your query doesn't fail due to type conversion:

Row	INPUT	TRY_TO_NUMBER(INPUT)
1	not a number	NULL

Figure 4.33 – Data type conversion with no failures

The TRY_ functions return the same result as the standard conversion functions when a valid numeric input is provided:

```
SELECT '100.2' AS input,
       TRY_TO_NUMBER(input);
```

As shown, the output of TRY_TO_NUMBER is similar to TO_NUMBER; the only difference is the TRY_ type of functions will not fail on an invalid input:

	INPUT	TRY_TO_NUMBER
1	100.2	100

Figure 4.34 – Type conversion with no fails on invalid input

4. Let's explore another common scenario, which is the conversion of string values into a BOOLEAN data type. Snowflake supports a variety of string values as a data type. As shown in the following query, the True, true, tRue, T, yes, on, and 1 string values are considered to be BOOLEAN value TRUE:

```
SELECT  TO_BOOLEAN('True'),
        TO_BOOLEAN('true'),
        TO_BOOLEAN('tRuE'),
        TO_BOOLEAN('T'),
        TO_BOOLEAN('yes'),
        TO_BOOLEAN('on'),
        TO_BOOLEAN('1');
```

As shown in the following output, all of these values converted successfully to TRUE:

	TO_BOOLEAN('TRUE')	TO_BOOLEAN('TRUE')	TO_BOOLEAN('TRUE')	TO_BOOLEAN('T')	TO_BOOLEAN('YES')	TO_BOOLEAN('ON')
1	TRUE	TRUE	TRUE	TRUE	TRUE	TRUE

Figure 4.35 – Converting string values to the Boolean type

5. Conversely, the `False`, `false`, `FalsE`, `f`, no, `off`, and `0` string values all convert to `FALSE`:

```
SELECT  TO_BOOLEAN('False'),
        TO_BOOLEAN('false'),
        TO_BOOLEAN('FalsE'),
        TO_BOOLEAN('f'),
        TO_BOOLEAN('no'),
        TO_BOOLEAN('off'),
        TO_BOOLEAN('0');
```

The following output shows the conversion results. All values are converted into a BOOLEAN `FALSE` value:

	TO_BOOLEAN('FALSE')	TO_BOOLEAN('FALSE')	TO_BOOLEAN('FALSE')	TO_BOOLEAN('F')	TO_BOOLEAN('NO')	TO_BOOLEAN('OFF')
1	FALSE	FALSE	FALSE	FALSE	FALSE	FALSE

Figure 4.36 – Converting string values to the Boolean type

6. Let's now convert a string value that contains a date. The `TO_DATE` function requires a string parameter that contains the date value. Optionally, you can specify a format as well and if the format is not supplied, the system defaults are picked up:

```
SELECT TO_DATE('2020-08-15'),
       DATE('2020-08-15'),
       TO_DATE('15/08/2020','DD/MM/YYYY');
```

The preceding conversion produces the following result:

TO_DATE('2020-08-15')	DATE('2020-08-15')	TO_DATE('15/08/2020','DD/MM/YYYY')
2020-08-15	2020-08-15	2020-08-15

Figure 4.37 – Converting string values that contain a date

7. Finally, let's try and convert to a timestamp. We will use the `TO_TIMESTAMP_NTZ` function, which is used for conversion to a timestamp with no time zones. Notice that

we have tried to convert a simple date string to a timestamp as well as the conversion of a proper timestamp:

```
SELECT TO_TIMESTAMP_NTZ ('2020-08-15'),
       TO_TIMESTAMP_NTZ ('2020-08-15 14:30:50');
```

As shown in the output, if only the date is provided to this function, the timestamp component defaults to `00:00:0.000`:

TO_TIMESTAMP_NTZ ('2020-08-15')	TO_TIMESTAMP_NTZ ('2020-08-15 14:30:50')
2020-08-15 00:00:00.000	2020-08-15 14:30:50.000

Figure 4.38 – Converting to the timestamp type

How it works...

Snowflake provides a variety of data type conversion functions, including TRY_ variants of many standard conversion functions. These functions attempt the requested conversion and return NULL instead of raising an error when the input value is invalid.

TRY_ functions are commonly used when loading staged files, parsing semi-structured data, or processing user-entered values where formats may not always be clean or predictable. This helps pipelines continue processing without failing because of a small number of bad records.

Standard conversion functions are typically used when strict data quality enforcement is required, and invalid values should halt execution. Any NULL values returned by TRY_ functions are often managed using COALESCE(), filtered from the result set, or routed for further review.

There's more...

Snowflake provides a wide range of data type conversion functions. The following table includes a sample of commonly used conversion functions. For brevity, the TRY_ variants of these functions are not listed here.

List of data type functions in Snowflake (excluding the `TRY_` **variant of these functions)**			
`TO_CHAR`	`TO_VARCHAR`		
`TO_BINARY`	`TO_VARIANT`		
`TO_DECIMAL`	`TO_NUMBER`	`TO_NUMERIC`	`TO_DOUBLE`

TO_BOOLEAN			
TO_DATE	DATE	TO_TIME	TIME
TO_TIME	TO_TIME	TO_TIMESTAMP	TO_TIMESTAMP_*
TO_GEOGRAPHY	ST_GEOGGROMGE0HASH	ST_GEAGRAPHYFROMWKB	ST_GEOGRAPHYFROMWKT

Table 4.1 – Some of the data type conversion functions in Snowflake

Managing context using different utility functions

This recipe provides examples of context management by using different Snowflake functions. These functions enable contextual data processing commonly required in ETL.

Getting ready

Ensure that you have access to a Snowflake account and privileges to execute SQL statements. The examples in this recipe can be run either in Snowsight or by using the Snowflake CLI. Some functions return values based on your current role, database, schema, and warehouse selections.

How to do it...

Perform the following steps to try this recipe:

1. This step elaborates on some of the most frequently used information in contextual processing, which is the current date. Snowflake provides the `CURRENT_DATE` function, which, as the name suggests, returns the current date in the default date format:

    ```
    SELECT CURRENT_DATE();
    ```

    A result set showing the output of `CURRENT_DATE` looks as follows:

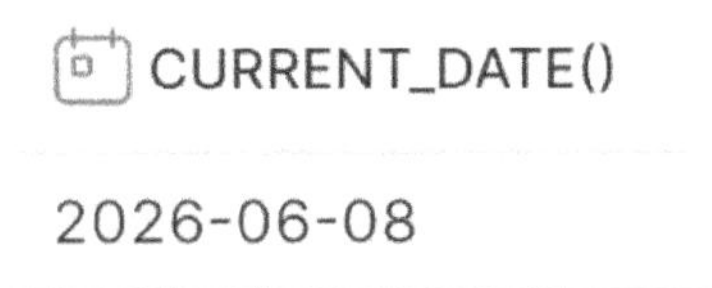

Figure 4.39 – Output of CURRENT_DATE

2. We can also combine the output of `CURRENT_DATE` with other processing logic. As an example, the following statement extracts the day name from the current date to determine whether we are processing during weekend timings or normal timings:

```
SELECT IFF (  DAYNAME(  CURRENT_DATE() ) IN ( 'Sat',
'Sun'), TRUE, FALSE) as week_end_processing_flag;
```

3. Similar to the current date, Snowflake provides the `CURRENT_TIMESTAMP` function, which, in addition to the date, also provides the time component:

```
SELECT CURRENT_TIMESTAMP();
```

4. You can also detect the client that a query is running from using the `CURRENT_CLIENT` context function. Depending on what method you are connecting via, the output of this function will vary:

```
SELECT CURRENT_CLIENT();
```

5. You can also find out the region of your Snowflake instance. This will be the region that you selected when you created your Snowflake instance:

```
SELECT CURRENT_REGION();
```

The output in this example shows the current region as Asia Pacific South East 2. Note that your output may differ depending on the region in which your Snowflake account is hosted. The cloud provider is included as a prefix in the region name; in this case, AWS indicates the cloud platform, and AP represents the Asia Pacific region:

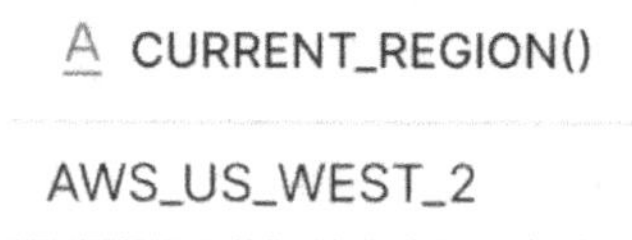

Figure 4.40 – Output showing the current region

6. Snowflake also provides security-specific contextual functions, for example, the current role function:

```
SELECT CURRENT_ROLE();
```

The output showing that the query is being run under the SYSADMIN role looks as follows:

CURRENT_ROLE()
SYSADMIN

Figure 4.41 – Output showing that the query is run under the SYSADMIN role

You can also use `CURRENT_ROLE()` within view definitions to implement conditional logic. For example, a view can include filters that return different subsets of data depending on the role executing the query. This approach uses standard SQL logic and is separate from Snowflake features such as row access or masking policies.

7. Similar to `CURRENT_ROLE()` is the `CURRENT_USER()` function, which, as the name suggests, returns the current user:

```
SELECT CURRENT_USER();
```

8. Finding out which database you are currently in is one of the most common actions. Snowflake provides the `CURRENT_DATABASE` function, which returns the database selected for the session. If there is no database selected, the function returns `NULL`:

```
USE DATABASE SNOWFLAKE_SAMPLE_DATA;
SELECT CURRENT_DATABASE();
```

9. Finding out which schema you are currently in is again one of the most common actions. Snowflake provides the `CURRENT_SCHEMA` function, which returns the schema selected for the session. If there is no schema selected, the function returns `NULL`:

```
USE DATABASE SNOWFLAKE_SAMPLE_DATA;
USE SCHEMA INFORMATION_SCHEMA;
SELECT CURRENT_SCHEMA();
```

10. You can also find out the current warehouse that has been selected to run the query by using the `CURRENT_WAREHOUSE` function:

```
SELECT CURRENT_WAREHOUSE();
```

How it works...

The context functions provide information about various elements, such as session, account, users, and so on, in the context of the executing query. You may want to perform slightly different processing based on the output of the context function. For example, say on the weekend, you would like to add a specific flag to your table. You can do that via the `CURRENT_DATE` context function. The results of the context functions change depending on when, where, and how they are being executed.

There's more...

At the time of writing, the following contextual functions are available in Snowflake:

General context	Session context	Session context object
CURRENT_CLIENT	CURRENT_ACCOUNT	CURRENT_DATABASE
CURRENT_DATE	CURRENT_ROLE	CURRENT_SCHEMA
CURRENT_REGION	CURRENT_SESSION	CURRENT_SCHEMAS
CURRENT_TIME	CURRENT_STATEMENT	CURRENT_WAREHOUSE
CURRENT_TIMESTAMP	CURRENT_TRANSACTION	INVOKER_ROLE
CURRENT_VERSION	CURRENT_USER	INVOKER_SHARE
LOCALTIME	LAST QUIERY ID	IS GRANTED TO_ NVOKER ROLE
LOCALTIMESTAMP	LAST_TRANSACTION	IS_ROLE_IN_SESSION
SYSDATE		

Table 4.2 – Contextual functions available in Snowflake

Using Dynamic Tables for data lifecycle automation

In this recipe, we will use Dynamic Tables to automate data refresh and transformation based on data freshness requirements rather than fixed schedules. Dynamic Tables allow you to declaratively define the contents of a target table using a SQL query, and Snowflake automatically maintains the table as underlying source data changes.

Unlike task-based pipelines, where execution is driven by schedules and explicit orchestration, Dynamic Tables are refreshed based on a target lag, which represents the maximum acceptable staleness of the data.

Getting ready

The steps in this recipe can be executed either through Snowsight or using the Snowflake CLI. This recipe builds on the staging-to-target pattern introduced in the Combining the concept of streams and tasks to build pipelines that process changed data on a schedule recipe. To avoid conflicts, separate tables are used if previous recipes have been executed.

How to do it...

Perform the following steps to create and use a Dynamic Table:

1. Start by creating a database and a staging table. This table simulates data arriving from an external source and serves as the source for the Dynamic Table:

```
CREATE OR REPLACE DATABASE STREAM_DEMO;
USE DATABASE STREAM_DEMO;

CREATE OR REPLACE TABLE CUSTOMER_STAGING_DT
(
  ID INTEGER,
  NAME STRING,
  STATE STRING,
  COUNTRY STRING);
```

2. Insert some initial data into the staging table:

```
INSERT INTO CUSTOMER_STAGING_DT VALUES
(1, 'JANE DOE', 'NSW', 'AU'),
(2, 'ALPHA', 'VIC', 'AU');
```

3. Create a Dynamic Table that selects data from the staging table. The Dynamic Table definition includes the `TARGET_LAG` and `WAREHOUSE` parameters that Snowflake will use to refresh the table:

```
CREATE OR REPLACE DYNAMIC TABLE CUSTOMER_DT
  TARGET_LAG = '1 MINUTE'
  WAREHOUSE = COMPUTE_WH
  REFRESH_MODE = AUTO
AS
```

```
SELECT
  ID,
  NAME,
  STATE,
  COUNTRY
FROM CUSTOMER_STAGING_DT;
```

The `TARGET_LAG` parameter specifies the maximum acceptable staleness of the data. Snowflake automatically schedules refreshes to ensure the Dynamic Table remains within this freshness window.

4. Query the Dynamic Table to validate that it contains the data from the source table:

```
SELECT * FROM CUSTOMER_DT;
```

You should see the two rows that were inserted into the staging table.

	# ID	A NAME	A STATE	A COUNTRY
1	1	JANE DOE	NSW	AU
2	2	ALPHA	VIC	AU

Figure 4.42 – Dynamic Table Load Results

5. Insert additional data into the source table to simulate new data arriving:

```
INSERT INTO CUSTOMER_STAGING_DT VALUES
(3, 'MIKE', 'ACT', 'AU'),
(4, 'TANGO', 'NT', 'AU');
```

6. After waiting for the Dynamic Table to refresh (within the defined target lag), query the Dynamic Table again:

```
SELECT * FROM CUSTOMER_DT;
```

You will now see the additional rows appear automatically, without explicitly running a task or managing a schedule.

	# ID	A NAME	A STATE	A COUNTRY
1	4	TANGO	NT	AU
2	3	MIKE	ACT	AU
3	1	JANE DOE	NSW	AU
4	2	ALPHA	VIC	AU

Figure 4.43 – Dynamic Table Updated Results

How it works...

Dynamic Tables in Snowflake provide a declarative approach to building data pipelines. Instead of defining when a transformation should run, you define what the transformed data should look like and how fresh it must be.

Snowflake continuously monitors changes to the source tables and refreshes the Dynamic Table as needed to satisfy the target lag. The refresh process is fully managed by Snowflake and uses the specified virtual warehouse for compute.

Dynamic Tables can also be chained together, allowing Snowflake to automatically derive and manage dependencies across multiple transformation layers. This creates a directed pipeline of Dynamic Tables without requiring explicit orchestration logic or task sequencing.

There's more...

Dynamic Tables are not intended to replace all task- and stream-based pipelines. Tasks and streams provide explicit control over execution order and are well suited for procedural or multi-step workflows. Dynamic Tables complement these approaches by offering a simpler, freshness-driven alternative for many transformation scenarios.

Dynamic Tables support multi-table transformations. You can use `INNER JOIN`, `CROSS JOIN`, and `OUTER JOIN` (with equality predicates) across any number of source tables, and Snowflake tracks changes to all of them for incremental refresh. `UNION ALL` is also supported incrementally. As a best practice, decompose complex logic into a pipeline of Dynamic Tables, for example, one layer for joins and another for aggregations, rather than combining everything into a single definition. Separating operators enables each step to refresh incrementally instead of reprocessing all data during every refresh.

In addition to fixed time-based values, `TARGET_LAG = DOWNSTREAM` can also be defined relative to downstream Dynamic Tables. This allows freshness requirements to propagate automatically through a pipeline, ensuring upstream tables refresh only when required by downstream consumers.

Operational visibility into Dynamic Tables is available through system functions. For example, the following query uses the `DYNAMIC_TABLE_REFRESH_HISTORY` table function to inspect refresh history, execution status, and potential errors:

```
SELECT *
FROM TABLE(INFORMATION_SCHEMA.DYNAMIC_TABLE_REFRESH_HISTORY());
```

This provides similar observability to task history, enabling monitoring and troubleshooting of Dynamic Table pipelines.

Get this book's PDF version and more

5

Data Protection and Security in Snowflake

For any data analytics solution, securing access to the data is of paramount importance. There are two components to security: authentication, letting a user connect, and authorization, determining what objects a connected user has access to. Snowflake provides discretionary access control and role-based access control through out-of-the-box and custom roles.

In this chapter, we will explore techniques for setting up role hierarchies, adding custom roles, and configuring default roles for users. We will also extend these foundational controls into more advanced governance capabilities including column-level security, row-level security, sensitive data classification, policy monitoring, data quality measurement, and auditing.

The following recipes will be covered in this chapter:

- Setting up custom roles and completing the role hierarchy
- Configuring and assigning a default role to a user
- Delineating user management from security and role management
- Configuring custom roles for managing access to highly secure data
- Setting up development, testing, pre-production, and production database hierarchies and roles
- Safeguarding the ACCOUNTADMIN role and users in the ACCOUNTADMIN role
- Implementing column-level security with masking policies
- Implementing row-level security with row access policies
- Classifying and tagging sensitive data

Technical requirements

The chapter assumes that you have a Snowflake account already set up. You can download the example project and code for this book by following the instructions in the ***Download the example code files*** section in the *Preface* of this book.

Setting up custom roles and completing the role hierarchy

In this recipe, we will introduce new custom roles and learn how and why to complete the role hierarchy. Custom roles allow organizations to group privileges around business functions such as development, analytics, or administration rather than granting broad access to individual users. Completing the role hierarchy helps simplify administration by allowing privileges to be inherited in a controlled and scalable manner across teams and environments. We will also understand how the role hierarchy works in Snowflake.

Getting ready

Before proceeding with this recipe, please ensure that the user you will use has access to the SECURITYADMIN role. Note that this recipe's steps can be run either in Snowflake Snowsight or the SnowSQL command-line client.

How to do it...

To create a new custom role, we need to have access to the SECURITYADMIN role, using which we will create a new custom role. The steps for this recipe are as follows:

1. We will start by creating a database called `DEV`:

   ```
   USE ROLE SYSADMIN;
   CREATE DATABASE DEV;
   ```

   The database should be created successfully.

2. Next, we will create a table called `CUSTOMER`, which we will use to grant privileges on:

   ```
   USE DATABASE DEV;
   CREATE TABLE CUSTOMER
   ( ID STRING,
   NAME STRING);
   ```

   The table should be created successfully.

3. Now, change your role to `SECURITYADMIN` so that you have the required privileges to create a new user and a new role:

```
USE ROLE SECURITYADMIN;
```

The `USE ROLE` statement should return with a success message (provided the user you are using has been granted permission to use the `SECURITYADMIN` role).

4. We will now create a new user, which we will use to demonstrate the role privileges:

```
CREATE USER dev_dba_user1 PASSWORD='Password123123' MUST_CHANGE_PASSWORD =
TRUE;
```

The new user is successfully created.

5. Log in as `dev_dba_user1` and try to run a `SELECT` query on the `CUSTOMER` table:

```
USE DATABASE DEV;
SELECT * FROM CUSTOMER;
```

The query will fail as this user does not have the required rights yet:

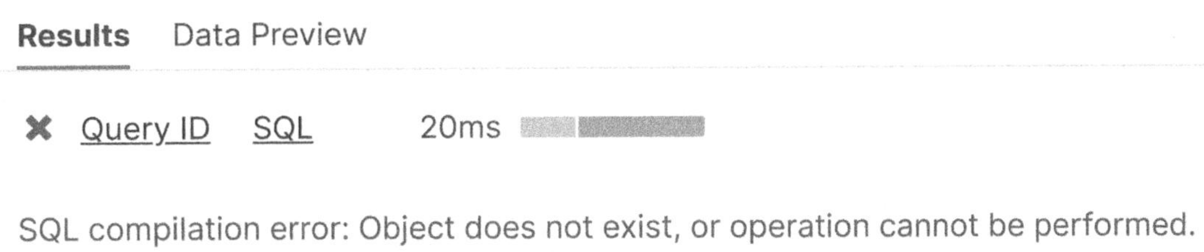

Figure 5.1 – Query failed as the user does not have the required rights yet

6. Log out of `dev_dba_user1` and log back in as the user used in *step 3*, who has access to the `SECURITYADMIN` role. We will now create a new role to manage access to the `DEV` database, hence the name `DEV_DBA`. The creation of a new role is straightforward, as shown in the following code:

```
USE ROLE SECURITYADMIN;
CREATE ROLE DEV_DBA;
```

The new role is successfully created:

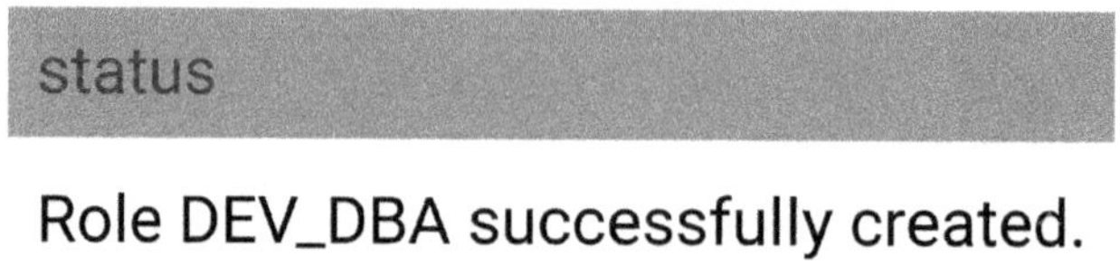

status
Role DEV_DBA successfully created.

Figure 5.2 – New role created

7. However, a new role has no default privileges after creation, which we can validate with the following SQL:

```
SHOW GRANTS TO ROLE DEV_DBA;
```

Zero grants are returned, signifying that the `DEV_DBA` role has no privileges yet:

created_on	privilege	granted_on	name	granted_to	grantee_name	grant_option	granted_by

Figure 5.3 – DEV_DBA has no privileges yet

8. Let's now provide the new role with some privileges on the `DEV` database. We will grant `ALL` privileges to the `DEV` database and the `DEV` database schemas, and explicit permission to the `DEV.PUBLIC.CUSTOMER` table:

```
GRANT ALL ON DATABASE DEV TO ROLE DEV_DBA;
GRANT ALL ON ALL SCHEMAS IN DATABASE DEV TO ROLE DEV_DBA;
GRANT ALL ON TABLE DEV.PUBLIC.CUSTOMER TO ROLE DEV_DBA;
SHOW GRANTS TO ROLE DEV_DBA;
```

The grant statements should execute successfully, and the output to the `SHOW GRANTS` statement will look as shown in the following screenshot.

created_on	privilege	granted_on	name	granted_to	grantee_name	grant_option	granted_by
2026-02-16 07:24:39.623 -0800	APPLYBUDGET	DATABASE	DEV	ROLE	DEV_DBA	false	SYSADMIN
2026-02-16 07:24:39.676 -0800	CREATE DATABASE ROLE	DATABASE	DEV	ROLE	DEV_DBA	false	SYSADMIN
2026-02-16 07:24:39.693 -0800	CREATE SCHEMA	DATABASE	DEV	ROLE	DEV_DBA	false	SYSADMIN
2026-02-16 07:24:39.648 -0800	EXECUTE AUTO CLASSIFICATION	DATABASE	DEV	ROLE	DEV_DBA	false	SYSADMIN
2026-02-16 07:24:39.608 -0800	MODIFY	DATABASE	DEV	ROLE	DEV_DBA	false	SYSADMIN
2026-02-16 07:24:39.633 -0800	MONITOR	DATABASE	DEV	ROLE	DEV_DBA	false	SYSADMIN
2026-02-16 07:24:39.658 -0800	USAGE	DATABASE	DEV	ROLE	DEV_DBA	false	SYSADMIN
2026-02-16 07:24:40.805 -0800	ADD SEARCH OPTIMIZATION	SCHEMA	DEV.PUBLIC	ROLE	DEV_DBA	false	SYSADMIN

Figure 5.4 – Output of the SHOW GRANTS statement

9. Let's now grant the DEV_DBA role to dev_dba_user1:

```
USE ROLE SECURITYADMIN;
GRANT ROLE DEV_DBA TO USER dev_dba_user1;
```

10. Log in as dev_dba_user1 and try to select from the CUSTOMER table:

```
USE ROLE DEV_DBA;
USE DATABASE DEV;
SELECT * FROM CUSTOMER;
```

The SELECT query will now work since dev_dba_user1 has access to the DEV_DBA role, and the DEV_DBA role has rights on the DEV database.

We have successfully created a custom role for use by **development database administrators** (**DBAs**). Similarly, you can set up additional roles according to your requirements.

How it works...

In Snowflake, privileges cannot be directly granted to a user. Privileges are granted to a role, and the role is then granted to one or more users.

There's more...

When creating a new custom role, it is recommended to complete the role hierarchy. Completing the role hierarchy refers to ensuring that the roles are set up so that all custom roles are granted to the SYSADMIN role. The concept is depicted in the following diagram:

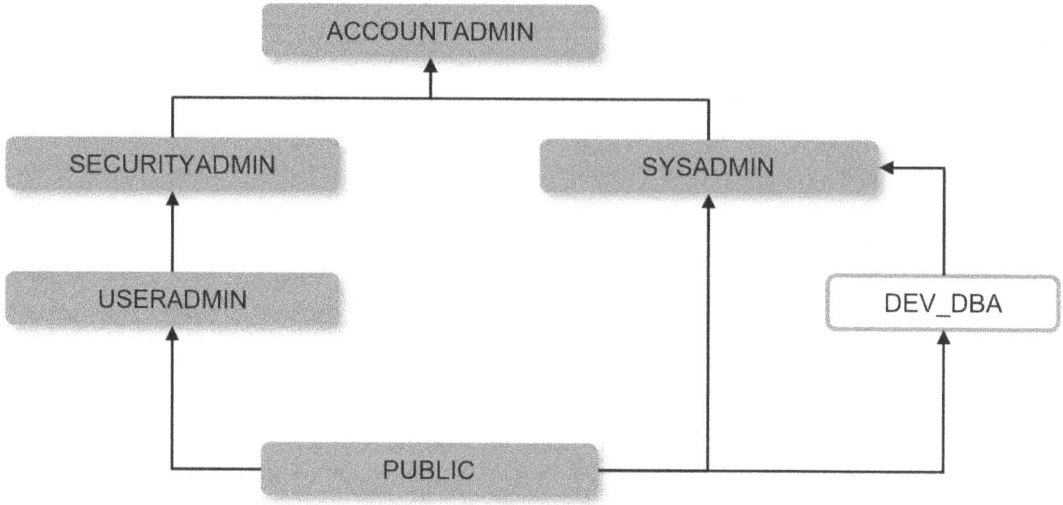

Figure 5.5 – Role hierarchy

Configuring and assigning a default role to a user

In this recipe, we will assign a default role to a user and understand the sequence in which the default role is determined for a session.

Getting ready

Before proceeding with this recipe, please ensure that the user you will use has access to the SECURITYADMIN role. Note that this recipe's steps can be run in either the Snowflake Snowsight or the SnowSQL command-line client.

How to do it...

To create a new user and grant a default role, we need to log in as a user who has access to the SECURITYADMIN role, using which we will create a new user. The steps for this recipe are as follows:

1. Create a new user, which we will call `marketing_user1`. Notice that no role has been granted to the user, and no default role has been specified:

   ```
   USE ROLE SECURITYADMIN;
   CREATE USER marketing_user1 PASSWORD='Password123123' MUST_CHANGE_PASSWORD
   = TRUE;
   ```

   The user will be created successfully.

2. Now, log in as `marketing_user1` and run the following query to view what the default role for the user is:

```
SELECT CURRENT_ROLE();
```

The output will show `PUBLIC` as the current role.

3. You can also validate the default role for `marketing_user1` by logging in to Snowflake Snowsight and viewing the available role in the top-right corner under the username. You will see that the `PUBLIC` role has been selected by default:

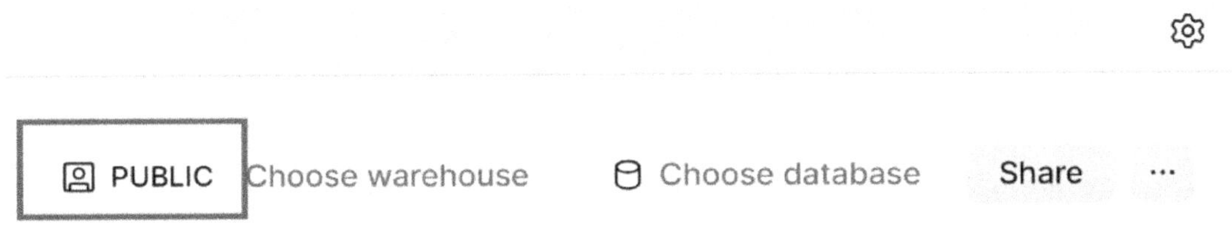

Figure 5.6 – Viewing the available roles in the UI

4. If you try to switch roles, you will see that only the roles granted to the user are available. In this example, the user has only been granted the PUBLIC role, although some Snowflake accounts (such as trial environments) may also include additional default roles such as `SNOWFLAKE_LEARNING_ROLE`.

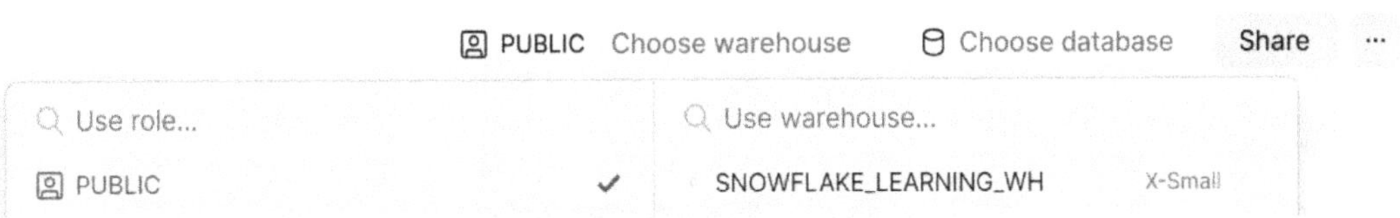

Figure 5.7 – Switching roles in Snowflake Snowsight

5. We will now log in as the user with access to the `SECURITYADMIN` role and assign a new role to `marketing_user1`:

```
USE ROLE SECURITYADMIN;
CREATE ROLE MKT_USER;
GRANT ROLE MKT_USER TO USER marketing_user1;
```

The role will be created and granted to the marketing user with a success message.

> **Note**
>
> The role has only been granted. It has not been set as the default role.

6. Granting a role and making it the default role are two related but separate actions. A role must first be granted to a user before it can be used as that user's default role. Granting a role does not automatically make it the default role, so the default role must be set separately when required. Let's now make the role the default role for the user:

```
USE ROLE SECURITYADMIN;
ALTER USER marketing_user1 SET DEFAULT_ROLE = 'FMKT_USER';
```

The default role for the user is updated with a success message.

7. Now, log in as `marketing_user1` and run the following query to view the user's default role. Make sure to open a new workspace if you are attempting this through Snowflake Snowsight.

```
SELECT CURRENT_ROLE();
```

The output will show `MKT_USER` as the current role:

CURRENT_ROLE()
MKT_USER

Figure 5.8 – Viewing the current role

8. You can also validate the default role for `marketing_user1` by logging in to Snowflake Snowsight and viewing the available role in the rightmost corner under the username. You will see that the `MKT_USER` role has been selected by default:

Figure 5.9 – Viewing the role from the UI

9. If you try and switch roles, you will see that you have the `MKT_ROLE` and `PUBLIC` roles available to you. `MKT_ROLE` is set as the default:

Figure 5.10 – Switching roles

A user may be granted several roles; however, if there is a specific role they will primarily be using, it is useful to set that as the user's default role to improve their experience.

How it works...

Setting a default role determines which granted role becomes the user's current role when a new session begins, unless another role is explicitly specified during connection. This improves the user experience because the user does not need to manually switch roles after each login.

A role must first be granted to a user before it can be set as that user's default role. Granting a role makes it available for use, while setting the default role determines which granted role is activated automatically at login.

This distinction is especially useful when users have multiple roles. For example, a user may have access to reporting, development, and administrative roles, while primarily working in only one of them during day-to-day activities.

There's more...

It is useful to understand how the current role for a session is determined. This can be easily understood through the following diagram:

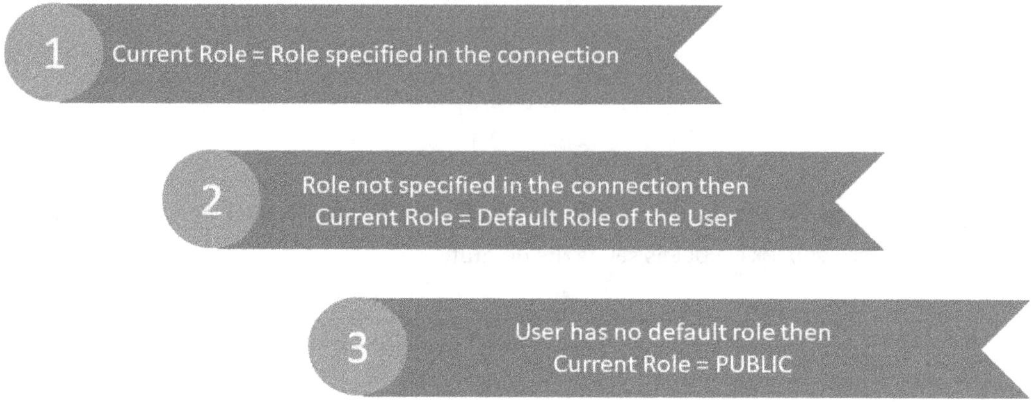

Figure 5.11 – Diagram showing how to check the role in a session

The preceding steps are explained in detail as follows:

- If the role is specified as part of the connection and the user has been granted the role, the role becomes the session's current role
- If no role was specified as part of the connection and the user has a default role, the default role becomes the session's current role
- If no role has been specified as part of the connection and the user does not have a default role, the current role is set to `PUBLIC`

You can specify the current role in the connection string for ETL/ELT jobs and avoid using the `USE ROLE` statement in every script, helping you simplify your code.

Delineating user management from security and role management

In this recipe, we will be using Snowflake's built-in roles to isolate access for operational teams that create users and roles and security teams that manage and control the access rights. The USERADMIN Snowflake role provides privileges for creating and managing users without requiring a higher privilege as with SECURITYADMIN. Therefore, the USERADMIN role can be granted to the operations team responsible for onboarding and offboarding users to your Snowflake instance.

Getting ready

Before proceeding with this recipe, please ensure that the user you will modify can use the SECURITYADMIN role. Note that this recipe's steps can be run in either the Snowflake Snowsight or the SnowSQL command-line client.

How to do it...

We will create a new user to whom we will grant the USERADMIN role. The steps for this recipe are as follows:

1. Create a new database that will be used to demonstrate privilege management:

```
USE ROLE SYSADMIN;
CREATE DATABASE test_database;
```

   The statement should run successfully.

2. Create a new user, which we will call `user_operations1`.

```
USE ROLE SECURITYADMIN;
CREATE USER user_operations1 PASSWORD='Password123123'
MUST_CHANGE_PASSWORD = TRUE;
```

   The user should be created successfully.

3. We will now grant the USERADMIN role to this user and make it their default role:

```
USE ROLE SECURITYADMIN;
GRANT ROLE USERADMIN TO USER user_operations1;
ALTER USER user_operations1 SET DEFAULT_ROLE = USERADMIN;
```

4. Let's now log in as the `user_operations1` user and validate the default role for the user:

```
SELECT CURRENT_ROLE();
```

   As expected, the current role for the user is set to USERADMIN:

CURRENT_ROLE()
USERADMIN

Figure 5.12 – Validating the default role

5. Let's now try to create a new user using the `user_operations1` user:

```
CREATE USER new_analyst1 PASSWORD='Password123123' MUST_CHANGE_PASSWORD =
TRUE;
```

The user is successfully created.

6. Let's now create a new role using the `user_operations1` user:

```
CREATE ROLE BA_ROLE;
```

The role should be created successfully.

7. We will now grant `BA_ROLE` to the `new_analyst1` user created previously and will also set it as the default role for `new_analyst1`:

```
GRANT ROLE BA_ROLE TO USER new_analyst1;
ALTER USER new_analyst1 SET DEFAULT_ROLE = BA_ROLE;
```

The role is granted, and the default role is set up with a success message.

8. Let's now try and grant `BA_ROLE` some privileges. Since we are performing this action as USERADMIN, the command should fail as USERADMIN is not allowed to manage privileges:

```
GRANT USAGE ON DATABASE test_database TO ROLE BA_ROLE;
```

The action fails with the following message:

SQL compilation error: Database 'TEST_DATABASE' does not exist or not authorized.

Figure 5.13 – Error message as the user is not authorized

9. Let's try the same action while logged in as a user who has access to the `SECURITYADMIN` role:

```
USE ROLE SECURITYADMIN;
GRANT USAGE ON DATABASE test_database TO ROLE BA_ROLE;
```

The privileges should be granted successfully.

How it works...

The built-in USERADMIN role is introduced explicitly in Snowflake to segregate user management from the rest of security management. The USERADMIN role provides the capability to create and manage users. It can also be used to create and grant roles to users. However, it does not have the privilege to grant privileges on objects such as databases, tables, views, and so on. Therefore, the USERADMIN role can easily be assigned to your operations team responsible for user provisioning. The USERADMIN role provides them with the required permissions without giving them the extra capability to assign privileges to objects. The following diagram shows the hierarchy:

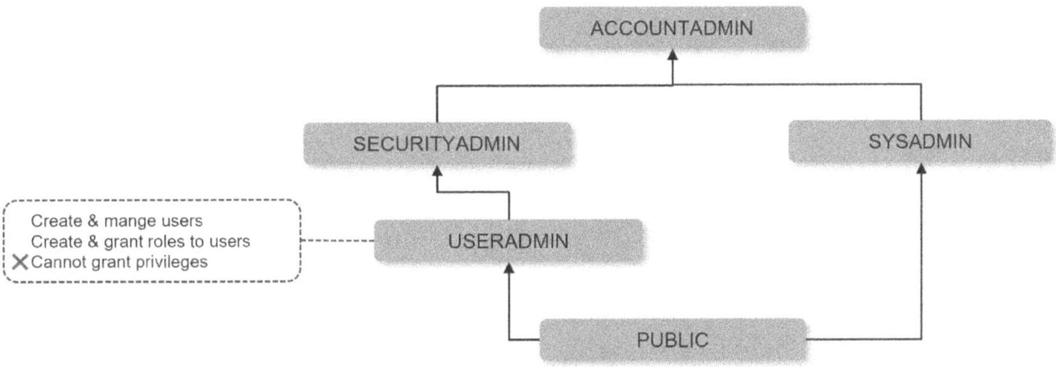

Figure 5.14 – Hierarchy diagram of user roles

As depicted in the preceding diagram, the **USER ADMIN** role is inherited by **SECURITY ADMIN**. Therefore, the **SECURITY ADMIN** role can do everything that **USER ADMIN** does, and it can also grant privileges on other objects.

Configuring custom roles for managing access to highly secure data

In this recipe, we will explore securing access to highly confidential data through a custom role. We will also explore how we can deny access to specific datasets, even to the administrative users.

Getting ready

Before proceeding with this recipe, please ensure that the user you will use can use the `SECURITYADMIN` role. Note that this recipe's steps can be run in either the Snowflake Snowsight or the SnowSQL command-line client.

How to do it...

We will create a new custom role and demonstrate how it can be configured to control access to sensitive data. The steps for this recipe are as follows:

1. Let's start by creating the database that will hold the sensitive data. In this database, we will also create a table that contains salary information:

```
USE ROLE SYSADMIN;
CREATE DATABASE sensitive_data;
CREATE TABLE SALARY
(
  EMP_ID INTEGER,
  SALARY NUMBER
);
```

   You should see the database and the table created successfully.

2. Next, we will create a role that will have access to this data:

```
USE ROLE SECURITYADMIN;
CREATE ROLE HR_ROLE;
```

   You should see the role created successfully.

3. Let's now grant the necessary privileges to this role. We will transfer the ownership of the database and the table that we previously created to this role:

```
GRANT OWNERSHIP ON TABLE sensitive_data.PUBLIC.SALARY TO ROLE HR_ROLE;
GRANT OWNERSHIP ON SCHEMA sensitive_data.PUBLIC TO ROLE HR_ROLE;
GRANT OWNERSHIP ON DATABASE sensitive_data TO ROLE HR_ROLE;
```

   You should see the statements execute successfully.

   At this point, we have effectively given `HR_ROLE` access to the `sensitive_data` database and have locked down access to all other roles.

4. Let's validate that no other role can access the data. As the SYSADMIN role, try to access the data in this table:

```
USE ROLE SYSADMIN;
SELECT * FROM sensitive_data.PUBLIC.SALARY;
```

You should see the following error:

SQL compilation error: Database 'SENSITIVE_DATA' does not exist or not authorized.

Figure 5.15 – Testing SYSADMIN's access to sensitive data

5. Let's check whether the ACCOUNTADMIN role can access the data:

```
USE ROLE ACCOUNTADMIN;
SELECT * FROM sensitive_data.PUBLIC.SALARY;
```

You should again get an error indicating that even the ACCOUNTADMIN role is unable to access the data:

SQL access control error: Insufficient privileges to operate on table 'SALARY'

Figure 5.16 – Testing ACCOUNTADMIN's access to sensitive data

6. The only way to access this data now is through the `HR_ROLE` role. We will now create a new user and add that user to the `HR_ROLE` role:

```
USE ROLE SECURITYADMIN;
CREATE USER hr_user1 PASSWORD='Password123123' MUST_CHANGE_PASSWORD = TRUE;
GRANT ROLE HR_ROLE to USER hr_user1;
```

The preceding query should complete successfully, with a new user created and the `HR_ROLE` role granted to the new user.

7. Let's now log in as `hr_user1` and see whether we can access the `SALARY` data:

```
USE ROLE HR_ROLE;
SELECT * FROM sensitive_data.PUBLIC.SALARY;
```

The `SELECT` query will successfully execute; however, zero rows are returned as we did not load any data into the table.

By not completing the role hierarchy, we have successfully limited access to sensitive data to one role.

How it works...

Snowflake recommends that you complete the role hierarchy when creating a new custom role. Completing the role hierarchy means that you grant the newly created role to the **SYSADMIN** role. This completes the role hierarchy and automatically inherits the role privileges to **SYSADMIN** and the **ACCOUNTADMIN** role. This is shown in the following diagram:

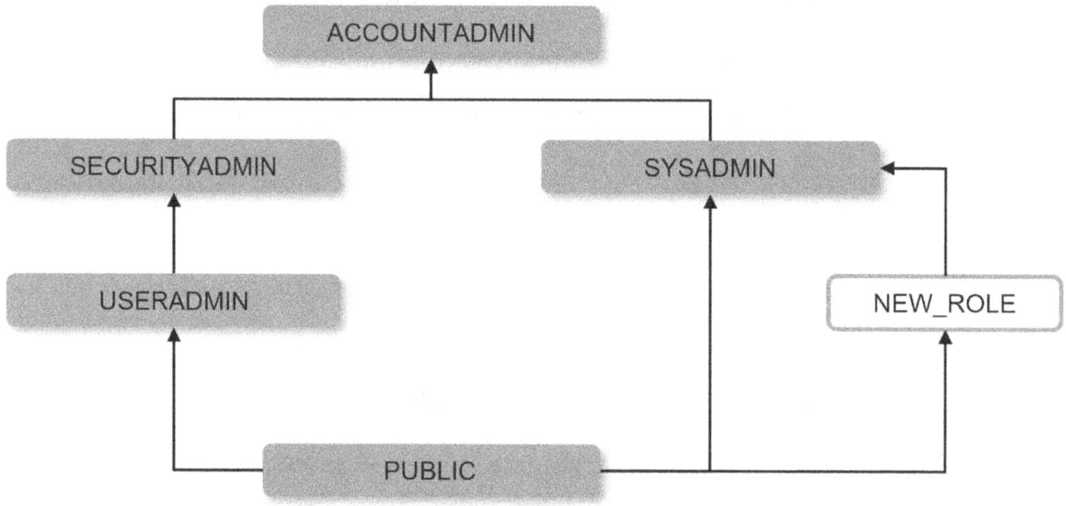

Figure 5.17 – Role hierarchy granting a newly created role to SYSTEM ADMIN

However, if there is sensitive data that you would not like even the administrators to see, you can break the role hierarchy and not grant the new role to **SYSADMIN**, as shown in the following diagram:

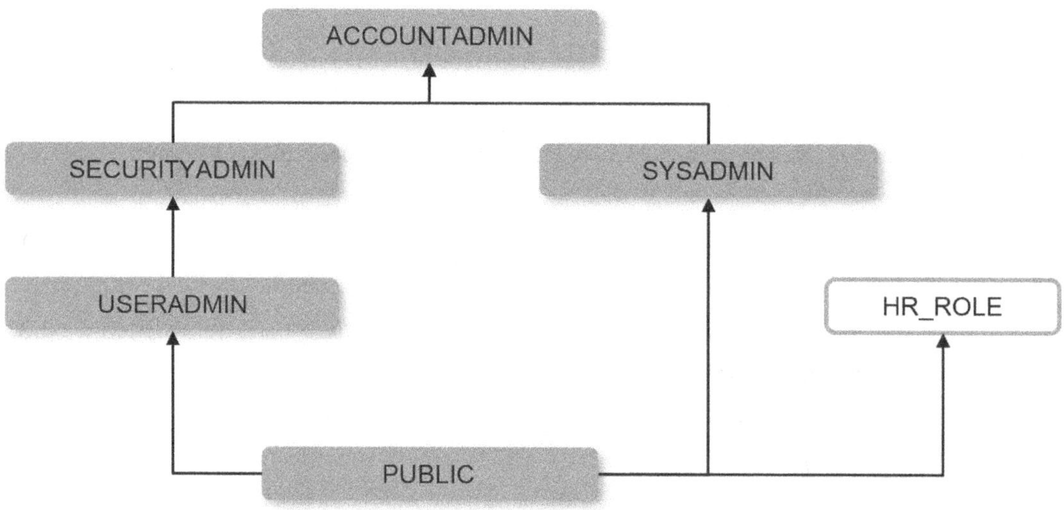

Figure 5.18 – Role hierarchy disabling the HR_ROLE role for administrators

HR_ROLE is not granted to the **SYSADMIN** role; therefore, **HR_ROLE** privileges given to **HR_ROLE** are not automatically inherited, effectively disabling access for the administrators.

This approach ensures that highly sensitive data remains accessible only to explicitly authorized roles and is not automatically inherited by broader administrative roles. In later recipes, we will enhance this model using dynamic masking and row-level security policies to provide even more granular protection.

Setting up development, testing, pre-production, and production database hierarchies and roles

This recipe will walk you through the setup of different environments, such as development, testing, pre-production, and production databases, and schemas, and configuring custom roles for managing access.

Getting ready

Before proceeding with this recipe, please ensure that the user you will use can use the `SECURITYADMIN` role. Note that this recipe's steps can be run in either the Snowflake Snowsight or the SnowSQL command-line client.

How to do it...

We will demonstrate the creation of development and production databases, roles, and users. The same concept can be extended if other environments are needed. The steps for this recipe are as follows:

1. Let's start by creating a new user who will act as a DBA for the development environment:

   ```
   USE ROLE SECURITYADMIN;

   CREATE USER dev_dba_1
   PASSWORD = 'Password123123'
   DEFAULT_ROLE = DEV_DBA_ROLE
   MUST_CHANGE_PASSWORD = TRUE;
   ```

   The user is created with a success message.

2. Next, we will create a role for the development DBA and grant it to the development user:

```
CREATE ROLE DEV_DBA_ROLE;
GRANT ROLE DEV_DBA_ROLE TO USER dev_dba_1;
```

The role is created and granted with a success message.

3. Next, we switch to the SYSADMIN role and create the development database:

```
USE ROLE SYSADMIN;
CREATE DATABASE DEV_DB;
```

The database is created with a success message.

4. With the database now created, it is time to grant full access to the `DEV_DBA_ROLE` role:

```
GRANT ALL ON DATABASE DEV_DB TO ROLE DEV_DBA_ROLE;
```

The specified privilege is granted to the role with a success message.

5. At this point, the `dev_dba_1` user has full rights to the `DEV_DB` database and can create objects and grant further permissions. Let's now create the production database, roles, and user using the same approach:

```
USE ROLE SECURITYADMIN;

CREATE USER prod_dba_1
PASSWORD = 'Password123123'
DEFAULT_ROLE = PROD_DBA_ROLE
MUST_CHANGE_PASSWORD = TRUE;
```

The user should be created successfully.

6. Next, we will create a role for the production DBA and grant it to the production user:

```
CREATE ROLE PROD_DBA_ROLE;
GRANT ROLE PROD_DBA_ROLE TO USER prod_dba_1;
```

This should complete with a success message.

7. Next, we switch to the SYSADMIN role and create the production database:

```
USE ROLE SYSADMIN;
CREATE DATABASE PROD_DB;
```

The production database is created successfully.

8. With the database now created, it is time to grant full access to the `PROD_DBA_ROLE` role:

```
GRANT ALL ON DATABASE PROD_DB TO ROLE PROD_DBA_ROLE;
```

This should complete with a success message.

9. At this point, the `prod_dba_1` user has full rights to the `PROD_DB` database and can create objects and grant further permissions.

We have successfully created production and development databases. The two databases are segregated, and only DBA users with the correct privileges can access their respective databases.

How it works...

Snowflake's role-based access control security model allows security administrators

to configure object security at a role level. Using role-based security, we have set up

a development database and production database segregated from each other in terms of access. The DBA user setup for the development database has full access to the development database but has no access to the production database. Since we have given full privileges to the DBA user, they can create additional schemas and other objects under the development database. Through this segregation and role assignment, you can free up your SYSADMIN users from development environment maintenance and delegate that function to specific users designated as DBAs for development environments.

Using the same principle, you can set up several different environments, such as test, system integration testing, pre-production, and so on, and manage them independently through different roles and privileges.

Safeguarding the ACCOUNTADMIN role and users in the ACCOUNTADMIN role

This recipe will walk you through techniques to safeguard the ACCOUNTADMIN role from unauthorized access and introduce redundancy in the role membership. The recipe will then walk you through the process of securing users in the ACCOUNTADMIN role through **multi-factor authentication** (**MFA**).

Getting ready

Before proceeding with this recipe, please ensure that you have access to the ACCOUNTADMIN role. Note that the steps in this recipe should be run through Snowflake Snowsight.

How to do it...

To introduce redundancy in the ACCOUNTADMIN role, we will create a new user and grant that user the ACCOUNTADMIN role. Next, we will enforce MFA using an authentication policy and apply it so that ACCOUNTADMIN users must enroll in MFA. The steps for this recipe are as follows:

1. Create a new user that we will give the ACCOUNTADMIN role using the syntax that follows. Make sure that you provide a *valid email address* for the user. The email address will be used in the next steps to set up MFA:

   ```
   USE ROLE SECURITYADMIN;

   CREATE USER second_account_admin
   PASSWORD = 'Password123123'
   EMAIL = 'john@doe.com'
   MUST_CHANGE_PASSWORD = TRUE;
   ```

   The new user is created successfully.

   > **Note**
   >
   > `MUST_CHANGE_PASSWORD = TRUE` forces the user to sign in and change their password via the web flow before using other interfaces.

2. Grant the ACCOUNTADMIN role to the newly created user:

   ```
   GRANT ROLE ACCOUNTADMIN TO USER second_account_admin;
   ```

   The role is successfully granted to the new user.

3. We are now going to configure the default role for the newly created user. We will set the default role of the new user to be SECURITYADMIN rather than ACCOUNTADMIN to ensure that there is no inadvertent use of the ACCOUNTADMIN role:

   ```
   ALTER USER second_account_admin
   SET DEFAULT_ROLE = SECURITYADMIN;
   ```

   The statement should execute successfully.

4. Verify that the user has ACCOUNTADMIN granted, and that the default role is set correctly:

   ```
   SHOW GRANTS TO USER second_account_admin;

   DESC USER second_account_admin;
   ```

5. Snowflake accounts require MFA for password users. To explicitly initiate MFA enrollment for the new administrative user, run the following command:

   ```
   ALTER USER second_account_admin ENROLL MFA;
   ```

   This command flags the user for MFA enrollment.

6. The user must now log in interactively to complete MFA configuration. Upon login, Snowflake will prompt the user to register a supported MFA method, such as:

   - A passkey (recommended)
   - An authenticator application (**Time-Based One-Time Password** (**TOTP**))

   For this recipe, select **Authenticator Application (TOTP)** during the Snowflake enrollment process. Snowflake will then display a QR code that must be scanned using a compatible TOTP authenticator application.

   Commonly supported authenticator applications include:

   - Microsoft Authenticator
   - Google Authenticator
   - Authy

7. After scanning, enter the six-digit code generated by the application to complete enrollment.

How it works...

When you sign up for a new Snowflake account, the first user created is automatically granted the ACCOUNTADMIN role. Because this user has full administrative control over the account, it is considered a best practice to create at least one additional user with the ACCOUNTADMIN role. This ensures administrative continuity in the event that one administrator is unable to access the account.

However, simply creating a secondary administrator is not sufficient. Because the ACCOUNTADMIN role inherits all administrative privileges within the Snowflake account, compromise of an ACCOUNTADMIN user could result in complete account takeover. For this reason, MFA must be enabled for all users granted this role.

Modern Snowflake accounts require MFA enrollment for password-based users. MFA adds a second factor of authentication in addition to the user's password. Even if a password is compromised, an attacker would still need access to the user's second authentication factor to gain entry.

Snowflake supports multiple MFA methods, including:

- Passkeys (phishing-resistant authentication using WebAuthn)
- Authenticator applications (TOTP)

TOTP-based authentication uses a standards-based algorithm (RFC 6238) that generates a rotating six-digit code every 30 seconds. Because it is vendor-neutral, any compatible authenticator application such as Microsoft Authenticator or Google Authenticator can be used.

For administrative users, phishing-resistant authentication methods such as passkeys are recommended in production environments. Regardless of the chosen method, enabling MFA significantly reduces the risk of unauthorized administrative access.

In addition to MFA protection, administrators should avoid using ACCOUNTADMIN as their default role and instead switch to it only when performing critical administrative tasks. This practice further limits exposure and reduces the risk of accidental misuse.

Implementing column-level security with masking policies

Role-based access control (**RBAC**) determines who can access an object in Snowflake. However, in many enterprise environments, granting access to a table is not sufficient control. Different users may require access to the same table while seeing different representations of sensitive data. Snowflake's dynamic data masking feature enables column-level security by rewriting query results at runtime based on execution context, such as the active role. This allows sensitive data to be protected without duplicating tables or creating separate views for each user group.

Getting ready

Before proceeding with this recipe, please ensure that the user you will use has access to the SYSADMIN, USERADMIN, and SECURITYADMIN roles, as these roles are used throughout the recipe to create objects, create roles, and grant privileges. Some environments may also require ACCOUNTADMIN to grant account-level privileges such as APPLY MASKING POLICY.

Note that this recipe's steps can be run in either the Snowflake Snowsight interface or the Snowflake CLI.

How to do it...

We will begin by creating a sample database, a schema, and a table that contains sensitive customer data. Next, we will create roles representing masked and unmasked access, define a masking policy for the `EMAIL` column, and apply the policy to the table. Finally, we will query the table under each role to verify that Snowflake returns different results based on the active role. The steps for this recipe are as follows:

1. Let's start by creating a simple table with sensitive data and a new user who will act as a DBA for the development environment:

```
USE ROLE SYSADMIN;

CREATE OR REPLACE DATABASE GOVERNANCE_DB;
CREATE OR REPLACE SCHEMA GOVERNANCE_DB.SECURITY;

CREATE OR REPLACE TABLE GOVERNANCE_DB.SECURITY.CUSTOMER_DATA
(
  CUSTOMER_ID NUMBER,
  FULL_NAME   STRING,
  EMAIL       STRING,
  REGION      STRING
);

INSERT INTO GOVERNANCE_DB.SECURITY.CUSTOMER_DATA (CUSTOMER_ID, FULL_NAME,
EMAIL, REGION) VALUES
  (1, 'JANE DOE', 'JANE.DOE@EXAMPLE.COM', 'EAST'),
  (2, 'JOHN DOE', 'JOHN.DOE@EXAMPLE.COM', 'WEST'),
  (3, 'PAT SMITH', 'PAT.SMITH@EXAMPLE.COM', 'EAST');
```

2. Next, we will create a role that sees masked data and a role that sees unmasked data:

```
USE ROLE USERADMIN;

CREATE OR REPLACE ROLE PII_MASKED;
CREATE OR REPLACE ROLE PII_FULL;
```

The role is created with a success message.

3. Grant access to the table for both roles; both roles can query the table, and the masking policy controls what they see.

```
USE ROLE SECURITYADMIN;

GRANT USAGE ON DATABASE GOVERNANCE_DB TO ROLE PII_MASKED;
GRANT USAGE ON SCHEMA GOVERNANCE_DB.SECURITY TO ROLE PII_MASKED;

GRANT SELECT ON TABLE GOVERNANCE_DB.SECURITY.CUSTOMER_DATA TO ROLE
PII_MASKED;
GRANT USAGE ON DATABASE GOVERNANCE_DB TO ROLE PII_FULL;
GRANT USAGE ON SCHEMA GOVERNANCE_DB.SECURITY TO ROLE PII_FULL;
GRANT SELECT ON TABLE GOVERNANCE_DB.SECURITY.CUSTOMER_DATA TO ROLE
PII_FULL;
```

4. Now create a masking policy for the `EMAIL` column. This policy returns the real email only when the active role is `PII_FULL`. Otherwise, it returns a masked value.

```
GRANT CREATE MASKING POLICY ON SCHEMA GOVERNANCE_DB.SECURITY TO ROLE
SECURITYADMIN;
GRANT APPLY MASKING POLICY ON ACCOUNT TO ROLE SECURITYADMIN;

CREATE OR REPLACE MASKING POLICY GOVERNANCE_DB.SECURITY.EMAIL_MASK
  AS (VAL STRING) RETURNS STRING ->
  CASE
    WHEN CURRENT_ROLE() = 'PII_FULL' THEN VAL
    ELSE '************'
  END;
```

5. Apply the masking policy to the EMAIL column.

```
USE ROLE SECURITYADMIN;

ALTER TABLE GOVERNANCE_DB.SECURITY.CUSTOMER_DATA
  MODIFY COLUMN EMAIL
  SET MASKING POLICY GOVERNANCE_DB.SECURITY.EMAIL_MASK;
```

6. Grant PII_MASKED to the user who should see masked values.

```
USE ROLE SECURITYADMIN;

GRANT ROLE PII_MASKED TO USER <YOUR_USER_NAME>;
```

7. For validation in this recipe, also grant PII_FULL to the same user.

```
GRANT ROLE PII_FULL TO USER <YOUR_USER_NAME>;
```

8. Validate masked behavior.

```
USE ROLE PII_MASKED;

SELECT CUSTOMER_ID, FULL_NAME, EMAIL, REGION
FROM GOVERNANCE_DB.SECURITY.CUSTOMER_DATA;
```

The query returns the rows successfully, but the EMAIL column values are masked because the session is using the PII_MASKED role, as shown in the following screenshot:

	# CUSTOMER_ID	A FULL_NAME	A EMAIL	A REGION
1	1	JANE DOE	************	EAST
2	2	JOHN DOE	************	WEST
3	3	PAT SMITH	************	EAST

Figure 5.19 – Under PII_MASKED, EMAIL is masked (************)

9. Validate unmasked behavior:

```
USE ROLE PII_FULL;
```

```
SELECT CUSTOMER_ID, FULL_NAME, EMAIL, REGION
FROM GOVERNANCE_DB.SECURITY.CUSTOMER_DATA;
```

The same query now returns the original `EMAIL` values because the session is using the `PII_FULL` role, which is authorized by the masking policy to view unmasked data, as shown in the following screenshot:

	# CUSTOMER_ID	A FULL_NAME	A EMAIL	A REGION
1	1	JANE DOE	JANE.DOE@EXAMPLE.COM	EAST
2	2	JOHN DOE	JOHN.DOE@EXAMPLE.COM	WEST
3	3	PAT SMITH	PAT.SMITH@EXAMPLE.COM	EAST

Figure 5.20 – Under PII_FULL, EMAIL shows the real value

How it works...

When Snowflake's masking policies implement column-level security by dynamically transforming query results at runtime, the underlying data stored in the table is not modified. Instead, whenever a protected column is referenced in a query, Snowflake evaluates the masking policy expression and returns a transformed value based on the execution context.

In this recipe, the masking policy uses `CURRENT_ROLE()` or `IS_ROLE_IN_SESSION()` to determine whether the active role is authorized to view unmasked data. When the query is executed using the `PII_FULL` role, the original value is returned. When executed using the `PII_MASKED` role, the policy returns a masked value. Because this evaluation happens during query execution, the same table can return different results depending on the role in use.

Snowflake intentionally separates the ability to create masking policies from the ability to apply them. Creating a masking policy requires the `CREATE MASKING POLICY` privilege on a schema, while attaching a masking policy to a column requires the global `APPLY MASKING POLICY` privilege. This separation supports centralized governance by allowing organizations to control who can enforce policies independently from who can define them.

Dynamic masking is enforced consistently across projections, filters, joins, and aggregations. This ensures that sensitive data cannot be exposed through alternative query patterns once a masking policy is attached to a column.

Implementing row-level security with row access policies

Row-level security is required when different users must query the same table but should only see a subset of rows based on business rules (for example, region, department, or tenant). Snowflake implements row-level security using row access policies, which evaluate to `TRUE` or `FALSE` for each row at query time. When a row access policy is bound to a table, Snowflake automatically filters rows based on the policy logic.

Getting ready

Before proceeding with this recipe, please ensure that the user you will use can use the `SECURITYADMIN` role. Note that this recipe's steps can be run in either the Snowflake Snowsight interface or the SnowSQL command-line client.

How to do it...

We will create a row access policy that restricts which rows are visible based on the roles enabled in the session. We will then apply the policy to the `REGION` column of the `CUSTOMER_DATA` table created in the *Implementing column-level security with masking policies* recipe.

1. Let's begin by verifying that the `CUSTOMER_DATA` table created earlier in this chapter exists and contains the sample rows that will be used in this recipe. We will reuse the same table so that row-level security can be layered on top of the column masking controls introduced previously:

   ```
   USE ROLE SYSADMIN;

   SELECT *
   FROM GOVERNANCE_DB.SECURITY.CUSTOMER_DATA;
   ```

   The query should return the sample rows that were inserted earlier in the chapter. We are selecting only non-sensitive columns here because the EMAIL column may still be subject to masking policies from the previous recipe.

2. Ensure the policy administrator can create row access policies in the schema:

   ```
   USE ROLE SECURITYADMIN;

   GRANT USAGE ON DATABASE GOVERNANCE_DB TO ROLE SECURITYADMIN;
   ```

```
GRANT USAGE ON SCHEMA GOVERNANCE_DB.SECURITY TO ROLE SECURITYADMIN;

GRANT CREATE ROW ACCESS POLICY ON SCHEMA GOVERNANCE_DB.SECURITY TO ROLE
SECURITYADMIN;
```

3. Create roles that represent row-level access:

```
USE ROLE USERADMIN;

CREATE OR REPLACE ROLE REGION_EAST;
CREATE OR REPLACE ROLE REGION_WEST;
CREATE OR REPLACE ROLE REGION_ALL;
```

4. Grant one region role to the user you are testing:

```
USE ROLE SECURITYADMIN;

GRANT ROLE REGION_EAST TO USER <YOUR_USER_NAME>;
-- OR:
-- GRANT ROLE REGION_WEST TO USER <YOUR_USER_NAME>;
-- OR:
-- GRANT ROLE REGION_ALL TO USER <YOUR_USER_NAME>;
```

Only one of these roles should be granted at a time when testing. The row access policy evaluates roles in sequence, so if multiple region roles are granted, the first matching condition will determine the result.

If you want to test a different region role, revoke the previously granted role before assigning a new one:

```
REVOKE ROLE REGION_EAST FROM USER <YOUR_USER_NAME>;
```

Then grant the new role:

```
GRANT ROLE REGION_WEST TO USER <YOUR_USER_NAME>;
```

5. Attaching a row access policy to a table requires the `APPLY ROW ACCESS POLICY` privilege:

```
USE ROLE ACCOUNTADMIN;

GRANT APPLY ROW ACCESS POLICY ON ACCOUNT TO ROLE SECURITYADMIN;
```

6. Create the row access policy that allows:
   - All rows when `REGION_ALL` is enabled
   - Only `EAST` rows when `REGION_EAST` is enabled
   - Only `WEST` rows when `REGION_WEST` is enabled

   We use `IS_ROLE_IN_SESSION()` so the policy can evaluate roles active in the session, including any secondary roles granted to the user. This allows the policy to determine access based on all roles available to the user rather than only the current role.

> **Note**
>
> In some Snowflake implementations, secondary roles may be disabled. If secondary roles are not enabled, the policy will evaluate only the primary role in the session.

```
USE ROLE SECURITYADMIN;

CREATE OR REPLACE ROW ACCESS POLICY
GOVERNANCE_DB.SECURITY.REGION_FILTER_POLICY
  AS (REGION_VAL STRING) RETURNS BOOLEAN ->
  CASE
    WHEN IS_ROLE_IN_SESSION('REGION_ALL') THEN TRUE
    WHEN IS_ROLE_IN_SESSION('REGION_EAST') THEN REGION_VAL = 'EAST'
    WHEN IS_ROLE_IN_SESSION('REGION_WEST') THEN REGION_VAL = 'WEST'
    ELSE FALSE
  END;
```

7. Attach the policy to the `REGION` column.

```
USE ROLE SECURITYADMIN;

ALTER TABLE GOVERNANCE_DB.SECURITY.CUSTOMER_DATA
```

```
ADD ROW ACCESS POLICY GOVERNANCE_DB.SECURITY.REGION_FILTER_POLICY
ON (REGION);
```

8. Let's now test the row access policy and confirm that it works alongside the masking controls introduced in the Implementing column-level security with masking policies recipe. Query the table using the `PII_MASKED` role:

```
USE ROLE PII_MASKED;

SELECT CUSTOMER_ID, FULL_NAME, EMAIL, REGION
FROM GOVERNANCE_DB.SECURITY.CUSTOMER_DATA
ORDER BY CUSTOMER_ID;
```

The query returns only the rows permitted by the row access policy based on the region role granted to the user. For example, if the user has been granted the `REGION_EAST` role (and only that role), the query will return only rows where the REGION column is `EAST`, while the `EMAIL` column remains masked because the session is using the `PII_MASKED` role, as shown in the following screenshot:

	# CUSTOMER_ID	A FULL_NAME	A EMAIL	A REGION
1	1	JANE DOE	************	EAST
2	3	PAT SMITH	************	EAST

Figure 5.21 – Masked and Region East policy applied

How it works...

A row access policy is a schema-level object that returns a `BOOLEAN` result for each row. When the policy is bound to a table column, Snowflake evaluates the policy at query time and filters out rows where the policy returns `FALSE`. Snowflake applies the row access policy automatically, so the caller cannot bypass it by changing query patterns.

In this recipe, the policy logic uses `IS_ROLE_IN_SESSION()` to determine whether a specific role is active in the session. Based on the roles available to the user, the policy evaluates the `REGION` column value and determines whether a row should be visible. Because this evaluation happens at query runtime, the same table can return different result sets depending on the user's role configuration. This allows row-level filtering to work seamlessly alongside the column masking logic introduced in the *Implementing column-level security with masking policies* recipe.

Classifying and tagging sensitive data

As organizations mature their security posture, they often move beyond manually applying policies to individual columns and instead adopt metadata-driven governance. Snowflake tags enable you to classify sensitive data consistently and then enforce protection rules at scale. In this recipe, you will create a sensitivity tag, assign it to a column, and reuse the existing masking policy from earlier in this chapter to enforce protection through tag-based masking. This allows sensitive data to be protected without duplicating tables or creating separate views for each user group.

Getting ready

Before proceeding with this recipe, please ensure that the user you will use can use the SECURITYADMIN role. Note that this recipe's steps can be run in either the Snowflake Snowsight interface or the SnowSQL command-line client.

Because this recipe builds on the previous row-level security example, a row access policy may still be active on the `CUSTOMER_DATA` table. To ensure all rows are visible during this recipe, grant the `REGION_ALL` role to the user being tested:

```
USE ROLE SECURITYADMIN;

GRANT ROLE REGION_ALL TO USER <YOUR_USER_NAME>;
```

This role allows the row access policy to return all rows, ensuring consistent results during validation.

How to do it...

We will create a tag to classify sensitive data, assign the tag to the `EMAIL` column in the `CUSTOMER_DATA` table, and then associate the existing masking policy with the tag so masking is applied automatically wherever the tag is used.

1. Let's begin by verifying that the `CUSTOMER_DATA` table and sample data created earlier in this chapter are still available. We will reuse the same table from the previous recipes so that tagging can be layered on top of the existing masking and row-level security examples. We are using the `PII_FULL` role so that the `EMAIL` column values can be viewed without masking during validation.

   ```
   USE ROLE PII_FULL;

   SELECT CUSTOMER_ID, FULL_NAME, EMAIL, REGION
   ```

```
FROM GOVERNANCE_DB.SECURITY.CUSTOMER_DATA
ORDER BY CUSTOMER_ID;
```

The query should return the sample rows that were created earlier in the chapter, including the unmasked `EMAIL` values.

2. Ensure `SECURITYADMIN` can create tags in the schema:

```
USE ROLE SECURITYADMIN;

GRANT USAGE ON DATABASE GOVERNANCE_DB TO ROLE SECURITYADMIN;
GRANT USAGE ON SCHEMA GOVERNANCE_DB.SECURITY TO ROLE SECURITYADMIN;

GRANT CREATE TAG ON SCHEMA GOVERNANCE_DB.SECURITY TO ROLE SECURITYADMIN;
```

3. Create a tag for sensitivity classification:

```
USE ROLE SECURITYADMIN;

CREATE OR REPLACE TAG GOVERNANCE_DB.SECURITY.SENSITIVITY_LEVEL;
```

Tags are schema objects created using `CREATE TAG`.

4. Remove the column-level masking policy so the tag-based policy can take effect. If the `EMAIL` column still has a masking policy directly assigned from the earlier recipe, that policy will override the tag-based masking policy.

```
ALTER TABLE GOVERNANCE_DB.SECURITY.CUSTOMER_DATA
  MODIFY COLUMN EMAIL
  UNSET MASKING POLICY;
```

5. Assign the sensitivity tag to the `EMAIL` column

```
ALTER TABLE GOVERNANCE_DB.SECURITY.CUSTOMER_DATA
  MODIFY COLUMN EMAIL
  SET TAG GOVERNANCE_DB.SECURITY.SENSITIVITY_LEVEL = 'CONFIDENTIAL';
```

6. Verify the tag assignment:

```
SELECT *
FROM TABLE(  GOVERNANCE_DB.INFORMATION_SCHEMA.TAG_REFERENCES_ALL_COLUMNS(
```

```
        'GOVERNANCE_DB.SECURITY.CUSTOMER_DATA',
        'TABLE'
    )
)
WHERE COLUMN_NAME = 'EMAIL';
```

7. Associate the existing masking policy with the tag. This creates a tag-based masking policy by setting the existing masking policy (`EMAIL_MASK`) on the tag.

```
ALTER TAG GOVERNANCE_DB.SECURITY.SENSITIVITY_LEVEL
  SET MASKING POLICY GOVERNANCE_DB.SECURITY.EMAIL_MASK;
```

8. Test the behavior using the existing `PII_MASKED` role:

```
USE ROLE PII_MASKED;

SELECT CUSTOMER_ID, FULL_NAME, EMAIL, REGION
FROM GOVERNANCE_DB.SECURITY.CUSTOMER_DATA
ORDER BY CUSTOMER_ID;
```

	# CUSTOMER_ID	A FULL_NAME	A EMAIL
1	1	JANE DOE	************
2	3	PAT SMITH	************

Figure 5.22 – Masked result from tagged policy

9. Test with `PII_FULL` role applied to see unmasked results

How it works...

Tags are metadata objects that can be assigned to Snowflake objects (including columns) to classify data for governance and security workflows. Once assigned, tags make it possible to identify sensitive data consistently and apply protection rules in a scalable, standardized way.

A tag-based masking policy combines tagging and masking policies by allowing a masking policy to be set on a tag. After the masking policy is associated with the tag, Snowflake automatically enforces the masking behavior on any column where the tag is applied (when the column's data type matches the masking policy signature).

In this recipe, we reused the `EMAIL_MASK` masking policy created earlier in the chapter and associated it with the `SENSITIVITY_LEVEL` tag. We then assigned that tag to the `EMAIL` column, which caused masking enforcement to occur through the tag. Finally, because a masking policy directly assigned to a column takes precedence over a tag-based masking policy, we explicitly unset the column-level masking policy first to ensure the tag-based policy was the enforcement mechanism in this recipe.

There's more...

While masking policies can be applied directly to individual columns, tag-based masking becomes significantly more valuable as environments scale.

When a masking policy is attached directly to a column, that column becomes tightly coupled to the policy. If the masking policy needs to be modified or replaced, Snowflake requires the policy to be detached from every column where it is applied before changes can be made. In environments with dozens or hundreds of protected columns, this can become operationally complex.

Tag-based masking centralizes enforcement. Instead of attaching a policy directly to each column, the masking policy is associated with a tag. Columns are then classified by assigning the tag. If the masking logic must change, administrators can update or replace the masking policy at the tag level, and the changes propagate automatically to every tagged column.

6

Performance and Cost Optimization

Snowflake provides powerful built-in capabilities for optimizing performance and cost through intelligent architecture and automation. Features such as result caching, automatic micro-partitioning, auto-scaling virtual warehouses, automatic clustering, and multi-cluster scaling reduce much of the traditional manual tuning required in legacy data warehouse platforms.

However, optimal performance in Snowflake is not accidental. While the platform abstracts away many physical design decisions, there remains significant opportunity to positively influence performance and cost efficiency through thoughtful table design, query analysis, workload management, and compute optimization. Decisions around clustering strategy, materialized views, warehouse sizing, and concurrency configuration can materially impact both execution speed and credit consumption.

In addition, Snowflake continues to evolve. Modern capabilities such as Warehouse Generations, **Query Acceleration Service** (**QAS**), and enhanced observability through Snowsight dashboards provide new mechanisms for scaling performance and controlling cost. Understanding how and when to use these features is essential for running an efficient Snowflake environment.

In this chapter, we explore practical techniques to analyze and optimize both performance and storage. We will examine how to interpret query plans, identify bottlenecks, tune compute resources, manage concurrency, reduce unnecessary storage costs, and leverage newer performance features to strike the right balance between speed and spend.

The following recipes are included in this chapter:

- Examining table schemas and deriving an optimal structure for a table
- Identifying query plans and bottlenecks
- Weeding out inefficient queries through analysis
- Identifying and reducing unnecessary Fail-safe and Time Travel storage usage
- Projections in Snowflake for performance
- Reviewing query plans to modify table clustering
- Optimizing virtual warehouse scale
- Optimizing warehouse generations and Query Acceleration Service (QAS)

Technical requirements

This chapter requires access to a modern internet browser (Chrome, Edge, Firefox, etc.) and access to the internet to connect to your Snowflake instance in the cloud.

You can download the example project and code for this book by following the instructions in the ***Download the example code files*** section in the *Preface* of this book.

Examining table schemas and deriving an optimal structure for a table

Although Snowflake automates many aspects of storage and performance management, table design still plays an important role in efficiency. Selecting appropriate data types and avoiding unnecessarily large column definitions can improve storage usage and support more efficient query processing. In this recipe, we will analyze a sample table design, compare it with an optimized version, and observe how thoughtful schema choices can reduce storage consumption and improve overall efficiency.

Getting ready

This recipe uses a public S3 bucket for a sample file that is loaded into an example table to demonstrate the concepts. You will need to be connected to your Snowflake instance via Snowsight.

How to do it...

We will create a new table with a not-so-optimal structure and load it with sample data. Later, we will optimize the table and load it with the same data and analyze the two tables' storage differences. The steps for this recipe are as follows:

1. We will start by using the SYSADMIN role to create a new database, schema, and table that will hold the sample data:

```
USE ROLE SYSADMIN;
CREATE DATABASE C6_R1;

CREATE SCHEMA RECIPES;

USE DATABASE C6_R1;
USE SCHEMA RECIPES;

CREATE TABLE CUSTOMER
(
  CustomerID VARCHAR(100),
  FName VARCHAR(1024),
  LName VARCHAR(1024),
  Email VARCHAR(1024),
  Date_Of_Birth VARCHAR(1024),
  City VARCHAR(1024),
  Country VARCHAR(1024)
);
```

   The table will be created successfully.

2. We will now create a file format object that defines how Snowflake should interpret the incoming CSV file during the load process:

```
CREATE FILE FORMAT CSV_FORMAT
     TYPE = CSV
     FIELD_DELIMITER = ','
     FIELD_OPTIONALLY_ENCLOSED_BY = '"'
     SKIP_HEADER = 1
     DATE_FORMAT = 'YYYY-MM-DD';
```

In this definition, `FIELD_DELIMITER` specifies that columns are separated by commas, `FIELD_OPTIONALLY_ENCLOSED_BY` allows text values to be wrapped in double quotes, `SKIP_HEADER = 1` instructs Snowflake to ignore the first row containing column headings, and `DATE_FORMAT` defines how date values in the file should be interpreted during loading.

3. Create a new external stage that points to the public S3 bucket containing the sample file used in this recipe. If the public bucket is unavailable, the same file can also be obtained from the chapter resources that can be found in the GitHub repository.

```
CREATE OR REPLACE STAGE C6_R1_STAGE url='s3://snowflake-cookbook/Chapter06/
r1'
FILE_FORMAT = CSV_FORMAT;
```

   This stage definition allows Snowflake to access the sample file directly from the external location using the file format created in the previous step.

4. List the files in the stage to ensure that you can connect to the S3 bucket:

```
LIST @C6_R1_STAGE;
```

   You should see a single file with the name `customers.csv` listed.

name
s3://snowflake-cookbook/ch6/r1/customers.csv

Figure 6.1 – Listing the files in the staging area

5. We will now load the sample data into the customer table:

```
COPY INTO CUSTOMER
FROM @C6_R1_STAGE;
```

   You will see 200 rows being loaded, as shown:

status	rows_parsed	rows_loaded
LOADED	200	200

Figure 6.2 – Sample data loaded

6. Let's now see how much space this table is consuming by using the following command:

```
SHOW TABLES;
```

The result will be a list of tables along with the size in bytes that the table is taking up:

A name	A database_name	A schema_name	A kind	A com	A cluster_b	# rows	# bytes
CUSTOMER	C6_R1	RECIPES	TABLE			200	13824

Figure 6.3 – List of tables with their sizes

7. We will now create a new customer table that has an optimized structure. The new table uses the `DATE` data type for the `Date_Of_Birth` field and the `NUMERIC` data type for the `CustomerID` field. We have also reduced the size of the other string fields to match the data contained in the table, as is best practice; however, this usually does not affect the table size:

```
CREATE TABLE CUSTOMER_OPT
(
  CustomerID DECIMAL(10,0),
  FName VARCHAR(50),
  LName VARCHAR(50),
  Email VARCHAR(50),
  Date_Of_Birth DATE,
  City VARCHAR(50),
  Country VARCHAR(50)
);
```

The table is created successfully.

8. Load the data into the new, optimized table:

```
COPY INTO CUSTOMER_OPT
FROM @C6_R1_STAGE;
```

You will see 200 rows being loaded, as shown:

status	rows_parsed	rows_loaded
LOADED	200	200

Figure 6.4 – Data loaded into the new, optimized table

9. Let's analyze the difference between the storage of the two tables:

```
SHOW TABLES;
```

As the results show, the optimized table is consuming 10% less storage than the original table. While for a small table the actual bytes difference is not significant, if you consider a table that is 1 TB in size, 10% less storage would equate to 100 GB.

A name	A database_name	A schema_name	A kind	A comment	A cluster_by	# rows	# bytes
CUSTOMER	C6_R1	RECIPES	TABLE			200	13824
CUSTOMER_OPT	C6_R1	RECIPES	TABLE			200	12800

Figure 6.5 – Difference between the storage of the two tables

How it works...

Assigning appropriate data types to your columns helps ensure that the table is stored and processed efficiently. Numeric and date data types are typically stored in a more compact internal format than character strings, which can reduce storage consumption when compared with storing the same values as text. In addition, when values are stored using their correct data types, Snowflake can evaluate joins, filters, and calculations without repeatedly converting strings into numbers or dates at query time.

Using character columns for numeric or date values can therefore increase both storage requirements and query overhead. Defining columns with the correct data types from the start is a recommended practice, and the benefits can become significant as table sizes grow.

Identifying query plans and bottlenecks

Snowflake provides detailed query execution profiles that help explain how a statement was processed and where time or resources were consumed. Learning how to read these profiles is an important skill when troubleshooting slow queries or optimizing workloads. In this recipe, we will execute a deliberately inefficient query, review its Query Profile, and identify common bottlenecks such as excessive table scans, unnecessary column retrieval, and avoidable data processing.

Getting ready

You will need to be connected to your Snowflake instance using Snowsight or the Snowflake CLI to complete this recipe. The example uses the SNOWFLAKE_SAMPLE_DATA database that is included with Snowflake accounts. Because the query scans a large amount of sample data, execution time will vary depending on the size of the virtual warehouse you are using. Larger warehouses will typically complete the query faster than smaller warehouses, but they will also consume credits at a higher rate.

How to do it...

We will be running a sample query using the TPCH sample dataset that is provided with Snowflake. The intent is to run an inefficient query, review its query plan, and identify which steps are using the most compute and contributing most to the overall query execution. The steps are as follows:

1. We will start by executing a sample query against Snowflake's built-in sample dataset. The SNOWFLAKE_SAMPLE_DATA database is provided by Snowflake and contains preloaded benchmark data, so no separate data loading step is required. If this query is executed using an X-Small virtual warehouse, it may take around 15–20 minutes to complete. Larger warehouses will typically complete the query faster, although they will consume credits at a higher rate.
   The SNOWFLAKE_SAMPLE_DATA database contains several schemas. For this recipe, we will use the TPCDS_SF10TCL schema before running the query:

   ```
   USE SCHEMA SNOWFLAKE_SAMPLE_DATA.TPCDS_SF10TCL;

   SELECT *
   FROM store_returns,date_dim
   WHERE sr_returned_date_sk = d_date_sk;
   ```

   You will see that the query has started executing. If you click on **Query ID**, you will be shown the unique query ID for your query. Clicking on the **Query ID** value will take you to the query profile page:

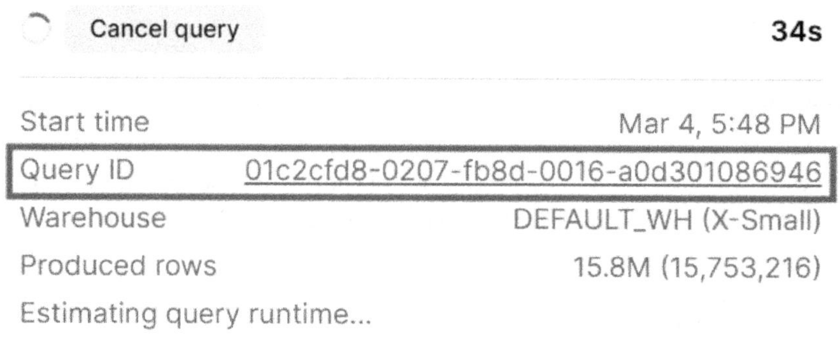

Figure 6.6 – Finding the query ID

2. On the query details page, click the **Query Profile** link to view the execution profile for the query:

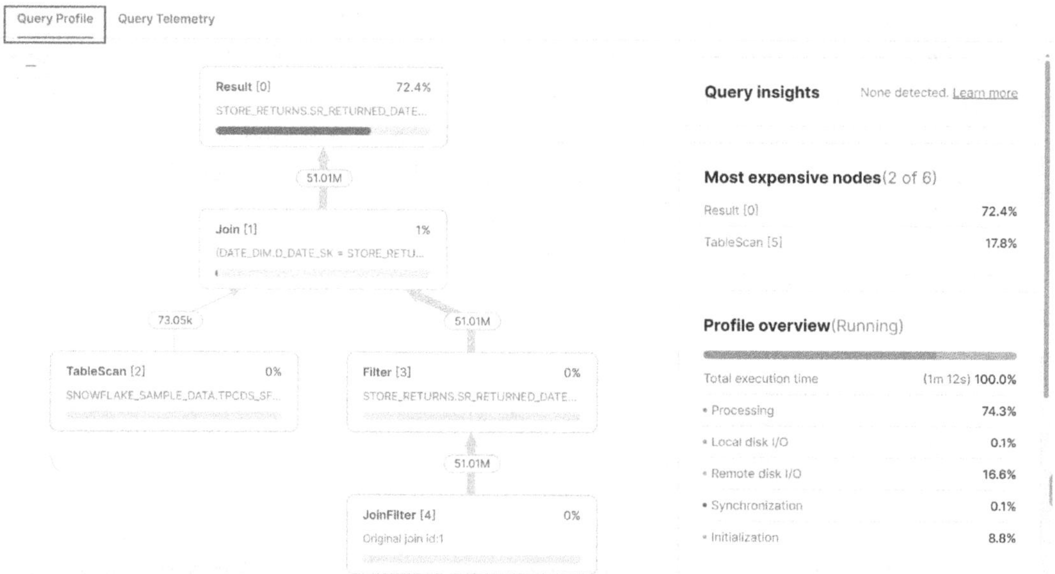

Figure 6.7 – Query profile page

The **Query Profile** page shows the execution plan of the query. It also shows information about the most expensive steps in the execution plan, which you can review to identify bottlenecks and issues.

3. We will start by analyzing the very first step, which is the **TableScan** step. The **TableScan** step occurs when the data is read from the table or, in other words, from storage. Read from storage is usually an expensive operation, and so any improvements

that you can perform here will result in an overall query improvement. So, go ahead and click the **TableScan** step to see more details. As seen in *Figure 6.8*, the query scanned 100.89 GB of data, and almost all the partitions of the table, which is far from ideal. Also, you will notice the query profile shows 21 columns being accessed, which is a result of `SELECT *` being used in the query:

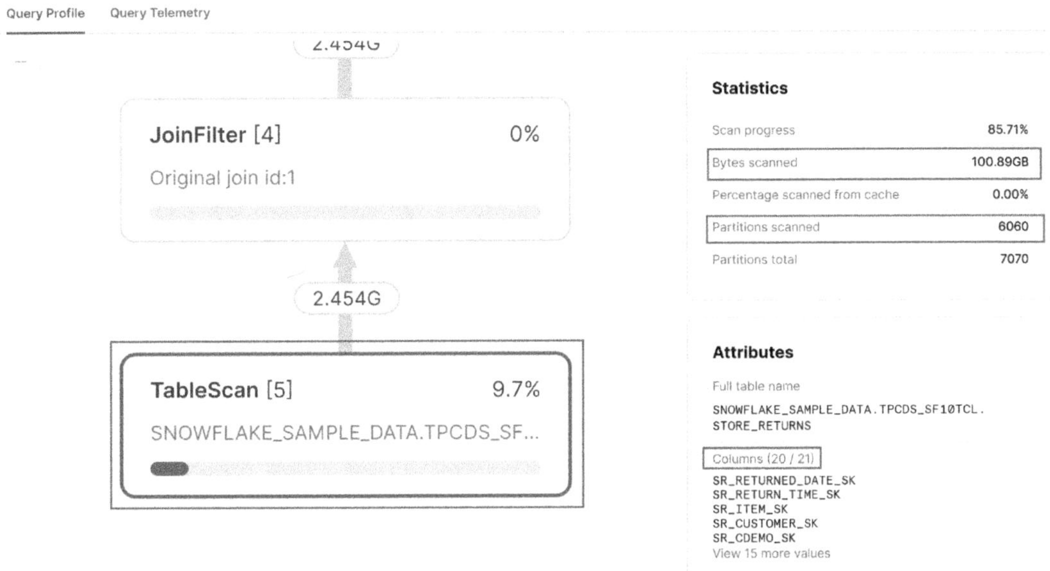

Figure 6.8 – TableScan details page

To optimize the query performance, we need to reduce the number of columns to just the columns that we actually need and, if possible, add a filter on the base table, which reduces the number of rows returned to only the ones we need.

4. Let's first reduce the number of columns that we are selecting. So, we replace `SELECT *` with just the four columns that we need:

```
USE SCHEMA SNOWFLAKE_SAMPLE_DATA.TPCDS_SF10TCL;

SELECT
d_year
,sr_customer_sk as ctr_customer_sk
,sr_store_sk as ctr_store_sk
,SR_RETURN_AMT_INC_TAX
```

```
FROM store_returns,date_dim
WHERE sr_returned_date_sk = d_date_sk;
```

You can see the Query Profile of the new query in *Figure 6.9*. As seen, the time taken to execute the query has come down to 7 minutes from 56 minutes. Additionally, the total bytes scanned have come down to 19.93 GB from 113 GB. This optimization is a direct result of not performing `SELECT *` but rather limiting it to just the columns we need.

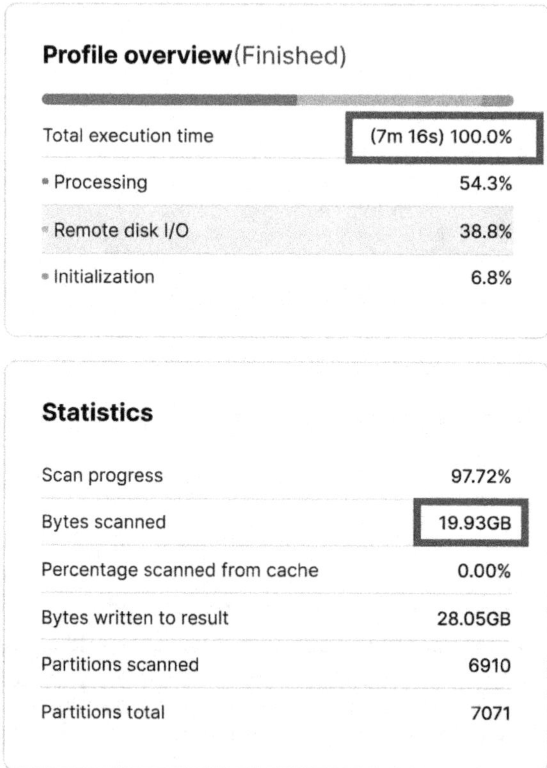

*Figure 6.9 – Query profile improvements after replacing SELECT **

5. Next, we will add a `WHERE` clause to the query to ensure we scan a limited number of partitions:

```
USE SCHEMA SNOWFLAKE_SAMPLE_DATA.TPCDS_SF10TCL;

SELECT

d_year,sr_customer_sk as ctr_customer_sk,sr_store_sk as
```

```
ctr_store_sk,SR_RETURN_AMT_INC_TAX

FROM store_returns,date_dim

WHERE sr_returned_date_sk = d_date_sk
AND d_year = 1999;
```

Looking at the Query Profile of this new query shows that the time taken to execute the query has come down further to 1 minute, and the number of bytes scanned has come down to 3.99 GB due to partition elimination introduced by the additional `WHERE` clause we added.

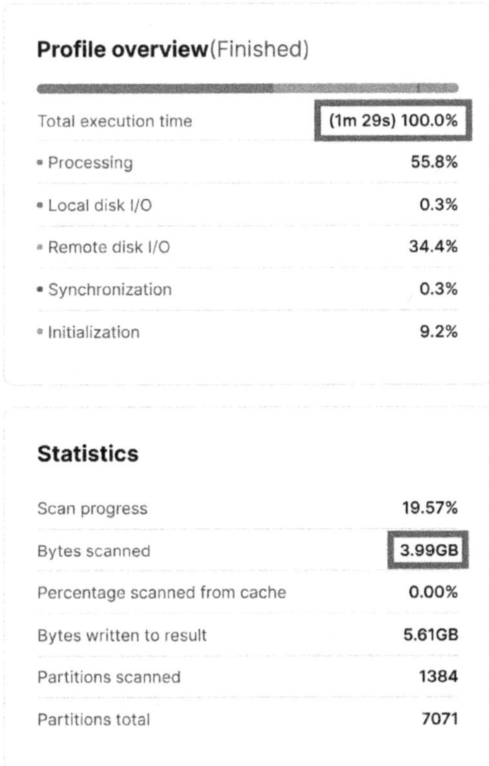

Figure 6.10 – Query profile improvements after we introduced the WHERE clause

How it works...

This recipe demonstrates how to make use of Query Profile to identify costly steps in your query execution. Although this recipe demonstrates how to improve table scan performance, you can identify other steps in your query execution and improve them using a similar approach.

In this recipe, we first selected all columns in the query, which required Snowflake to scan more data than was necessary. As a general query optimization best practice, select only the columns required by the query. Doing so can reduce the amount of data scanned during the initial table read and can also improve later processing steps by reducing the volume of data moved through the execution plan. Similarly, applying filter predicates, such as `WHERE` conditions, as early as possible can reduce the number of rows processed by subsequent steps. In this example, adding a filter for the year 1999 resulted in fewer partitions being scanned and improved overall query performance.

Weeding out inefficient queries through analysis

Snowflake provides detailed query history and execution metrics that can be used to identify inefficient SQL statements. Queries that run longer than expected, scan excessive amounts of data, or consume unnecessary compute resources are strong candidates for review. In this recipe, we will query the `QUERY_HISTORY` view in the `SNOWFLAKE.ACCOUNT_USAGE` schema to identify queries with high elapsed time or large scan volumes. Based on those results, we can determine which queries may benefit from optimization.

Getting ready

You will need to be connected to your Snowflake instance via Snowsight or the Snowflake CLI client to execute this recipe.

How to do it...

The steps for this recipe are as follows:

1. We will start by selecting all rows from the `QUERY_HISTORY` view and ordering them by the time taken to execute:

```
USE ROLE ACCOUNTADMIN;
USE SNOWFLAKE;
SELECT QUERY_ID, QUERY_TEXT, EXECUTION_TIME,USER_NAME
FROM SNOWFLAKE.ACCOUNT_USAGE.query_history
ORDER BY EXECUTION_TIME DESC;
```

As shown in *Figure 6.11*, the results will vary based on the queries executed in your Snowflake environment and the amount of query history available in the `ACCOUNT_USAGE` view.

	QUERY_ID	QUERY_TEXT	EXECUTION_TIME	USER_NAME
1	01c2cff9-0207-f689-0016-a0d301093322	SELECT * FROM store_returns,date_dim WHERE sr_returned_date_sk = d_d	3368026	KBELANGER
2	01c2cfd8-0207-fb8d-0016-a0d301086946	SELECT * FROM store_returns,date_dim WHERE sr_returned_date_sk = d_c	651174	KBELANGER
3	01c2d096-0207-f92f-0016-a0d30108adf6	SELECT_year, sr_customer_sk as ctr_customer_sk, sr_store_sk as ctr_store	435241	KBELANGER

Figure 6.11 – List of queries with the time taken to execute

You will need to focus on the `EXECUTION_TIME` column and analyze queries that have taken too long to execute. In our case, we will focus on the first query in the list and try and analyze the profile for that query. To do so, copy the `QUERY_ID` of the query.

2. Next, navigate to the **Query history** page to locate the query using its `QUERY_ID`. From the left navigation menu, select **Monitoring**, then choose **Query history**.

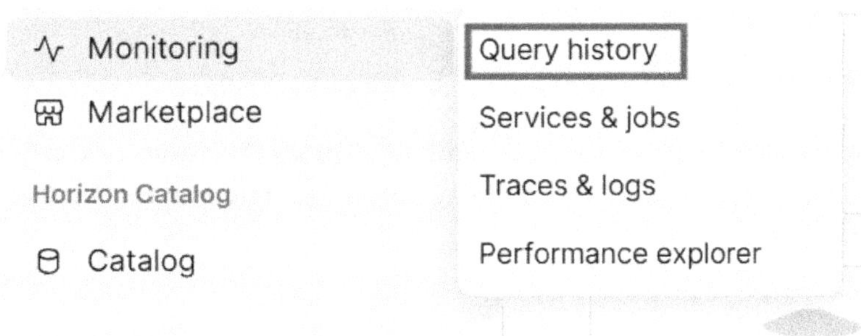

Figure 6.12 – Navigating to the Query history page

3. On the **Query history** page, select **Filters** to open the filtering options and select **Query ID** as the filter criteria. Paste the `QUERY_ID` that you copied in the previous step into the filter field and click **Apply Filters**. This will return the single query in the results, allowing you to open it and review its details and performance characteristics.

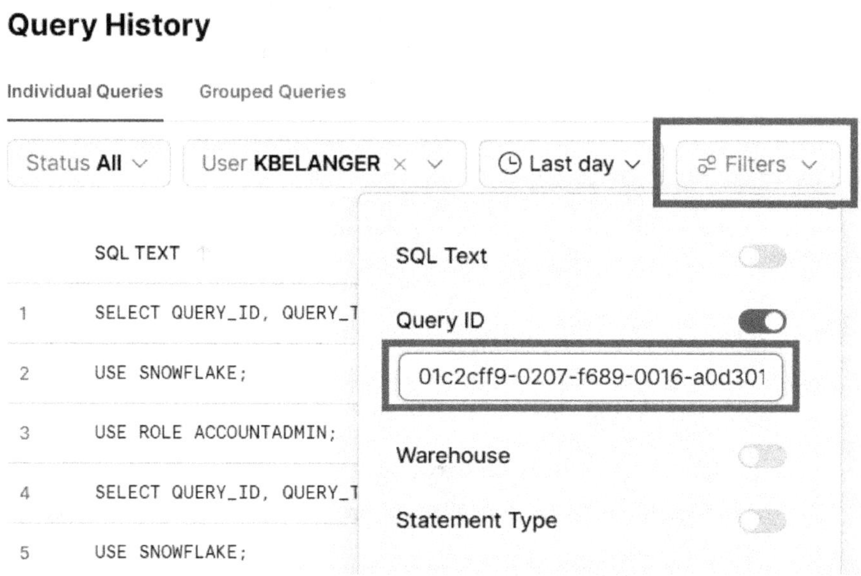

Figure 6.13 – Selecting Query ID as the filter criteria

4. Click **Query ID** on the result set and then **Query Profile** at the top of the screen, which will result in the query details being displayed. Here, you can analyze the query for inefficiencies.

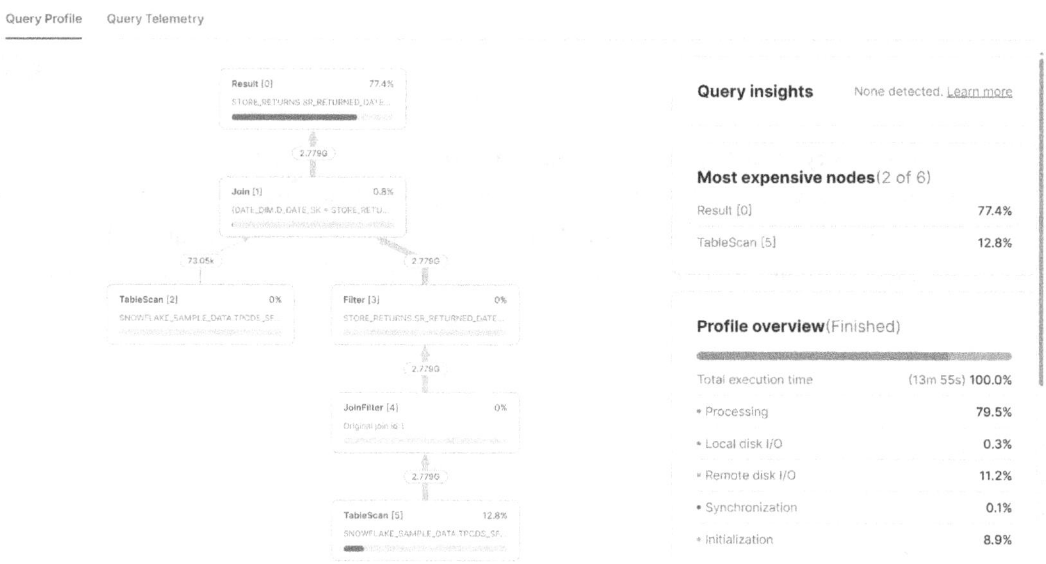

Figure 6.14 – Query profile page

In previous steps, we focused on queries that have a long execution time. When improving performance, it is also beneficial to improve queries that execute too frequently, even if they do not take that much time for a single execution. Any small improvements on such queries will result in a much more significant performance gain since the query runs frequently.

5. To identify such queries, we need to group the queries and find the aggregated time. We will remove `QUERY_ID` from our query for grouping purposes since it is unique and would stop the result set from aggregating. However, removing the `QUERY_ID` removes the ability to look at the query profile; therefore, we will generate a hash of the query text and use that as a `PSEUDO_QUERY_ID`:

```
USE ROLE ACCOUNTADMIN;
USE SNOWFLAKE;
SELECT QUERY_TEXT, USER_NAME, HASH(QUERY_TEXT) AS PSEUDO_QUERY_ID ,
COUNT(*) AS NUM_OF_QUERIES, SUM(EXECUTION_TIME) AS AGG_EXECUTION_TIME

FROM SNOWFLAKE.ACCOUNT_USAGE.query_history
GROUP BY QUERY_TEXT, USER_NAME
ORDER BY AGG_EXECUTION_TIME DESC;
```

You should see a result similar to *Figure 6.15*. Notice the `PSEUDO_QUERY_ID` and `NUM_OF_QUERIES` columns. What we would like to do is analyze the query in row 2. For that, we first need to find the actual `QUERY_ID`. To achieve that, copy the `PSEUDO_QUERY_ID` column and follow the next step:

A QUERY_TEXT	A USER_NAME	# PSEUDO_QUERY_ID	# NUM_OF_QUERIES
select date_trunc(hour, CONVERT_TIMEZONE(	KBELANGER	-272538368834755579	1
select /*+ param_value(ENABLE_UNQUOTED_	KBELANGER	-211054918945146800	7
select SYSTEM$BOOTSTRAP_DATA_REQUEST	KBELANGER	-5538996166537179803	3

Figure 6.15 – Grouped queries with aggregated execution times

6. We will take the `PSEUDO_QUERY_ID` column copied from the previous step and use it in the next query, where we find out the actual `QUERY_ID`:

```
SELECT
QUERY_ID,
QUERY_TEXT,
```

```
USER_NAME,
HASH(QUERY_TEXT) AS PSEUDO_QUERY_ID
FROM SNOWFLAKE.ACCOUNT_USAGE.QUERY_HISTORY
WHERE HASH(QUERY_TEXT) = replace_with_pseudo_query_id;
```

The result will look similar to the following screenshot. You will get one or many rows for the same `QUERY_TEXT`. Copy any `QUERY_ID` and repeat *steps 3* and *4* to analyze it.

	QUERY_ID	QUERY_TEXT	USER_NAME	PSEUDO_QUERY_ID
1	01c0dbcb-0207-3155-0016-a0d3000ccee2	select /*+ param_value(ENABLE_UNQUOT	KBELANGER	-211054918945146800
2	01c0dbc5-0207-3155-0016-a0d3000cce3a	select /*+ param_value(ENABLE_UNQUOT	KBELANGER	-211054918945146800
3	01c0dbcb-0207-3393-0016-a0d3000cf46a	select /*+ param_value(ENABLE_UNQUOT	KBELANGER	-211054918945146800
4	01c0dbca-0207-3518-0016-a0d3000d12a6	select /*+ param_value(ENABLE_UNQUOT	KBELANGER	-211054918945146800
5	01c0dbc5-0207-3155-0016-a0d3000cce1a	select /*+ param_value(ENABLE_UNQUOT	KBELANGER	-211054918945146800
6	01c0dbca-0207-3518-0016-a0d3000d12aa	select /*+ param_value(ENABLE_UNQUOT	KBELANGER	-211054918945146800
7	01c0dbca-0207-3393-0016-a0d3000cf40a	select /*+ param_value(ENABLE_UNQUOT	KBELANGER	-211054918945146800

Figure 6.16 – Finding the actual query ID

How it works...

You can use the `QUERY_HISTORY` view to identify badly performing queries based on various criteria, including execution time, bytes scanned, and more. Once you identify the `QUERY_ID` of an inefficient query, use the **History** tab to bring up the query profile of that query and analyze and improve the query.

Identifying and reducing unnecessary Fail-safe and Time Travel storage usage

Snowflake provides powerful data protection features such as Time Travel and Fail-safe, allowing historical data recovery and protection against accidental data loss. While these features are valuable for many production tables, they may be unnecessary for short-lived transient workloads such as staging or intermediate ELT processing tables.

In this recipe, we will simulate a fictitious ELT process in which a temporary table is used to hold intermediate data. That data is then processed and aggregated into a target table, after which the temporary data is removed. This scenario helps illustrate when transient or temporary table types may be more appropriate than permanent tables in order to reduce storage overhead.

Getting ready

You will need access to a Snowflake account with permission to create databases and tables. This recipe uses Snowflake's built-in sample data, which is available in the `SNOWFLAKE_SAMPLE_DATA` database included with most Snowflake accounts. Specifically, the example is based on data from the TPCH benchmark dataset and uses it to simulate an ELT staging workload.

No separate data download or loading process is required because the sample data is already available within Snowflake.

How to do it...

The steps for this recipe are as follows:

1. We will start by creating a new database and a table that will load through fictitious ELT processes. The table that we will create is modeled after the structure of the `LINEITEM` table from Snowflake's built-in TPCH sample dataset located in the `SNOWFLAKE_SAMPLE_DATA` database. It is created here as an interim processing table to simulate data that is loaded and used temporarily by an ELT process:

```
CREATE DATABASE C6_R4;
CREATE TABLE lineitem_interim_processing (
     L_ORDERKEY NUMBER(38,0),
     L_PARTKEY NUMBER(38,0),
     L_SUPPKEY NUMBER(38,0),
     L_LINENUMBER NUMBER(38,0),
     L_QUANTITY NUMBER(12,2),
     L_EXTENDEDPRICE NUMBER(12,2),
     L_DISCOUNT NUMBER(12,2),
     L_TAX NUMBER(12,2),
     L_RETURNFLAG VARCHAR(1),
     L_LINESTATUS VARCHAR(1),
     L_SHIPDATE DATE,
     L_COMMITDATE DATE,
     L_RECEIPTDATE DATE,
     L_SHIPINSTRUCT VARCHAR(25),
     L_SHIPMODE VARCHAR(10),
     L_COMMENT VARCHAR(44)
);
```

The table should be created successfully.

2. Now we will create another table to simulate a table used by reporting tools. This table will contain aggregated information:

```
CREATE TABLE order_reporting (
    Order_Ship_Date DATE,
    Quantity NUMBER(38,2),
    Price NUMBER(38,2),
    Discount NUMBER(38,2)
);
```

   The table should be created successfully.

3. Next, we will insert data into the temporary table. However, before that, we will delete all existing data from this interim table as the intent is to simulate a step in ELT processing.

```
DELETE FROM lineitem_interim_processing;

INSERT INTO lineitem_interim_processing
SELECT * FROM
snowflake_sample_data.tpch_sf1.lineitem
WHERE l_shipdate BETWEEN dateadd(day, -365,
  to_date('1998-12-31')) AND to_date('1998-12-31');
```

   You should see a large number of rows inserted into the temporary table, as shown in the following output:

number of rows inserted
689291

Figure 6.17 – Data inserted into the temporary table

4. Next, we will aggregate data into our reporting table, but we will delete the last 7 days' worth of data from the table before doing so (again, we are just doing this to simulate a real-world process):

```
DELETE FROM order_reporting WHERE Order_Ship_Date >
  dateadd(day, -7, to_date('1998-12-01'));
```

5. On the first run, you will see no rows being deleted as there is no data in the `order_reporting` table; but after the first run, the `DELETE` command will result in some rows being removed:

```
INSERT INTO order_reporting
SELECT
    L_SHIPDATE AS Order_Ship_Date,
    SUM(L_QUANTITY) AS Quantity,
    SUM(L_EXTENDEDPRICE) AS Price,
    SUM(L_EXTENDEDPRICE * L_DISCOUNT) AS Discount
FROM lineitem_interim_processing
WHERE Order_Ship_Date NOT IN (SELECT Order_Ship_Date
  FROM order_reporting)
GROUP BY Order_Ship_Date;
```

   This should result in a small number of rows being inserted into the `order_reporting` table. However, in subsequent runs, the number of rows will reduce to 7 as we are only deleting and re-inserting the last 7 days' worth of data.

6. As we do not need the data in the temporary table anymore, we will now delete all the data from it:

```
DELETE FROM lineitem_interim_processing;
```

   This will result in all rows being deleted from the temporary table.

7. Now, to simulate an ELT process, run *steps 3* to *6* a couple of times. Once done, we will query Snowflake metadata to uncover some facts about this ELT process.
8. Let's query the table storage information from the metadata. Note that the metadata can take 2-3 hours to refresh, so it is best to run the following final steps after waiting for 2-3 hours:

```
USE ROLE ACCOUNTADMIN;
SELECT * FROM C6_R4.INFORMATION_SCHEMA.TABLE_STORAGE_METRICS
WHERE TABLE_CATALOG='C6_R4';
```

   The `LINEITEM_INTERIM_PROCESSING` table shows `ACTIVE_BYTES` as `0`, but `TIME_TRAVEL_BYTES` is not `0`. Although this table is being used for temporary purposes, it unnecessarily contributes to the storage costs by storing Time Travel data:

TABLE_NAME	ID	CLONE_GROUP_ID	IS_TRA	ACTIVE_BYTES	TIME_TRAVEL_BYTES
LINEITEM_INTERIM_PROCESSING	5644290	5644290	NO	0	61412352
ORDER_REPORTING	5645314	5645314	NO	6144	22528

Figure 6.18 – Data inserted into the temporary table

9. We can recreate the interim processing table by using the `TRANSIENT` keyword, which will ensure that the table does not store Time Travel data or Fail-safe data, therefore reducing storage costs.

```
DROP TABLE lineitem_interim_processing;
CREATE TRANSIENT TABLE lineitem_interim_processing (
     L_ORDERKEY NUMBER(38,0),
     L_PARTKEY NUMBER(38,0),
     L_SUPPKEY NUMBER(38,0),
     L_LINENUMBER NUMBER(38,0),
     L_QUANTITY NUMBER(12,2),
     L_EXTENDEDPRICE NUMBER(12,2),
     L_DISCOUNT NUMBER(12,2),
     L_TAX NUMBER(12,2),
     L_RETURNFLAG VARCHAR(1),
     L_LINESTATUS VARCHAR(1),
     L_SHIPDATE DATE,
     L_COMMITDATE DATE,
     L_RECEIPTDATE DATE,
     L_SHIPINSTRUCT VARCHAR(25),
     L_SHIPMODE VARCHAR(10),
     L_COMMENT VARCHAR(44)
);
```

How it works...

There are three types of tables in Snowflake: **permanent**, **temporary**, and **transient**. By default, a new table is created as a permanent table, which means that it has the Time Travel and Fail-safe functionalities enabled. Both of these functionalities contribute to the storage. In the case of a temporary table used to store data temporarily, it is much better to create that table as a transient table, as Time Travel and Fail-safe are disabled for such tables.

It is advisable to keep a check on the tables in your Snowflake system. Suppose you spot tables with large amounts of bytes in the Time Travel and Fail-safe bytes columns but have a low number (or even 0) in the active bytes column. In that case, it is likely that the table is used as a temporary table and may be created as a transient or temporary table.

There's more...

Snowflake provides multiple data protection mechanisms that influence storage consumption. Understanding how these mechanisms work can help you choose the appropriate table type for your workload.

Snowflake tables support Time Travel, which allows users to query historical versions of data for a configurable retention period. The retention period is controlled using the `DATA_RETENTION_TIME_IN_DAYS` parameter. When this retention period expires, the data enters Fail-safe, a seven-day recovery window managed by Snowflake that is intended for disaster recovery scenarios.

For permanent tables, Fail-safe cannot be disabled. This means that even if the Time Travel retention period is set to zero days, Snowflake will still retain the data in Fail-safe for seven additional days.

For workloads such as staging, ELT processing, or other transient data pipelines where historical recovery is not required, Snowflake offers transient tables. Transient tables support Time Travel but do not include Fail-safe, which can significantly reduce storage costs for large or frequently refreshed datasets.

Choosing the appropriate table type, permanent, transient, or temporary, based on the workload characteristics can help balance data protection requirements with storage cost optimization.

Projections in Snowflake for performance

Snowflake does not implement projections as a native database construct. Instead, Snowflake provides materialized views, which can be used to optimize query performance for common access patterns. Materialized views store the results of a query physically and are automatically maintained by Snowflake as the underlying base tables change. This allows frequently executed queries to retrieve precomputed results instead of recalculating them each time.

Materialized views are particularly useful when queries repeatedly filter, join, or aggregate large tables in similar ways. By materializing the results of these operations, Snowflake can significantly reduce query execution time and compute consumption for those workloads.

This recipe demonstrates how to create and use a materialized view in Snowflake to improve query performance.

Getting ready

To complete this recipe, you will need access to a Snowflake account with privileges to create tables, materialized views, and virtual warehouses. You should also be connected to your Snowflake environment using Snowsight or the Snowflake CLI.

The examples in this recipe use Snowflake sample data to demonstrate how materialized views can improve query performance by precomputing and maintaining query results.

How to do it...

Let's start by creating a table in a database, followed by generating a large dataset to demonstrate how materialized views improve efficiency. The steps for this recipe are as follows:

1. We will start by creating a new database:

   ```
   CREATE DATABASE C6_R5;
   ```

   The database should be created successfully.

2. Moreover, we shall execute a configuration change for the following steps so that Snowflake does not use caching:

   ```
   ALTER SESSION SET USE_CACHED_RESULT=FALSE;
   ```

3. Let's create a simple table called `SENSOR_DATA` to hold the demo data. The table will have data observed by a sensor, starting with the create timestamp (`CREATE_TS`) for each row, followed by the sensor identifier (`SENSOR_ID`), and the third column is a measurement taken by the sensor (`SENSOR_READING`):

   ```
   CREATE OR REPLACE TABLE SENSOR_DATA(
      CREATE_TS BIGINT,
      SENSOR_ID BIGINT,
      SENSOR_READING INTEGER
   );
   ```

   The table should be created successfully.

4. Now that we have successfully created a table to hold our dataset, we can generate and insert demo data into the table. Let's generate 1 billion sensor observations that are randomly generated. `CREATE_TS` will be populated by a sequence automatically generated by the Snowflake system, using the `SEQ8` function. The data type is `BIGINT` to

allow large numbers to be stored. The next column is also a BIGINT data type, generated by the UNIFORM Snowflake function. The third column, SENSOR_READING, uses a definition similar to the previous column. To generate 1 billion rows, Snowflake's GENERATOR function has been used and has been passed a value of 1000000000 (1 billion) to its parameter. This would allow 1 billion rows to be generated with randomly generated data in parallel. *Please note that this step will take some time to execute*:

```
INSERT INTO SENSOR_DATA
SELECT
    (SEQ8())::BIGINT AS CREATE_TS
    ,UNIFORM(1,9999999,RANDOM(11111))::BIGINT SENSOR_ID
    ,UNIFORM(1,9999999,RANDOM(22222))::INTEGER SENSOR_READING
FROM TABLE(GENERATOR(ROWCOUNT => 1000000000))
ORDER BY CREATE_TS;
```

As a result, a billion rows should be inserted with randomly generated data.

5. Let's now introduce the concept of clustering. **Clustering** is a well-known technique for enabling data distribution into small, *related* storage blocks. We can also say that the data is a cluster of values with respect to a particular column. Clustering generally involves sorting data; that is, each micro-partition will have sorted data. This helps get to a required micro-partition quickly, and sorting allows efficiently getting to an individual row within the micro-partition. Let's first enable clustering on the CREATE_TS column. The following command enables clustering using the values of this column. The CLUSTER BY clause is used for this:

```
ALTER TABLE SENSOR_DATA  CLUSTER BY (CREATE_TS);
```

> **Note**
>
> This command should complete almost immediately but note that the redistribution of data based on the new clustering key can take some time and occurs in the background.

6. Let's run a couple of queries on each of the columns to understand the issue:

```
SELECT
COUNT(*) CNT
,AVG(SENSOR_READING) MEAN_SENSOR_READING
```

```
FROM SENSOR_DATA WHERE CREATE_TS
BETWEEN 100000000 AND 100001000;
```

The output of the preceding code is as follows:

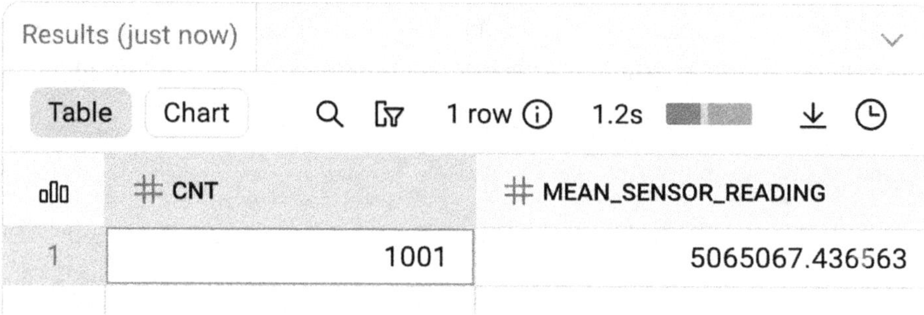

Figure 6.19 – Execution time for a query using the CREATE_TS (clustered) column

Here is another query to understand the issue:

```
SELECT COUNT(*) CNT, AVG(SENSOR_READING)  MEAN_SENSOR_READING FROM
SENSOR_DATA WHERE SENSOR_ID BETWEEN 100000 AND 101000;
```

The output of the preceding code is as follows:

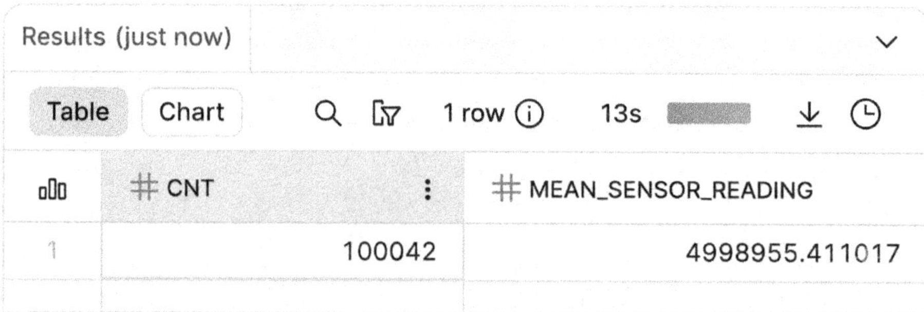

Figure 6.20 – Execution time for a query using the SENSOR_ID (unclustered) column

7. The preceding queries generate the same (or close to the same) number of records/average readings, but the query runtimes are substantially different. The second query was more than 10,000 times slower. This provides us with the insight that the table is not optimized for two different access patterns. To solve this, let's create a materialized

view on our SENSOR_DATA table, then we shall include the three columns in the SENSOR_DATA table, but this time using SENSOR_ID for clustering data:

```
CREATE OR REPLACE MATERIALIZED VIEW MV_SENSOR_READING       (CREATE_TS,
SENSOR_ID, SENSOR_READING)
CLUSTER BY (SENSOR_ID) AS
SELECT CREATE_TS, SENSOR_ID, SENSOR_READING
FROM SENSOR_DATA;
```

The materialized view should be created successfully as a result of the preceding query. Please note that the view creation will take some time.

8. Let's revisit the second query in *step 6* that did not perform well before. With improved clustering, we should see a reduction in execution time for the query when run against the newly created materialized view, MV_SENSOR_READING:

```
SELECT COUNT(*) CNT, AVG(SENSOR_READING)  MEAN_SENSOR_READING
FROM MV_SENSOR_READING
WHERE SENSOR_ID BETWEEN 100000 AND 101000;
```

The output of the preceding code is as follows:

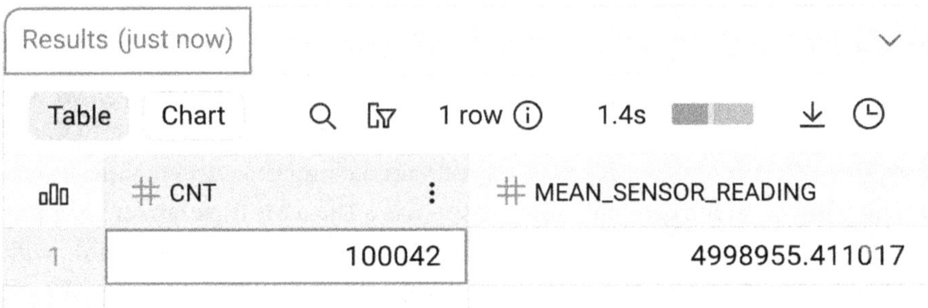

Figure 6.21 – Query execution is faster when using an MV

How it works...

Now that we have taken a detailed look at the process for creating a materialized view for a table, let's look at the internal workings of a materialized view as shown in *Figure 6.22*. We can see how Snowflake manages it and ensures a dynamic link to the original table, as well as reflecting the changes consistently and in real time:

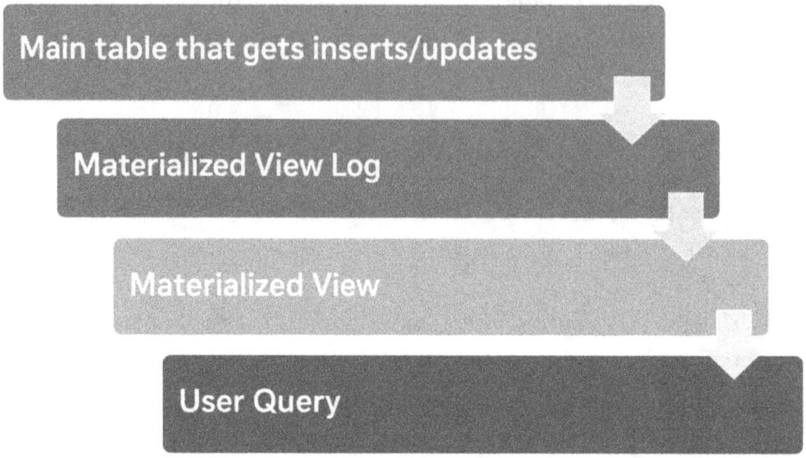

Figure 6.22 – MV internal workings

The link between a transactional table that needs to have a materialized view is maintained using a log. The log keeps track of the changes that happen to the source table and, in real time, runs the process to update the materialized view. This is done as consistent transactions and at scale. The logic or aggregation function defined in the materialized view is applied based on any changes in data in the materialized view source table.

There's more...

In the preceding example, we had a one-to-one corresponding materialized view created over our table, which was as good as creating a **CREATE TABLE AS SELECT** (**CTAS**) table from the original table. The benefit here is that a table created using the CTAS technique is not dynamically linked to the original table. As soon as a **Data Manipulation Language** (**DML**) operation is executed on the original table, the CTAS table or the derived table will be rendered stale and will not reflect the original table's changes. Materialized views, on the other hand, are updated systemically and automatically.

Another benefit is that Snowflake has smart routing or query tuning. The Snowflake query engine can intercept queries that are written against the main table, and if a materialized view is present for that table and the materialized view can answer the query, it automatically routes the query to the materialized view.

Another consideration when creating a materialized view is the elastic sizing capability of Snowflake virtual warehouses. Creating a materialized view can require significant compute resources because Snowflake must scan the source table and generate the precomputed results. For larger tables, temporarily increasing the warehouse size can reduce the time required for the initial build.

In this example, the warehouse is increased before the materialized view is created and then returned to its normal size afterward:

```
ALTER WAREHOUSE <NAME> SET WAREHOUSE_SIZE=XXXLARGE;
CREATE OR REPLACE MATERIALIZED VIEW MV_SENSOR_READING
  (CREATE_TS, SENSOR_ID, SENSOR_READING)
CLUSTER BY (SENSOR_ID) AS
SELECT CREATE_TS, SENSOR_ID, SENSOR_READING
FROM SENSOR_DATA;
ALTER WAREHOUSE <NAME> SET WAREHOUSE_SIZE=MEDIUM;
```

This approach can shorten the initial creation time of the materialized view while avoiding the cost of running a larger warehouse longer than necessary.

Reviewing query plans to modify table clustering

Snowflake provides the option to configure clustering keys for tables so that larger tables can benefit from partition pruning. This recipe will analyze query plans in conjunction with table structures and identify whether a new clustering key will improve query performance.

Getting ready

The steps in this recipe can be run either in the Snowflake Snowsight or the Snowflake CLI command-line client.

How to do it...

Let's start by creating and populating a table in Snowflake. We will simulate data being inserted into the table regularly, resulting in an increased size on disk and an increased number of partitions. The steps for this recipe are as follows:

1. Create a new database, followed by the creation of a table that will hold the transaction data:

```
CREATE DATABASE C6_R6;

CREATE TABLE TRANSACTIONS
(
  TXN_ID STRING,
  TXN_DATE DATE,
  CUSTOMER_ID STRING,
  QUANTITY DECIMAL(20),
  PRICE DECIMAL(30,2),
  COUNTRY_CD STRING
);
```

2. Next, we will populate this table with dummy data using the SQL given in the code block that follows. Note that we will run this step *8–10 times repeatedly* to ensure that a large amount of data is inserted into the `TRANSACTIONS` table and many micro-partitions are created. Also note that each run adds 10 million rows to the table:

```
INSERT INTO TRANSACTIONS
SELECT
    UUID_STRING() AS TXN_ID
    ,DATEADD(DAY,UNIFORM(1, 500, RANDOM()) * -1,
      '2020-10-15') AS TXN_DATE
    ,UUID_STRING() AS CUSTOMER_ID
    ,UNIFORM(1, 10, RANDOM()) AS QUANTITY
    ,UNIFORM(1, 200, RANDOM()) AS PRICE
    ,RANDSTR(2,RANDOM()) AS COUNTRY_CD
FROM TABLE(GENERATOR(ROWCOUNT => 10000000));
```

3. Now that enough data has been populated, we will run a sample query simulating a report that needs to access the last 30 days of data and check the profile of this query:

```
SELECT * FROM TRANSACTIONS
WHERE TXN_DATE BETWEEN DATEADD(DAY, -31, '2020-10-15')
  AND '2020-10-15';
```

4. Once the preceding query is complete, check the profile of this query by clicking the row count at the bottom, then selecting **Query ID** in the dialog box that appears:

Figure 6.23 – Navigating to the query profile via the query ID

5. Clicking **Query ID** will take you to the **Query profile** page. Click **Query profile**, which will take you to the profile page, where on the right-hand side will be the **Profile overview** pane, as shown in *Figure 6.24*:

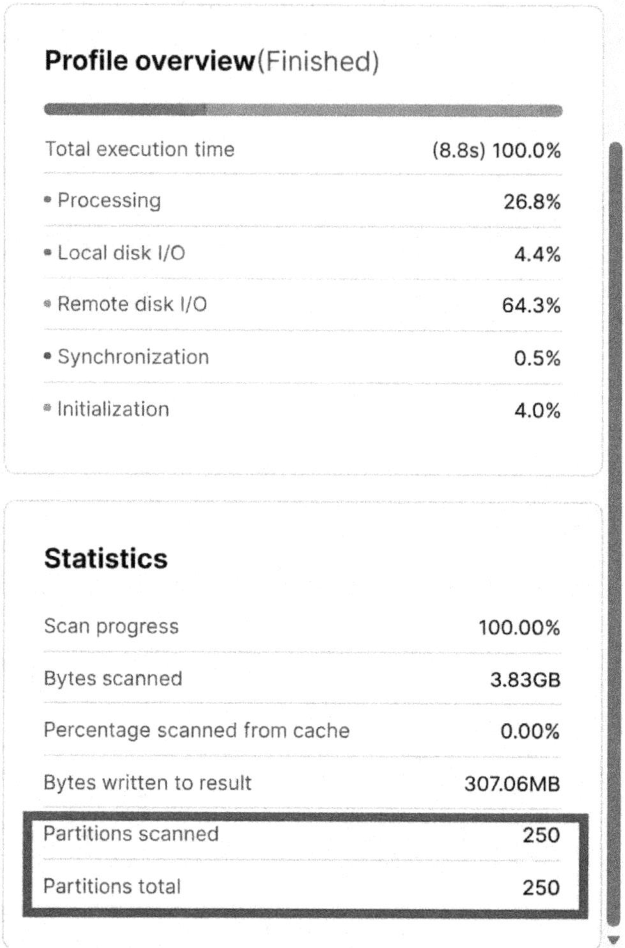

Figure 6.24 – Query profile overview

You will observe that the number of total partitions and the number of partitions scanned are the same. This indicates that there is no partition pruning occurring, and there is a likelihood that a better clustering key will provide us with the desired partition pruning.

6. Since our query is filtering on TXN_DATE, we can change the clustering key to TXN_DATE. In production scenarios, you will need to analyze many queries to find the most common filter clause for large tables and use it in the clustering key. For our example, we will change the clustering key to TXN_DATE, as shown in the following code snippet:

    ```
    ALTER TABLE TRANSACTIONS CLUSTER BY ( TXN_DATE );
    ```

    The statement should immediately execute with a success message.

    > **Note**
    >
    > The re-clustering is not immediate, and Snowflake might take some time to re-cluster the data; therefore, it is advised to wait for some time before continuing with the next step.

7. Now that re-clustering is complete, we will rerun the same query and investigate whether the clustering key has improved performance:

    ```
    SELECT * FROM TRANSACTIONS
    WHERE TXN_DATE BETWEEN DATEADD(DAY, -31, '2020-10-15') AND '2020-10-15';
    ```

    When we look at the query profile of the re-executed query, we notice that the number of partitions scanned has dramatically reduced, resulting in less data being processed, and there is a much quicker query response:

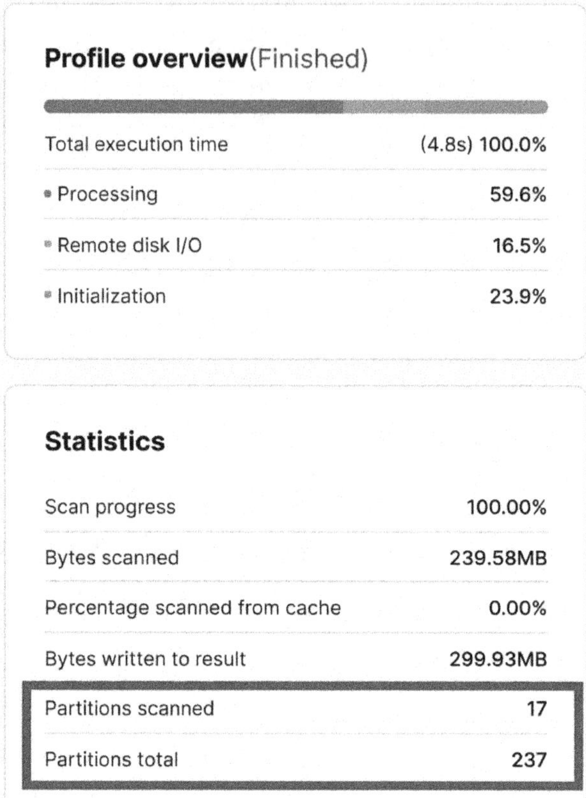

Figure 6.25 – Query profile overview after rerunning the query

The changed clustering key has resulted in only the required partitions being scanned and therefore improves performance and reduces costs.

How it works...

Snowflake automatically partitions tables, where the partitions are added as new data is added into a table. Over time, as data is added to the table, the partitions may not be contiguous anymore, resulting in similar values for a given column being distributed over several micro-partitions. In the scenario explained in the recipe, the last 30 days of data is distributed across all partitions, requiring a full table scan every time, even when a `WHERE` clause is provided. Re-clustering the table redistributes the data such that the data for a given date is combined into a few partitions. When the same query is rerun, now a small number of partitions are scanned, resulting in better query performance.

There's more...

Snowflake stores table data in compressed micro-partitions and relies heavily on micro-partition metadata (such as minimum and maximum values per column) to prune data during query execution. When pruning is effective, Snowflake can skip scanning many micro-partitions entirely, which reduces the amount of data scanned and improves query performance.

In today's Snowflake accounts, natural clustering during bulk loads may already provide strong pruning for common access patterns, especially when data is loaded in an ordered way. In those cases, defining a clustering key may not produce a noticeable improvement because there is little additional pruning to gain. For the purpose of this recipe, the data is intentionally inserted in a scrambled order to reduce natural clustering and make clustering improvements easier to observe.

It is also important to understand that defining a clustering key does not instantly reorganize the table. When a clustering key is set, Snowflake maintains clustering asynchronously and improvements may appear gradually as background re-clustering takes place. For this reason, it is common to re-run the test query after some time and compare the query profile again.

Finally, when comparing before and after query profiles, be aware that Snowflake may serve results from the result cache if the same query is executed repeatedly without underlying changes. Disabling cached results for the session can help ensure you are measuring actual execution behavior when validating performance changes.

Optimizing virtual warehouse scale

This recipe explores how to determine the appropriate size for a virtual warehouse and how to identify when a warehouse needs to scale vertically (larger size) or horizontally (multi-cluster configuration). By generating a concurrent workload and analyzing warehouse load and query execution statistics in Snowsight, we can determine whether a warehouse is constrained by compute resources or by concurrency limits.

Getting ready

In this recipe, we will use Snowflake sample datasets to generate a concurrent query workload. Snowflake provides the `SNOWFLAKE_SAMPLE_DATA` database, which includes several benchmark datasets. For this recipe, we will use the TPCDS sample data, which is distinct from the TPCH benchmark data used in earlier examples.

We will also use Snowsight monitoring tools to analyze warehouse utilization and query execution characteristics.

How to do it...

Let's generate a concurrent workload on a virtual warehouse and observe how it behaves under load. By monitoring running and queued queries in Snowsight and reviewing query execution details, we can determine whether the warehouse should be scaled vertically (larger size) or horizontally (additional clusters) to better support the workload. The steps for this recipe are as follows:

1. Begin by creating a dedicated virtual warehouse for this recipe so the workload and monitoring results are isolated from other activity in your account. Using a smaller warehouse size makes it easier to observe concurrency limits and queued queries:

```
CREATE OR REPLACE WAREHOUSE WH_SCALE_TEST
WAREHOUSE_SIZE = 'XSMALL'
AUTO_SUSPEND = 60
AUTO_RESUME = TRUE
INITIALLY_SUSPENDED = TRUE;
```

2. Now set the schema to the Snowflake sample dataset so we can generate a query workload for this recipe:

```
USE DATABASE SNOWFLAKE_SAMPLE_DATA;
USE SCHEMA TPCDS_SF10TCL;
```

3. Execute the following analytical query that processes a significant amount of data. The following query joins large tables from the TPC-DS dataset:

```
USE DATABASE SNOWFLAKE_SAMPLE_DATA;
USE SCHEMA TPCDS_SF10TCL;
USE WAREHOUSE WH_SCALE_TEST;

SELECT
 d_year,
 SUM(ss_sales_price) AS total_sales
FROM store_sales
JOIN date_dim
ON store_sales.ss_sold_date_sk = date_dim.d_date_sk
GROUP BY d_year
ORDER BY d_year;
```

4. Open multiple SQL tabs in Snowsight and paste the query into each tab. Because each tab starts with a new session context, ensure that the database, schema, and warehouse are set before running the query. Then execute the query in each tab at approximately the same time to generate a concurrent workload against the `WH_SCALE_TEST` warehouse.

5. Next, we will monitor the warehouse activity. In Snowsight, use the left navigation menu and expand the Compute category. Then select the **Warehouses** submenu item and choose the `WH_SCALE_TEST` warehouse. In the monitoring view, select the **Hour** tab to match the time range shown in this example. The graph displays running queries and queued queries. Running queries represent active execution, while queued queries indicate that the warehouse has reached its concurrency limits.

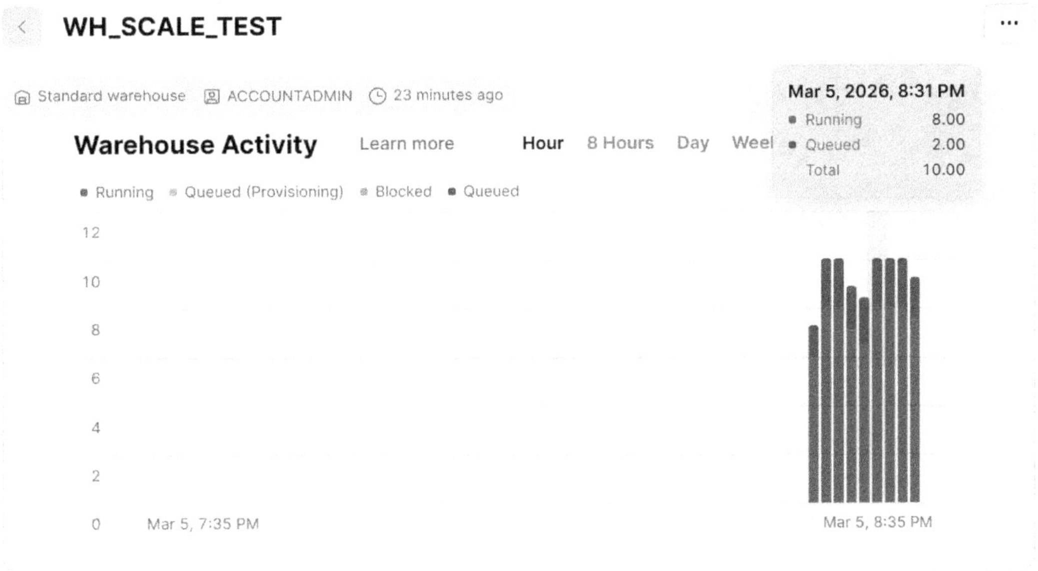

Figure 6.26 – Warehouse load monitoring

Each bar in *Figure 6.26* represents the average number of queries running on the warehouse and the average number of queued queries during a 5-minute window. The window is represented by each bar. Let's zoom in to the cluster of queries shown in the preceding screenshot:

At **8:31 P.M.**, the warehouse load from running queries was **8** running and **2** queued queries. The number of queries queued is more or less proportional to the number of queries running in the warehouse. This shows that the vertical scale is adequate for the workload, and horizontal scaling (scaling out) is required. In such circumstances, it is recommended to use a multi-cluster warehouse. That allows more queries to be admitted into execution, and fewer queries to wait in the queue.

6. The next step is to drill deep into one of the queries and see whether there is an opportunity for scaling up (also called vertical scaling). For that, Snowflake provides insight into the execution of individual queries. To do that, scroll down to the **Query History** section. This will display the list of queries that have executed, are in execution at that time, or are waiting for execution. Let's select a running query for this example; look at the last row. Then, click on the value of the **Query ID** column. This should take the user to the details page for the query:

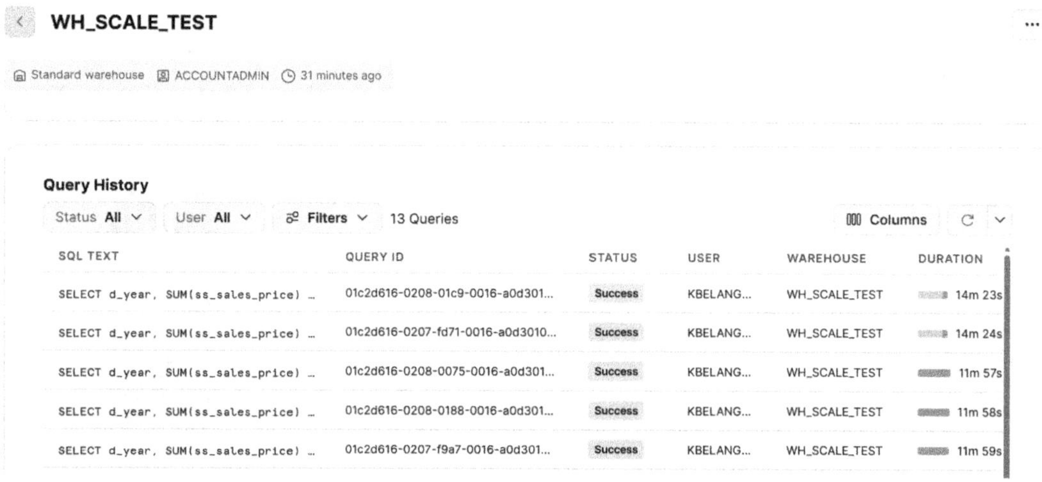

Figure 6.27 – History window

7. Let's investigate the details of the second query in the list by selecting the row. When you click the query, you will be taken to statistics collected by Snowflake around the execution of the query and resource consumption:

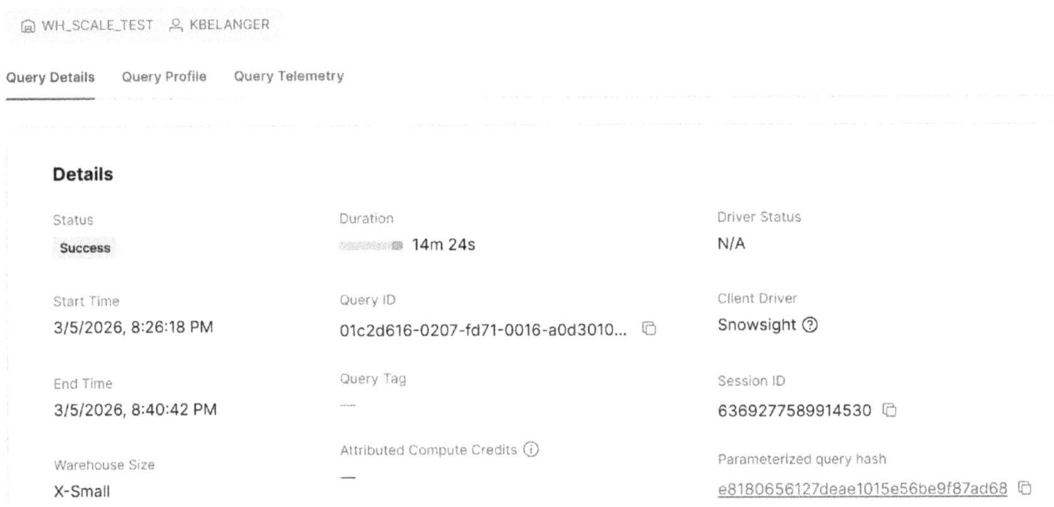

Figure 6.28 – Details page of the selected query

8. Let's click the **Query Profile** tab in this view. The view will change and show two frames. The one on the left will show the execution graph and different nodes. Each node represents a step in the execution. This shows the steps that consumed more resources or time. You can click and get statistics for individual steps.
   The tab toward the right-hand side provides detailed statistics on the execution of the query.

9. If queries frequently appear in the queued state, the warehouse may require horizontal scaling. Horizontal scaling can be achieved by configuring the warehouse as a multi-cluster warehouse, allowing more queries to run concurrently.

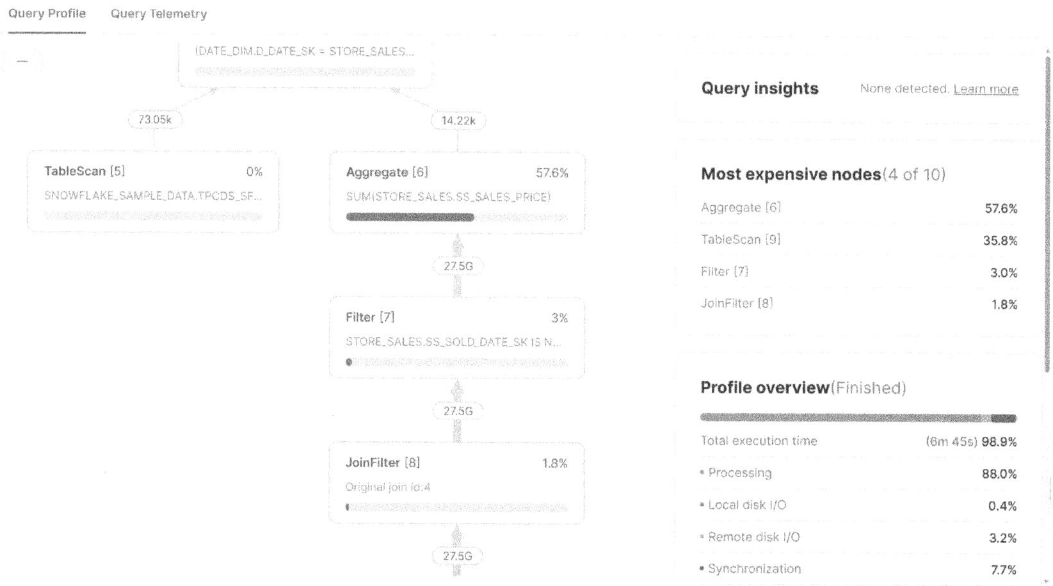

Figure 6.29 – Zoomed-in view of the most expensive node

10. Next, select a step in the **Query Profile** graph to examine the statistics for that portion of the query. Pay particular attention to the Spilling metrics. If the profile shows bytes spilled to local storage, the query required more memory than was available in the warehouse. If bytes spilled to remote storage appear, the data volume exceeded both memory and local disk capacity.

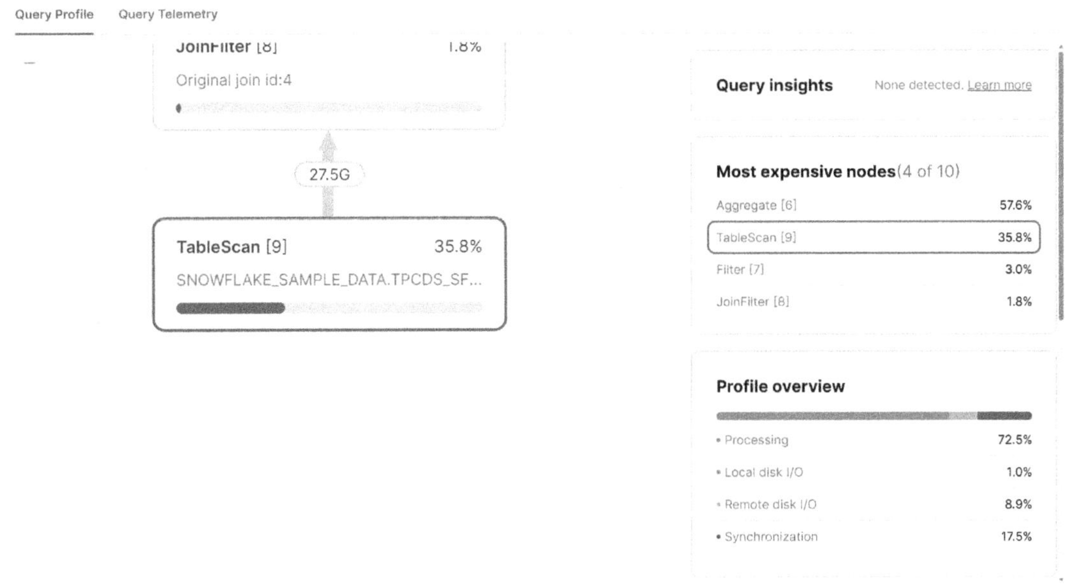

Figure 6.30 – Zoomed-in view of Spilling metrics

How it works...

In this recipe, we generated a concurrent workload against a dedicated virtual warehouse and then used Snowsight monitoring views to observe how the warehouse behaved under load. This allowed us to determine whether the workload was constrained by concurrency (too many queries competing for execution slots) or by the resources available to each query (compute and memory).

Snowflake provides two primary scaling approaches for virtual warehouses. When many queries are submitted at the same time and a portion of them spend time in a queued state, the workload is typically constrained by concurrency. In this situation, horizontal scaling is appropriate, which is achieved by configuring the warehouse as a multi-cluster warehouse so additional clusters can execute queries in parallel and reduce queueing. For example, the following statement configures the warehouse to automatically scale between one and three clusters based on workload demand:

```
ALTER WAREHOUSE WH_SCALE_TEST
SET MIN_CLUSTER_COUNT = 1
    MAX_CLUSTER_COUNT = 3
    SCALING_POLICY = STANDARD;
```

This configuration allows Snowflake to add additional clusters when query demand increases and reduce clusters when demand decreases, helping to minimize queued queries while controlling costs.

When queries are able to start executing but run slowly due to resource constraints, vertical scaling may be required. Increasing the warehouse size provides more compute resources and more memory per query, which can reduce execution time for large scans, joins, sorts, and aggregations. One of the clearest indicators of memory pressure is spilling in the Query Profile. Local spilling occurs when intermediate data cannot fit in memory and must be written to local disk, which is slower than memory and introduces additional I/O overhead. Remote spilling indicates that intermediate data exceeded local storage capacity and required remote storage, which adds network latency and typically has a much larger performance impact.

By correlating warehouse-level monitoring (running versus queued queries) with query-level statistics (execution time and spilling), you can make informed decisions about whether to scale out, scale up, or both, and provision a warehouse configuration that meets workload performance needs while controlling cost.

Optimizing warehouse generations and Query Acceleration Service (QAS)

Snowflake provides multiple ways to improve query performance, including scaling virtual warehouses or distributing workloads across clusters. In addition to these traditional scaling methods, Snowflake offers the **Query Acceleration Service** (**QAS**), which can speed up certain large scan-heavy queries by automatically leveraging additional serverless compute resources. In this recipe, we will execute a large analytical query, observe its performance, enable QAS, and compare how the query execution changes when QAS is available.

Getting ready

We will use the Snowflake sample dataset to generate a large analytical workload. Specifically, the `SNOWFLAKE_SAMPLE_DATA` database and the `TPCDS_SF10TCL` schema will be used, which contain large tables suitable for performance testing.

To ensure consistent performance observations during the recipe, cached results will be disabled for the session so that each query execution performs actual compute work rather than returning a cached result.

How to do it...

Let's begin by preparing a warehouse and running a query that scans a large dataset. We will first observe the baseline performance and then enable the QAS to compare how the query execution changes. The steps for this recipe are as follows:

1. Create a dedicated warehouse for this recipe so the workload and results are isolated from other activity. Use an small warehouse to make the baseline query performance easier to observe:

```
CREATE OR REPLACE WAREHOUSE WH_QAS_TEST
  WAREHOUSE_SIZE = 'SMALL'
  AUTO_SUSPEND = 60
  AUTO_RESUME = TRUE
  INITIALLY_SUSPENDED = TRUE;
```

2. Use the Snowflake sample dataset that contains large tables suitable for analytical workload testing. In this recipe, we will use the `SNOWFLAKE_SAMPLE_DATA` database and the `TPCDS_SF10TCL` schema, which contains TPC-DS benchmark tables suitable for performance testing.

```
USE DATABASE SNOWFLAKE_SAMPLE_DATA;
USE SCHEMA TPCDS_SF10TCL;
```

3. Disable result caching for the session so that each query execution performs actual compute work.

```
ALTER SESSION SET USE_CACHED_RESULT = FALSE;
```

4. Activate the warehouse created for this recipe.

```
USE WAREHOUSE WH_QAS_TEST;
```

5. Run the following scan-heavy analytical query against the STORE_SALES table. This query is designed to scan a large volume of data with aggregation, making it a good candidate for the Query Acceleration Service:

```
SELECT
    ss_store_sk,
    SUM(ss_sales_price) AS total_sales
```

```
FROM STORE_SALES
GROUP BY ss_store_sk
ORDER BY total_sales DESC;
```

After the query completes, note the total execution time and record the Query ID from the results panel. These details will be used in the following steps to evaluate whether the query is a good candidate for the QAS.

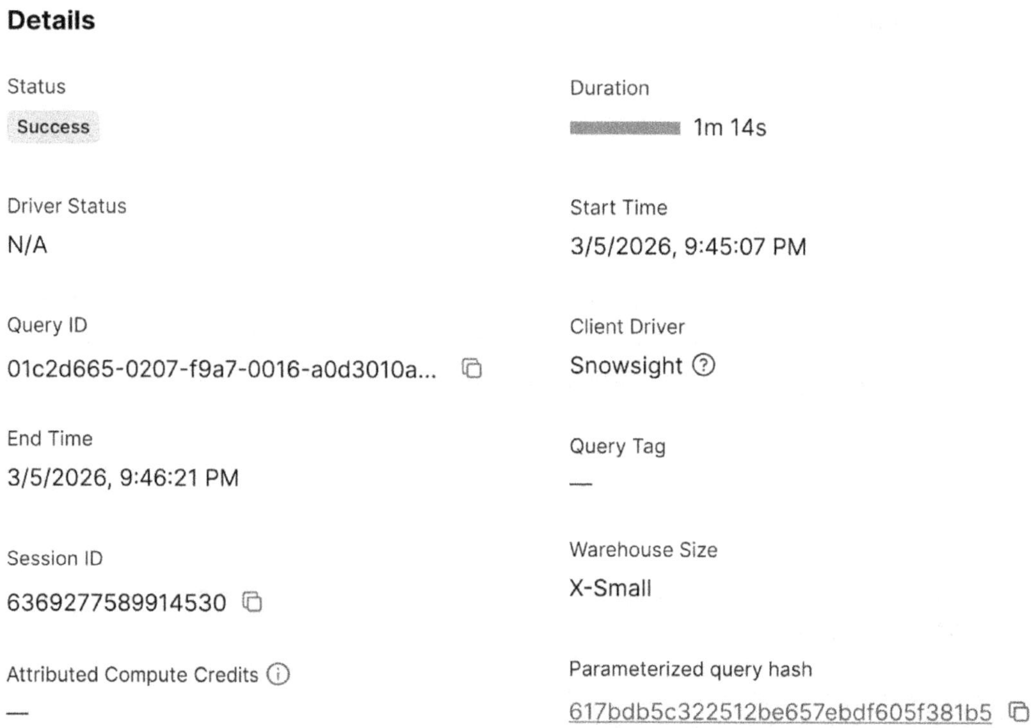

Figure 6.31 – First query execution result

6. After the query completes, capture its Query ID so we can evaluate whether it is eligible for QAS.

```
SELECT LAST_QUERY_ID();
```

7. Use the Query ID returned in the previous step with `SYSTEM$ESTIMATE_QUERY_ACCELERATION`. This function helps determine whether the query is eligible for QAS and, if it is, returns estimated execution times for different

scale factors. Snowflake documents this as the recommended way to assess a previously executed query.

```
SELECT PARSE_JSON(SYSTEM$ESTIMATE_QUERY_ACCELERATION('<query_id>'));
```

If the query is eligible, the result will include an `estimatedQueryTimes` object, an `originalQueryTime`, and an `upperLimitScaleFactor`. If the query is not eligible, the output will include an `ineligibleReason`, such as `NO_LARGE_ENOUGH_SCAN`. In the result below we see that this query is eligible.

Figure 6.32 – Query acceleration test results

8. Enable QAS on the warehouse.

```
ALTER WAREHOUSE WH_QAS_TEST
SET ENABLE_QUERY_ACCELERATION = TRUE;
```

9. Set a modest maximum scale factor for the warehouse. The scale factor controls the maximum additional serverless compute Snowflake may use for eligible queries. The `QUERY_ACCELERATION_MAX_SCALE_FACTOR` parameter defines the maximum additional serverless compute Snowflake may use to accelerate eligible queries. A value of 2 allows Snowflake to use up to twice the warehouse's compute resources when accelerating qualifying queries.

```
ALTER WAREHOUSE WH_QAS_TEST
SET QUERY_ACCELERATION_MAX_SCALE_FACTOR = 2;
```

10. Run the same query from *Step 3* again after enabling QAS.

```
SELECT
    ss_store_sk,
    SUM(ss_sales_price) AS total_sales
FROM STORE_SALES
WHERE ss_sold_date_sk BETWEEN 2450815 AND 2451179
GROUP BY ss_store_sk
ORDER BY total_sales DESC;
```

After the query completes, compare the execution time and Query Profile with the baseline run from *Step 3*. If the query is a good candidate for QAS, you may observe a reduction in elapsed time or changes in how Snowflake distributed the query workload.

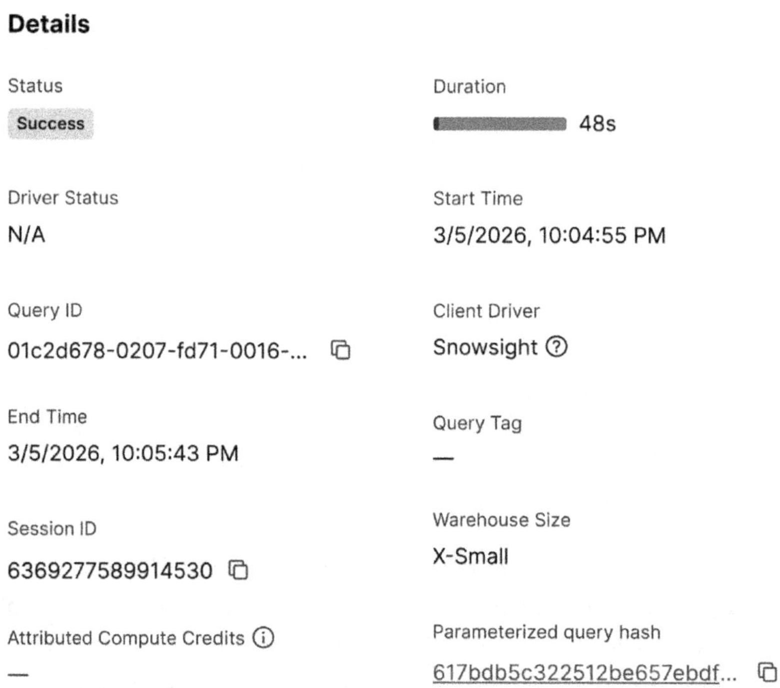

Figure 6.33 – Second Query execution result

11. Compare the second execution with the baseline run by reviewing the query details and query profile in Snowsight. If the query was a good candidate for QAS, you may see a reduction in elapsed time. Snowflake also notes that performance improvements can fluctuate because QAS depends on server availability, so the benefit is not guaranteed on every run.
12. To identify additional candidate queries for QAS, query the `QUERY_ACCELERATION_ELIGIBLE` view. Use this view for identifying queries and warehouses that might benefit from the service.

How it works...

Virtual warehouses normally execute queries using only the compute resources assigned to that warehouse. When a query scans large volumes of data, the work must be processed by the nodes within the warehouse, which can make large analytical queries take longer unless the warehouse size is increased.

QAS introduces an additional mechanism that can speed up certain queries without requiring the warehouse itself to be resized. When this feature is enabled, Snowflake may temporarily use additional compute resources outside the warehouse to help process portions of an eligible query. These extra resources focus primarily on scan and filtering operations, allowing large datasets to be processed in parallel and reducing the overall time required to complete the query.

Because these resources are provided outside the warehouse, they are billed as serverless compute rather than standard warehouse credits. To control how much additional compute Snowflake is allowed to use, the warehouse parameter `QUERY_ACCELERATION_MAX_SCALE_FACTOR` defines an upper limit on the amount of extra compute that can be applied to a query.

Not every query will benefit from this feature. Snowflake determines eligibility automatically based on the query plan and workload characteristics. Queries that scan large tables with selective filters or aggregations are more likely to benefit because part of the processing can be distributed across additional compute resources. Smaller queries or queries that already execute efficiently within the warehouse may not use the service at all.

In this recipe, the query was executed first without query acceleration to establish a baseline. After enabling the feature, the same query was executed again so that the query profile and execution time could be compared. This approach helps determine whether the workload is a good candidate for query acceleration and whether the performance improvement justifies the additional serverless compute usage.

Get this book's PDF version and more

Scan the QR code (or go to `packtpub.com/unlock`). Search for this book by name, confirm the edition, and then follow the steps on the page.

UNLOCK NOW

Note: Keep your invoice handy. Purchases made directly from Packt don't require an invoice.

7

Secure Data Sharing

Traditional data warehouse solutions typically share data by extracting it and transferring it through mechanisms such as FTP, APIs, or file delivery. A major drawback of this approach is that as soon as the data is exported, it can begin to fall out of sync with the source system. It also introduces additional operational overhead related to data movement, storage, and security.

Snowflake addresses these challenges with its secure data sharing capabilities, which allow organizations to share live data directly from their Snowflake environment without copying or moving the underlying data. This approach reduces operational complexity, lowers costs, and ensures that consumers always access the most up-to-date version of the data.

In this chapter, you will learn how to share data with other Snowflake accounts as well as with organizations that do not yet have a Snowflake account. You will also explore how Snowflake Marketplace enables organizations to distribute and consume data products more broadly through a governed marketplace experience.

The following recipes will be covered in this chapter:

- Sharing a table with another Snowflake account
- Sharing data through a view with another Snowflake account
- Sharing a complete database with another Snowflake account and setting up future objects
- Creating reader accounts and configuring them for non-Snowflake sharing
- Sharing an object with a non-Snowflake user
- Keeping costs in check when sharing data with non-Snowflake users
- Publishing a data share to the Snowflake Internal Marketplace

Technical requirements

This chapter requires access to a modern internet browser (Chrome, Edge, Firefox, or similar) and access to the internet to connect to your Snowflake account in the cloud.

You can download the example project and code for this book by following the instructions in the ***Download the example code files*** section in the *Preface* of this book.

Sharing a table with another Snowflake account

In this recipe, we will share a basic table with another Snowflake account by creating a share and assigning the necessary privileges. In Snowflake, a share is a secure object that allows specific database objects, such as tables or views, to be made available to other Snowflake accounts without copying or moving the underlying data. The share acts as the mechanism that defines what data is accessible and who can access it.

Getting ready

You will need to be connected to your Snowflake instance via Snowsight to execute this recipe. We will act as a data provider and share data with *another* Snowflake account that will act as the data consumer. Therefore, you will need to know the consumer Snowflake account and, more specifically, you will need to know the consumer account name.

Since we will be creating and consuming a share, which is an account-level activity, you must use a role with the privileges required to create and manage shares. In many environments, this is the ACCOUNTADMIN role.

For this recipe, the consumer account must either reside in the same cloud platform and region as the provider account, or the shared data must be replicated to the consumer's region using Snowflake replication features. If you are creating a second Snowflake trial account to act as the consumer, ensure it is created in the same region and cloud as the provider account to simplify the exercise.

How to do it...

We will be creating a table and populating that table with some sample data. We will share that table further in this recipe. The steps are as follows:

1. We will start by creating a new database, followed by the creation of a table that will hold some transaction data:

```
CREATE DATABASE C7_R1;

USE WAREHOUSE DEFAULT_WH;
```

```
CREATE TABLE TRANSACTIONS
(
  TXN_ID STRING,
  TXN_DATE DATE,
  CUSTOMER_ID STRING,
  QUANTITY DECIMAL(20),
  PRICE DECIMAL(30,2),
  COUNTRY_CD STRING
);
```

2. Next, we will populate this table with a thousand rows of dummy data using the following SQL command:

```
INSERT INTO TRANSACTIONS
SELECT
    UUID_STRING() AS TXN_ID
    ,DATEADD(DAY,UNIFORM(1, 500, RANDOM()) * -1, '2020-10-15') AS TXN_DATE
    ,UUID_STRING() AS CUSTOMER_ID
    ,UNIFORM(1, 10, RANDOM()) AS QUANTITY
    ,UNIFORM(1, 200, RANDOM()) AS PRICE
    ,RANDSTR(2,RANDOM()) AS COUNTRY_CD
FROM TABLE(GENERATOR(ROWCOUNT => 1000));
```

You should see a thousand rows inserted into the table.

3. Next, we will create the share object through which we will share the table. You will need to use the `ACCOUNTADMIN` role to create the share. To do so, run the following SQL:

```
USE ROLE ACCOUNTADMIN;
CREATE SHARE share_trx_data;
```

4. Next, we need to provide various permissions to the newly created share object to ensure that the sharing works correctly. The first two permissions that we need to provide are the `USAGE` permissions on the database and the `public` schema in which our table is created. To do so, run the following SQL:

```
GRANT USAGE ON DATABASE C7_R1 TO SHARE share_trx_data;
GRANT USAGE ON SCHEMA C7_R1.public TO SHARE share_trx_data;
```

The grants should succeed with a success message.

5. Finally, we will provide the `SELECT` permissions on the transaction table to the share object. Note that you can provide the `SELECT` permission to more than one table, which will result in each of the tables having permissions to then be shared. To do so, run the following SQL:

```
GRANT SELECT ON TABLE C7_R1.public.transactions TO SHARE
share_trx_data;
```

   The grant should succeed with a success message.

6. At this point, we have created the share, added the required objects to it, and granted the necessary permissions. Now, we are ready to add the consumer to the share. To do so, we must first obtain the Snowflake account locator for the consumer account.
   In most cases, the consuming organization will provide their account locator. If you are working with another Snowflake account that you control, you can retrieve the account locator directly from Snowflake by executing the following command:

```
SELECT CURRENT_ACCOUNT();
```

   The result of this query returns the account locator for the current Snowflake account. This value is what you will use when adding the consumer account to the share.

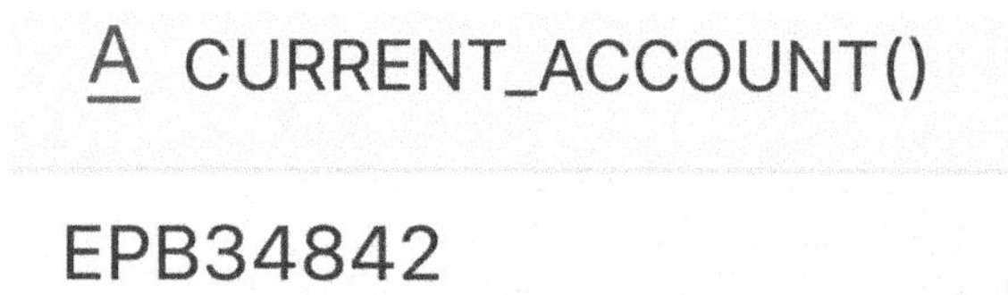

Figure 7.1 – Ascertaining the account locator from the Snowflake Snowsight

7. Let's now add the consumer to the share. Please ensure that you replace the placeholder text `consumer_account_locator_here` with the appropriate consumer number. To do so, run the following SQL:

```
ALTER SHARE share_trx_data ADD ACCOUNT=consumer_account_locator_name_here;
```

   At this point, we have, as a data provider, successfully shared a table with a consumer. Our next steps are to log in *as the consumer* and create a database using the share so that the consuming account can read the table.

> **Note**
>
> For secure data sharing, either your consumer should exist in the same region and cloud as the provider account or data should be replicated to the consumer region and cloud.

8. For the next steps, log in to the consumer account as an `ACCOUNTADMIN` role and configure the share to be usable, and the shared table can then be queried. First, we list all the shares and validate that the new share does appear in our system. To do so, run the following command:

```
USE ROLE ACCOUNTADMIN;
SHOW SHARES;
```

The query will execute with the following output:

kind	owner_account	name	database_name
INBOUND	IFZJGKM.DOL_KEITH_LAB_KRXBTD	SHARE_TRX_DATA	
INBOUND	SNOWFLAKE	ACCOUNT_USAGE	SNOWFLAKE
INBOUND	SFSALESSHARED.SFC_SAMPLES_PROD3	SAMPLE_DATA	SNOWFLAKE_SAMPLE.

Figure 7.2 – List of shares available to the consumer

As you can see, there is an inbound share with the name of `SHARE_TRX_DATA`, which is the share object shared by the provider. However, there is no database attached to the share. A database must be attached to the share by the consumer before someone can query it.

9. Let's now run the `DESCRIBE` command on the share to view what is contained in the share. To do so, run the following SQL:

```
USE ROLE ACCOUNTADMIN;
DESC SHARE provider_account_locator_here.SHARE_TRX_DATA;
```

The query will execute with the following output:

kind	name	shared_on
DATABASE	<DB>	2020-10-29 12:47:17.53.559 -0700
SCHEMA	<DB>.PUBLIC	2020-10-29 12:47:17.08.008 -0700
TABLE	<DB>.PUBLIC.TRANSACTIONS	2020-10-29 12:47:17.22.056 -0700

Figure 7.3 – Output of the describe share command

The output of running the `DESCRIBE` command shows that the share contains a database, that the database contains a schema called `PUBLIC`, and that there is a single table called `TRANSACTIONS` in that schema. Do note that the shared database's name is shown as <DB>, which is because you (as a consumer) have not attached any database to the share.

10. We will now create and attach a database to the share. To do so, execute the following SQL:

```
CREATE DATABASE SHR_TRANSACTIONS FROM SHARE
provider_account_locator_here.SHARE_TRX_DATA;
```

11. Let's now rerun the `DESCRIBE` command on the share to validate that the database is attached to the share. To do so, run the following SQL:

```
USE ROLE ACCOUNTADMIN;
DESC SHARE provider_account_locator_here.SHARE_TRX_DATA;
```

The query will execute with the following output:

kind	name	shared_on
DATABASE	SHR_TRANSACTIONS	2020-10-29 12:47:17.559 -0700
SCHEMA	SHR_TRANSACTIONS.PUBLIC	2020-10-29 12:47:18.008 -0700
TABLE	SHR_TRANSACTIONS.PUBLIC.TRANSACTI	2020-10-29 12:47:22.056 -0700

Figure 7.4 – Validating whether the database is attached to the share

You will notice that the previous output from the DESCRIBE command showed <DB> as a placeholder. But after a database was created pointing to the share, the describe output clearly shows the attached database, which is SHR_TRANSACTIONS.

12. At this point, we (as consumers) can query the TRANSACTIONS table just like how we would query any other table:

```
USE ROLE ACCOUNTADMIN;
SELECT * FROM SHR_TRANSACTIONS.PUBLIC.TRANSACTIONS;
```

You will be shown the data from the table, as shown:

TXN_ID	TXN_DATE	CUSTOMER_ID	QUANTITY	PRICE	COUNTRY_CD
ed58ec30-e033...	2019-12-16	385b7145-a53f...	10	189.00	oJ
26764eb9-768d...	2020-03-25	bcc95cd8-e861...	1	149.00	a5
962427f1-510d-...	2020-08-31	ce705904-6fe1-...	2	93.00	EV

Figure 7.5 – Querying the TRANSACTIONS table as a data consumer

You can now grant access to this database and the table(s) to other roles so that the shared data is accessible by others in the consumer Snowflake account.

How it works...

The concept of sharing can best be understood through *Figure 7.6*, which describes the steps we took in this recipe. The `transactions` table exists in the Provider account within the C7_R1 database. The share object called `share_trx_data` contains the `transactions` table within. Think of that as a soft reference to the table since the table hasn't been copied or moved, but rather the share is merely pointing to the table.

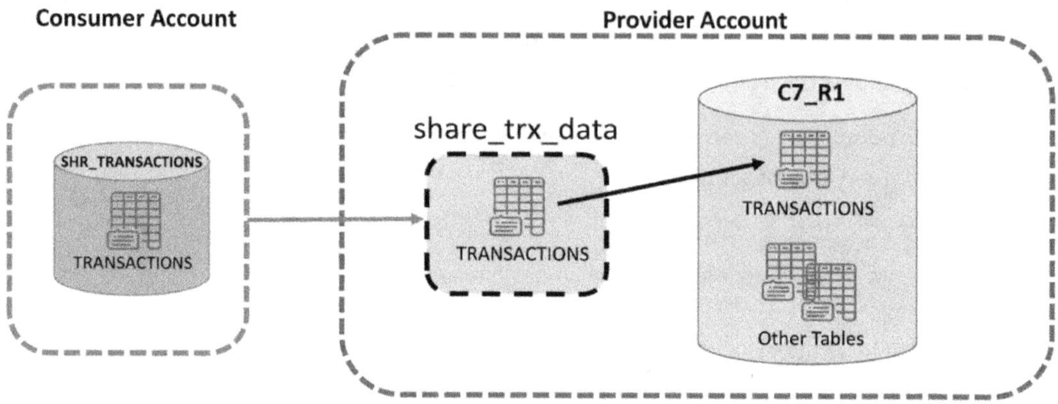

Figure 7.6 – Sharing in Snowflake illustrated

Once the share is created and has all the required objects, one or more consumer accounts can access the share, making the share available to them within their account. However, to use the shared data, the consumer account must create a database on top of the share, which is shown as the `shr_transactions` database on the consumer side. After a database is created pointing to the share, the tables inside the share can be queried like any other table.

Sharing data through a view with another Snowflake account

Through this recipe, we will share data through a secure view to another Snowflake account. We will create the secure view, create a share, and assign the necessary grants for the view and the share to function correctly. If you need to share data from multiple databases, creating a secure view and sharing it is the recommended approach based on Snowflake best practices.

Getting ready

You will need to be connected to your Snowflake instance via Snowsight or the CLI client to execute this recipe. We will act as a data provider and share data with another Snowflake account that will act as the data consumer. Therefore, you will need to know the consumer Snowflake account and, more specifically, you will need to know the consumer account name.

Since we will create and consume a share, which is an account-level activity, `ACCOUNTADMIN`-level access is required on the Snowflake accounts that will act as the provider and the consumer.

How to do it...

We will start by creating two databases with one table each. We will populate the tables with some sample data. Further along in the recipe, we will create a secure view on these tables and share that view. The steps for this recipe are as follows:

1. We will start by creating a new database, followed by creating a table that will hold the customer name data:

```
CREATE DATABASE C7_R2_DB1;
CREATE TABLE CUSTOMER
(
  CUST_ID NUMBER,
  CUST_NAME STRING
);
```

   The command should succeed with a success message stating that the `CUSTOMER` table was created successfully.

2. Next, we will populate this table with a thousand rows of dummy data using the provided SQL:

```
INSERT INTO CUSTOMER
SELECT
    SEQ8() AS CUST_ID,
    RANDSTR(10,RANDOM()) AS CUST_NAME
FROM TABLE(GENERATOR(ROWCOUNT => 1000));
```

   You should see a thousand rows inserted into the table.

3. Next, we will create an additional database, followed by creating a table that will hold the customer address data:

```
CREATE DATABASE C7_R2_DB2;
CREATE TABLE CUSTOMER_ADDRESS
(
  CUST_ID NUMBER,
  CUST_ADDRESS STRING
);
```

   The command should succeed with a success message stating that the `CUSTOMER_ADDRESS` table was created successfully.

4. Next, we will populate this table with a thousand rows of dummy data using the provided SQL:

```
INSERT INTO CUSTOMER_ADDRESS
SELECT
    SEQ8() AS CUST_ID,
    RANDSTR(50,RANDOM()) AS CUST_ADDRESS
FROM TABLE(GENERATOR(ROWCOUNT => 1000));
```

   You should see a thousand rows inserted into the table.

5. Next, we will create a third database, which will contain our view. To do so, run the following SQL:

```
CREATE DATABASE VIEW_SHR_DB;
```

   The command should succeed with a success message stating that the database was created successfully.

6. Let's now create the secure view, in which we will combine data from the `CUSTOMER` and `CUSTOMER_ADDRESS` tables. To do so, run the following SQL:

```
CREATE SECURE VIEW CUSTOMER_INFO AS
SELECT CUS.CUST_ID, CUS.CUST_NAME, CUS_ADD.CUST_ADDRESS
FROM C7_R2_DB1.PUBLIC.CUSTOMER CUS
INNER JOIN C7_R2_DB2.PUBLIC.CUSTOMER_ADDRESS CUS_ADD
ON CUS.CUST_ID = CUS_ADD.CUST_ID;
```

7. Let's now validate that the view works correctly. To do so, run the following SQL:

```
SELECT * FROM CUSTOMER_INFO;
```

   You should see a thousand rows with random data returned as the result as shown:

CUST_ID	CUST_NAME	CUST_ADDRESS
0	jdmQH5GA1J	LXAYxsldzqseAt1S30TXsc1Qx23n0lyptbXpKoNkbVJogatg5V
1	scCydZ9tl3	gCY89nx7pLYG9rwRSslaxXLJkNexvnQ5DsuWzSkwslu9XBI9IC
2	AHCRo5Vg9S	zhbDyr4Od3ZHPRdgCtHv5OTkZsKyeYlejnHJgtHkauzrO4RR

Figure 7.7 – Validating the view

8. Next, we will create the SHARE object through which we will share the view. You will need to use the ACCOUNTADMIN role to create the share. To do so, run the following SQL:

```
USE ROLE ACCOUNTADMIN;
CREATE SHARE share_cust_data;
```

9. Next, we need to provide various permissions to the newly created share object to ensure that the sharing works correctly. The first two permissions that we need to provide are the USAGE permissions on the database and the public schema in which our view is created. To do so, run the following SQL:

```
GRANT USAGE ON DATABASE VIEW_SHR_DB TO SHARE share_cust_data;
GRANT USAGE ON SCHEMA VIEW_SHR_DB.public TO SHARE share_cust_data;
```

10. When sharing data from a secure view, we also need to provide the REFERENCE_USAGE privileges on the databases that contain the underlying tables. To do so, run the following SQL:

```
GRANT REFERENCE_USAGE ON DATABASE C7_R2_DB1 TO SHARE
share_cust_data;
GRANT REFERENCE_USAGE ON DATABASE C7_R2_DB2 TO SHARE
share_cust_data;
```

11. Finally, we will provide the SELECT permissions on the CUSTOMER_INFO view to the SHARE object. To do so, run the following SQL:

```
GRANT SELECT ON VIEW VIEW_SHR_DB.public.CUSTOMER_INFO
TO SHARE share_cust_data;
```

By this point, we have created a view that combines data from two different databases. We have also defined a share and granted the necessary privileges on the view so it can be accessed through the share. The next step is to add the consumer account to the share.

12. To add the consumer account to the share, we must first obtain the Snowflake account locator for the consumer account. In most cases, the consuming organization will provide their account locator directly. However, if you are working with another

Snowflake account that you control, you can retrieve the account locator from within Snowflake by executing the following command:

```
SELECT CURRENT_ACCOUNT();
```

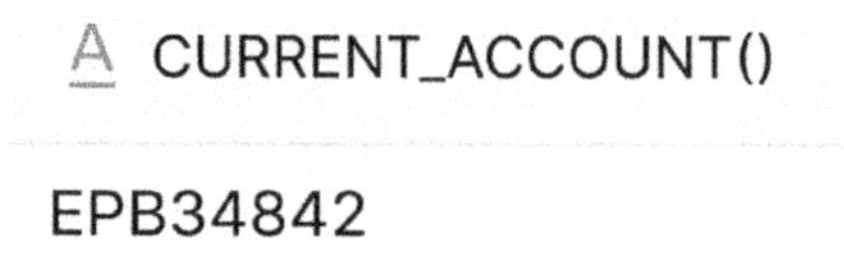

Figure 7.8 – Ascertaining the account name from the Snowflake Snowsight URL

13. Let's now add the consumer to the share. Please ensure that you replace the following placeholder text with the appropriate consumer account locator. To do so, run the following SQL:

```
ALTER SHARE share_cust_data ADD ACCOUNT=consumer_account_locator_here;
```

At this point, we have, as a data provider, successfully shared a secure view with a consumer. The next step is to log in *as the consumer* and create a database using the share so that the consuming account can read the table.

> **Note**
>
> Note
>
> For secure data sharing, either your consumer should exist in the same region and cloud as the provider account or data should be replicated to the consumer region and cloud.

14. For the next steps, log in to the consumer account as an `ACCOUNTADMIN` and configure the share to be usable, and the shared view can be queried. First, we list all the shares and validate that the new share does appear in our system. To do so, run the following command:

```
USE ROLE ACCOUNTADMIN;
SHOW SHARES;
```

The query will execute with the following output:

kind	name	database_name
INBOUND	.SHARE_CUST_DATA	
INBOUND	SFC_SAMPLES.SAMPLE_DATA	SNOWFLAKE_SAMPL...
INBOUND	SNOWFLAKE.ACCOUNT_US...	SNOWFLAKE

Figure 7.9 – List of shares available to the consumer

As you can see, there is an inbound share with the name of `share_cust_data`, which is the share object shared by the provider. However, there is no database attached to the share. A database must be attached to the share by the consumer before someone can query it.

15. Let's run the `DESCRIBE` command on the share to view what is contained in the share. To do so, run the following SQL:

```
USE ROLE ACCOUNTADMIN;
DESC SHARE provider_account_locator_here.SHARE_CUST_DATA;
```

The query will execute with the following output:

kind	name ↓
DATABASE	<DB>
SCHEMA	<DB>.PUBLIC
VIEW	<DB>.PUBLIC.CUSTOMER_INFO

Figure 7.10 – Output of the describe share command

The output of running the `DESCRIBE` command shows that the share contains a database, that the database contains a schema called `PUBLIC`, and that there is a single view called `CUSTOMER_INFO` in that schema. Do note that the shared database's name is shown as `<DB>`, which is because you (as a consumer) have not attached any database to the share.

16. We will now create and attach a database to the share. To do so, execute the following SQL:

```
CREATE DATABASE SHR_CUSTOMER FROM SHARE
provider_account_locator_here.SHARE_CUST_DATA;
```

17. Let's now run the `DESCRIBE` command again on the share to validate that the database is attached to the share. To do so, run the following SQL:

```
USE ROLE ACCOUNTADMIN;
DESC SHARE provider_account_locator_here.SHARE_CUST_DATA;
```

The query will execute with the following output:

kind	name
DATABASE	SHR_CUSTOMER
SCHEMA	SHR_CUSTOMER.PUBLIC
VIEW	SHR_CUSTOMER.PUBLIC.CUSTOMER_INFO

Figure 7.11 – Validating that the database is attached to the share

You will notice that the previous output from the `DESCRIBE` command showed `<DB>` as a placeholder. But after a database was created pointing to the share, the describe output clearly shows the attached database, which in this case is `SHR_CUSTOMER`.

18. At this point, we (as consumers) can query the `CUSTOMER_INFO` view just like how we would query any other table:

```
USE ROLE ACCOUNTADMIN;
SELECT * FROM SHR_CUSTOMER.PUBLIC.CUSTOMER_INFO;
```

You will be shown the data from the view, as shown:

CUST_ID	CUST_NAME	CUST_ADDRESS
0	jdmQH5GA1J	LXAYxsldzqseAt1S30TXsc1Qx23n0lyptbXpKoNkbVJogatg5V
1	scCydZ9tl3	gCY89nx7pLYG9rwRSslaxXLJkNexvnQ5DsuWzSkwslu9XBl9lC
2	AHCRo5Vg9S	zhbDyr4Od3ZHZPRdgCtHv5OTkZsKyeYlHejnHJgtHkauzrO4RR

Figure 7.12 – Querying the CUSTOMER_INFO view as a consumer

19. You can now grant access to this database and the view to other roles so that the shared data is accessible to others in the consumer Snowflake account.

How it works...

A variety of objects can be shared with a consumer through Snowflake data sharing, including sharing entire databases, entire schemas, individual tables, and views. Sharing a view is somewhat similar to how a table is shared; however, some additional steps are required when sharing data through a view.

A view that is shared through Snowflake Secure Data Sharing must be created as a secure view. Secure views prevent consumers from accessing information about the view definition or the underlying tables by disabling certain internal query optimizations. This ensures that consumers can query the view's results without gaining visibility into the objects used to produce those results.

Additionally, you must grant reference usage to the share object on the tables underlying the view so that the share can run the SQL in the view definition successfully.

Sharing a complete database with another Snowflake account and future objects

We will share a complete database through this recipe and include all the schemas, tables, and views within that database. We will also configure future grants so that any new objects created in the database are automatically included in the share.

Getting ready

You will need to be connected to your Snowflake instance via Snowsight or the CLI client to execute this recipe. We will act as a data provider and share data with another Snowflake account that will act as the data consumer. Therefore, you will need to know the consumer Snowflake account and, more specifically, you will need to know the consumer account name.

Since we will create and consume a share, which is an account-level activity, ACCOUNTADMIN-level access is required on the Snowflake accounts that will act as the provider and the consumer.

How to do it...

We will create a database that will initially contain a single table. We will share the database first and then create another table in the database. Then we will demonstrate how to share this new (and other future tables) by running a simple GRANT statement. The steps are as follows:

1. We will start by creating a new database, followed by the creation of a sample table:

```
USE ROLE ACCOUNTADMIN;
CREATE DATABASE C7_R3;
CREATE TABLE CUSTOMER
(
  CUST_ID NUMBER,
  CUST_NAME STRING
);
```

2. Next, we will create the SHARE object through which we will share the table. You will need to use the ACCOUNTADMIN role to create the share. To do so, run the following SQL:

```
USE ROLE ACCOUNTADMIN;
CREATE SHARE share_cust_database;
```

3. Next, we need to provide various permissions to the newly created share object to ensure that the sharing works correctly. The two permissions that we need to provide are the USAGE permissions on the database and the public schema in which our table is created. To do so, run the following SQL:

```
GRANT USAGE ON DATABASE C7_R3 TO SHARE share_cust_database;
GRANT USAGE ON SCHEMA C7_R3.public TO SHARE share_cust_database;
```

4. Next, we will provide the SELECT permissions on all existing tables to the share object. To do so, run the following SQL:

```
GRANT SELECT ON ALL TABLES IN SCHEMA C7_R3.public TO
SHARE share_cust_database;
```

5. At this point, we have created the share and granted the necessary privileges on the database objects that will be shared. The next step is to add the consumer account to the share.

   To do this, we must first obtain the Snowflake account locator for the consumer account. In most cases, the consuming organization will provide their account locator directly. However, if you are working with another Snowflake account that you control, you can retrieve the account locator from within Snowflake by executing the following command:

   ```
   SELECT CURRENT_ACCOUNT();
   ```

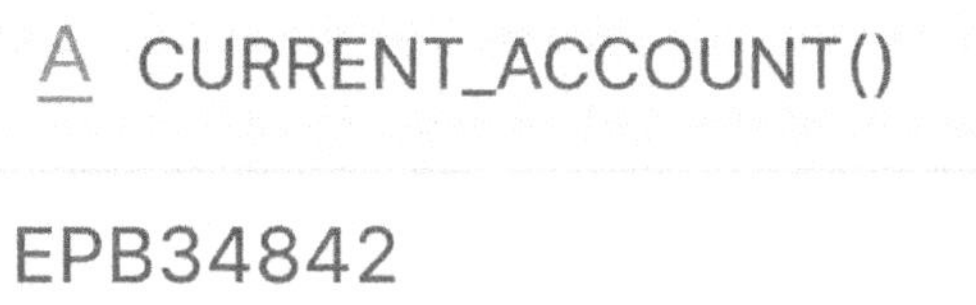

Figure 7.13 – Ascertaining the account name from the Snowflake Snowsight URL

6. Let's now add the consumer to the share. Please ensure that you replace the placeholder text with the appropriate consumer locator. To do so, run the following SQL:

   ```
   ALTER SHARE share_cust_database ADD ACCOUNT=consumer_account_locator_here;
   ```

   At this point, we have, as a data provider, successfully shared a database and existing table(s) contained in that database with a consumer.

7. Let's now run the `DESCRIBE` command on the share object to see what tables are being shared. To do so, run the following command:

   ```
   DESC SHARE share_cust_database;
   ```

   The query will execute with the following output:

kind	name
DATABASE	C7_R3
SCHEMA	C7_R3.PUBLIC
TABLE	C7_R3.PUBLIC.CUSTOMER

Figure 7.14 – List of objects contained in the share

You will notice a single table by the name of `CUSTOMER`, which is part of the share.

8. Now we will create an additional table in the shared database to demonstrate how to share future tables. To do so, run the following SQL:

```
USE C7_R3;
CREATE TABLE CUSTOMER_ADDRESS
(
  CUST_ID NUMBER,
  CUST_ADDRESS STRING
);
```

9. Now that we have added a new table to the shared database, let's check whether the new table is automatically shared. To do so, run the following command:

```
DESC SHARE share_cust_database;
```

The query will execute with the following output:

kind	name
DATABASE	C7_R3
SCHEMA	C7_R3.PUBLIC
TABLE	C7_R3.PUBLIC.CUSTOMER

Figure 7.15 – New table NOT added to the share

10. As you can see, there is still only a single table shared by the name of `CUSTOMER` and the `CUSTOMER_ADDRESS` table is not added to the share automatically:

To ensure that any newly created table(s) are added to the share, we need to provide the `SELECT` permissions on all existing tables in the database to the share object. To do so, run the following SQL:

```
GRANT SELECT ON ALL TABLES IN SCHEMA C7_R3.public TO
SHARE share_cust_database;
```

Note that this `GRANT` statement affected two objects. If there were more tables in the database, the count would be higher.

11. Let's again check whether the new table is now added to the share. To do so, run the following command:

```
DESC SHARE share_cust_database;
```

The query will execute with the following output:

kind	name
DATABASE	C7_R3
SCHEMA	C7_R3.PUBLIC
TABLE	C7_R3.PUBLIC.CUSTOMER
TABLE	C7_R3.PUBLIC.CUSTOMER_ADDRESS

Figure 7.16 – New table added to the share after privileges granted

You will now see that both tables are shared and will be available to the consumers of the share.

You can configure the statement in *step 10* to execute on a recurring schedule using Snowflake's tasks feature. This will ensure that any new tables in the database are automatically shared.

How it works...

Snowflake does not add newly added tables and views to a share object automatically. This is by design and likely done to ensure that new objects' security is not inadvertently compromised. Suppose you have requirements that all objects (existing and new) in a particular database should be shared with the consumers, in that case, you can run the `GRANT SELECT ON ALL` statement regularly to ensure that any new tables are shared. Alternatively, you can use the `Task` functionality in Snowflake to schedule this statement's execution at regular intervals.

It is worth noting that Snowflake does provide a mechanism through which you can grant privileges on future objects in a database; however, that mechanism is not valid for share objects. Future grants are typically used when assigning privileges to roles within an account, but they cannot be applied when granting privileges to a share.

Creating reader accounts and configuring them for non-Snowflake sharing

In this recipe, you will create a reader account and configure it so that users outside your organization can access shared data even if they do not operate their own Snowflake environment.

Reader accounts allow a Snowflake provider to create and manage a Snowflake account on behalf of a consumer. The provider controls access, manages users, and is responsible for the compute resources used by the reader account.

Getting ready

You must be connected to your Snowflake account using Snowsight to complete this recipe. Since creating a reader account is an account-level operation, you must be logged in using the `ACCOUNTADMIN` role. In this recipe, we will act as a data provider and create a reader account that will later be used to share data with non-Snowflake consumers.

How to do it...

Follow these steps to create and configure a Reader Account:

1. Ensure that your current role is `ACCOUNTADMIN`:

   ```
   USE ROLE ACCOUNTADMIN;
   ```

   Reader accounts can only be created by the `ACCOUNTADMIN` role.

2. Create the reader account using the `CREATE MANAGED ACCOUNT` command:

   ```
   CREATE MANAGED ACCOUNT RA_FOR_SUP
   ADMIN_NAME = SP_ACCOUNT_ADMIN
   ADMIN_PASSWORD = 'StrongPassword123!'
   TYPE = READER;
   ```

This creates a reader account named RA_FOR_SUP and defines SP_ACCOUNT as the administrative user for that account.

3. Verify the reader account using the following command:

```
SHOW MANAGED ACCOUNTS;
```

The output will include the account URL and account locator required to access the reader account.

account_name	cloud	region	account_locator	created_on	account_url
RA_FOR_SUP	aws	AWS_US_WEST_2	GBB62082	2026-03-11 16:39:50	https://ifzjgkm-ra_for_sup.snowflakecomputing.com

Figure 7.17 – Reader account URL link

4. Log in to the Reader Account using the account URL returned in the previous step. Please note that it can take several minutes for a newly created Reader Account to be fully provisioned. If the account is not yet available, you may receive a temporary error such as a 403 Forbidden message. If this occurs, wait a few minutes and try again. Once the account is available, log in using the following credentials:

```
ADMIN_NAME = SP_ACCOUNT_ADMIN
ADMIN_PASSWORD = 'StrongPassword123!'
```

5. A newly created reader account only contains a single user acting as the reader account's administrative user. In the same way as we set up a regular Snowflake account, we must create new users and other objects to configure the reader account properly. First, we will need to create a new user and grant them the SYSADMIN and SECURITYADMIN roles. This new user will act as the administrator for the reader account and will be able to create and manage objects and users as required. To do so, run the following SQL:

```
USE ROLE SECURITYADMIN;

CREATE USER SP_SYSADMIN
PASSWORD='StrongPassword123!'
DEFAULT_ROLE = SYSADMIN
MUST_CHANGE_PASSWORD = TRUE;
```

You should see a message stating that the user was created successfully.

6. Now we will grant this new user the `SYSADMIN` and `SECURITYADMIN` roles so that the user can create new objects and new users within the reader account. To do so, run the following SQL:

```
GRANT ROLE SYSADMIN TO USER SP_SYSADMIN;
GRANT ROLE SECURITYADMIN TO USER SP_SYSADMIN;
```

7. You will see a success message stating that the statement was executed successfully. The `SP_SYSADMIN` user can now use both the `SYSADMIN` and `SECURITYADMIN` roles. Note that we reused the same user for both roles. If required, you can create separate users for each of these roles.

8. We will now create a virtual warehouse for the reader account since the reader account does not have a virtual warehouse by default. To create the virtual warehouse, run the following SQL:

```
USE ROLE ACCOUNTADMIN;

CREATE WAREHOUSE SP_VW
WITH
WAREHOUSE_SIZE = 'SMALL'
WAREHOUSE_TYPE = 'STANDARD'
AUTO_SUSPEND = 300
AUTO_RESUME = TRUE
INITIALLY_SUSPENDED = TRUE;
```

9. Since we are creating a virtual warehouse as the `ACCOUNTADMIN` role, we must grant other roles privileges to this virtual warehouse. Which roles you grant privileges to will depend on your requirements. In this case, we will grant `USAGE` privileges to the `PUBLIC` role so that any user in the reader account can use the virtual warehouse. We will also grant `ALL` privileges on the virtual warehouse to the `SYSADMIN` role so that the `SYSADMIN` role can manage the virtual warehouse. To do so, run the following SQL:

```
GRANT USAGE ON WAREHOUSE SP_VW TO ROLE PUBLIC;
GRANT ALL ON WAREHOUSE SP_VW TO ROLE SYSADMIN;
```

10. We have configured the reader account and created a new user with `SYSADMIN` and `SECURITYADMIN` privileges. We have created a new virtual warehouse that users in the reader account can use to run their queries. You can now share data from the provider

account to the reader account as you would typically do with any other consumer account. You will follow that by creating users in the reader account who will be querying that shared data.

How it works...

Snowflake provides multiple methods for sharing data, including sharing with other Snowflake customers and sharing with organizations that do not operate their own Snowflake environment. Sharing with another Snowflake customer is straightforward because the consumer already has a Snowflake account that can receive the share.

When sharing with a non-Snowflake customer, Snowflake must provide a way for the consumer to log in and access the shared data. Snowflake enables this through reader accounts, which are Snowflake accounts created and managed by the data provider. You can think of a reader account as a Snowflake account that exists under the control of the provider account.

Each reader account has its own account URL through which users can log in and access shared data. By default, a newly created reader account does not contain any virtual warehouses, databases, or users beyond the administrative user created during the reader account setup process. As a result, the provider must configure additional users, roles, and a virtual warehouse so that consumers can run queries against the shared data.

It is important to note that compute usage in a reader account is billed to the provider account that created it. For this reason, providers should monitor and control warehouse usage within reader accounts to manage compute costs effectively.

Once the reader account is configured, sharing data with it is similar to sharing with any other Snowflake account. The provider simply uses the reader account's account locator in the sharing statement to grant access to the share.

Snowflake also supports distributing data products through **Listings** and the **Snowflake Marketplace**, which provide a governed way to share data with a broader audience. This capability is covered later in this chapter.

Sharing an object with a non-Snowflake user

Snowflake supports sharing data with both Snowflake users and organizations that do not yet use Snowflake. When sharing with a non-Snowflake user, a Reader Account must be created to allow the recipient to access the shared data without requiring their own Snowflake account.

In this recipe, we will create a new Reader Account, share a table and a view with that account, and then grant the required privileges.

Getting ready

You will need to be connected to your Snowflake instance via Snowsight or the CLI client to execute this recipe. We will act as a data provider and create a reader account that can subsequently be used to share data with non-Snowflake users.

Since we will be creating a reader account, which is an account-level activity, `ACCOUNTADMIN`-level access is required.

How to do it…

To share data with a non-Snowflake user, the first step is to set up a reader account, with which we can then share the data. The steps for this recipe are as follows:

1. We will start by creating a new reader account. To do so, run the following SQL:

```
USE ROLE ACCOUNTADMIN;
CREATE MANAGED ACCOUNT SH_NON_SF_ACCOUNT TYPE=READER,
ADMIN_NAME = 'READER_ADMIN',
ADMIN_PASSWORD='<password_of_your_choice>';
```

   The command should succeed with the following message. Please make a note of the `accountName` and `loginUrl` values from the output:

Row	status
1	{"accountName": "BE52113", "loginUrl": "https://be52113.ap-southeast-2.snowflakecomputing.com"}

Figure 7.18 – New reader account created

   From the preceding output, `BE52113` is the account identifier, and `https://be52113.ap-southeast-2.snowflakecomputing.com` is the URL through which you will access the reader account.

2. Next, use a browser to navigate to the URL in the preceding step and log in using the username and password you provided in *Step 1*.

> **Note**
>
> It can take some time to provision a reader account, and until it is provisioned, you might get a 403 forbidden error message when trying to access it.

3. We will create a virtual warehouse for the reader account since the reader account does not have a virtual warehouse by default. To create the virtual warehouse, run the following SQL:

```
USE ROLE ACCOUNTADMIN;
CREATE WAREHOUSE SP_VW WITH
WAREHOUSE_SIZE = 'SMALL' WAREHOUSE_TYPE = 'STANDARD'
AUTO_SUSPEND = 300 AUTO_RESUME = TRUE
INITIALLY_SUSPENDED = TRUE;
```

   Note that we have created a small standard virtual warehouse to conserve costs. You can create a virtual warehouse as per your needs.

4. Since we are creating a virtual warehouse as the `ACCOUNTADMIN` role, we must grant other role privileges to this virtual warehouse. Which roles you grant privileges to will be dependent on your requirements. In this case, we will grant `USAGE` privileges to the `PUBLIC` role so that any user in the reader account can use the virtual warehouse. We will also grant `ALL` privileges in the virtual warehouse to the `SYSADMIN` role so that the `SYSADMIN` role can manage the virtual warehouse. To do so, run the following SQL:

```
GRANT USAGE ON WAREHOUSE SP_VW TO ROLE PUBLIC;
GRANT ALL ON WAREHOUSE SP_VW TO ROLE SYSADMIN;
```

   You will see a success message stating that the statements were executed successfully.

5. We have configured the reader account with a new virtual warehouse that users in the reader account can use to run their queries. Now, we will share data from the provider account to the reader account. To do so, log back in to the provider account.
6. Create a sample table in the provider account. To do so, run the following SQL:

```
CREATE DATABASE CUSTOMER_DATA;
CREATE TABLE STORE_SALES AS
SELECT * FROM SNOWFLAKE_SAMPLE_DATA.TPCDS_SF10TCL.STORE_SALES
LIMIT 1000;
```

   You will see a success message stating that the table was created successfully.

7. Now, we will create a secure view on top of the `STORE_SALES` table. Please note that it is not possible to share data through a standard view, and you must create a secure view if you need to share. To do so, run the following SQL:

```
USE DATABASE CUSTOMER_DATA;
CREATE OR REPLACE SECURE VIEW STORE_SALES_AGG
AS
SELECT SS_SOLD_DATE_SK,SUM(SS_NET_PROFIT) AS SS_NET_PROFIT
FROM CUSTOMER_DATA.PUBLIC.STORE_SALES
GROUP BY 1;
```

8. Let's now create a share object. To do so, run the following SQL:

```
USE ROLE ACCOUNTADMIN;
CREATE SHARE share_sales_data;
```

You should see a success message stating that the share was created successfully.

9. Next, we will perform the necessary grants to include the objects in the share. To do so, run the following SQL:

```
GRANT USAGE ON DATABASE CUSTOMER_DATA TO SHARE share_sales_data;
GRANT USAGE ON SCHEMA CUSTOMER_DATA.public TO SHARE
share_sales_data;
GRANT SELECT ON VIEW CUSTOMER_DATA.PUBLIC.STORE_SALES_AGG
TO SHARE share_sales_data;
```

Each of the preceding `GRANT` statements should execute successfully.

10. We will now share the data with the reader account. To do so, run the following SQL and use the `accountName` value that you noted in *step 1*:

```
ALTER SHARE share_sales_data ADD ACCOUNT=<reader_account_name_here>;
```

You should see the preceding statement execute successfully.

11. Now, log back in to the reader account using the URL that you noted down in *step 1*. Once inside the reader account, create a new database from the share object. To do so, run the following SQL:

```
USE ROLE ACCOUNTADMIN;
CREATE DATABASE SALES FROM SHARE
<provider_account_name_here>.share_sales_data;
```

We should be able to select from the view in the database created from the share. To do so, run the following SQL:

```
SELECT * FROM SALES.PUBLIC.STORE_SALES_AGG;
```

This should run successfully with the following results:

SS_SOLD_DATE_SK	SS_NET_PROFIT
2451154	-928455.27

Figure 7.19 – Selecting from the shared secure view

With this last step, the process of sharing to a non-Snowflake user is complete.

How it works...

Snowflake provides various methods for sharing data, including sharing with other Snowflake customers, and sharing with non-Snowflake customers. While sharing with another Snowflake customer is a straightforward process, it is slightly more involved for a non-Snowflake customer.

When sharing with a non-Snowflake customer, you need a mechanism to allow them to log in to Snowflake. This is done by creating a new reader account, which, as the name suggests, is mainly for reading the shared data. A reader account can be thought of as a child account and, as such, it consumes the compute resources of its parent account. The reader account must be set up with a new virtual warehouse to allow the execution of queries.

Once the reader account is all set up, sharing data is relatively straightforward and simply requires the reader's account name. The account name is used in the sharing statement to enable sharing. In this recipe, we shared data through a view rather than a table. Snowflake doesn't support sharing data from a standard view, but instead requires the creation of a secure view.

Keeping costs in check when sharing data with non-Snowflake users

Snowflake allows data to be shared not only with other Snowflake accounts but also with organizations that do not yet operate their own Snowflake environment. In these scenarios, access to shared data is provided through a reader account. A reader account is created and managed by the data provider and enables external users to access shared data through a Snowflake-managed environment without requiring their own Snowflake deployment. Because reader accounts execute queries using the provider's compute resources, the compute costs generated by those queries are billed to the Snowflake account that created the reader account.

In this recipe, you will learn how to manage and limit the compute costs associated with reader accounts so that data can be shared with non-Snowflake users while keeping compute usage predictable and under control.

Getting ready

You will need to be connected to your Snowflake instance via Snowsight or another SQL client to execute this recipe. This recipe assumes that the Reader Account created in the previous recipe is already configured and that a virtual warehouse named SP_VW exists to support queries executed by users in the Reader Account.

The steps in this recipe are performed within the Reader Account rather than the provider account because the resource monitor will be used to control compute consumption generated by users of the Reader Account.

Since resource monitors are account-level objects, you must use the ACCOUNTADMIN role to complete the steps in this recipe.

How to do it...

To limit the compute costs associated with a Reader Account, connect to the Reader Account and log in using a user with the ACCOUNTADMIN role. We will then create a resource monitor and attach it to the warehouse used by that account. The steps for this recipe are as follows:

1. We first switch to the `ACCOUNTADMIN` role:

```
USE ROLE ACCOUNTADMIN;
```

Next, create a resource monitor that will limit the number of credits that can be consumed during a given period:

```
CREATE RESOURCE MONITOR RM_READER_ACCOUNT
WITH
  CREDIT_QUOTA = 100
  FREQUENCY = MONTHLY
  START_TIMESTAMP = IMMEDIATELY
  TRIGGERS
    ON 80 PERCENT DO NOTIFY
    ON 100 PERCENT DO SUSPEND;
```

> **Note**
>
> This resource monitor limits compute consumption to 100 credits per month. When usage reaches 80% of the quota, Snowflake generates a notification. When 100% of the quota is reached, the monitor suspends the warehouse to prevent further credit consumption.

2. After creating the resource monitor, attach it to the warehouse used by the reader account:

```
ALTER WAREHOUSE SP_VW
SET RESOURCE_MONITOR = RM_READER_ACCOUNT;
```

By attaching the resource monitor to the warehouse, all compute activity executed through that warehouse will count toward the defined credit quota.

3. To verify that the resource monitor was created successfully, run the following command:

```
SHOW RESOURCE MONITORS;
```

This should run successfully with the following results:

A name	A credit_quota	A used_credits	A remaining_credits	A level	A frequency
RM_READER_ACCOUNT	100.00	0.00	100.00	WAREHOUSE	MONTHLY

Figure 7.20 – Results from show resource monitors

4. You can also verify that the warehouse is associated with the monitor by running the following command:

```
SHOW WAREHOUSES LIKE 'SP_VW';
```

The output will show the `RESOURCE_MONITOR` column indicating the monitor assigned to the warehouse.

A resource_monitor	# actives	# pendings	# failed	# suspended	A uuid	A se
RM_READER_ACCOUNT	0	0	0	2	596791124	STAN

Figure 7.21 – Results from show warehouses

Snowflake will now continuously track credit consumption against the defined quota and enforce the configured actions when thresholds are reached.

How it works...

When sharing data with a non-Snowflake customer, a reader account provides the mechanism for that customer to access Snowflake without maintaining their own Snowflake environment. A reader account can be thought of as a child account that operates within the provider's Snowflake environment. Because reader accounts use the provider's compute resources, all query processing costs are billed to the parent account.

Without controls in place, users in the reader account could run large or inefficient queries that consume significant compute resources. Resource monitors provide a mechanism to control this consumption by defining a credit quota over a specified time period.

In this recipe, we created a resource monitor with a monthly credit quota and attached it to the `SP_VW` warehouse used by the reader account. As queries run against that warehouse, Snowflake tracks credit consumption against the defined quota. When the configured threshold is reached, Snowflake automatically executes the specified action, in this case suspending the warehouse, to prevent additional credit usage.

Using resource monitors allows data providers to safely share data with external users while maintaining predictable and controlled compute costs.

Publishing a data share to the Snowflake Internal Marketplace

Snowflake Secure Data Sharing allows organizations to share data directly between Snowflake accounts without copying or transferring the underlying data. Earlier in this chapter, you explored how to share data directly with other Snowflake accounts and how to provide access to non-Snowflake users through reader accounts.

As organizations grow, managing large numbers of direct shares can become difficult. To address this challenge, Snowflake provides the Internal Marketplace, which allows organizations to publish datasets as internal data products that can be discovered and installed by other accounts within the same Snowflake organization.

Internal Marketplace listings allow data providers to publish governed datasets while making them easily discoverable across teams. Instead of manually configuring shares between accounts, consumers can browse the Internal Marketplace and install the datasets they need.

In this recipe, you will publish an existing data share as an Internal Marketplace listing, allowing other Snowflake accounts in your organization to discover and install the dataset.

Getting ready

You should be connected to your Snowflake account using Snowsight.

This recipe reuses the share `share_trx_data`, which was created earlier in this chapter in the recipe *Sharing a table with another Snowflake account*. That share will be used as the data source for the Internal Marketplace listing.

To create organizational listings in the Snowflake Internal Marketplace, you must use the `ACCOUNTADMIN` role (or a role with equivalent privileges).

Your Snowflake account must also belong to a Snowflake organization, which enables the Internal Marketplace capability.

How to do it...

To publish a data share as a private Snowflake Marketplace listing, perform the following steps. Run the following command:

1. First, ensure you are using the `ACCOUNTADMIN` role.

```
USE ROLE ACCOUNTADMIN;
```

2. We will need to verify that the share created earlier in the chapter exists.

```
SHOW SHARES;
```

Locate `SHARE_TRX_DATA` in the results.

3. Confirm that the share contains the expected objects. To do so, run the following command:

```
SHOW GRANTS TO SHARE SHARE_TRX_DATA;
```

This command returns the database objects that have been granted access to the share.

	created_on	privilege	granted_on	name	granted_to
1	2026-03-11 15:47	USAGE	DATABASE	C7_R1	SHARE
2	2026-03-11 15:47	USAGE	SCHEMA	C7_R1.PUBLIC	SHARE
3	2026-03-11 15:48	SELECT	TABLE	C7_R1.PUBLIC.TRANSACTIONS	SHARE

Figure 7.22 – Results from share grants

4. Open Snowsight and navigate to **Catalog** -> **Internal Marketplace**.

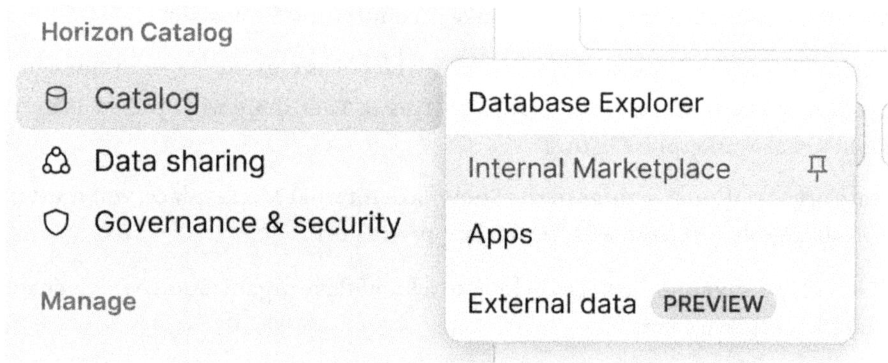

Figure 7.23 – Snowsight menu to Internal Marketplace

5. Select **+ Create listing** to begin creating a new internal listing.

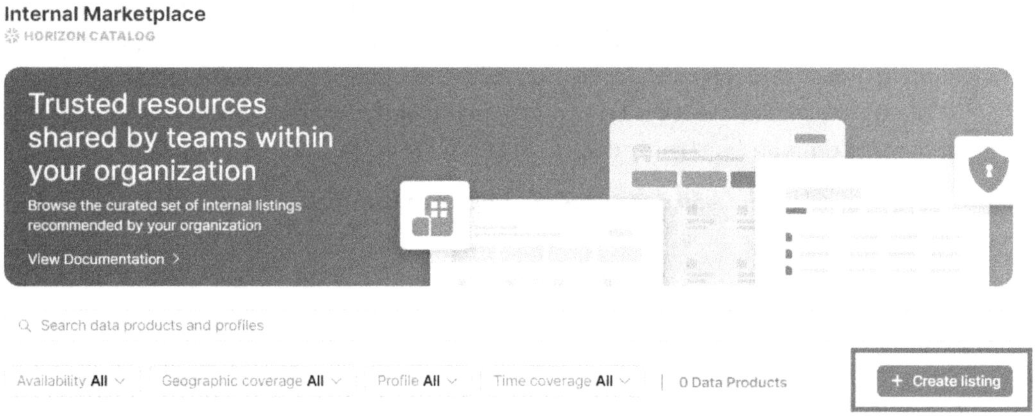

Figure 7.24 – Create Listing button

6. When prompted for the **Listing title**, enter the following value: `Transaction Data Sample`, and click **Save**.

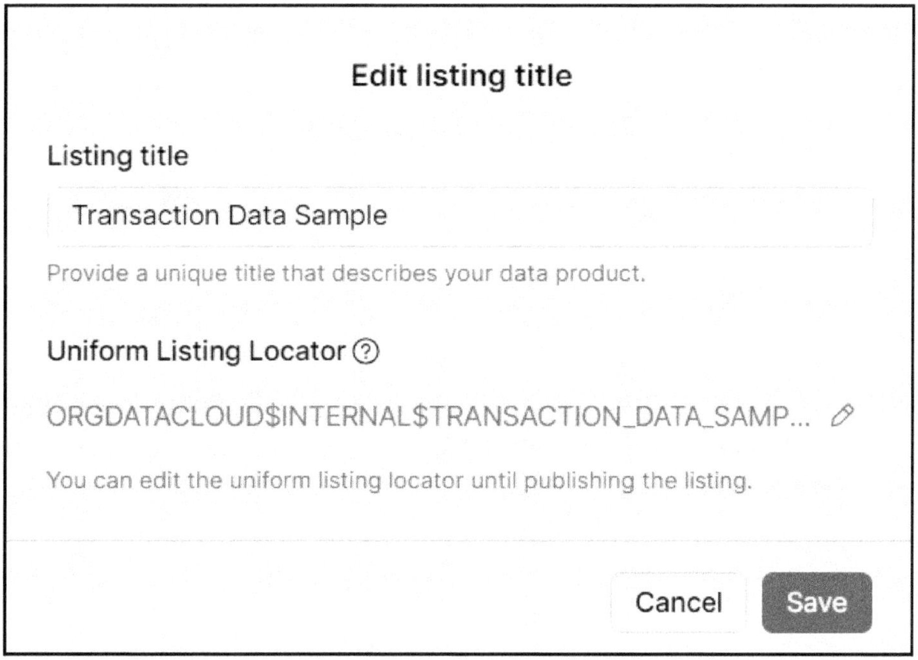

Figure 7.25 – Listing name

7. This will bring you to the Internal Marketplace listing page. Here you can configure additional information for the listing. Set the **Description** to the following: Sample transaction dataset shared internally through the Snowflake Internal Marketplace. This dataset contains example transaction records used for demonstrations and internal analytics experimentation.

8. Locate and select the **Add data product** button in the upper-right corner.

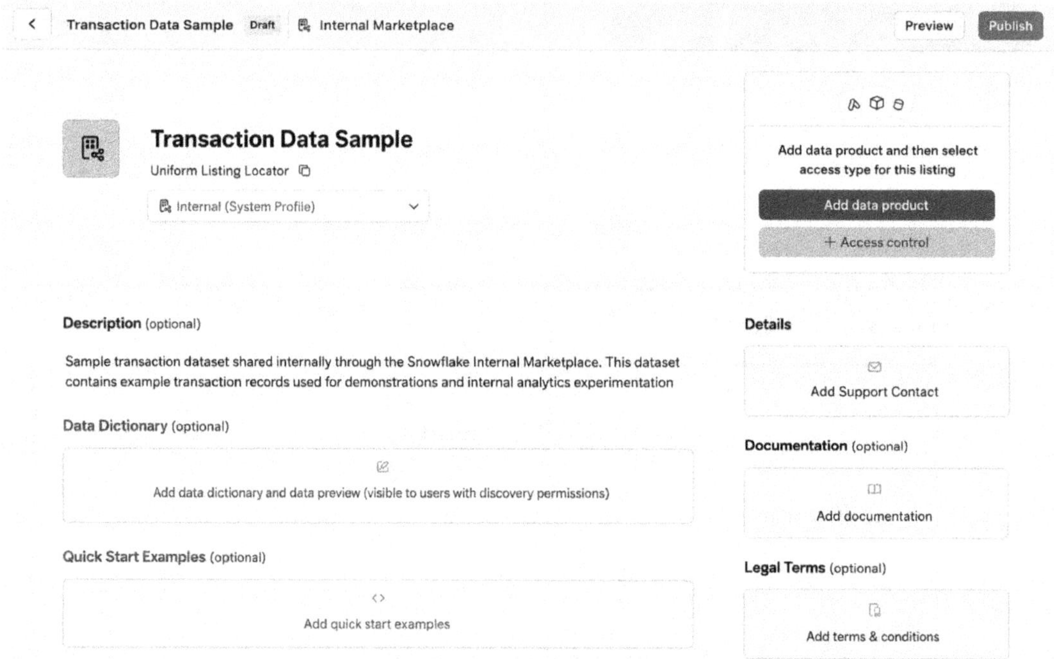

Figure 7.26 – Internal Marketplace Listing page

9. Select the data product to add. For this recipe, select the **TRANSACTIONS** table located in the **PUBLIC** schema of the **C7_R1** database. After selecting the table, click **Done**, and then select **Save**.

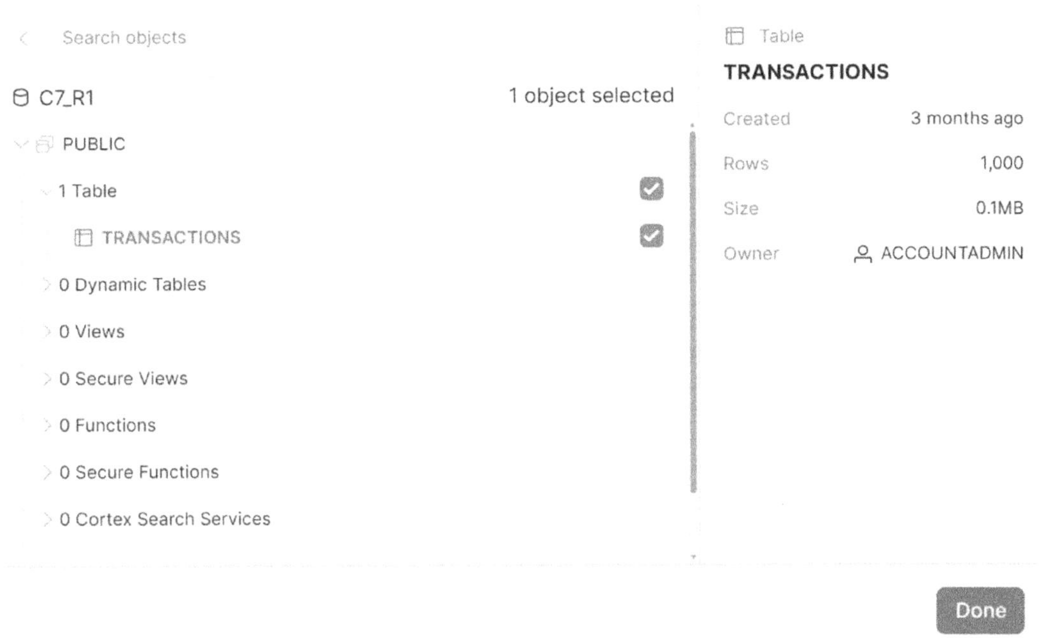

Figure 7.27 – Selecting the data product

10. Next, configure access to the listing. Select the **+ Access control** button to define which accounts can discover and access the listing.

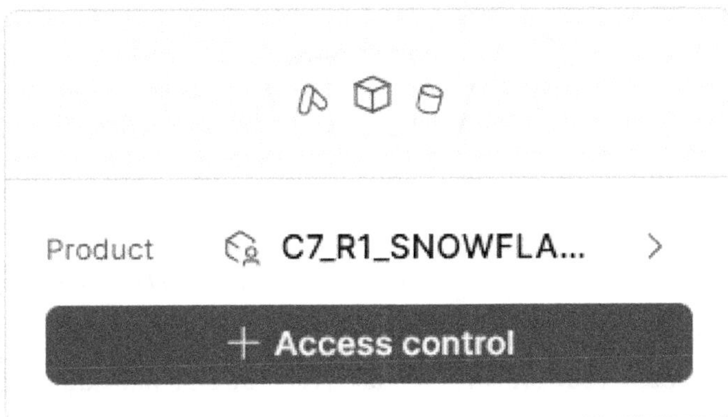

Figure 7.28 – Access Control button

11. Choose who can access the data product and who can discover it. You may select an entire organization or selected accounts and roles. For this recipe, select the account you are currently using. You may use the same selection for **Allow discovery**.

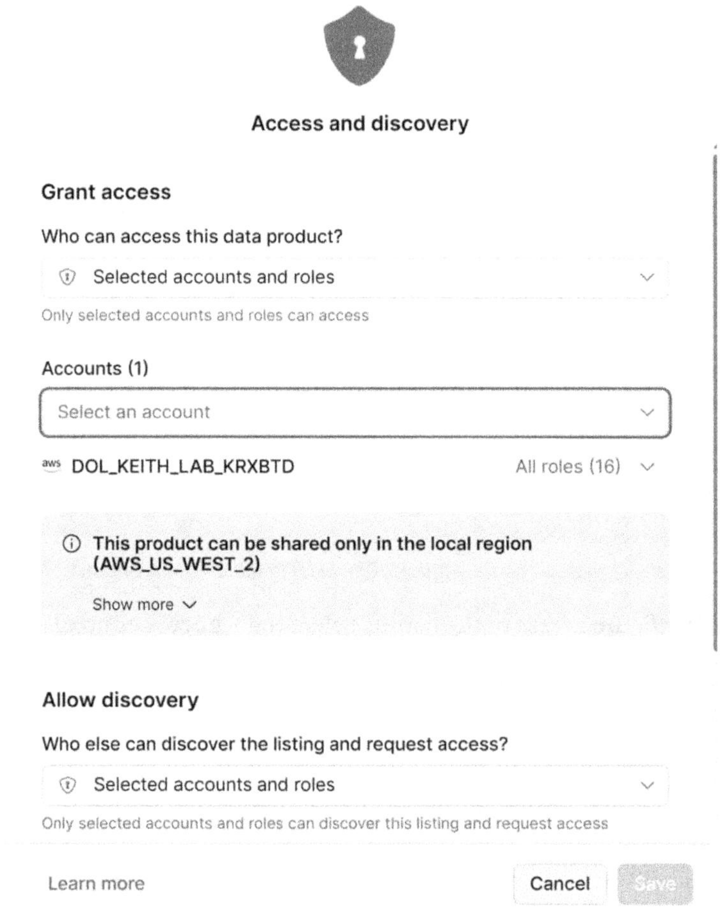

Figure 7.29 – Setting access and discovery

12. To complete the access configuration, you must also define the request approval flow. Select **Manage requests** in Snowflake, provide an email address for notifications, and select the roles that are allowed to approve requests. For this recipe, select the **ACCOUNTADMIN** role and then click **Done**.

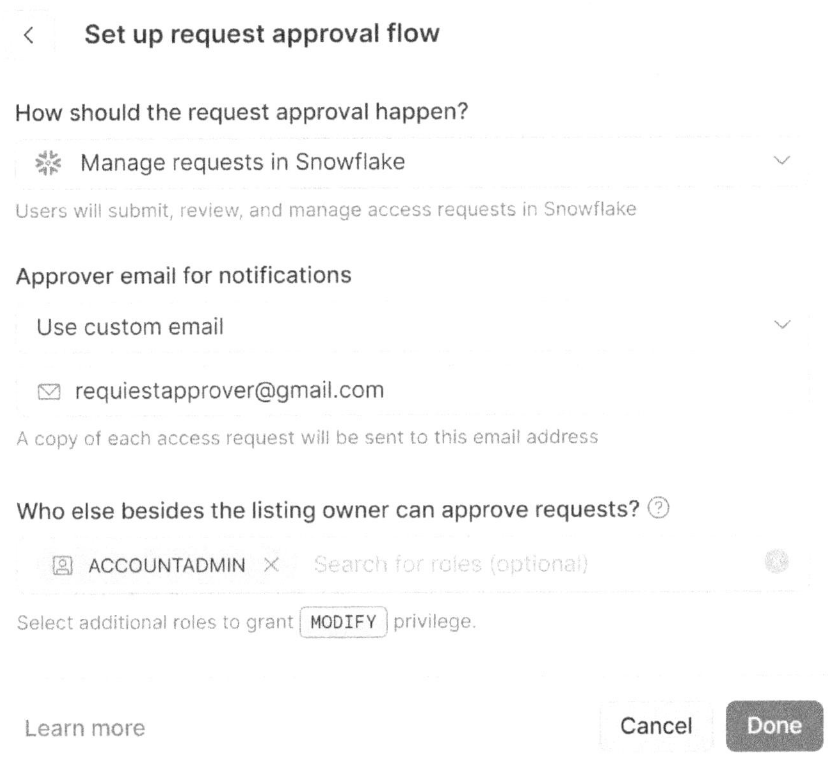

Figure 7.30 – Set up request approval flow

Before the listing can be published, all required fields must be completed. The remaining required field is **Support contact**. Select **Add Support Contact** and provide an email address that consumers can use if they require assistance.

Figure 7.31 – Adding a support contact

13. After all required information has been provided, the **Publish** button becomes available in the upper-right corner. Click **Publish** to publish the listing.

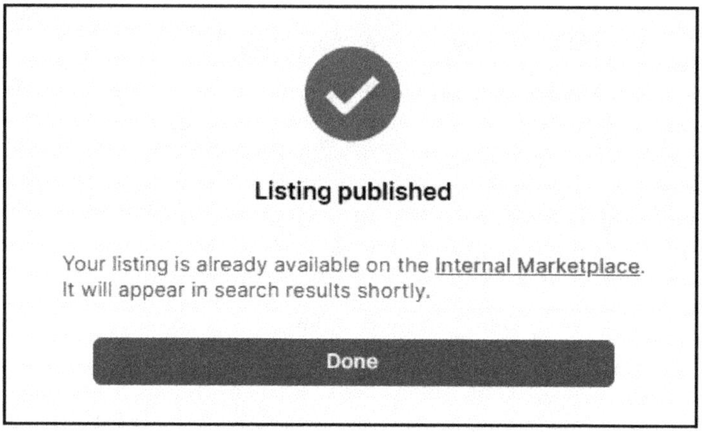

Figure 7.32 – Listing published

14. You can now navigate back to **Catalog** -> **Internal Marketplace** to see the published listing as it appears in the Internal Marketplace.

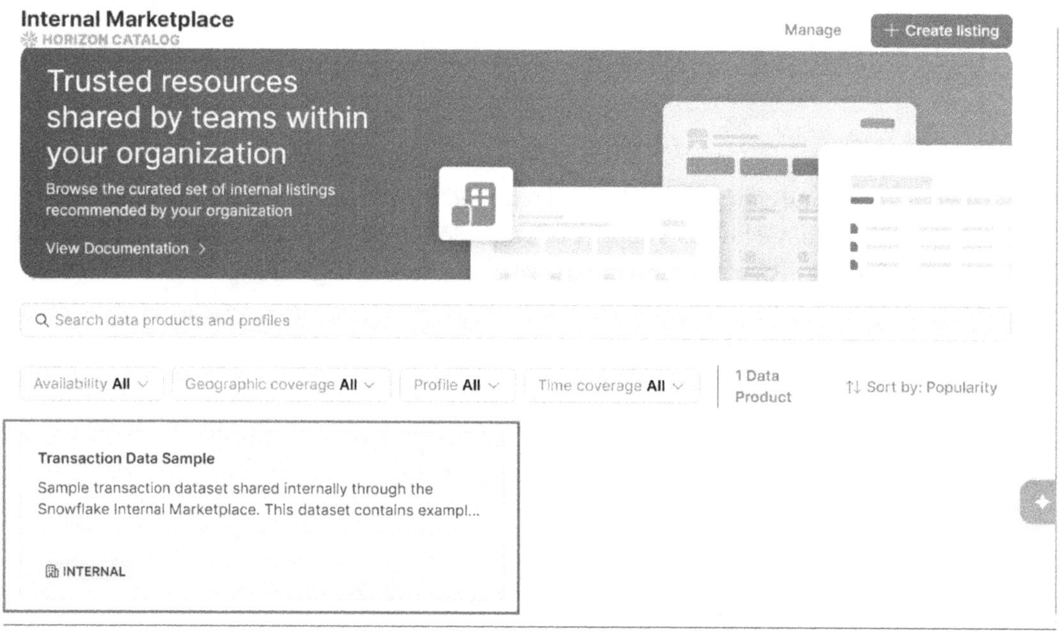

Figure 7.33 – Marketplace Listing

How it works...

The Snowflake Internal Marketplace provides a structured way for organizations to distribute data products across accounts within the same Snowflake organization. Instead of manually configuring direct shares between accounts, providers can publish datasets as listings that are discoverable through the Internal Marketplace.

Under the hood, Marketplace listings are built on top of Snowflake's Secure Data Sharing architecture. The listing created in this recipe references the existing share `SHARE_TRX_DATA`, which was created earlier in the chapter. The share still controls the actual data access, while the listing provides the metadata and discovery mechanism that allows other accounts to find and request access to the dataset.

When a consumer installs the listing from the Internal Marketplace, Snowflake automatically creates a database in the consumer account that references the provider's shared data. Queries executed against that database are processed in the consumer account, but the data itself remains in the provider account. This means that the provider maintains full control over the underlying data while consumers always access the most current version.

After installing the listing, the consumer can locate the newly created database in Snowsight and query the shared data just as they would any other Snowflake database. For example:

```
SELECT *
FROM <installed_database>.PUBLIC.TRANSACTIONS
LIMIT 10;
```

The database name will depend on the name chosen during the installation process. Although the consumer queries the data using standard SQL, the underlying data remains in the provider account and is not copied into the consumer account.

The Internal Marketplace also introduces governance capabilities that go beyond traditional direct shares. Providers can control which accounts can discover the listing, who is allowed to request access, and which roles can approve those requests. This allows organizations to safely distribute curated datasets across departments while maintaining centralized control and visibility.

By publishing a dataset through the Internal Marketplace, organizations can move from ad-hoc sharing to a data product model, where governed datasets are cataloged, documented, and discoverable across the enterprise.

Get this book's PDF version and more

Scan the QR code (or go to packtpub.com/unlock). Search for this book by name, confirm the edition, and then follow the steps on the page.

UNLOCK NOW

Note: Keep your invoice handy. Purchases made directly from Packt don't require an invoice.

8

Back to the Future with Time Travel

Dealing with data issues is never a pleasant task, especially when it is unclear when data was changed or whether it has been lost altogether. Snowflake provides a powerful capability to address these challenges through its Time Travel feature, which allows you to access historical data and recover from unintended changes.

In this chapter, we explore how Time Travel can be used to investigate and recover from data issues, and how it can be combined with cloning to simplify debugging and environment management.

The following topics will be covered in this chapter:

- Using Time Travel to return to the state of data at a particular time
- Using Time Travel to recover from the accidental loss of table data
- Identifying dropped databases, tables, and other objects and restoring them using Time Travel
- Using Time Travel in conjunction with cloning to improve debugging
- Using cloning to set up new environments based on the production environment rapidly
- Managing Time Travel and cloning retention policies for governance

Technical requirements

This chapter requires access to a modern internet browser (Chrome, Edge, Firefox, and so on) and access to the internet to connect to your Snowflake instance in the cloud.

You can download the example project and code for this book by following the instructions in the ***Download the example code files*** section in the *Preface* of this book.

Using Time Travel to return to the state of data at a particular time

In this recipe, we will use Snowflake's Time Travel feature to query a table as it existed at a specific point in time. Unlike recovering data after it has been modified or restoring objects that have been dropped, Time Travel can also be used to inspect historical versions of data without making any changes to the underlying table. This capability is useful for troubleshooting, auditing, and validating how data looked before a change occurred.

Getting ready

You will need to be connected to your Snowflake instance via Snowsight to execute this recipe.

How to do it...

We will create a table and populate that table with some sample data. Further on in the recipe, we will run an update on this table and demonstrate how to recover to a point before the data was updated. The steps are as follows:

1. We will create a new database, followed by creating a table containing some sample customer data. We will use sample data provided by Snowflake to populate this table. To do so, run the following SQL:

```
USE ROLE SYSADMIN;
USE WAREHOUSE DEFAULT_WH;

CREATE DATABASE C8_R1;
CREATE TABLE CUSTOMER AS
SELECT * FROM SNOWFLAKE_SAMPLE_DATA.TPCDS_SF10TCL.
  CUSTOMER
LIMIT 100000;
```

2. Let's validate that data has successfully been populated in the customer table. To do so, run the following SQL:

```
SELECT * FROM CUSTOMER LIMIT 100;
```

You should see a result similar to the following:

C_CUSTOMER_	C_CUSTOMER_IID	C_CURRENT_CD	C_CURRENT_HD	C_CURRENT_AD	C_FIRST_SHIPT	C_FIRST_SALES_	C_SALUTATION	C_FIRST_NAME	C_LAST_NAME	C_PREFERRED_
18891201	AAAAAAAAB...	1672603	1484	7455518	2451793	2451763	Miss	Edna	Figueroa	N
18891202	AAAAAAAAA...	1664822	3607	10618745	2450648	2450618	Dr.	Helen	Estes	Y
18891203	AAAAAAAA...	909382	1243	18451857	2452041	2452011	Sir	William	Unger	N
18891204	AAAAAAAE...	1833396	4666	13386336	2449280	2449250	Mr.	Charles	Reed	N

Figure 8.1 – Validating the customer table data

3. Make a note of the current time before running an update on the customer table. We will use this timestamp to see the data as it existed before our update:

```
SELECT CURRENT_TIMESTAMP;
```

You should see the result shown in the following screenshot. Copy the timestamp value somewhere as we will use it later in the recipe:

CURRENT_TIMESTAMP
2026-03-23 15:42:00.241 -0700

Figure 8.2 – Viewing the current timestamp

4. Let's now run `UPDATE` on the customer table. We will update the email address column for all rows. To do so, run the following SQL:

```
UPDATE CUSTOMER SET C_EMAIL_ADDRESS = 'john.doe@gmail.com';
```

5. Validate that the email address column has indeed been updated for the whole table. To do so, run the following SQL:

```
SELECT DISTINCT C_EMAIL_ADDRESS FROM CUSTOMER;
```

You should see the result shown in the following screenshot:

Row	C_EMAIL_ADDRESS
1	john.doe@gmail.com

Figure 8.3 – A single distinct value for the email address after the update

6. We will now use Snowflake's Time Travel functionality to view the data as it existed before the update. We will use the timestamp and the AT syntax to travel back to how the table's data looked at or before a specific time. To do that, run the following SQL:

```
SELECT DISTINCT C_EMAIL_ADDRESS
FROM CUSTOMER AT
(TIMESTAMP => '2026-03-23 16:03:42.696 -0700'::TIMESTAMP_LTZ);
```

You will see that almost 100,000 email addresses will be returned (rather than a single email address as in the previous step). The result should look similar to the following:

C_EMAIL_ADDRESS
Melinda.Mcdonald@S2y6OCshd.edu
Glenda.Gomez@Fyig2tnhFYdRf.edu
Mason.Roberts@iGC20e1MPvLR.edu
Bobby.Presley@L8QuISIHHc.org

Figure 8.4 – Email address data before the update was run

This indicates that we have been able to view the table's data through Time Travel as it existed before the UPDATE query was run.

7. If needed, you can now select all rows from the table and use them in various ways as per your requirements. To do that, run the following SQL:

```
SELECT *
FROM CUSTOMER AT
(TIMESTAMP => '2026-03-23 16:03:42.696 -0700'::timestamp_tz);
```

8. The AT syntax in Time Travel is handy when you know the exact timestamp you would like to travel to. However, if you are not 100% sure when the update was made, you can

use the `BEFORE` syntax and provide an approximate timestamp. To do so, run the following SQL:

```
SELECT *
FROM CUSTOMER before
(TIMESTAMP => '2026-03-23 16:03:42.696 -0700'::timestamp_tz);
```

Notice that the timestamp we have provided corresponds to the approximate time at which the `UPDATE` statement was executed. As a result of the SQL, you should see an output similar to the following screenshot (note that you may see only one updated email address if the timestamp you provided is not correct; in that case, gradually move the timestamp back by one minute at a time until all the email addresses are returned):

C_EMAIL_ADDRESS
Conrad.Samuels@KLbidv1dROr3z0E.com
Juana.Hahn@8J2HH2eEps.edu
Garrett.Roderick@iES5pM7NOCQ.edu
James.Jenkins@vmmD8NIGAyGEa.org

Figure 8.5 – Data before a particular timestamp

The preceding steps show how you can undo the effects of `UPDATE` statements by restoring the data to how it existed at a specific point in time.

How it works...

In this recipe, we used the `AT` and `BEFORE` syntax to retrieve historical data at or before a specific timestamp through an SQL extension referred to as **Time Travel**. Time Travel provides the capability to access data that has been historically changed or deleted. It enables users to access and restore changes to data in tables, schemas, and databases. The functionality even allows restoring complete databases and schemas after they may have been dropped.

Snowflake achieves this powerful feature by retaining a copy of changed or deleted data for a specified period. Snowflake tracks this copy of data through the metadata it maintains for each table and object. When a Time Travel query is executed, the Snowflake query engine can search through metadata to access and retrieve the historical data.

By default, when you make changes to a permanent table's data, historical data is retained for one day. However, in Enterprise Edition and higher, you can set the retention to be up to 90 days, allowing you to undo, access or restore changes up to 90 days in the past.

Using Time Travel to recover from the accidental loss of table data

This recipe will go through a scenario of accidental data loss after a `DELETE` query has been executed, affecting data in a table. We will demonstrate how we can recover data after it has been deleted accidentally.

Getting ready

You will need to be connected to your Snowflake instance via Snowsight to execute this recipe.

How to do it…

We will create a table and populate that table with some sample data. Further on in the recipe, we will run `DELETE` on this table and demonstrate how to recover to a point before the data was deleted. The steps for this recipe are as follows:

1. Create a new database and then create a table containing sample customer data. We will use sample data provided by Snowflake to populate this table. To do so, run the following SQL:

```
CREATE DATABASE C8_R2;
CREATE TABLE CUSTOMER AS
SELECT * FROM SNOWFLAKE_SAMPLE_DATA.TPCDS_SF10TCL.
  CUSTOMER
LIMIT 100000;
```

2. Let's validate that data has successfully been populated in the customer table. To do so, run the following SQL:

```
SELECT * FROM CUSTOMER LIMIT 100;
```

You should see a result similar to the following:

C_CUSTOMER_	C_CUSTOMER_ID	C_CURRENT_CD	C_CURRENT_HD	C_CURRENT_ADDR	C_FIRST_SHIPTO	C_FIRST_SALES_	C_SALUTATION	C_FIRST_NAME	C_LAST_NAME	C_PREFERRED_
18891201	AAAAAAAAAB...	1672603	1484	7455518	2451793	2451763	Miss	Edna	Figueroa	N
18891202	AAAAAAAAAA...	1664822	3607	10618745	2450648	2450618	Dr.	Helen	Estes	Y
18891203	AAAAAAAAA...	909382	1243	18451857	2452041	2452011	Sir	William	Unger	N
18891204	AAAAAAAAAE...	1833396	4666	13386336	2449280	2449250	Mr.	Charles	Reed	N

Figure 8.6 – Validating the data in the customer table

3. Let's now simulate an accidental DELETE on the customer table. To do so, run the following SQL:

```
DELETE FROM CUSTOMER;
```

The command should run successfully without any errors.

4. Validate that all rows from the table have been deleted. To do so, run the following SQL:

```
SELECT * FROM CUSTOMER;
```

No rows will be returned as a result of the preceding query.

5. We will first query the query history to identify which query deleted all the rows. To do so, run the following SQL:

```
SELECT QUERY_ID, QUERY_TEXT, DATABASE_NAME, SCHEMA_NAME,
  QUERY_TYPE
FROM TABLE(INFORMATION_SCHEMA.QUERY_HISTORY())
WHERE QUERY_TYPE = 'DELETE'
AND EXECUTION_STATUS = 'SUCCESS'
AND DATABASE_NAME = 'C8_R2';
```

This query returns all successfully executed DELETE queries that were executed successfully on the C8_R2 database. An example result is shown in the following screenshot. Make a note of the value(s) in the QUERY_ID column as we will use these value(s) in the next step:

QUERY_ID	QUERY_TEXT	DATABASE_NAME	SCHEMA_NAME	QUERY_TYPE
019825cd-0438-0033-0000-002fd30330bd	DELETE FROM CUSTOMER;	C8_R2	PUBLIC	DELETE

Figure 8.7 – Querying the query history

6. Let's now use Snowflake's Time Travel functionality to view the data as it existed before the `DELETE` query was run. We will use the timestamp and the `BEFORE` syntax to travel back to how the table looked before the `DELETE` query was executed. To do that, run the following SQL:

```
SELECT *
FROM CUSTOMER BEFORE
(STATEMENT => '019825cd-0438-0033-0000-002fd30330bd');
```

You will see that all 100,000 rows will be returned rather than an empty table. The result will be like what is shown here:

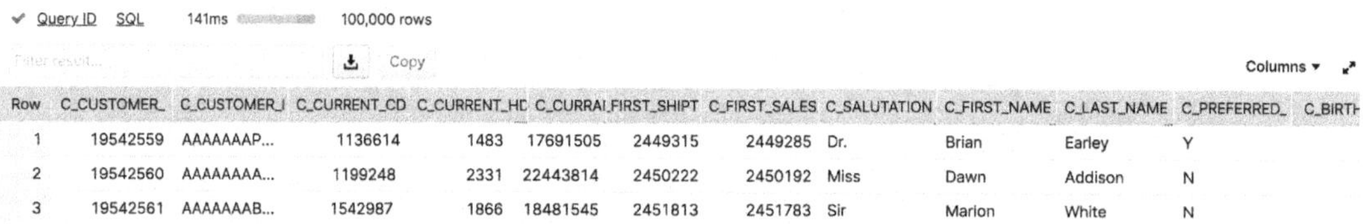

Query ID SQL 141ms 100,000 rows

Row	C_CUSTOMER_	C_CUSTOMER_I	C_CURRENT_CD	C_CURRENT_HC	C_CURRAI	FIRST_SHIPT	C_FIRST_SALES	C_SALUTATION	C_FIRST_NAME	C_LAST_NAME	C_PREFERRED_	C_BIRTH
1	19542559	AAAAAAAP...	1136614	1483	17691505	2449315	2449285	Dr.	Brian	Earley	Y	
2	19542560	AAAAAAAA...	1199248	2331	22443814	2450222	2450192	Miss	Dawn	Addison	N	
3	19542561	AAAAAAAB...	1542987	1866	18481545	2451813	2451783	Sir	Marion	White	N	

Figure 8.8 – Viewing the data before the DELETE query was run

This indicates that we have been able to view the table's data through Time Travel as it existed before the `DELETE` query was run.

> **Note**
>
> You should replace the query ID in the preceding statement with the query ID of the statement you would have run.

7. You can now undo the `DELETE` action by reinserting this data into the table by using Time Travel. To do that, run the following SQL:

```
INSERT INTO CUSTOMER
SELECT *
FROM CUSTOMER BEFORE
(STATEMENT => '019825cd-0438-0033-0000-002fd30330bd');
```

8. Validate that the data has indeed been restored by running the following SQL:

```
SELECT * FROM CUSTOMER;
```

You should see 100,000 rows returned as a result of the preceding query. The results are as shown:

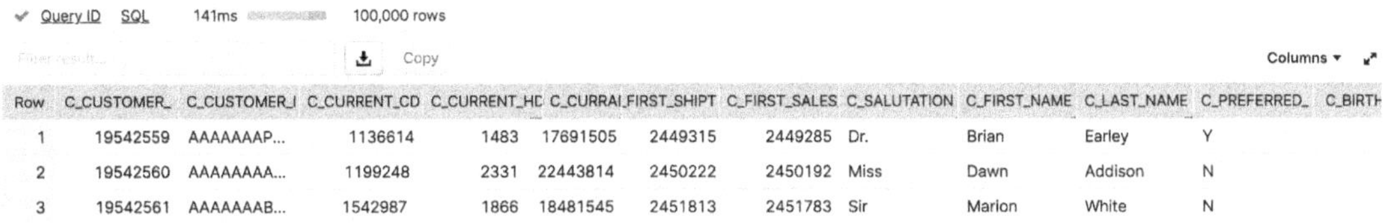

Row	C_CUSTOMER_	C_CUSTOMER_I	C_CURRENT_CD	C_CURRENT_HD	C_CURRAI	FIRST_SHIPT	C_FIRST_SALES	C_SALUTATION	C_FIRST_NAME	C_LAST_NAME	C_PREFERRED_	C_BIRTH
1	19542559	AAAAAAAP...	1136614	1483	17691505	2449315	2449285	Dr.	Brian	Earley	Y	
2	19542560	AAAAAAAA...	1199248	2331	22443814	2450222	2450192	Miss	Dawn	Addison	N	
3	19542561	AAAAAAAB...	1542987	1866	18481545	2451813	2451783	Sir	Marion	White	N	

Figure 8.9 – Validating the restored data

The preceding steps show how an erroneous SQL statement's detrimental effects may be reversed easily by restoring the data as it existed before that statement was run.

How it works...

In this recipe, we used the `STATEMENT` syntax to retrieve deleted data as it existed before the specified `DELETE` query was executed. Using this approach, we can access and retrieve data that was deleted by a `DELETE` query or retrieve data that was changed through other queries, such as `UPDATE`. The `STATEMENT` syntax accepts a `QUERY_ID` value, and returns the data as it existed before that query was executed.

Referred to as **Time Travel**, Snowflake achieves this powerful feature by retaining a copy of the modified or deleted data for a specified period of time. Snowflake tracks this data copy through the metadata it maintains for each table and object. When a Time Travel query is run, the Snowflake query engine can access and retrieve historical data via metadata.

Identifying dropped databases, tables, and other objects and restoring them using Time Travel

Time Travel can be used to recover tables, schemas, and even complete databases. In this recipe, let's look at a scenario where a database and other objects have been deleted. We will identify what has been deleted and recover them back to the previous state.

Getting ready

You will need to be connected to your Snowflake instance via Snowsight or the CLI client to execute this recipe.

How to do it...

We will first create a database, then two schemas in that database, and some tables within those schemas. We will then gradually delete the tables, schemas, and eventually the complete database. Then we will try to recover them through the Time Travel feature. The steps for this recipe are as follows:

1. Start by creating a new database, followed by a schema. To do so, run the following SQL:

```
CREATE DATABASE C8_R3;
CREATE SCHEMA SCHEMA1;
```

2. Next, create a test table called `CUSTOMER` in this schema. We will use sample data provided by Snowflake to populate this table. To do so, run the following SQL:

```
CREATE TABLE CUSTOMER AS
SELECT * FROM SNOWFLAKE_SAMPLE_DATA.TPCDS_SF10TCL.
  CUSTOMER
LIMIT 100000;
```

   You should see a success message stating that the table was created successfully.

3. Next, create another test table called `CUSTOMER_ADDRESS` in this schema. Again, use sample data provided by Snowflake to populate this table. To do so, run the following SQL:

```
CREATE TABLE CUSTOMER_ADDRESS AS
SELECT * FROM SNOWFLAKE_SAMPLE_DATA.TPCDS_SF10TCL.CUSTOMER_ADDRESS
LIMIT 100000;
```

   You should see a success message stating that the table was created successfully.

4. Next, create another schema by the name of `SCHEMA2`. To do so, run the following SQL:

```
USE DATABASE C8_R3;
CREATE SCHEMA SCHEMA2;
```

5. Next, create a test table called `INVENTORY` in this schema. Use sample data provided by Snowflake to populate this table. To do so, run the following SQL:

```
CREATE TABLE INVENTORY AS
SELECT * FROM SNOWFLAKE_SAMPLE_DATA.TPCDS_SF10TCL.INVENTORY
LIMIT 100000;
```

You should see a success message stating that the table was created successfully.

If you expand the database tree on the left pane of the Snowflake web UI, you should see the following structure of the database, schemas, and tables that we just created:

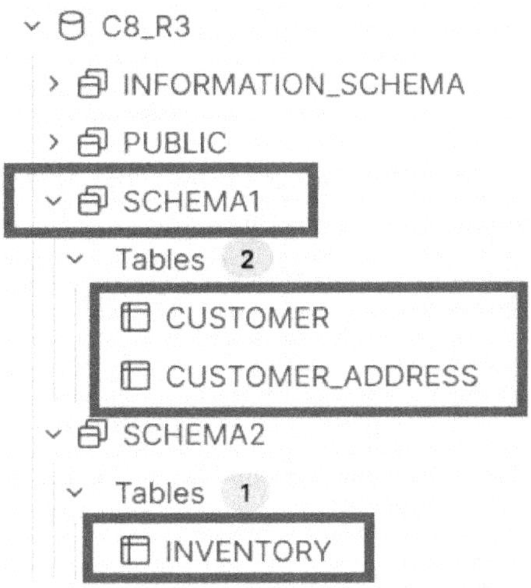

Figure 8.10 – Structure of the database, schemas, and tables

6. Let's now drop the customer table from the schema. To do so, run the following SQL:

```
USE SCHEMA SCHEMA1;
DROP TABLE CUSTOMER;
```

If you now expand and refresh the database tree on the left pane of the Snowflake web UI, you should see that the customer table is now deleted, as shown:

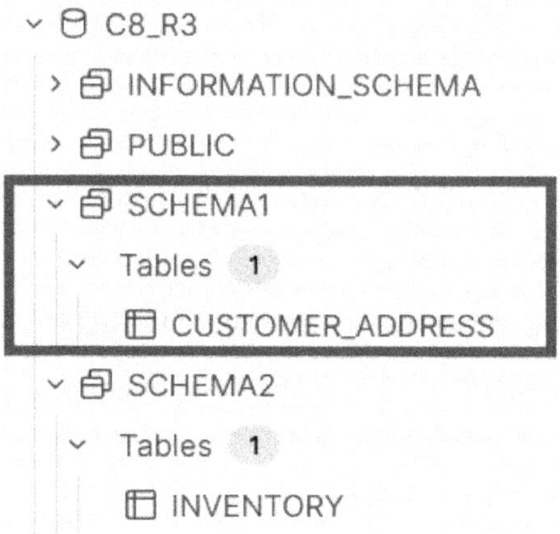

Figure 8.11 – Customer table deleted

7. If at any time you want to find out the tables that may have been dropped programmatically, you can run the following query to identify such tables:

```
USE ROLE ACCOUNTADMIN;

SELECT TABLE_CATALOG, TABLE_SCHEMA,TABLE_NAME,
ID,CLONE_GROUP_ID, TABLE_CREATED, TABLE_DROPPED
FROM INFORMATION_SCHEMA.TABLE_STORAGE_METRICS WHERE
TABLE_CATALOG = 'C8_R3';
```

This should show you all the schemas and the tables within the C8_R3 database. The result is as shown:

TABLE_NAME	ID	CLONE_GROUP_ID	TABLE_CREATED	TABLE_DROPPED
CUSTOMER	320514	320514	2026-06-13 17:08:01.927 -0700	2026-06-13 17:08:37.232 -0700
CUSTOMER_ADDRE	321538	321538	2026-06-13 17:08:16.390 -0700	null

Figure 8.12 – Schemas and tables in the C8_R3 database

Tables that have been dropped will have a non-null date value in the `TABLE_DROPPED` column.

8. Let's now restore the dropped table. To do so, simply run the following SQL:

```
USE SCHEMA SCHEMA1;
UNDROP TABLE CUSTOMER;
```

9. Validate that the table is indeed available now by running the following SQL:

```
SELECT COUNT(*) FROM CUSTOMER;
```

The query should succeed and should show 100,000 rows in the count column. This indicates that you can query the table and that the table has been restored successfully.

10. Let's now drop the whole `SCHEMA1` schema. To do so, run the following SQL:

```
DROP SCHEMA SCHEMA1;
```

If you now expand and refresh the database tree on the left pane of the Snowflake web UI, you should see that the `SCHEMA1` schema is nowhere to be seen:

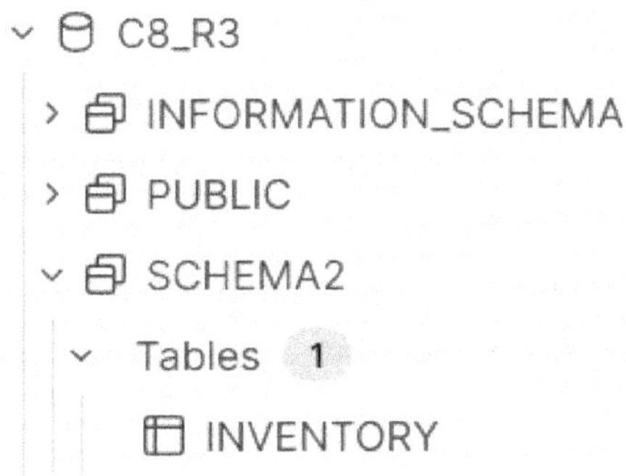

Figure 8.13 – Dropping the SCHEMA1 schema

11. Let's now restore the schema. To do so, run the following SQL:

```
UNDROP SCHEMA SCHEMA1;
```

If you now expand and refresh the database tree on the left pane of the Snowflake web UI, you should see that the `SCHEMA1` schema has reappeared along with its child tables:

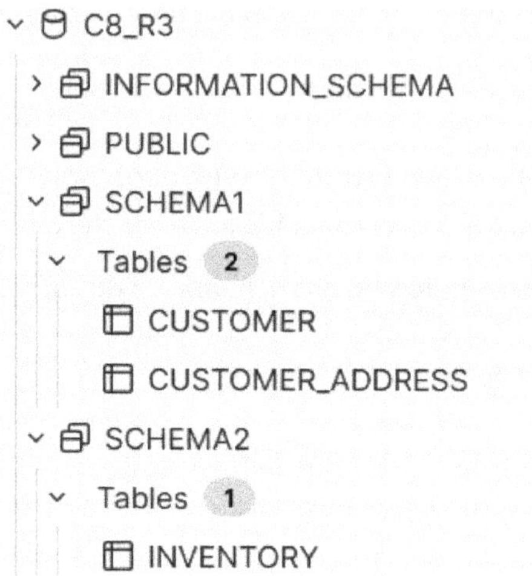

Figure 8.14 – The SCHEMA1 schema restored

You can now query the tables in that schema as usual as the schema has been restored and is available for querying.

UNDROP is not limited to just tables and schemas. Similar to how we dropped and restored a schema, you can run UNDROP on complete databases to restore them after they have been deleted.

How it works...

In Snowflake, each table is maintained in the metadata within the cloud services layer. The table's actual data is maintained in object storage (S3, Azure Blob Storage, and so on). When a table is dropped in Snowflake, it is marked as deleted in the metadata, but the table's underlying data remains. When the UNDROP command is run on a dropped table, Snowflake changes the table's deleted status back to undeleted, in effect restoring the table immediately.

Using Time Travel in conjunction with cloning to improve debugging

Often, debugging data issues requires restoring data to a point and rerunning the process. It is typically required in traditional databases to make an actual copy of your production system's data. Additionally, if you require data as it existed at a specific time or in a specific state, it is almost impossible to achieve that without significant effort. The Snowflake Time Travel feature combined with cloning simplifies that process. In this recipe, we will create a clone of a complete database at a point in time so that the development team can use the cloned version to validate and debug their code.

Getting ready

You will need to be connected to your Snowflake instance via Snowsight or the CLI client to execute this recipe.

How to do it...

We will create a database, two schemas, and then some tables within those schemas. We will then add some sample data in these tables, followed by inserting additional sample data into the tables. Then we will create a clone of this database. The steps are as follows:

1. Create a new database called PRODUCTION_DB, representing a database that contains production data. Also create a schema called SRC_DATA, which represents raw data from source systems. To do so, run the following SQL:

```
CREATE DATABASE PRODUCTION_DB;
CREATE SCHEMA SRC_DATA;
```

   The command should succeed with a success message.

2. Next, create a test table called INVENTORY in this schema. We will use sample data provided by Snowflake to populate this table. To do so, run the following SQL:

```
CREATE TABLE INVENTORY AS
SELECT * FROM SNOWFLAKE_SAMPLE_DATA.TPCDS_SF10TCL.INVENTORY
LIMIT 100000;
```

   You should see a success message stating that the table was created successfully.

3. Next, create another test table called ITEM in this schema. Again, use sample data provided by Snowflake to populate this table. To do so, run the following SQL:

```
CREATE TABLE ITEM AS
SELECT * FROM SNOWFLAKE_SAMPLE_DATA.TPCDS_SF10TCL.ITEM
LIMIT 100000;
```

   You should see a success message stating that the table was created successfully.

4. Next, create another schema by the name of ACCESS_LAYER. To do so, run the following SQL:

```
USE DATABASE PRODUCTION_DB;
CREATE SCHEMA ACCESS_LAYER;
```

The commands should succeed with a success message.

5. Next, create a test table called `STORE_SALES` in this schema. We will use sample data provided by Snowflake to populate this table. To do so, run the following SQL:

```
CREATE TABLE STORE_SALES AS
SELECT * FROM SNOWFLAKE_SAMPLE_DATA.TPCDS_SF10TCL.STORE_SALES
LIMIT 100000;
```

You should see a success message stating that the table was created successfully.

6. If you expand the database tree on the Snowflake web UI's left pane, you should see the following structure of the database, schemas, and tables that we just created:

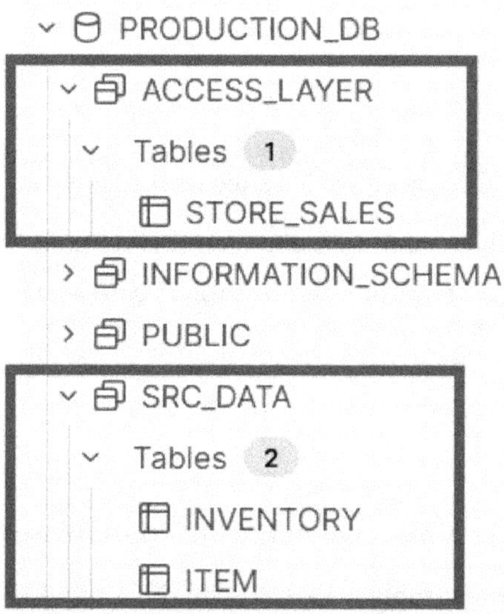

Figure 8.15 – Database, schemas, and tables structure

7. We have now created a database hierarchy similar to one that might exist in a production system. Let's now note the current timestamp, as we will need it later to clone our production database as it existed at a specific point in time. To do so, run the following SQL:

```
SELECT CURRENT_TIMESTAMP;
```

8. Let's also check the count of rows in each table so that when we clone the database in conjunction with Time Travel, we can demonstrate the database is cloned before

additional data is added to the table. To do so, run the following SQL statements one by one and note the row counts of each table:

```
SELECT COUNT(*) FROM PRODUCTION_DB.SRC_DATA.INVENTORY;
SELECT COUNT(*) FROM PRODUCTION_DB.SRC_DATA.ITEM;
SELECT COUNT(*) FROM PRODUCTION_DB.ACCESS_LAYER.STORE_SALES;
```

You should see 100,000 rows in each table.

9. We will now insert more data into all the tables in our PRODUCTION_DB database, simulating how a regular ETL run may execute every day. To do so, run the following SQL statements several times:

```
INSERT INTO PRODUCTION_DB.SRC_DATA.INVENTORY
SELECT * FROM SNOWFLAKE_SAMPLE_DATA.TPCDS_SF10TCL.INVENTORY
LIMIT 20000;

INSERT INTO PRODUCTION_DB.SRC_DATA.ITEM
SELECT * FROM SNOWFLAKE_SAMPLE_DATA.TPCDS_SF10TCL.ITEM
LIMIT 20000;

INSERT INTO PRODUCTION_DB.ACCESS_LAYER.STORE_SALES
SELECT * FROM SNOWFLAKE_SAMPLE_DATA.TPCDS_SF10TCL.STORE_SALES
LIMIT 20000;
```

Running these statements will insert new rows into the tables in the PRODUCTION_DB database and increase the row count from the initial 100,000 rows we loaded in those tables.

10. Let's now clone the PRODUCTION_DB database into the DEV_1 database, and while doing so, we'll also go back to when the table only had the initial set of rows. To do so, run the following SQL:

```
CREATE DATABASE DEV_1 CLONE PRODUCTION_DB AT(TIMESTAMP => '<replace with
the timestamp from step#7>'::timestamp_tz);
```

If you now expand and refresh the database tree on the left pane of the Snowflake web UI, you should see that the DEV_1 database has been created with the exact structure of the PRODUCTION_DB database:

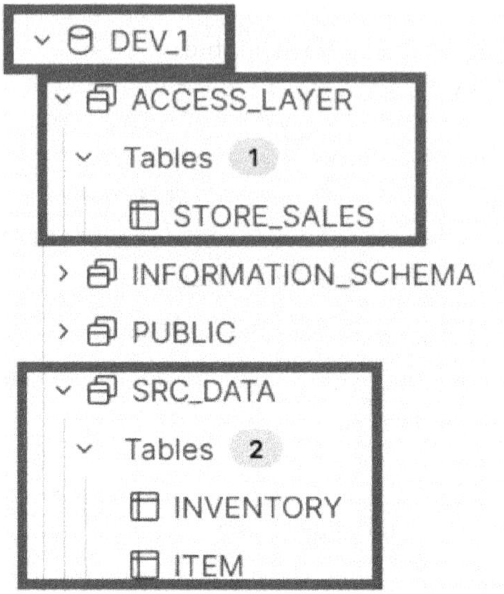

Figure 8.16 – DEV_1 database structure

11. Since we used Time Travel with cloning, the `DEV_1` database is cloned from the `PRODUCTION_DB` database; however, it should contain only the 100,000 rows that were initially inserted into the tables. Let's validate that by running `COUNT` queries on the tables in the `DEV_1` database. To do so, run the following SQL statements:

```
SELECT COUNT(*) FROM DEV_1.SRC_DATA.INVENTORY;
SELECT COUNT(*) FROM DEV_1.SRC_DATA.ITEM;
SELECT COUNT(*) FROM DEV_1.ACCESS_LAYER.STORE_SALES;
```

    You should see 100,000 rows in each table.

12. Now you can perform your development and debugging activities on this cloned database. Any changes you make to the `DEV_1` database will not impact anything in the `PRODUCTION_DB` database.

Using this cloning technique and Time Travel, you can make clones of a database as it existed at a point in time. Therefore, you get a more flexible method to develop and debug using production data without impacting the production data itself.

How it works...

In Snowflake, within the cloud services layer, information for each table is stored in the metadata. However, the table's actual data is stored in object storage (S3, Azure Blob Storage, and so on). The metadata for each table maintains references to the actual data in the object storage. This architecture allows Snowflake to track changes to a table transparently to the user; therefore, when you have updated a table, the data that existed before the update is retained for some time, allowing Snowflake to perform Time Travel.

Since references to actual data are maintained in the metadata, Snowflake can configure new tables and set up the metadata references to point to existing data, a phenomenon known as **cloning**. A cloned table and its parent table are in effect pointing to the same physical data. Snowflake also allows mixing cloning and Time Travel; as demonstrated in this recipe, you can create clones of objects as they existed at a point in time. This feature can be convenient when development teams are trying to debug production issues and may require the data to be in a state that it existed in on a particular day. You can simply clone the whole production database into a new database as of the required point in time without incurring any additional costs.

Using cloning to set up new environments based on the production environment rapidly

In traditional database and data warehousing systems, setting up a new development environment can be a lengthy and costly process. It typically involves replicating the production structures in a new development database and then copying a subset of production data for testing and development purposes. The process can be time-consuming and prone to errors, as it involves running table DDLs in a new environment and then inserting the sample data. Creating one or several new environments based on an existing production environment is a straightforward process in Snowflake. In this recipe, we will explore how we can use the cloning capabilities to create new development environments in a matter of minutes.

Getting ready

You will need to be connected to your Snowflake instance via Snowsight to execute this recipe.

How to do it...

In this recipe, we will configure and review Time Travel retention settings at different levels and observe how these settings apply to cloned objects. The steps are as follows:

1. Let's start by creating a new database called `PRD`, representing a production environment. We will also create three schemas called `SRC_DATA`, `INTEGRATED_DATA`, and `REPORTING_DATA`. To do so, run the following SQL:

```
CREATE DATABASE PRD;
CREATE SCHEMA SRC_DATA;
CREATE SCHEMA INTEGRATED_DATA;
CREATE SCHEMA REPORTING_DATA;
```

The commands should succeed with a success message.

2. Next, create a series of tables in these databases. To do so, run the following SQL statements:

```
USE SCHEMA SRC_DATA;
CREATE TABLE CUSTOMER AS
SELECT * FROM SNOWFLAKE_SAMPLE_DATA.TPCH_SF1.CUSTOMER;

USE SCHEMA SRC_DATA;
CREATE TABLE LINEITEM AS
SELECT * FROM SNOWFLAKE_SAMPLE_DATA.TPCH_SF1.LINEITEM;

USE SCHEMA INTEGRATED_DATA;
CREATE TABLE ORDERS AS
SELECT * FROM SNOWFLAKE_SAMPLE_DATA.TPCH_SF1.ORDERS;
```

Each of these should complete successfully.

3. Next, create a reporting view, which we will use later to verify that views also get cloned. To do so, run the following SQL:

```
USE SCHEMA REPORTING_DATA;
CREATE VIEW REVENUE_REPORT AS
SELECT
L_RETURNFLAG,
L_LINESTATUS,
SUM(L_QUANTITY) AS SUM_QTY,
SUM(L_EXTENDEDPRICE) AS SUM_BASE_PRICE,
SUM(L_EXTENDEDPRICE * (1-L_DISCOUNT)) AS SUM_DISC_PRICE,
SUM(L_EXTENDEDPRICE * (1-L_DISCOUNT) * (1+L_TAX)) AS SUM_CHARGE,
AVG(L_QUANTITY) AS AVG_QTY,
AVG(L_EXTENDEDPRICE) AS AVG_PRICE,
AVG(L_DISCOUNT) AS AVG_DISC,
COUNT(*) AS COUNT_ORDER
FROM PRD.SRC_DATA.LINEITEM
WHERE L_SHIPDATE <= DATEADD(DAY, -90, TO_DATE('1998-12-01'))
GROUP BY L_RETURNFLAG,L_LINESTATUS;
```

You should see a success message stating that the view was created successfully.

4. If you expand the database tree on the left pane of the Snowflake web UI, you should see the following structure of the database, schemas, and tables that we just created:

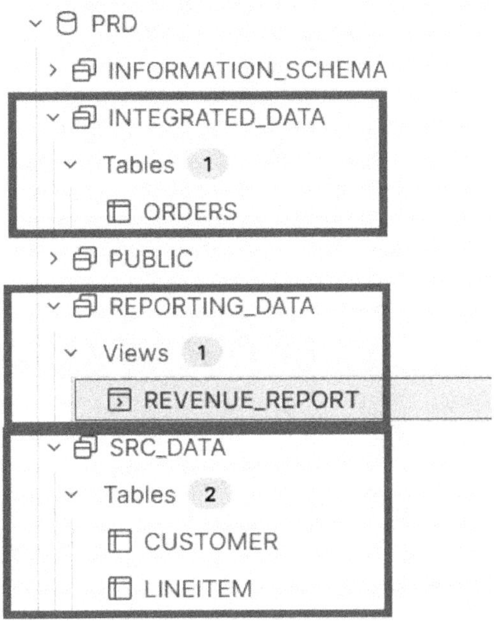

Figure 8.17 – Structure of database, schemas, and tables that we just created

5. We will now create a brand-new development environment based on the PRD database, including its data. To do so, we will use Snowflake's clone functionality as shown here:

```
CREATE DATABASE DEV_DB_1 CLONE PRD;
```

6. Let's validate that the new environment has all the required objects. To do so, expand the database tree on the left pane of the Snowflake web UI; you should see the following structure of database, schemas, tables, and views:

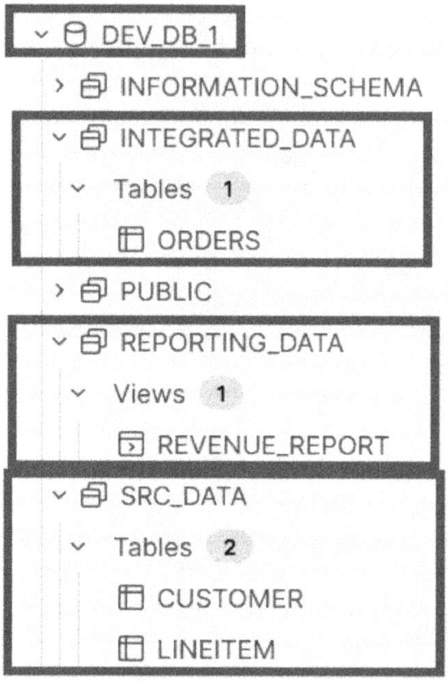

Figure 8.18 – Cloned schemas, tables, and views in the development database

As you will observe, all tables and views have been cloned successfully.

7. Let's validate that there is actual data in the cloned tables. To do so, run the following SQL statements:

```
SELECT COUNT(*) FROM DEV_DB_1.SRC_DATA.CUSTOMER;
```

8. Similarly, let's validate that there is actual data in the cloned views. To do so, run the following SQL statements:

```
SELECT COUNT(*) FROM DEV_DB_1.REPORTING_DATA.REVENUE_REPORT;
```

9. At this point, we have successfully created a development environment from the production environment. If needed, we can create as many clones of the `PRD` database as we want. We can even clone the `DEV_DB_1` database further if needed.

10. Let's create a testing environment from the production environment. To do so, run the following SQL:

```
CREATE DATABASE TEST_1 CLONE PRD;
```

The database will be successfully created, and you can validate that it has all the required schemas, tables, and views created.

11. You can even create a new development environment from the existing development environment. To do so, run the following SQL:

```
CREATE DATABASE DEV_DB_2 CLONE DEV_DB_1;
```

The database will be successfully created, and you can validate that it has all the required schemas, tables, and views created.

How it works...

In Snowflake, each database, schema, and table is represented as metadata in the cloud service layer. A table's actual data is maintained in object storage (that is, S3, Azure Blob Storage, and so on). This approach allows Snowflake to make clones of existing objects without actually copying data. Each cloned object points to the same data in the object storage. Snowflake takes care of the fact that if data is updated in the original tables, it is not reflected in the cloned tables, and vice versa. If a query updates the cloned data in the development database, it doesn't impact the production database.

Managing Time Travel and cloning retention policies for governance

In this recipe, we will explore how to manage Time Travel and cloning retention policies in Snowflake to support governance, recovery requirements, and cost control. While Time Travel is enabled by default, its retention period can be configured at the database, schema, and table levels. Understanding and managing these settings ensures that historical data is available when needed, while avoiding unnecessary storage overhead. We will also examine how retention settings impact cloning operations and how they can be validated and audited using Snowflake metadata.

Getting ready

You will need to be connected to your Snowflake instance via Snowsight to execute this recipe.

How to do it...

In this recipe, we will configure and review Time Travel retention settings at different levels and observe how these settings impact governance and cloning behavior. The steps are as follows:

1. Let's set the appropriate role and create a database for this recipe. This ensures we are working in an isolated environment and have the necessary privileges to configure retention settings:

   ```
   USE ROLE SYSADMIN;

   CREATE OR REPLACE DATABASE C8_R6;
   USE DATABASE C8_R6;
   USE SCHEMA PUBLIC;
   ```

   The commands should succeed with a success message.

2. Next, create a table using sample data. This table will be used to demonstrate how retention settings can be applied and managed:

   ```
   CREATE OR REPLACE TABLE CUSTOMER AS
   SELECT *
   FROM SNOWFLAKE_SAMPLE_DATA.TPCDS_SF10TCL.CUSTOMER
   LIMIT 100000;
   ```

3. Review the current Time Travel retention settings. By default, Snowflake applies a retention period, which can be viewed using the `SHOW` command:

   ```
   SHOW DATABASES LIKE 'C8_R6';
   SHOW SCHEMAS LIKE 'PUBLIC';
   SHOW TABLES LIKE 'CUSTOMER';
   ```

   In the results, locate the `retention_time` column to identify the current retention period applied at each level.

retention_time
1

Figure 8.19 – Retention Time Value

4. Let's modify the retention period at the database level. This sets a default retention period for all objects created within the database:

```
ALTER DATABASE C8_R6
SET DATA_RETENTION_TIME_IN_DAYS = 3;
```

5. We will now override the retention period at the table level. This demonstrates how more granular control can be applied when certain tables require longer recovery windows:

```
ALTER TABLE CUSTOMER
SET DATA_RETENTION_TIME_IN_DAYS = 5;
```

6. Now we can validate that the updated retention settings have been applied. This step confirms that the table-level setting overrides the database-level configuration:

```
SHOW TABLES LIKE 'CUSTOMER';
```

retention_time
5

Figure 8.20 – Customer Table Retention Time

Verify that the retention time reflects the updated value.

7. Create a clone of the table. Cloning allows us to create a copy of the table without duplicating the underlying data:

```
CREATE OR REPLACE TABLE CUSTOMER_CLONE
CLONE CUSTOMER;
```

8. Now review the retention settings for the cloned table. This confirms that cloning preserves the retention configuration from the source object:

```
SHOW TABLES LIKE 'CUSTOMER_CLONE';
```

   Observe that the retention time for the cloned table matches the source table.

9. Let's modify the retention period on the cloned table. This demonstrates that once a clone is created, its retention settings can be managed independently of the source table:

```
ALTER TABLE CUSTOMER_CLONE
SET DATA_RETENTION_TIME_IN_DAYS = 1;
```

10. Finally, you can validate the updated retention setting on the cloned table:

```
SHOW TABLES LIKE 'CUSTOMER_CLONE';
```

   Verify that the retention time now reflects the updated value.

How it works...

In this recipe, we configured Time Travel retention settings at the database and table levels and observed how those settings influence data recovery capabilities and cloning behavior in Snowflake.

Time Travel retention is controlled by the `DATA_RETENTION_TIME_IN_DAYS` parameter, which can be set at the database, schema, or table level. When set at a higher level, such as the database, it provides a default retention period for objects created within that scope. More granular control can be applied by overriding this setting at the table level, as demonstrated in this recipe.

Snowflake retains historical data for the duration of the configured retention period. This allows users to query or restore data to a previous state within that window. Increasing the retention period extends the recovery window but also increases the amount of historical data Snowflake must maintain.

When a table is cloned, Snowflake creates a new object that initially inherits the structure, data, and configuration of the source table, including its Time Travel retention setting. However, once the clone is created, it becomes an independent object. This allows retention settings on the cloned table to be modified without impacting the source table.

Cloning in Snowflake is metadata-based, meaning that no physical data is copied at the time of creation. Instead, both the source and cloned objects reference the same underlying micro-partitions until changes are made. This makes cloning an efficient mechanism for creating new environments or testing scenarios while still preserving the ability to manage retention policies independently.

Understanding how retention settings are applied and inherited is important for balancing recovery requirements with storage considerations. By configuring retention appropriately at different levels, organizations can ensure that critical data remains recoverable while avoiding unnecessary storage overhead.

Get this book's PDF version and more

Scan the QR code (or go to `packtpub.com/unlock`). Search for this book by name, confirm the edition, and then follow the steps on the page.

UNLOCK NOW

Note: Keep your invoice handy. Purchases made directly from Packt don't require an invoice.

9

Advanced SQL Techniques

In this chapter, you will explore advanced SQL techniques that help unlock the full analytical and operational power of Snowflake. While basic SQL can answer simple business questions, modern data platforms require more sophisticated approaches for handling time-based data, performing trend analysis, managing uniqueness, supporting transactional workloads, and deriving insights through advanced analytical functions.

These capabilities are especially valuable in data warehousing, reporting, and data engineering environments where accuracy, scalability, and maintainability are essential. Snowflake provides a rich and continually evolving SQL feature set, far beyond what can be covered in a single chapter. The recipes included here represent a carefully selected group of practical techniques that data professionals frequently rely on when building modern analytical solutions.

The following recipes will be covered in this chapter:

- Managing timestamp data
- Extracting calendar intelligence from date and time data
- Performing unique counts and approximate distinct analysis
- Managing transactions in Snowflake
- Ordered analytics over window frames
- Generating sequences in Snowflake
- Using `QUALIFY` to simplify filtering of window functions
- Creating and using user-defined data types

Let's get started!

Technical requirements

The recipes in this chapter work on Snowflake's Snowsight, as well as Snowflake CLI. You can download the example project and code for this book by following the instructions in the ***Download the example code files*** section in the *Preface* of this book.

Managing timestamp data

Working with date and time values is one of the most common and error-prone tasks in data engineering. Source systems often deliver timestamp data in different formats, inconsistent time zones, or text-based files that must be interpreted correctly during ingestion.

Snowflake provides a robust set of date and timestamp functions that make it possible to standardize these values, convert between formats, and accurately manage time zone behavior.

In this recipe, you will learn how to load and convert timestamp values using both standard ISO and non-standard formats, understand how the `DATE` data type values interact with timestamp inputs, and use session parameters to control time zone handling. These techniques are especially valuable when integrating data from multiple systems across regions or when ensuring accurate reporting across time zones.

Getting ready

You will need access to a Snowflake environment and permission to create databases and tables. The SQL statements in this recipe can be executed in Snowsight.

How to do it...

In the following steps, you will work through common date and timestamp scenarios in Snowflake. You will convert string values into dates, observe how timestamps interact with `DATE` columns, and use session parameters to manage time zone behavior during processing. The steps are as follows:

1. The `DATE` data type is used for storing date values in columns in Snowflake tables. A date is typically composed of the year, month, and the day of the month separated by hyphens (`YYYY-MM-DD`). Let's create a table called `C9R1_DATE_TEST`, where we will store a date value in a string. We will use the `to_date` function to convert the string value

into a valid date format. The function accepts two parameters: the string value to be converted and the format of the input string:

```
CREATE DATABASE C9_R1;
CREATE TABLE c9r1_date_test (date_id INTEGER, date_value DATE);
INSERT INTO c9r1_date_test (date_id, date_value)
Values
(1, to_date('2019-12-19','YYYY-MM-DD'));
```

The DATE data type is not limited to accepting just dates. It can also accept timestamp values. However, it will ignore the time component of the input:

```
INSERT INTO c9r1_date_test (date_id, date_value)
VALUES
(2, TO_TIMESTAMP('2019.12.21 04:00:00', 'YYYY.MM.DD HH:MI:SS'));
```

Another variation is to use the `to_date` function but pass the time component only. It can take time values, but it assumes the value of January 1, 1970, for the date, thus completely ignoring the date value:

```
INSERT INTO c9r1_date_test (date_id, date_value)
VALUES
(3, TO_DATE ('08:00:00', 'HH:MI:SS'));
```

2. Let's now run a query so that we can select data from the table:

```
SELECT * FROM c9r1_date_test;
```

The result of the query is as follows:

DATE_ID	DATE_VALUE
1	2019-12-19
2	2019-12-21
3	1970-01-01

Figure 9.1 – Query result showing the date values

The table shows that a timestamp value can be stored in a `DATE` type column. Here, Snowflake ignores the timestamp's time component. The third row shows that the `DATE_VALUE` column will accept the date value, even if nothing is provided.

3. Now, let's create a new table with a `TIMESTAMP` type column to demonstrate how Snowflake manages time zones:

```
CREATE TABLE c9r1_ts_test (ts_id INTEGER, ts_value TIMESTAMP);
```

4. We shall now investigate the session object and how it can be used to manage time zones. The session holds various objects, where each object has a default value. To find out the values of all the objects in the session that are related to the time zone, run the following command:

```
SHOW PARAMETERS LIKE '%TIMEZONE%' IN SESSION;
```

The results are as follows:

Row	key	value	default	level	description	type
1	JDBC_FORMAT_DATE...	false	false		When true, ResultSet...	BOOLEAN
2	JDBC_USE_SESSION_...	false	false		When true, JDBC driv...	BOOLEAN
3	TIMEZONE	America/Los_Angeles	America/Los_Angeles		time zone	STRING

Figure 9.2 – Output of running a query on the session object

5. In the case of the `TIMEZONE` object stored in the session, the default value is `America/Los_Angeles`. This value can be changed by running the `ALTER SESSION` command. Snowflake uses standard **Internet Assigned Numbers Authority** (**IANA**) time zone names, such as America/New_York, Europe/London, and Asia/Tokyo, when working with time zone-aware data. A complete list of supported time zone names is maintained by the IANA. In practice, most users simply specify the appropriate region and city combination for their time zone.

6. To set the user-defined value for the time zone that will be used with our data, use the following statement:

```
ALTER SESSION SET TIMEZONE='Australia/Sydney';
```

The command should execute successfully.

7. Let's now rerun the command for the session to view the updated value:

```
SHOW PARAMETERS LIKE '%TIMEZONE%' IN SESSION;
```

The preceding statement will generate the following output. Here, we can see that the **value** column has been updated, but the values under the **default** column remain unchanged:

Row	key	value	default	level	description	type
1	JDBC_FORMAT_DATE...	false	false		When true, ResultSet...	BOOLE
2	JDBC_USE_SESSION_...	false	false		When true, JDBC driv...	BOOLE
3	TIMEZONE	Australia/Sydney	America/Los_Angeles	SESSION	time zone	STRIN

Figure 9.3 – Output of the query in step 8

8. Now, let's insert a timestamp value:

```
INSERT INTO c9r1_ts_test (ts_id, ts_value)
VALUES (1, '2020-11-19 22:00:00.000');
```

9. Now, select the data from this table by running the following command:

```
SELECT * FROM c9r1_ts_test;
```

You should see the following results:

TS_ID	TS_VALUE
1	2020-11-19 22:00:00.000

Figure 9.4 – No change/interpretation of the time zone

10. Now, let's change another session parameter that controls how Snowflake manages timestamp data. Snowflake supports several timestamp data types, including TIMESTAMP_NTZ (No Time Zone), TIMESTAMP_LTZ (Local Time Zone), and TIMESTAMP_TZ (Time Zone). The TIMESTAMP_TYPE_MAPPING session parameter controls which timestamp type Snowflake uses when a generic TIMESTAMP data type

is specified. For this example, we will update the value of the TIMESTAMP_TYPE_MAPPING parameter by executing the following SQL statements:

```
ALTER SESSION SET TIMESTAMP_TYPE_MAPPING = 'TIMESTAMP_LTZ';
ALTER SESSION SET TIMEZONE = 'Australia/Sydney';
CREATE OR REPLACE TABLE c9r1_test_ts (ts TIMESTAMP);
INSERT INTO c9r1_test_ts VALUES ('2020-11-19 22:00:00.000');
SELECT ts FROM c9r1_test_ts;
```

The result will generate a column called **TS** in the table, as well as a value, as shown in the following screenshot:

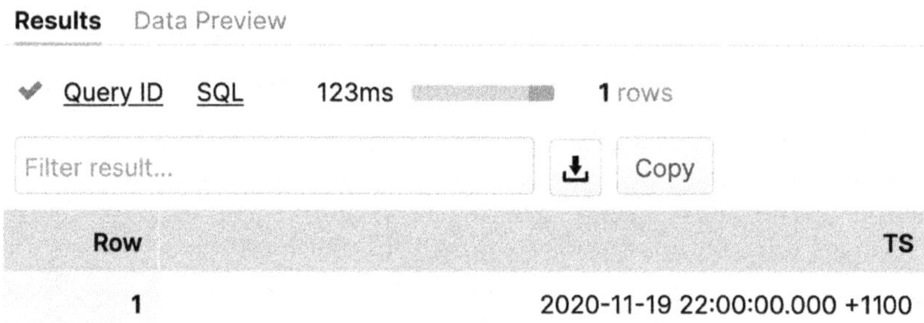

Figure 9.5 – The time zone is shown, along with the time difference compared with GMT

11. Now, let's see how Snowflake handles a timestamp value from a different time zone. Execute the following code. Unlike the previous example, the inserted timestamp includes a +0800 offset from UTC, which corresponds to the time zone used in Perth, Australia:

```
CREATE OR REPLACE TABLE c9r1_test_ts (ts TIMESTAMP);
INSERT INTO c9r1_test_ts VALUES ('2020-11-19 22:00:00.000 +0800');
SELECT ts FROM c9r1_test_ts;
```

The output is shown in the following screenshot:

Figure 9.6 – Timestamp adjusted by + 3 hours due to a session time zone change

Here, we can see that Snowflake has converted the incoming timestamp to the session time zone we configured. Because there is a three-hour difference between the source and session time zones, the timestamp rolls over to the following day.

How it works...

When a timestamp value is inserted into a `DATE` column, Snowflake stores only the calendar date and discards the time portion. If a time-only value is converted to a `DATE`, Snowflake defaults the date portion to `1970-01-01`, which is commonly used as the Unix epoch reference date.

For timestamp processing, Snowflake uses session and account-level parameters to control how date and time values are interpreted and displayed. Parameters such as `TIMEZONE` and `TIMESTAMP_TYPE_MAPPING` influence whether timestamp values are stored without a time zone or converted relative to the current session time zone.

These settings are especially important when loading data from multiple regions or source systems, as consistent configuration helps prevent reporting errors and unexpected timestamp shifts.

Extracting calendar intelligence from date and time data

In this recipe, you will learn how to use Snowflake date functions to derive valuable calendar attributes from a date value. Common examples include the day of the month, day of the week, week of the year, month name, quarter, and other fields frequently used in reporting and analytics.

These capabilities are especially important in data warehousing, where dates often serve as core dimensions for trend analysis, period comparisons, fiscal reporting, and operational dashboards. You will also explore business-friendly functions such as identifying the first or last day of a month and generating reusable calendar reference data.

Along the way, this recipe highlights important considerations related to Snowflake week calculations, including how session settings can influence the start of the week and affect reporting results. By the end of the recipe, you will be able to build a utility calendar table that can be reused across analytical workloads.

Getting ready

You will need access to a Snowflake environment and permission to create database objects if you plan to build the calendar table shown later in this recipe. The SQL statements can be executed using either Snowsight or the Snowflake CLI.

How to do it...

In this recipe, you will generate a reusable set of calendar dates and progressively enrich them with common reporting attributes such as day, month, year, month boundaries, quarter-end dates, and descriptive labels. This pattern is commonly used when building calendar dimensions for analytics and reporting workloads. The steps are as follows:

1. First, we will use the `seq4()` function to generate a list of numbers from 0 to 364. These numbers will be added to the first date of the year 2021. To generate 365 rows, use the following code, which uses the `GENERATOR()` function:

   ```
   SELECT (to_date('2020-01-01') + seq4()) cal_dt
   FROM TABLE(GENERATOR(ROWCOUNT => 365));
   ```

   The output will look similar to the following. Here, we are showing the first five rows of the dataset, starting with January 1, 2020. The table contains a single column called `CAL_DT`. This column will be used in the subsequent steps as input to different extractor functions so that we can extract date parts:

Row	CAL_DT
1	2020-01-01
2	2020-01-02
3	2020-01-03
4	2020-01-04
5	2020-01-05

Figure 9.7 – First five rows of the sample date dataset

2. Now that we have the foundation set up, we can start adding functions so that we can extract date parts. In this step, we will extract the day, month, and year from the date using the `DATE_PART()` function:

```
SELECT (to_date('2020-01-01') + seq4()) cal_dt,
DATE_PART(day, cal_dt) as cal_dom, --day of month
DATE_PART(month, cal_dt) as cal_month, --month of year
DATE_PART(year, cal_dt) as cal_year --year
FROM TABLE(GENERATOR(ROWCOUNT => 365));
```

The result is as follows:

Row	CAL_DT	CAL_DOM	CAL_MONTH	CAL_YEAR
1	2020-01-01	1	1	2020
2	2020-01-02	2	1	2020
3	2020-01-03	3	1	2020
4	2020-01-04	4	1	2020
5	2020-01-05	5	1	2020
6	2020-01-06	6	1	2020
7	2020-01-07	7	1	2020
8	2020-01-08	8	1	2020

Figure 9.8 – Date components

3. Now that we have the basic parts of the date extracted, we can enrich it with more fields. We are going to add the first and last day of the month against each date in our dataset. We will add two columns, as shown in the following code:

```
SELECT
(to_date('2021-01-01') + seq4()) cal_dt
,DATE_PART(day, cal_dt) as cal_dom --day of month
,DATE_PART(month, cal_dt) as cal_month --month of year
,DATE_PART(year, cal_dt) as cal_year --year
,DATE_TRUNC('month', CAL_DT) as cal_first_dom
,DATEADD('day', -1,
  DATEADD('month', 1,
  DATE_TRUNC('month', CAL_DT))) as cal_last_dom
FROM TABLE(GENERATOR(ROWCOUNT => 365));
```

The output is as follows:

Row	CAL_DT	CAL_DOM	CAL_MONTH	CAL_YEAR	CAL_FIRST_DOM	CAL_LAST_DOM
1	2021-01-01	1	1	2021	2021-01-01	2021-01-31
2	2021-01-02	2	1	2021	2021-01-01	2021-01-31
3	2021-01-03	3	1	2021	2021-01-01	2021-01-31
4	2021-01-04	4	1	2021	2021-01-01	2021-01-31
5	2021-01-05	5	1	2021	2021-01-01	2021-01-31
6	2021-01-06	6	1	2021	2021-01-01	2021-01-31

Figure 9.9 – Last and first date of the month

The result set contains two new columns: `CAL_FIRST_DOM` and `CAL_LAST_DOM`. Here, we can see that for January 2021, the values of `CAL_FIRST_DOM` and `CAL_LAST_DOM` are 2021-01-01 and 2021-01-31, respectively. The `DATE_TRUNC()` function has been used with month as a parameter to get the first day of the month. For arriving at the last day of the month, we start by getting to the first day of the month, then add a month to the date, and then, finally, subtract a day to get to the last day of the month.

4. Now, let's add the month name to the dataset. Snowflake provides the MONTHNAME function, which returns the English name of the month for a given date. The following query adds a CAL_MONTH_NAME column to our calendar dataset:

```
SELECT (to_date('2021-01-01') + seq4()) cal_dt,
DATE_PART(day, cal_dt) as cal_dom, --day of month,
```

```
DATE_PART(month, cal_dt) as cal_month, --month of year,
DATE_PART(year, cal_dt) as cal_year, --yearSS,
DATE_TRUNC('month', CAL_DT) cal_first_dom,
DATEADD('day', -1,
  DATEADD('month', 1,
  DATE_TRUNC('month', CAL_DT))) cal_last_dom
, MONTHNAME(CAL_DT) AS cal_month_name
FROM TABLE(GENERATOR(ROWCOUNT => 365));
```

A partial output is shown in the following screenshot. Here, we can see some data rows corresponding to January and February 2021:

CAL_DT	CAL_DOM	CAL_MONTH	CAL_YEAR	CAL_FIRST_DOM	CAL_LAST_DOM	CAL_MONTH_NAME
2021-01-01	1	1	2021	2021-01-01	2021-01-31	January
2021-01-02	2	1	2021	2021-01-01	2021-01-31	January
2021-01-03	3	1	2021	2021-01-01	2021-01-31	January
2021-01-04	4	1	2021	2021-01-01	2021-01-31	January
2021-01-05	5	1	2021	2021-01-01	2021-01-31	January

Figure 9.10 – Using the DECODE() function to generate the month's name in English

We can map the numeric month to the name of the month using the `DECODE` function, which takes the month's numeric value and spits out the month's name. This has been made possible due to the list of key-value pairs we provided to the `DECODE` function.

5. Now, let's add a column to our dataset that captures the quarter's end against each date. We will use the `DATE_TRUNC` function, which will be passed alongside the `'quarter'` parameter, to manage this. The process is similar to the one we used to arrive at the end of the month for each month. The following code shows the new `CAL_QTR_END_DT` column, which represents the last date of the quarter:

```
SELECT (to_date('2021-01-01') + seq4()) cal_dt
,DATE_PART(day, cal_dt) as cal_dom --day of month
,DATE_PART(month, cal_dt) as cal_month --month of year
,DATE_PART(year, cal_dt) as cal_year --yearSS
,DATE_TRUNC('month', CAL_DT) cal_first_dom
,DATEADD('day', -1,
  DATEADD('month', 1,
  DATE_TRUNC('month', CAL_DT))) cal_last_dom
,MONTHNAME(CAL_DT) AS cal_month_name
```

```
,DATEADD('day', -1,
  DATEADD('month', 3,
  DATE_TRUNC('quarter', CAL_DT))) as CAL_QTR_END_DT

FROM TABLE(GENERATOR(ROWCOUNT => 365));
```

The output of this query can be seen in the following screenshot:

CAL_DT	CAL_DOM	CAL_MONTH	CAL_YEAR	CAL_FIRST_DOM	CAL_LAST_DOM	CAL_MONTH_NAME	CAL_QTR_END_DT
2021-01-01	1	1	2021	2021-01-01	2021-01-31	January	2021-03-31
2021-01-02	2	1	2021	2021-01-01	2021-01-31	January	2021-03-31
2021-01-03	3	1	2021	2021-01-01	2021-01-31	January	2021-03-31
2021-01-04	4	1	2021	2021-01-01	2021-01-31	January	2021-03-31
2021-01-05	5	1	2021	2021-01-01	2021-01-31	January	2021-03-31

Figure 9.11 – Calendar generation for use in BI/Analytics

A new column has been added that shows the end of the quarters for March and April 2021. The end of quarter dates for the two months are March 31, 2021 and June 30, 2021.

Now that we have the SQL devised, the next step is to create a utility table with an appropriate name and then store the output in that table so that it can be used in an ETL process. The preceding SQL can also be extended as we can add important dates related to the fiscal calendar or any other calendar that's important to a business.

How it works...

This recipe uses Snowflake's `GENERATOR()` table function to create a synthetic row set without requiring a source table. By specifying a `ROWCOUNT` of `365`, Snowflake returns one row for each day of the year. The `seq4()` function generates an incrementing numeric sequence beginning at zero, which can be added to a starting date to produce a continuous range of calendar dates.

Once the base date set is created, functions such as `DATE_PART()` extract commonly used reporting attributes including day of month, month number, and year. These derived values are frequently used in dashboards, filtering logic, and time-based aggregations.

Additional date intelligence is created using `DATE_TRUNC()` and `DATEADD()`. These functions make it possible to calculate the first day of a month, the last day of a month, quarter boundaries, and other reusable business calendar values.

The MONTHNAME() function is used to return the English name of the month associated with each date. This improves readability for reporting outputs and dimension tables while simplifying the SQL compared to manually mapping month numbers to month names.

By persisting this logic into a utility calendar table, organizations can standardize time-based reporting logic and avoid repeating date calculations across ETL pipelines, dashboards, and analytical workloads.

Performing unique counts and approximate distinct analysis

Calculating unique values across large datasets is a common requirement in analytics, but it can become computationally expensive at scale. Exact distinct counts often require significant processing, especially when grouping over billions of rows.

Snowflake provides both traditional exact distinct counting and high-performance approximate cardinality estimation through the `APPROX_COUNT_DISTINCT` function, which is based on the **HyperLogLog** (**HLL**) algorithm.

In this recipe, you will compare exact and approximate counting techniques, understand the tradeoff between speed and precision, and learn when approximate distinct counts are a practical choice for large analytical workloads. Unique counts for rows in distributed systems are a compute-intensive process. Snowflake uses a distributed algorithm that is state of the art. This technique is different from those used in other databases. It is faster but, at the same time, approximate. The recipe shall show you how to use the uniqueness functions that are available in Snowflake.

Getting ready

You will need access to a Snowflake environment with access to the `SNOWFLAKE_SAMPLE_DATA` database. The SQL statements in this recipe can be executed using either Snowsight or the Snowflake CLI. An X-Small warehouse is sufficient for demonstration purposes.

How to do it...

The following steps use Snowflake's TPCH sample dataset to demonstrate several counting techniques at scale. You will begin with a basic row count, then calculate exact distinct customer counts by order priority, and finally compare those results with an approximate distinct count using Snowflake's built-in estimation functions.

This example helps illustrate how different counting methods can be applied depending on reporting requirements, data volume, and performance goals. The steps are as follows:

1. First, let's perform a simple `SELECT` query on the `ORDERS` table, which is available in the `SNOWFLAKE_SAMPLE_DATA` database and the `TPCH_SF1000` schema. We shall query `1000` rows from the dataset:

```
select *
from "SNOWFLAKE_SAMPLE_DATA"."TPCH_SF1000"."ORDERS"
sample row (1000 rows);
```

   The output can be seen in the following screenshot. Please note that it took 20 seconds for Snowflake to query the 1.5 billion rows in the table. Here, Snowflake has already queried the table; it has collected metadata and cached some data, which will help with subsequent queries:

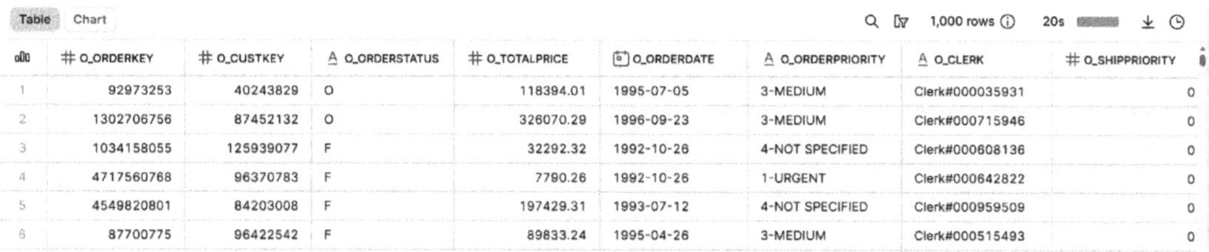

Table Chart 1,000 rows 20s

	# O_ORDERKEY	# O_CUSTKEY	A O_ORDERSTATUS	# O_TOTALPRICE	O_ORDERDATE	A O_ORDERPRIORITY	A O_CLERK	# O_SHIPPRIORITY
1	92973253	40243829	O	118394.01	1995-07-05	3-MEDIUM	Clerk#000035931	0
2	1302706756	87452132	O	326070.29	1996-09-23	3-MEDIUM	Clerk#000715946	0
3	1034158055	125939077	F	32292.32	1992-10-26	4-NOT SPECIFIED	Clerk#000608136	0
4	4717560768	96370783	F	7790.26	1992-10-26	1-URGENT	Clerk#000642822	0
5	4549820801	84203008	F	197429.31	1993-07-12	4-NOT SPECIFIED	Clerk#000959509	0
6	87700775	96422542	F	89833.24	1995-04-26	3-MEDIUM	Clerk#000515493	0

Figure 9.12 – Sample output

2. Next, we will execute a count on the `O_CUSTKEY` column while applying grouping to `O_ORDERPRIORITY`. The goal of this analysis is to determine which order priorities occur most frequently for each customer. Since we are working with synthetic data, the goal is to demonstrate the functionality rather than derive meaningful business insights:

```
select
O_ORDERPRIORITY
,count(O_CUSTKEY)
from "SNOWFLAKE_SAMPLE_DATA"."TPCH_SF1000"."ORDERS"
group by 1
order by 1;
```

   We were able to get the result in almost 12 seconds, as shown in the following screenshot:

	O_ORDERPRIORITY	COUNT(O_CUSTKEY)
1	1-URGENT	300002709
2	2-HIGH	300005966
3	3-MEDIUM	299995087
4	4-NOT SPECIFIED	299993557
5	5-LOW	300002681

Figure 9.13 – Simple count results

3. Now, let's make things a bit difficult for Snowflake. We will calculate the same count but with a variation this time. Here, we will apply a `DISTINCT` function to the `O_CUSTKEY` column so that customers with repeat orders are counted once. However, to stop Snowflake from using results from its cache, we will alter the session and set `USE_CACHED_RESULT` to `FALSE`, and then execute the query so that we do a distinct count over customers:

```
ALTER SESSION SET USE_CACHED_RESULT = FALSE;

SELECT O_ORDERPRIORITY
,count(DISTINCT O_CUSTKEY)
from "SNOWFLAKE_SAMPLE_DATA"."TPCH_SF1000"."ORDERS"
group by 1
order by 1;
```

The result can be seen in the following screenshot:

Table Chart 5 rows 1m 40s

	O_ORDERPRIORITY	COUNT(DISTINCT O_CUSTKEY)
1	1-URGENT	97803539
2	2-HIGH	97802436
3	3-MEDIUM	97799688
4	4-NOT SPECIFIED	97799505
5	5-LOW	97802711

Figure 9.14 – Distinct count values

Please note that it took 1 minute and 40 seconds to get these five results on an X-Small warehouse.

4. Now, let's run a similar query, but this time with the APPROX_COUNT_DISTINCT function on the O_CUSTKEY column, rather than with the COUNT(DISTINCT ...) function we used in *step 3*:

```
select O_ORDERPRIORITY
,APPROX_COUNT_DISTINCT(O_CUSTKEY)
from "SNOWFLAKE_SAMPLE_DATA"."TPCH_SF100"."ORDERS"
group by 1
order by 1;
```

As expected, the result is similar to the previous step's outcome, but it is not the same, as shown in the following screenshot. Please note that the execution times shown in this example were captured using an Extra Small virtual warehouse. Your results may vary depending on warehouse size, caching, and workload characteristics.

Table Chart 5 rows 8.0s

	O_ORDERPRIORITY	APPROX_COUNT_DISTINCT(O_CUSTKEY)
1	1-URGENT	9336831
2	2-HIGH	9504205
3	3-MEDIUM	9396256
4	4-NOT SPECIFIED	9385399
5	5-LOW	9298539

Figure 9.15 – Approximate counts

Let's look at the count for the 1-URGENT category in the O_ORDERPRIORITY column. The approximate method returns a count of about 97.5 million, while the result from the exact count was 97.8 million. This results in an error of around 0.23 percent, while at the same time, the query execution time has come down to 17.29 seconds from almost 2 minutes. For use cases that do not require exact counts, it can be cost-effective to use an approximate method.

How it works...

The key concept in this recipe is the difference between exact distinct counting and approximate distinct counting. The COUNT(DISTINCT column) function returns the precise number of unique values, but on very large, distributed datasets it can consume more processing time and compute resources.

Snowflake also provides APPROX_COUNT_DISTINCT, which is functionally equivalent to HLL. HLL is a probabilistic algorithm designed to estimate the number of unique values in a dataset, also known as its cardinality.

For example, the set {3,6,2,5,6,1,7} contains six unique values, so its cardinality is 6. Rather than storing and comparing every distinct value directly, HLL uses compact mathematical estimation techniques to approximate the result with high efficiency and low memory usage.

This makes APPROX_COUNT_DISTINCT especially useful for large-scale analytics, dashboards, exploratory queries, and workloads where a small variance from the exact answer is acceptable in exchange for faster performance and lower compute cost. When exact precision is required, such as financial or regulatory reporting, COUNT(DISTINCT ...) remains the preferred option.

Managing transactions in Snowflake

Snowflake is an **atomicity, consistency, isolation, and durability** (**ACID**)-compliant platform. ACID is a set of transaction properties that help ensure data remains valid and reliable during operations that modify it, even in the presence of errors or failures.

In this recipe, you will learn how to use transactions in Snowflake, including how transaction scope, isolation behavior, commits, rollbacks, and session management work together to ensure data consistency.

Getting ready

You will need access to a Snowflake environment. The SQL statements in this recipe can be executed using either Snowsight or the Snowflake CLI.

How to do it...

The following steps demonstrate how transactions are controlled in Snowflake using BEGIN, COMMIT, and ROLLBACK. You will create a simple example involving debit and credit entries across two tables, where both changes must succeed together to preserve balance and data integrity.

You will also review how transaction behavior is influenced by the current session and how stored procedures can be used to manage multi-step transactional logic. These examples help illustrate when explicit transaction control is useful in real-world data processing scenarios. The steps are as follows:

1. Let's create a database called CHAPTER9:

```
CREATE DATABASE CHAPTER9;
USE CHAPTER9;
```

2. In this database, create two tables. One table will be used to store account debits, while the other will store account credits. The tables will be updated/inserted as part of a transaction:

```
CREATE TABLE c9r4_credit (
account int
,amount int
,payment_ts timestamp
);
```

The preceding statement creates a table called `C9R4_CREDIT`. The table contains an `ACCOUNT` column to store the account number, an `AMOUNT` column to store the transaction amount, and a `PAYMENT_TS` column to record when the transaction occurred.

3. Similar to the `C9R4_CREDIT` table, we will now create a table called `C9R4_DEBIT`:

```
CREATE TABLE c9r4_debit (
account int
,amount int
,payment_ts timestamp
);
```

Both tables we've created contain a column called `payment_ts`. This column is of the timestamp type and will store timestamp data when it is inserted.

4. This stored procedure is designed to simulate a balanced debit-and-credit transaction across two tables. It first inserts a row into the debit table and then inserts the corresponding row into the credit table when processing completes successfully. A conditional error has been intentionally included for even-numbered account values so that a later step can demonstrate rollback behavior. When that condition is triggered during execution, the transaction is reversed and no partial data is committed.

   At this stage, you are only creating the stored procedure. The expected result is a successful procedure creation message.

```
CREATE OR REPLACE PROCEDURE sp_adjust_credit
(PARAM_ACCT FLOAT, PARAM_AMT FLOAT)
RETURNS STRING
LANGUAGE JAVASCRIPT
```

```
AS
$$
var ret_val = "";
var sql_command_debit = "";
var sql_command_credit = "";

sql_command_debit = "INSERT INTO CHAPTER9.PUBLIC.C9R4_DEBIT VALUES ("
    + PARAM_ACCT + "," + PARAM_AMT + ", CURRENT_TIMESTAMP());";

sql_command_credit = "INSERT INTO CHAPTER9.PUBLIC.C9R4_CREDIT " +
    "SELECT * FROM CHAPTER9.PUBLIC.C9R4_DEBIT " +
    "WHERE CHAPTER9.PUBLIC.C9R4_DEBIT.payment_ts > " +
    "(SELECT IFF(MAX(payment_ts) IS NULL, TO_DATE('1970-01-01'),
MAX(payment_ts)) " +
    "FROM CHAPTER9.PUBLIC.C9R4_CREDIT);";

snowflake.execute({sqlText: "BEGIN WORK;"});

try {
    snowflake.execute({sqlText: sql_command_debit});

    if ((PARAM_ACCT % 2) === 0) {
        snowflake.execute({sqlText: "DELETE FROM table_0123456789;"});
    }

    snowflake.execute({sqlText: sql_command_credit});
    snowflake.execute({sqlText: "COMMIT WORK;"});

    ret_val = "Succeeded";
} catch (err) {
    snowflake.execute({sqlText: "ROLLBACK WORK;"});
    ret_val = "Failed: " + err.message;
}

return ret_val;
$$;
```

Let's review how the stored procedure manages the transaction. The `sp_adjust_credit()` procedure accepts two FLOAT parameters:

- `PARAM_ACCT` – account number
- `PARAM_AMT` – transaction amount

When executed, the procedure begins a transaction, inserts a row into the debit table, and then inserts the corresponding row into the credit table. If processing completes successfully, the transaction is committed and the procedure returns succeeded.

A conditional failure path has also been included for demonstration purposes. If an even-numbered account value is supplied, the procedure intentionally references a non-existent table, causing an exception. The transaction is then rolled back, and an error message is returned.

5. Let's disable `AUTOCOMMIT` for clearer transaction control.

```
ALTER SESSION SET AUTOCOMMIT = FALSE;
```

6. Now execute the stored procedure using an odd-numbered account value. This example uses account number `1`, so the transaction should complete successfully.

```
    CALL sp_adjust_credit(1,100);
```

Expected result:

	A SP_ADJUST_CREDIT
1	Succeeded

Figure 9.16 – Successfully deploying a stored procedure

7. Verify that both tables were updated.

```
SELECT * FROM c9r4_credit;

SELECT * FROM c9r4_debit;
```

Both tables should contain the new transaction row.

	ACCOUNT	AMOUNT	PAYMENT_TS
1	1	100	2026-04-25 17:21:40.544
2	1	100	2026-04-25 17:54:03.014

Figure 9.17 – Rows in the c9r4_credit table

Similarly, for the `c9r4_debit` table, we should get the following output:

	ACCOUNT	AMOUNT	PAYMENT_TS
1	1	100	2026-04-25 17:21:40.544
2	1	100	2026-04-25 17:54:03.014

Figure 9.18 – Rows in the c9r4_debit table

8. Execute the stored procedure using an even-numbered account value. This example uses account number 2, which activates the intentional failure condition.

```
CALL sp_adjust_credit(2,200);
```

The procedure attempts to reference a table that does not exist, which raises an exception. The exception is caught by the JavaScript CATCH block defined in the stored procedure, where a ROLLBACK is issued to undo the transaction and prevent partial data from being committed.

You should receive an error similar to the following:

	SP_ADJUST_CREDIT
1	Failed: SQL compilation error: Object 'TABLE_0123456789' does not exist or not authorized.

Figure 9.19 – Error resulting from a missing table

9. Re-run the queries from *step 7*. The failed transaction should not have added any new rows.
10. We temporarily disabled `AUTOCOMMIT` so transaction behavior could be observed more clearly. Re-enable the default behavior so future SQL statements automatically commit unless explicitly controlled within a transaction.

```
ALTER SESSION SET AUTOCOMMIT = TRUE;
```

How it works...

Snowflake manages transactions in a manner similar to many traditional relational database systems. Multiple SQL statements can be grouped into a single transaction, so they succeed or fail as one unit of work. This behavior supports ACID principles discussed earlier and helps preserve data consistency during data modification operations.

A transaction typically begins explicitly with `BEGIN` (or `BEGIN WORK`) and is completed with either `COMMIT` or `ROLLBACK`.

- `COMMIT` makes all changes in the transaction permanent
- `ROLLBACK` reverses all changes made since the transaction began

In this recipe, the stored procedure performs multiple related operations within a single transaction. When the procedure completes successfully, both the debit and credit inserts are committed together. When the simulated error is triggered, control moves to the exception handler, which issues a rollback so that no partial data remains.

This pattern is especially valuable in real-world workloads where multiple dependent changes must remain synchronized. If one step fails, the entire transaction can be reversed to maintain accurate and trustworthy data.

Ordered analytics over window frames

The window functions are one of the most powerful features available in SQL for analytical workloads. They allow calculations to be performed across related rows while still returning detailed row-level results. In Snowflake, window functions are especially useful for identifying trends, ranking results, calculating moving averages, and producing cumulative totals over time.

These techniques are commonly used in financial analysis, customer behavior modeling, operational reporting, and marketing analytics where patterns across sequences of rows provide valuable insight. Rather than collapsing data into grouped summaries, window functions preserve the underlying rows while adding analytical context.

In this recipe, you will learn how Snowflake performs ordered analytics over window frames using a sample dataset of customer deposits. You will use functions such as running totals, moving averages, and other ordered calculations to analyze activity across time.

Getting ready

You will need access to a Snowflake environment. The SQL statements in this recipe can be executed using either Snowsight or the Snowflake CLI.

This recipe generates a sample dataset with three columns:

- `customer_id`
- `deposit_dt`
- `deposit`

The data represents deposits made by customers on specific dates and will be used to demonstrate ordered analytical calculations.

How to do it...

Start by generating the sample data used throughout this recipe. The following step creates a view that returns customer deposit activity, which will then be used to demonstrate ordered analytics and window frame calculations. The steps are as follows:

1. The following query will be used to generate the base data that will be used to implement a view. We will use the `CHAPTER9` database for this:

```
create database chapter9; // create if not exists
use chapter9;
create or replace view c9r5_vw as
select
    mod(seq4(),5) as customer_id
    ,(mod(uniform(1,100,random()),5) + 1)*100 as deposit
    ,dateadd(day, '-' || seq4(), current_date()) as deposit_dt
from
  table
    (generator(rowcount => 365));
```

2. Query the view to review the generated sample data.

```
SELECT * FROM c9r5_vw;
```

The view returns 365 rows of sample deposit activity. `CUSTOMER_ID` contains five repeating customer values (0 through 4). `DEPOSIT` rotates through the values 100, 200, 300, 400, and 500. The `DEPOSIT_DT` column begins with the current date and extends backward across the generated time period.

A sample of the output is shown in the following screenshot:

	# CUSTOMER_ID	# DEPOSIT	DEPOSIT_DT
1	0	200	2026-04-25
2	1	200	2026-04-24
3	2	100	2026-04-23
4	3	200	2026-04-22
5	4	200	2026-04-21
6	0	300	2026-04-20

Figure 9.20 – Sample data representing transactions generated on different dates

3. Now that we have created a view, let's use this dataset to run a few window functions available in Snowflake. Let's start by highlighting customers who made a single deposit amounting to more than the cumulative sum of their last two deposits:

```
SELECT
      customer_id,
      deposit_dt,
      deposit,
      deposit >
      COALESCE(SUM(deposit) OVER (
                  PARTITION BY customer_id
                  ORDER BY deposit_dt
                  ROWS BETWEEN 2 PRECEDING AND 1 PRECEDING)
       , 0) AS hi_deposit_alert
FROM c9r5_vw
ORDER BY
      customer_id, deposit_dt desc;
```

This query generates a column that shows `TRUE` or `FALSE`, depending on the fact that a customer made a deposit more than the sum of their last two deposits. The output is as follows:

	# CUSTOMER_ID	DEPOSIT_DT	# DEPOSIT	0|1 HI_DEPOSIT_ALERT
1	0	2026-04-25	300	FALSE
2	0	2026-04-20	400	FALSE
3	0	2026-04-15	200	FALSE
4	0	2026-04-10	300	FALSE
5	0	2026-04-05	300	FALSE
6	0	2026-03-31	500	FALSE
7	0	2026-03-26	400	TRUE
8	0	2026-03-21	100	FALSE
9	0	2026-03-16	200	FALSE

Figure 9.21 – Comparing each customer's deposit with the sum of their two preceding deposits

The output demonstrates how the analytical calculation evaluates each deposit within the context of prior deposits for the same CUSTOMER_ID. The window function uses the ordering of DEPOSIT_DT to compare the current row against earlier transactions in the customer's history. The HI_DEPOSIT_ALERT column is set to TRUE when the current deposit exceeds the comparison value calculated from those prior rows.

4. We can use many other functions for the window ranges. Similarly, window ranges can have different configurations.
   In this step, the window definition is expanded to include all prior deposits for the current customer. Rather than calculating a running total, the query computes the average of the previous deposits and compares it to the current deposit value. This allows you to identify deposits that are higher than the customer's historical average, which can be useful for detecting unusual activity or changes in behavior.

```
SELECT
      customer_id,
      deposit_dt,
      deposit,
      COALESCE(AVG(deposit) OVER (
                PARTITION BY customer_id
                ORDER BY deposit_dt
                ROWS BETWEEN UNBOUNDED PRECEDING AND 1 PRECEDING)
       , 0) as past_average_deposit,
      deposit >  past_average_deposit AS hi_deposit_alert
FROM
     c9r5_vw

WHERE CUSTOMER_ID = 3
```

```
ORDER BY
      customer_id, deposit_dt desc;
```

The output is as follows:

	CUSTOMER_ID	DEPOSIT_DT	DEPOSIT	PAST_AVERAGE_DEPOSIT	HI_DEPOSIT_ALERT
46	3	2025-09-09	400	288.888	TRUE
47	3	2025-09-04	300	288.461	TRUE
48	3	2025-08-30	300	288.000	TRUE
49	3	2025-08-25	500	279.166	TRUE
50	3	2025-08-20	400	273.913	TRUE
51	3	2025-08-15	100	281.818	FALSE
52	3	2025-08-10	500	271.428	TRUE
53	3	2025-08-05	400	265.000	TRUE
54	3	2025-07-31	300	263.157	TRUE
55	3	2025-07-26	300	261.111	TRUE
56	3	2025-07-21	100	270.588	FALSE

Figure 9.22 – Comparing the current deposit to the average of all the previous deposits of a customer

We have also added a column that calculates the past average deposit for the customer with `CUSTOMER_ID = 3`. This is then compared with the current value of the deposit to generate an alert.

How it works...

Window functions in Snowflake perform calculations across a set of related rows while still returning a result for each underlying row. Unlike traditional aggregate functions, window functions do not collapse multiple rows into a single summary row. Instead, they preserve row-level detail and add analytical calculations alongside it.

A window is typically defined using three components:

- `PARTITION BY` groups related rows, such as all records for the same customer
- `ORDER BY` establishes the sequence of rows within each partition, often by date or timestamp
- The window frame defines which rows relative to the current row should be included in the calculation.

For example, a query might analyze each customer's deposits in date order and compare the current deposit to the previous two deposits or to the historical average of all earlier deposits.

This makes window functions especially useful for running totals, moving averages, rankings, trend analysis, anomaly detection, and many other analytical workloads.

Generating sequences in Snowflake

Generating unique values is a common requirement in data platforms. While many modern architectures now use hash-based or distributed key strategies, numeric sequences remain a familiar and useful option in scenarios such as technical row identifiers, legacy integrations, ordered inserts, and simple surrogate key generation.

Snowflake supports both standalone `SEQUENCE` objects and auto-incrementing table columns. In this recipe, you will learn how these features work, where they can be applied effectively, and practical considerations when using sequences in modern analytical environments.

Getting ready

You will need access to a Snowflake environment. The SQL statements in this recipe can be executed using either Snowsight or the Snowflake CLI.

How to do it...

In the following steps, you will create several Snowflake sequences and observe how sequence values are generated. You will then use sequences to populate table columns both explicitly during inserts and implicitly through column default definitions. These examples demonstrate common approaches for generating unique numeric identifiers in Snowflake. The steps are as follows:

1. Create a database for this recipe and define a basic `SEQUENCE`. This sequence uses Snowflake's default behavior, beginning at 1 and incrementing by 1 each time a new value is requested.

   ```
   CREATE DATABASE C9_R6;
   CREATE SEQUENCE SEQ1;
   ```

   The sequence should succeed and show the following message:

	status
1	Sequence SEQ1 successfully created.

   Figure 9.23 – SEQUENCE creation message given by Snowflake

2. Now, Retrieve values from the sequence.

   ```
   SELECT SEQ1.NEXTVAL;
   ```

You will see a value of 1 being returned, as shown here:

	# NEXTVAL
1	1

Figure 9.24 – Initializing a sequence

3. Now that the sequence has been incremented, if we perform the same `SELECT` statement again, we will get the next value in the sequence, which will be 2. Run the following SQL to check the next value:

```
SELECT SEQ1.NEXTVAL;
```

The result is shown in the following screenshot:

	# NEXTVAL
1	2

Figure 9.25 – The next value of the sequence on the second call

> **Note**
>
> Snowflake sequences are designed to generate unique values, but the returned numbers may not always appear consecutive or in display order. In distributed systems, gaps can occur, and result ordering is not guaranteed unless an explicit `ORDER BY` clause is used.

4. Let's request multiple sequence values in a single statement.

```
SELECT SEQ1.NEXTVAL,SEQ1.NEXTVAL,SEQ1.NEXTVAL;
```

Each reference returns a unique value, even when the sequence is called multiple times within the same query.

	# NEXTVAL	# NEXTVAL	# NEXTVAL
1	401	402	403

Figure 9.26 – Series of calls made to the sequence and order of execution

5. Now, create a `SEQUENCE` with custom starting and increment values. This sequence begins at `777` and increases by `100` for each new value generated.

```
CREATE SEQUENCE SEQ_SPECIAL
START WITH =  777
INCREMENT BY = 100;
```

The sequence should be created successfully, and you should see the following message:

A status
Sequence SEQ_SPECIAL successfully created.

Figure 9.27 – Successful sequence creation

6. Let's test the preceding sequence by running the following SQL:

```
SELECT SEQ_SPECIAL.NEXTVAL,
       SEQ_SPECIAL.NEXTVAL,
       SEQ_SPECIAL.NEXTVAL;
```

This command's output will show that this sequence starts at 777 and increments by 100, as shown here:

# NEXTVAL	# NEXTVAL	# NEXTVAL
777	877	977

Figure 9.28 – Effect of INTERVAL on SEQUENCE

The returned values demonstrate the configured starting point and increment pattern.

7. Now, let's create a table that will use sequence-generated identifiers.

```
CREATE TABLE T1
(
  CUSTOMER_ID INTEGER,
  CUSTOMER_NAME STRING
);
```

8. We will follow that by creating a sequence that will be used for populating auto-increment values in the `CUSTOMER_ID` column:

```
CREATE SEQUENCE T1_SEQ;
```

9. We shall now use the `SEQUENCE` in the `INSERT INTO` statement to populate the data:

```
INSERT INTO T1
SELECT T1_SEQ.NEXTVAL,
       RANDSTR(10, RANDOM())
FROM TABLE(GENERATOR(ROWCOUNT => 500));
```

You will see that 500 rows have been inserted into this table.

10. Now, let's perform a query on the inserted data.

```
SELECT * FROM T1;
```

The `CUSTOMER_ID` column should now contain incrementing values generated during the insert, as shown in the following screenshot:

	# CUSTOMER_ID	A CUSTOMER_NAME
1	1	au9AtA36g6
2	2	OgH89CyGJt
3	3	DF44bgOM2H
4	4	LV2FbbXVz9
5	5	f0U0bfogxN
6	6	0f6s9ok1FQ
7	7	Tkp8mX7o3v
8	8	V6iZx1oxtk
9	9	qr8Kj05CdE

Figure 9.29 – GENERATOR used with explicit calls to SEQUENCE

11. Now create a second table that uses a sequence as the default column value.

```
CREATE SEQUENCE T2_SEQ;
CREATE TABLE T2
(
  CUSTOMER_ID INTEGER DEFAULT T2_SEQ.NEXTVAL,
  CUSTOMER_NAME STRING
);
```

With this design, Snowflake automatically generates the identifier when no value is supplied.

12. Let's insert some data into this table but omit `CUSTOMER_ID` while inserting.

```
INSERT INTO T2 (CUSTOMER_NAME)
SELECT RANDSTR(10, RANDOM())
FROM
  TABLE
    (generator(rowcount => 500));
```

Because the column has a default sequence value, Snowflake automatically assigns a unique identifier to each row.

13. Let's check the data in the table by running the following SQL:

```
SELECT * FROM T2;
```

The output is as follows:

# CUSTOMER_ID	A CUSTOMER_NAME
1	TKfMFBb4ag
2	jW98uMbmaz
3	GBVEJQWd7d
4	sPjoG9XfCr
5	Kd8BFmN3vL
6	KDHqtkHoui
7	uWm5wNWTMg
8	mlHBvemvsh
9	gct4fWXAKR

Figure 9.30 – GENERATOR used with an implicit SEQUENCE

As we can see, the `CUSTOMER_ID` column has automatically been assigned an incremental value since we set up the column default value to be `NEXTVAL` of the sequence.

How it works...

Sequences in Snowflake are database objects used to generate unique numeric values that automatically increment according to a defined interval. By default, a sequence begins at 1 and increments by 1, although custom starting values and increment patterns can also be specified.

Sequence values are designed to be unique across multiple statements, sessions, and concurrent workloads. If several users or processes request sequence values at the same time, Snowflake ensures that each request receives a distinct value without collision.

Sequences can be used in several ways. A common pattern is assigning technical identifiers or auto-incrementing values to table columns. This can be done by explicitly calling NEXTVAL during an INSERT, or by defining a column default that automatically retrieves the next sequence value when rows are loaded.

It is important to note that, like many distributed database platforms, Snowflake sequences are not guaranteed to be gap-free. Values may be skipped due to concurrency, caching, rollbacks, or parallel execution. For this reason, sequences should be used when uniqueness is required, rather than when uninterrupted numbering is expected.

Using QUALIFY to simplify filtering of window functions

In the earlier recipe, *Ordered analytics over window frames*, you learned how Snowflake window functions can analyze related rows while preserving row-level detail. Those same functions are widely used in analytics, but they are equally valuable in data engineering workloads such as deduplication, change data capture, Type 2 dimensions, and Data Vault processing.

In many SQL platforms, filtering the results of a window function often requires an additional subquery or common table expression, which can make otherwise simple queries harder to read and maintain.

Snowflake provides the QUALIFY clause to simplify this pattern. QUALIFY allows you to filter rows after window functions have been evaluated, making queries more concise and easier to understand.

In this recipe, you will learn how to use QUALIFY with functions such as ROW_NUMBER, RANK, and DENSE_RANK. You will use it to simplify common patterns such as selecting the most recent row per business key, returning top-ranked results, removing duplicate records, and streamlining warehouse loading logic.

Getting ready

You will need access to a Snowflake environment. The SQL statements in this recipe can be executed using Snowsight.

How to do it...

In the following steps, you will create a small sample table and use Snowflake's QUALIFY clause to simplify common filtering patterns based on window functions. The examples demonstrate practical use cases such as selecting the most recent row per business key, returning top-ranked results, and removing duplicate records without the need for nested subqueries. The steps are as follows:

1. Begin by creating a sample table for this recipe. This table will store sample customer sales transactions used throughout the recipe.

```
CREATE OR REPLACE DATABASE C9_R7;

CREATE OR REPLACE TABLE C9_R7_SALES
(
    CUSTOMER_ID INTEGER,
    ORDER_DT DATE,
    SALES_AMT NUMBER(10,2)
);
```

2. Now insert sample rows into the table. The sample data includes multiple rows for each customer so ranking and deduplication examples can be demonstrated.

```
INSERT INTO C9_R7_SALES VALUES
(101,'2026-01-05',125.00),
(101,'2026-02-10',175.00),
(101,'2026-03-15',150.00),
(102,'2026-01-12',220.00),
(102,'2026-02-18',220.00),
(103,'2026-01-08',95.00),
(103,'2026-03-01',140.00),
(103,'2026-03-20',140.00);
```

3. Let's , review the source data before applying analytical logic.

```
SELECT *
FROM C9_R7_SALES
ORDER BY CUSTOMER_ID, ORDER_DT;
```

This confirms the rows that will be used in the remaining examples.

	CUSTOMER_	ORDER_DT	SALES_AMT
1	101	2026-01-05	125.00
2	101	2026-02-10	175.00
3	101	2026-03-15	150.00
4	102	2026-01-12	220.00
5	102	2026-02-18	220.00
6	103	2026-01-08	95.00
7	103	2026-03-01	140.00
8	103	2026-03-20	140.00

Figure 9.31 – Sample sales data used in the QUALIFY examples

4. Now let's return the most recent row for each customer.

```
SELECT CUSTOMER_ID,
       ORDER_DT,
       SALES_AMT
FROM C9_R7_SALES
QUALIFY ROW_NUMBER() OVER
       (PARTITION BY CUSTOMER_ID ORDER BY ORDER_DT DESC) = 1;
```

`ROW_NUMBER()` assigns a sequence within each customer group, starting with the newest date. `QUALIFY` then keeps only the latest row.

	CUSTOMER_ID	ORDER_DT	SALES_AMT
1	101	2026-03-15	150.00
2	102	2026-02-18	220.00
3	103	2026-03-20	140.00

Figure 9.32 – Customer latest row results

5. Let's now Identify the highest sales value for each customer:

```
SELECT CUSTOMER_ID,
       ORDER_DT,
       SALES_AMT
FROM C9_R7_SALES
```

```
QUALIFY RANK() OVER
      (PARTITION BY CUSTOMER_ID ORDER BY SALES_AMT DESC) = 1;
```

This query ranks rows by sales amount within each customer group. If multiple rows share the highest value, each tied row is returned.

	# CUSTOMER_ID	ORDER_DT	# SALES_AMT
1	101	2026-02-10	175.00
2	102	2026-01-12	220.00
3	102	2026-02-18	220.00
4	103	2026-03-01	140.00
5	103	2026-03-20	140.00

Figure 9.33 – Customer latest row results

> **Note**
>
> In the sample data, customer `102` has two transactions with the same `SALES_AMT` of `220.00`, so both rows are returned with a rank of `1`. This illustrates an important difference between `RANK()` and `ROW_NUMBER()`: `RANK()` preserves ties, while `ROW_NUMBER()` assigns a unique sequence even when values are the same.

6. Now, let's return the top two rows per customer by sales amount.

```
SELECT CUSTOMER_ID,
       ORDER_DT,
       SALES_AMT
FROM C9_R7_SALES
QUALIFY ROW_NUMBER() OVER
       (PARTITION BY CUSTOMER_ID ORDER BY SALES_AMT DESC) <= 2;
```

This pattern is useful when selecting the top-N records within each business key.

	# CUSTOMER_ID	ORDER_DT	# SALES_AMT
1	101	2026-02-10	175.00
2	101	2026-03-15	150.00
3	102	2026-01-12	220.00
4	102	2026-02-18	220.00
5	103	2026-03-01	140.00
6	103	2026-03-20	140.00

Figure 9.34 – Top 2 Customer rows

7. Let's now examine a common scenario that removes duplicate business rows while retaining the most recent occurrence.

```
SELECT CUSTOMER_ID,
       ORDER_DT,
       SALES_AMT
FROM C9_R7_SALES
QUALIFY ROW_NUMBER() OVER
       (
         PARTITION BY CUSTOMER_ID, SALES_AMT
         ORDER BY ORDER_DT DESC
       ) = 1;
```

This approach is commonly used in data warehousing and ingestion pipelines where duplicate records must be consolidated while preserving the latest version.

	CUSTOMER_ID	ORDER_DT	SALES_AMT
1	101	2026-02-10	175.00
2	103	2026-01-08	95.00
3	103	2026-03-20	140.00
4	101	2026-03-15	150.00
5	102	2026-02-18	220.00
6	101	2026-01-05	125.00

Figure 9.35 – Lates duplicate version

8. For our final step, let's compare this with the traditional subquery approach.

```
SELECT CUSTOMER_ID,
       ORDER_DT,
       SALES_AMT
FROM
(
    SELECT CUSTOMER_ID,
           ORDER_DT,
           SALES_AMT,
           ROW_NUMBER() OVER
           (PARTITION BY CUSTOMER_ID ORDER BY ORDER_DT DESC) AS RN
    FROM C9_R7_SALES
)
WHERE RN = 1;
```

This returns the same result as the earlier QUALIFY ROW_NUMBER() example that selected the most recent row for each customer, but it requires an additional nested query. The QUALIFY clause often provides a cleaner and more maintainable alternative.

How it works...

When Snowflake executes a query containing window functions, calculations such as `ROW_NUMBER()`, `RANK()`, and `DENSE_RANK()` are performed across the logical row sets defined in the `OVER()` clause. Once those values have been produced, the `QUALIFY` clause can filter the rows based on the windowed results.

This allows filtering logic to remain in the same query block rather than requiring an outer query or common table expression. Window functions operate over logical row sets defined by the `OVER()` clause:

- `PARTITION BY` separates rows into groups, such as one group per customer
- `ORDER BY` determines ranking or sequencing within each group
- The window function then calculates a result for each row inside that partition

In this recipe, `ROW_NUMBER()` was used when only one row should be retained, such as the latest row per customer. `RANK()` was used when tied values should be preserved, which is why customer 102 returned more than one row for the highest sales amount.

This pattern is especially useful in data warehousing and engineering workloads where developers frequently need to deduplicate source data, retain current dimension rows, isolate top-performing records, or simplify SQL used in slowly changing dimension and Data Vault processing.

Creating and using user-defined data types

As Snowflake data initiatives grow within organizations, many tables begin to share common groups of columns that are reused across the account. Typical examples include customer attributes, address information, contact details, financial fields, and metadata columns used for auditing, lineage, and historical tracking. Repeating these definitions across many tables can increase development effort and lead to inconsistent implementations.

Snowflake supports user-defined data types, including structured object types that allow related attributes to be defined once and reused across multiple database objects. This can simplify schema design, improve consistency, and reduce repetitive DDL maintenance.

In this recipe, we will focus on a dimensional modeling use case by creating a structured metadata type containing common columns frequently used across dimension tables.

Getting ready

You will need access to a Snowflake environment. The SQL statements in this recipe can be executed using either Snowsight or the Snowflake CLI.

How to do it...

In many data warehouse environments, dimension tables repeatedly require the same metadata columns to support historical tracking, auditing, and lineage. Common examples include `EFFECTIVE_START_DT`, `EFFECTIVE_END_DT`, `IS_CURRENT`, `CREATED_TS`, `UPDATED_TS`, `SOURCE_SYSTEM_CD`, and `LOAD_BATCH_ID`.

Rather than redefining these related columns in every table, the following steps demonstrate how to create a structured user-defined type once and reuse it across multiple dimension tables. The steps are as follows:

1. Begin by creating a database for this recipe and setting the working context. This database will store the user-defined type and sample dimension tables used in the recipe.

```
CREATE OR REPLACE DATABASE C9_R8;

USE DATABASE C9_R8;
USE SCHEMA PUBLIC;
```

2. Now create a structured user-defined type for common dimension metadata columns. This object groups commonly repeated metadata attributes into a reusable definition.

```
CREATE OR REPLACE TYPE DIMENSION_METADATA AS OBJECT(
    EFFECTIVE_START_DT DATE,
    EFFECTIVE_END_DT DATE,
    IS_CURRENT BOOLEAN,
    CREATED_TS TIMESTAMP_NTZ,
    UPDATED_TS TIMESTAMP_NTZ,
    SOURCE_SYSTEM_CD VARCHAR(25),
    LOAD_BATCH_ID NUMBER(18,0)
);
```

3. Now instead of defining several metadata columns individually, the table now references a single structured type, improving consistency and reducing repetitive DDL.

```
CREATE OR REPLACE TABLE DIM_CUSTOMER
(
    CUSTOMER_KEY NUMBER,
    CUSTOMER_ID VARCHAR(50),
    CUSTOMER_NAME VARCHAR(100),
    METADATA DIMENSION_METADATA
);
```

4. Let's run the following query to review the table structure to understand how the metadata type is applied.

```
DESCRIBE TABLE DIM_CUSTOMER;
```

This output shows that the `METADATA` column is defined as a structured `OBJECT` type based on the `DIMENSION_METADATA` definition. Rather than creating separate physical columns for each metadata attribute, Snowflake stores them as a single structured column.

	name	type	kind	null?	de
1	CUSTOMER_KEY	NUMBER(38,0)	COLUMN	Y	null
2	CUSTOMER_ID	VARCHAR(50)	COLUMN	Y	null
3	CUSTOMER_NAME	VARCHAR(100)	COLUMN	Y	null
4	METADATA	C9_R8.PUBLIC.DIMENSION_METADATA	COLUMN	Y	null

Figure 9.36 – Metadata columns as a structured object

5. Let's Insert sample rows into the dimension table. The metadata values are inserted as a structured object that aligns with the user-defined type.

```
INSERT INTO DIM_CUSTOMER
SELECT
  1,
  'C1001',
  'ACME INDUSTRIES',
  OBJECT_CONSTRUCT(
    'EFFECTIVE_START_DT','2025-01-01'::DATE,
    'EFFECTIVE_END_DT','9999-12-31'::DATE,
    'IS_CURRENT',TRUE,
    'CREATED_TS',CURRENT_TIMESTAMP()::TIMESTAMP_NTZ,
    'UPDATED_TS',CURRENT_TIMESTAMP()::TIMESTAMP_NTZ,
    'SOURCE_SYSTEM_CD','ERP',
    'LOAD_BATCH_ID',1001::NUMBER(18,0)
  )::DIMENSION_METADATA
UNION ALL
SELECT
  2,
  'C1002',
```

```
    'NORTHWIND RETAIL',
    OBJECT_CONSTRUCT(
      'EFFECTIVE_START_DT','2025-02-01'::DATE,
      'EFFECTIVE_END_DT','9999-12-31'::DATE,
      'IS_CURRENT',TRUE,
      'CREATED_TS',CURRENT_TIMESTAMP()::TIMESTAMP_NTZ,
      'UPDATED_TS',CURRENT_TIMESTAMP()::TIMESTAMP_NTZ,
      'SOURCE_SYSTEM_CD','CRM',
      'LOAD_BATCH_ID',1002::NUMBER(18,0)
    )::DIMENSION_METADATA;;
```

6. Now you can query the table to review the stored metadata.

```
  SELECT CUSTOMER_KEY,
  CUSTOMER_ID,
  CUSTOMER_NAME,
  METADATA
FROM DIM_CUSTOMER;
```

As seen in the following figure, the metadata is stored as a single structured column while still preserving all underlying attributes.

A CUSTOMER_NAM	{ } METADATA
ACME INDUSTRIES	{ "EFFECTIVE_START_DT": "2025-01-01", "EFFECTIVE_END_DT": "9999-12-31", "IS_CURRENT": true, "CREATED_TS":
NORTHWIND RETAIL	{ "EFFECTIVE_START_DT": "2025-02-01", "EFFECTIVE_END_DT": "9999-12-31", "IS_CURRENT": true, "CREATED_TS":

Figure 9.37 – Top 2 stored metadata

7. The `METADATA` column stores a structured object, but you can still reference individual attributes directly using object notation.

```
SELECT CUSTOMER_NAME,
       METADATA:EFFECTIVE_START_DT,
       METADATA:IS_CURRENT,
       METADATA:SOURCE_SYSTEM_CD
FROM DIM_CUSTOMER;
```

The following figure shows the specific metadata values from the statement above.

	CUSTOMER_NAME	METADATA:EFFECTIVE_START_DT	METADATA:IS_CURRENT	METADATA:SOURCE_SYSTEM_CD
1	ACME INDUSTRIES	2025-01-01	TRUE	ERP
2	NORTHWIND RETAIL	2025-02-01	TRUE	CRM

Figure 9.38 – Individual metadata values

8. You can also view the user-defined types available in the schema.

```
SHOW TYPES;
```

This returns the structured type that has been created and is available for reuse.

How it works...

Snowflake **user-defined types** (**UDTs**) allow you to define reusable type definitions that can be applied across multiple tables. In this recipe, we used a structured UDT based on an `OBJECT` type, which groups multiple related attributes into a single logical column.

When the `DIMENSION_METADATA` type is created, Snowflake defines a schema for the object, including the attribute names and their corresponding data types. Any column defined using this type must conform to that structure. This provides a level of consistency similar to defining multiple columns, but with the flexibility of storing them as a single object.

In the table definition, the `METADATA` column is not expanded into separate physical columns. Instead, it is stored as a single structured object. This is why the `DESCRIBE TABLE` output shows one column of type `DIMENSION_METADATA`, rather than multiple metadata columns.

When inserting data, the `OBJECT_CONSTRUCT` function is used to build an object that matches the defined structure. The explicit cast to `DIMENSION_METADATA` ensures that the object conforms to the expected schema. Without this cast, Snowflake treats the value as a generic semi-structured object rather than a typed structure.

When querying the data, individual attributes are accessed using object notation, for example, `METADATA:EFFECTIVE_START_DT`. This allows you to work with the structured data in a way that is similar to querying regular columns, while still maintaining the benefits of a reusable grouped definition.

This approach is particularly useful when multiple tables share the same group of related attributes. By defining the structure once, you can enforce consistency across your data model while reducing repetitive DDL and improving maintainability.

> **Note**
>
> While UDTs help standardize column structures, changes to a type definition do not automatically propagate to existing tables or data. Updates to a type may require modifying dependent objects.

Get this book's PDF version and more

Scan the QR code (or go to `packtpub.com/unlock`). Search for this book by name, confirm the edition, and then follow the steps on the page.

10

Extending Snowflake Capabilities

Snowflake provides far more than a platform for querying and storing data. As data initiatives grow in complexity, organizations must extend Snowflake to support custom logic, data processing, and governance at scale. Traditionally, this extensibility has been achieved through programmatic constructs such as **user-defined functions** (**UDFs**) and Snowpark, enabling developers to embed business logic and data transformations directly within the platform.

However, modern data platforms require more than code alone. Governance, security, and data classification must scale alongside data growth. Snowflake enables this through metadata-driven capabilities such as tags and policy-based controls, allowing organizations to enforce rules dynamically without modifying underlying data structures. These governance capabilities complement programmatic extensions by enabling behavior to be modified without requiring changes to application logic.

In this chapter, you will explore how to extend Snowflake using both approaches. You will begin with programmatic extensibility using UDFs and Snowpark, and then transition into governance-based extensibility using tags and dynamic data masking. Together, these capabilities demonstrate how Snowflake can be extended not only through code, but also through centralized, policy-driven design.

The following recipes will be covered in this chapter:

- Creating a scalar user-defined function using SQL
- Creating a table user-defined function using SQL
- Creating a scalar user-defined function using JavaScript
- Creating a table user-defined function using JavaScript
- Processing data using Snowpark
- Transforming and writing data using Snowpark

- Applying tags to support policy-based governance
- Implementing dynamic data masking using tags

Technical requirements

This chapter requires access to a modern internet browser (Chrome, Microsoft Edge, Firefox, and so on) and access to the internet to connect your Snowflake instance to the cloud.

You can download the example project and code for this book by following the instructions in the ***Download the example code files*** section in the *Preface* of this book.

Creating a scalar user-defined function using SQL

Snowflake provides the capability to create UDFs that extend the platform by enabling custom logic not available out of the box. Snowflake supports creating UDFs using several languages, including SQL, JavaScript, Python, Java, and Scala. In this chapter, we will focus on SQL and JavaScript UDFs, both of which can return either scalar or tabular results.

In this recipe, we will create SQL-based scalar UDFs and demonstrate how to invoke them in different query scenarios. A scalar UDF returns a single value for each row processed, making it useful for encapsulating reusable logic within SQL queries.

Getting ready

You will need access to a Snowflake environment. The SQL statements in this recipe can be executed using either Snowsight or the Snowflake CLI.

How to do it...

We will be creating a series of UDFs to demonstrate the various SQL UDF capabilities provided by Snowflake. We will start by creating a relatively simple UDF and will slowly increase the complexity of the UDFs that we create. The basic syntax of creating a SQL function is straightforward and as follows:

```
CREATE FUNCTION <name> ( [ <arg_name> <arg_data_type> ] )
RETURNS <result_data_type>
AS '<function_definition_in_SQL>'
```

The following steps use this syntax to create and invoke several SQL-based scalar UDFs, beginning with a simple example and gradually introducing more advanced functionality.

1. Let's start by creating a database in which we will create our SQL scalar UDFs. To do so, execute the following command:

```
CREATE DATABASE C10_R1;
```

2. Next, we will create a relatively simple UDF that squares the value that is provided as the input:

```
CREATE FUNCTION square(val float)
RETURNS float
AS
$$
  val * val
$$
;
```

The function should be created with a success message. Notice that the body of the function has been enclosed between the $$ symbols. You can use either the $$ symbols or enclose the function body between single quotes.

3. We can now test this function by calling it in a `SELECT` statement. To do so, run the following command:

```
SELECT square(5);
```

The statement will output the value `25` as expected.

4. Let's create a slightly more complicated function that can apply a tax percentage (10% in this case) and return the profit after tax deduction. To do so, run the following command:

```
CREATE FUNCTION profit_after_tax(cost float, revenue float)
RETURNS float
AS
$$
  (revenue - cost) * (1 - 0.1)
$$
;
```

The function should be created successfully.

5. Let's now call the function with a simple `SELECT` statement, as shown below:

```
SELECT profit_after_tax(100,120);
```

The call returns 18 as a result, which indicates that the profit before tax was $20 and 10% was subtracted to leave us with $18.

6. We can also call this UDF in several places in the SQL. This UDF can be used in the `SELECT` list or the `WHERE` clause and pretty much any place where a scalar value can be used, for example, joins. Let's call this UDF in the `SELECT` list and the `WHERE` clause as follows:

```
SELECT
    DD.D_DATE,
    SUM(profit_after_tax(SS_WHOLESALE_COST, SS_SALES_PRICE)) AS real_profit
FROM SNOWFLAKE_SAMPLE_DATA.TPCDS_SF10TCL.STORE_SALES SS
INNER JOIN SNOWFLAKE_SAMPLE_DATA.TPCDS_SF10TCL.DATE_DIM DD
    ON SS.SS_SOLD_DATE_SK = DD.D_DATE_SK
WHERE DD.D_DATE BETWEEN '2003-01-01' AND '2003-12-31'
  AND profit_after_tax(SS_WHOLESALE_COST, SS_SALES_PRICE) < -50
GROUP BY DD.D_DATE;
```

7. We are trying to return only those results in this query where the `profit_after_tax` was negative and less than -$50, which is the sales that made a significant loss. The results are shown as follows:

D_DATE	REAL_PROFIT
2003-01-01	-153011149.065
2003-01-02	-152977353.948

Figure 10.1 – Output of calling the profit_after_tax UDF

The preceding example demonstrated the creation and use of a simple scalar SQL UDF. Scalar UDFs can be used in most places in a SQL statement, including in `SELECT`, `WHERE`, and `GROUP BY` clauses.

How it works...

Snowflake provides the capability to create UDFs using familiar SQL syntax. The most commonly used type of UDF is a scalar UDF, which returns a single value for each row processed. Within a UDF body, you can use standard SQL expressions, including arithmetic operations, conditional logic, and calls to other UDFs.

Creating a table user-defined function using SQL

Snowflake provides the capability to create UDFs that extend the platform by enabling custom logic not available out of the box. Snowflake supports creating UDFs using several languages, including SQL, JavaScript, Python, Java, and Scala. In this recipe, we will focus on SQL and JavaScript UDFs, both of which can return either scalar or tabular results.

In this recipe, we will create SQL-based table UDFs and demonstrate how to invoke them in various scenarios. A table UDF returns multiple rows and columns, allowing you to encapsulate reusable query logic that produces relational results.

Getting ready

You will need access to a Snowflake environment. The SQL statements in this recipe can be executed using either Snowsight or the Snowflake CLI.

How to do it

We will create a series of UDFs to demonstrate the SQL table UDF capabilities provided by Snowflake. We will begin by exploring an existing `TABLE` function provided by Snowflake and reviewing the results it returns.

1. Let's start by creating a database in which we will create our SQL tabular UDFs. To do so, execute the following command:

```
CREATE DATABASE C10_R2;
USE DATABASE C10_R2;
USE SCHEMA PUBLIC;
```

2. Next, we will run an out-of-the-box `TABLE` function provided by Snowflake to see how to call `TABLE` functions and review the results returned by those functions. To do so, run the following command:

```
SELECT *
FROM TABLE(information_schema.query_history_by_session())
ORDER BY start_time;
```

The preceding query should show results similar to the following; however, do note that you will get different results depending on how many other queries you have run:

Row	QUERY_ID	QUERY_TEXT	DATABASE_NA	SCHEMA_NAME	QUER
1	019a4342-0...	CREATE DATABASE...	NULL	NULL	CREA
2	019a4342-0...	USE DATABASE C10...	C10_R2	PUBLIC	USE
3	019a4342-0...	USE SCHEMA PUBL...	C10_R2	PUBLIC	USE

Figure 10.2 – Output of the query_history_by_session table function

The vital aspect to note here is that we have just called a `TABLE` function. Since a `TABLE` function returns multiple rows and columns, the result we see in the previous step is in a relational table format.

It is also important to note that the call must be enclosed within a `TABLE(<functionname>)` statement when calling a `TABLE` function.

3. Let's now create a relatively simple `TABLE` function using SQL. The function will return the name of a location and the time zone that the location has.
The basic syntax of creating a SQL function is straightforward and as follows:

```
CREATE FUNCTION <name> ( [ <arg_name> <arg_data_type> ] )
RETURNS TABLE ( <output_col_name> <output_col_type> [, <output_col_name>
<output_col_type> ... ] )
AS '<function_definition_in_SQL>'
```

Using the previous syntax, we will create a new UDF and call the UDF in a SQL statement.

4. To keep things simple, we will use hardcoded values. Run the following SQL to create this function:

```
CREATE FUNCTION LocationTimeZone()
RETURNS TABLE(LocationName String, TimeZoneName String)
as
$$
    SELECT 'Sydney', 'GMT+11'
    UNION
    SELECT 'Auckland', 'GMT+13'
    UNION
```

```
    SELECT 'Islamabad', 'GMT+5'
    UNION
    SELECT 'London', 'GMT'
$$;
```

The function should be successfully created.

5. Let's now call this function. To do so, run the following SQL:

```
SELECT * FROM TABLE(LocationTimeZone());
```

You will see the following output:

Row	LOCATIONNAME	TIMEZONENAME
1	Sydney	GMT+11
2	Auckland	GMT+13
3	Islamabad	GMT+5
4	London	GMT

Figure 10.3 – Output from calling the Table UDF LocationTimeZone

6. Note that you can treat this output as any other relational table, so you can add `WHERE` clauses and select only particular columns. To do so, run the following SQL:

```
SELECT TimeZoneName FROM TABLE(LocationTimeZone())
WHERE LocationName = 'Sydney';
```

Predictably, the output has only the row for `Sydney` and only one column in the result set.

7. We do not necessarily have to hardcode values in a `TABLE` function. We can select from existing tables and even join tables within our function definition. Let's create such a `TABLE` function that joins data from two tables to produce an output:

```
CREATE FUNCTION CustomerOrders()
RETURNS TABLE(CustomerName String, TotalSpent Number(12,2))
as
$$
```

```
    SELECT C.C_NAME AS CustomerName, SUM(O.O_TOTALPRICE) AS TotalSpent
    FROM SNOWFLAKE_SAMPLE_DATA.TPCH_SF1.ORDERS O
    INNER JOIN SNOWFLAKE_SAMPLE_DATA.TPCH_SF1.CUSTOMER C
    ON C.C_CUSTKEY = O.O_CUSTKEY
    GROUP BY C.C_NAME
$$;
```

The creation of the function should be successful.

8. Let's call this function to review the output. To do so, run the following SQL:

```
SELECT * FROM TABLE(CustomerOrders());
```

You will see an output like what is shown here, and the function will return around 100,000 rows:

Row	CUSTOMERNAME	TOTALSPENT
1	Customer#000044485	3480299.61
2	Customer#000055624	2442812.17
3	Customer#000041861	2262921.26
4	Customer#000003296	1392250.10
5	Customer#000000307	3866167.74

Figure 10.4 – Output from calling the CustomerOrders UDF

9. Let's assume that we want to get the `TotalSpent` value for only a single customer. We are going to alter the function so that it can take the customer name as a parameter. To do so, run the following command:

```
CREATE FUNCTION CustomerOrders(CustomerName String)
RETURNS TABLE(CustomerName String, TotalSpent Number(12,2))
as
$$
    SELECT C.C_NAME AS CustomerName, SUM(O.O_TOTALPRICE) AS TotalSpent
    FROM SNOWFLAKE_SAMPLE_DATA.TPCH_SF1.ORDERS O
    INNER JOIN SNOWFLAKE_SAMPLE_DATA.TPCH_SF1.CUSTOMER C
    ON C.C_CUSTKEY = O.O_CUSTKEY
```

```
        WHERE C.C_NAME = CustomerName
        GROUP BY C.C_NAME
$$;
```

The function should be created successfully.

10. Before we go any further, it is essential to understand that we have created two functions here. One function is called `CustomerOrders`, which does not take any parameters, and there's another with the same name, which accepts the name as a parameter. To demonstrate this, run the following SQL:

```
SHOW FUNCTIONS LIKE '%CustomerOrders%';
```

You will see the following output, which explains that two functions are created:

created_on	name	schema_name	is_builtin	is_aggregate	is_ansi	min_num_argum	max_num_argu	arguments
2021-02-13 ...	CUSTOMER...	PUBLIC	N	N	N	0	0	CUSTOMERORDERS() RETURN
2021-02-13 ...	CUSTOMER...	PUBLIC	N	N	N	1	1	CUSTOMERORDERS(VARCHAR)

Figure 10.5 – Output from step 14 showing two UDFs with the same name

11. Let's now call the new function by passing in a customer name as a parameter:

```
SELECT * FROM TABLE(CustomerOrders('Customer#000062993'));
```

This should succeed, with a single row demonstrating that only the rows for the specified customer are returned.

The examples in this recipe demonstrated Snowflake's built-in `TABLE` functions and the creation of new `Table` UDFs. `Table` UDFs differ from Scalar UDFs in their return type, which is of the `Table` type in the case of Table UDFs.

How it works

`TABLE` functions are a powerful way of defining UDFs in Snowflake, with several built-in system functions provided as `TABLE` functions. You can find a list of Snowflake `TABLE` functions at `https://docs.snowflake.com/en/sql-reference/functions-table`.

There are two key aspects to understand when working with `TABLE` functions. First, a `TABLE` function can return multiple rows and columns, and therefore its output is presented in a relational format. Second, unlike scalar functions, `TABLE` functions cannot be called directly within expressions. Instead, they must be invoked using the `TABLE()` construct so that their results can be used within a query.

Creating a scalar user-defined function using JavaScript

In this recipe, we will be walking you through the creation of JavaScript-based *Scalar* UDFs and demonstrating the usage of JavaScript-based UDFs.

Getting ready

You will need to be connected to your Snowflake instance via the Web UI or the SnowSQL client to execute this recipe.

How to do it

We will create a series of UDFs to demonstrate the JavaScript UDF capabilities provided by Snowflake. We will begin with a simple UDF and gradually increase the complexity of the examples. The basic syntax for creating a JavaScript-based UDF is similar to that of a SQL UDF, with one key difference: if the `LANGUAGE` attribute is not specified, the UDF defaults to SQL. The syntax for a JavaScript-based UDF is as follows:

```
CREATE FUNCTION <name> ( [ <arg_name> <arg_data_type> ] )
RETURNS <result_data_type>
[ LANGUAGE JAVASCRIPT ]
AS <function_definition_in_SQL>
```

You can find the detailed syntax at `https://docs.snowflake.com/en/sql-reference/sql/create-function`. The following steps use this syntax to create and invoke several JavaScript-based scalar UDFs, beginning with a simple example and gradually introducing more advanced functionality:

1. Let's start by creating a database in which we will create our JavaScript-based scalar UDF. To do so, execute the following command:

   ```
   CREATE DATABASE C10_R3;
   ```

2. Next, we will create a very simple UDF that squares the value that is provided as the input. Note that compared to a SQL UDF, we must capitalize the parameter name in the function definition when defining an input parameter in a JavaScript UDF. This can be seen in the following code, where the input parameter `val` is used in uppercase as `VAL`:

   ```
   CREATE FUNCTION square(val float)
   RETURNS float
   ```

```
LANGUAGE JAVASCRIPT
AS
  'return VAL * VAL;'
;
```

This function should be created with a success message.

3. We can now test this function by calling it in a SELECT statement. To do so, run the following command:

```
SELECT square(5);
```

The statement will output the value 25 as expected.

4. We will now demonstrate how to create a recursive UDF using JavaScript. For the demonstration, we will be creating a simple factorial function that will recursively call itself to calculate the factorial of the input value:

```
CREATE FUNCTION factorial(val float)
RETURNS float
LANGUAGE JAVASCRIPT
AS
$$
    if ( VAL == 1 ){
        return VAL;
    }
    else{
        return VAL * factorial(VAL -1);
    }
$$
;
```

The function creation should complete successfully.

5. Let's try out the factorial function by invoking the function in a SELECT statement, as follows:

```
SELECT factorial(5);
```

This should result in the value 120 being returned. As demonstrated in the preceding examples, JavaScript-based UDFs can be relatively straightforward to implement;

however, it is worth noting that they also provide more powerful features, such as recursion capabilities.

How it works

Like other databases, Snowflake provides the capability to create UDFs. Unlike many other databases, Snowflake also allows UDFs to be written in JavaScript, enabling more advanced procedural logic within your functions.

The overall syntax for creating a JavaScript-based UDF is similar to that of a SQL UDF; however, you must explicitly specify `LANGUAGE JAVASCRIPT`. JavaScript UDFs execute within a restricted, sandboxed environment, which limits certain capabilities such as system-level access.

Creating a table user-defined function using JavaScript

Snowflake provides capabilities for creating UDFs that can be used to extend the system and perform operations not available out of the box. Snowflake supports two languages for creating UDFs: SQL and JavaScript. Either type of UDF can return scalar or table results. In this recipe, we will create JavaScript-based table UDFs and demonstrate how to call them in various scenarios.

Getting ready

You will need access to a Snowflake environment. The SQL statements in this recipe can be executed using either Snowsight or the Snowflake CLI.

How to do it

We will create a series of UDFs to demonstrate the capabilities of JavaScript-based table UDFs in Snowflake. We will begin by exploring an existing `TABLE` function and then create our own functions of increasing complexity.

The basic syntax for creating a JavaScript table UDF is as follows:

```
CREATE FUNCTION <name> ( [ <arg_name> <arg_data_type> ] )
RETURNS TABLE ( <output_col_name> <output_col_type>
[, <output_col_name> <output_col_type> ... ] )
[ LANGUAGE JAVASCRIPT ]
AS <function_definition_in_SQL>
```

You can find the detailed syntax at `https://docs.snowflake.com/en/sql-reference/sql/create-function.html`.

1. Let's start by creating a database in which we will create our SQL tabular UDFs. To do so, execute the following command:

```
CREATE DATABASE C10_R4;
USE DATABASE C10_R4;
USE SCHEMA PUBLIC;
```

2. Next, we will run an out-of-the-box `TABLE` function provided by Snowflake to see how to call `TABLE` functions and review the results returned by those functions. We will use the function to generate rows of random data; it is a handy function for various scenarios. The function is aptly called `GENERATOR`. Let's call this function to generate 10 rows of data. To do so, run the following command:

```
SELECT seq4() AS incremental_id, random() AS a_random_
  number
FROM TABLE(generator(rowcount => 10));
```

This should return 10 rows, as shown in the following screenshot:

Row	INCREMENTAL_ID	A_RANDOM_NUMBER
1	0	1319172314325829327
2	1	7287171906336155199
3	2	1471939173074368979
4	3	1446911816204395330
5	4	3570717189561876932
6	5	8748051370615372015
7	6	9163926763116258811
8	7	-166691577935958742
9	8	-1882923199411928270
10	9	-3889428872739052128

Figure 10.6 – Random data produced by the GENERATOR table function

The important aspect to note here is that we have just called a `TABLE` function. Since a `TABLE` function returns multiple rows and columns, the preceding result is in a relational table format. It is also important to note that the call must be enclosed within a `TABLE(<functionname>)` statement when calling a `TABLE` function.

3. Let's now create a relatively simple `TABLE` function using JavaScript. The function will return the two-letter ISO code for a country. To keep things simple, we will use hardcoded values for this initial example. Run the following SQL to create this function:

```
CREATE FUNCTION CountryISO()
RETURNS TABLE(CountryCode String, CountryName String)
LANGUAGE JAVASCRIPT
AS
$$
   {
   processRow: function f(row, rowWriter, context){
       rowWriter.writeRow({COUNTRYCODE: "AU",COUNTRYNAME:
         "Australia"});
       rowWriter.writeRow({COUNTRYCODE: "NZ",COUNTRYNAME:
        "New Zealand"});
       rowWriter.writeRow({COUNTRYCODE: "PK",COUNTRYNAME:
        "Pakistan"});
       }
    }
$$;
```

Snowflake interacts with user-defined `TABLE` functions through callback functions during the execution of a query. The preceding code used the `processRow` callback function to process rows and return them to the function output. Please note that we simply wrote three rows in the same callback function. Depending on your requirements, you may be processing a single row per callback.

Note that we have specified the language as JavaScript, and very importantly, we are using the uppercase `COUNTRYCODE` and `COUNTRYNAME` in the function definition. It is a requirement in Snowflake JavaScript UDFs that these are capitalized.

4. Let's now call this function. To do so, run the following SQL:

```
SELECT * FROM TABLE(CountryISO());
```

You will see the following output produced:

Row	COUNTRYCODE ↓	COUNTRYNAME
1	AU	Australia
2	NZ	New Zealand
3	PK	Pakistan

Figure 10.7 – Output from the CountryISO UDF

5. Note that you can treat this output as any other relational table, so you can add `WHERE` clauses and select only particular columns. To do so, run the following SQL:

```
SELECT COUNTRYCODE FROM TABLE(CountryISO()) WHERE
CountryCode = 'PK';
```

Predictably, the output has only the row for Pakistan and only the `COUNTRYCODE` column.

6. We do not necessarily have to hardcode values in a `TABLE` function. Instead, we can select data from the existing table and process each row. Let's create such a JavaScript-based `TABLE` function, which processes values for each row of a table and produces the count of characters for the input:

```
CREATE FUNCTION StringSize(input String)
RETURNS TABLE (Size FLOAT)
LANGUAGE JAVASCRIPT
AS
$$
{
    processRow: function f(row, rowWriter, context) {
      rowWriter.writeRow({SIZE: row.INPUT.length});
    }
}
$$;
```

The creation of the function should be successful with a success message.

7. Let's call this function to review the output. We can now call this function for a single value, which is not very useful; however, let's call it for a single value to demonstrate the concept:

```
SELECT * FROM TABLE(StringSize('TEST'));
```

As expected, you will see the value 4 returned as a result. But this is not especially useful, and we could have easily achieved the same result from a scalar function instead.

8. However, you can join this newly created TABLE function with another table and have the TABLE function process multiple rows. To do this, run the SQL as follows:

```
SELECT * FROM
SNOWFLAKE_SAMPLE_DATA.TPCH_SF1.NATION,
TABLE(StringSize(N_NAME));
```

The query produces the following output.

N_NATIONKEY	N_NAME	↓ N_REGIONK	N_COMMENT	SIZE
0	ALGERIA	0	haggle. carefully final deposi...	7
1	ARGENTINA	1	al foxes promise slyly accord...	9
2	BRAZIL	1	y alongside of the pending d...	6
3	CANADA	1	eas hang ironic, silent packa...	6
4	EGYPT	4	y above the carefully unusua...	5
5	ETHIOPIA	0	ven packages wake quickly. ...	8
6	FRANCE	3	refully final requests. regular,...	6

Figure 10.8 – Output from the StringSize UDF processing multiple rows

9. This approach of using TABLE functions is particularly powerful and allows you to create exciting functionality. An example of a TABLE function being used is the FLATTEN function provided out of the box by Snowflake.
In the preceding steps, the creation of a TABLE function using the JavaScript language was discussed. We also demonstrated how a TABLE function could be joined with a table and process multiple rows through that mechanism.

How it works

`TABLE` functions are a powerful way of defining UDFs in Snowflake. Several built-in system functions are implemented as `TABLE` functions. You can find a list of Snowflake `TABLE` functions at `https://docs.snowflake.com/en/sql-reference/functions-table`.

`TABLE` functions created using JavaScript are particularly powerful because they enable procedural logic that is not always practical using standard SQL-based UDFs. By leveraging JavaScript, you can use variables, control flow, and iterative logic to generate and manipulate output rows in a flexible manner.

Processing data using Snowpark

Snowflake provides native development capabilities through Snowpark, allowing data engineers to process data directly within Snowflake using familiar programming constructs. Snowpark supports multiple languages, including Python, Java, and Scala, and provides a DataFrame-based programming model.

If you are familiar with Apache Spark, Snowpark offers a similar approach for working with data, enabling operations such as loading data, applying transformations, and displaying results without requiring external clusters or moving data out of Snowflake.

In this recipe, we will use Snowpark with Python to perform a series of transformations that demonstrate how to process data directly within Snowflake.

Getting ready

You will need access to a Snowflake environment. Create a Snowflake notebook within a workspace and ensure that it is connected to a role and warehouse. If prompted, select or set a database and schema for the notebook execution context. A Snowpark session is automatically available within the notebook environment. The examples in this recipe are intended to be executed sequentially within a Snowflake notebook using Python cells.

How to do it

Snowpark is used to load data from a table, apply transformations, and display the results. These steps demonstrate how Snowpark enables working with data using a DataFrame-based programming model.

1. Begin by creating a Python cell and importing the required Snowpark libraries. These libraries provide the functionality needed to retrieve the active session, reference columns, and perform aggregation operations.

   ```
   from snowflake.snowpark.context import get_active_session
   from snowflake.snowpark.functions import col
   ```

   If executed successfully, no error message will be returned.

2. Let's retrieve the active Snowpark session. Within a Snowflake notebook, a connection to Snowflake is already established when a role and warehouse are selected. This step retrieves the active session associated with that connection.

   ```
   session = get_active_session()
   ```

   If executed successfully, no error message will be returned.

3. Next, load the `CUSTOMER` table into a DataFrame.

   ```
   df = session.table("SNOWFLAKE_SAMPLE_DATA.TPCH_SF1.CUSTOMER")
   ```

   This creates a DataFrame reference. No data is displayed at this stage because Snowpark does not execute the query until an action, such as `show()`, is called.

4. Now let's display sample rows from the `CUSTOMER` table.

   ```
   df.show()
   ```

   The following figure shows an example of the output returned.

```
3    df.show()
```

Executed 7 minutes ago

```
-------------------------------------------------------------------------------------------
|"C_CUSTKEY"  |"C_NAME"            |"C_ADDRESS"                              |"C_NATIONKEY"
-------------------------------------------------------------------------------------------
|60001        |Customer#000060001  |9Ii4zQn9cX                               |14
|60002        |Customer#000060002  |ThGBMjDwKzkoOxhz                         |15
|60003        |Customer#000060003  |Ed hbPtTXMTAsgGhCr4HuTzK,Md2             |16
|60004        |Customer#000060004  |NivCT2RVaavl,yUnKwBjDyMvB42WayXCnky      |10
|60005        |Customer#000060005  |1F3KM3ccEXEtI, B22XmCMOWJMl              |12
|60006        |Customer#000060006  |3isiXW651fa8p                            |22
```

Figure 10.9 – Output of the CUSTOMER DataFrame

5. Apply a filter to return only rows where `C_NATIONKEY` equals `14`, and display the result.

```
df_filtered = df.filter(col("C_NATIONKEY") == 14)
df_filtered.show()
```

   Only rows matching the filter condition should appear in the output.

6. Now select the relevant columns from the filtered DataFrame and display the result.

```
df_selected = df_filtered.select(
    col("C_CUSTKEY"),
    col("C_NAME"),
    col("C_ACCTBAL")
)
df_selected.show()
```

   This reduces the dataset to only the columns required for analysis.

7. Finally, sort the selected data by account balance in descending order and display the result.

```
df_sorted = df_selected.sort(col("C_ACCTBAL").desc())
df_sorted.show()
```

   The following figure shows the reduced set of columns sorted by account balance.

```
3    df.show()
```

Executed 7 minutes ago

```
------------------------------------------------------------------------------------------
|"C_CUSTKEY"  |"C_NAME"            |"C_ADDRESS"                          |"C_NATIONKEY"
------------------------------------------------------------------------------------------
|60001        |Customer#000060001  |9Ii4zQn9cX                           |14
|60002        |Customer#000060002  |ThGBMjDwKzkoOxhz                     |15
|60003        |Customer#000060003  |Ed hbPtTXMTAsgGhCr4HuTzK,Md2         |16
|60004        |Customer#000060004  |NivCT2RVaavl,yUnKwBjDyMvB42WayXCnky  |10
|60005        |Customer#000060005  |1F3KM3ccEXEtI, B22XmCMOWJMl          |12
|60006        |Customer#000060006  |3isiXW651fa8p                        |22
```

Figure 10.10 – Reduced and sorted DataFrame output

How it works

Snowflake Snowpark provides a DataFrame-based programming model that allows data to be processed using familiar constructs while remaining entirely within Snowflake. When working with Snowpark, operations such as loading data, filtering rows, selecting columns, and sorting results are defined as transformations on a DataFrame.

These transformations are not executed immediately. Instead, Snowpark builds a logical plan representing the sequence of operations to be performed. Execution occurs only when an action, such as `show()`, is called. This behavior is commonly referred to as lazy execution.

In this recipe, each call to `show()` triggered the execution of the DataFrame and returned results to the notebook. Behind the scenes, Snowpark translated the DataFrame operations into SQL and executed them within Snowflake's compute engine.

This approach allows data to remain in Snowflake while still enabling flexible and expressive data transformations. By leveraging Snowpark, complex data processing logic can be written in Python while taking advantage of Snowflake's scalability and performance.

Transforming and writing data using Snowpark

Snowpark enables data transformations to be performed directly within Snowflake using a DataFrame-based programming model. In addition to reading and transforming data, Snowpark also allows the results of those transformations to be written back to Snowflake tables.

In this recipe, Snowpark is used to load data, apply transformations, and persist the results to a new table within Snowflake.

Getting ready

You will need access to a Snowflake environment. Create a Snowflake notebook within a workspace and ensure that it is connected to a role and warehouse.

How to do it

Snowpark is used to load data from an existing table, apply transformations, and persist the results to a new table within Snowflake.

1. Begin by importing the required Snowpark libraries. These provide the functionality needed to retrieve the active session, reference columns, and perform aggregation operations.

   ```
   from snowflake.snowpark.context import get_active_session
   from snowflake.snowpark.functions import col, sum as sum_
   ```

   If executed successfully, no error message will be returned.

2. Let's retrieve the active Snowpark session. Within a Snowflake notebook, a connection to Snowflake is already established when a role and warehouse are selected. The `get_active_session()` function accesses that connection so it can be used for DataFrame operations.

   ```
   session = get_active_session()
   ```

   If executed successfully, no error message will be returned.

3. Next, you will load the `ORDERS` table into a DataFrame.

   ```
   orders_df = session.table("SNOWFLAKE_SAMPLE_DATA.TPCH_SF1.ORDERS")
   ```

   This creates a DataFrame reference. No data is displayed at this stage because Snowpark does not execute the query until an action is called.

4. Let's display sample rows from the `ORDERS` table.

   ```
   orders_df.show()
   ```

   The following figure confirms that the data has been loaded successfully.

```
orders_df.show()

Executed just now

-----------------------------------------------------------------------------------------------------
|"O_ORDERKEY"  |"O_CUSTKEY"  |"O_ORDERSTATUS"  |"O_TOTALPRICE"  |"O_ORDERDATE"  |"O_ORDERP
-----------------------------------------------------------------------------------------------------
|3000001       |145618       |F                |30175.88        |1992-12-17     |4-NOT SPE
|3000002       |1481         |O                |297999.63       |1995-07-28     |1-URGENT
|3000003       |127432       |O                |345438.38       |1997-11-04     |5-LOW
|3000004       |47423        |O                |135965.53       |1996-06-13     |4-NOT SPE
|3000005       |84973        |F                |209937.09       |1992-09-12     |5-LOW
|3000006       |135136       |O                |140186.32       |1996-09-26     |1-URGENT
|3000007       |78841        |F                |298655.07       |1992-04-13     |5-LOW
```

Figure 10.11 – ORDERS DataFrame output

5. Now let's aggregate total revenue by customer. This groups the data by customer and calculates total revenue.

```
customer_revenue_df = orders_df.group_by(col("O_CUSTKEY")) \
    .agg(sum_(col("O_TOTALPRICE")).alias("TOTAL_REVENUE"))

customer_revenue_df.show()
```

The `show()` function executes the transformation and displays the aggregated results.

```
--------------------------------
|"O_CUSTKEY"  |"TOTAL_REVENUE"  |
--------------------------------
|74321        |499209.06        |
|40787        |492069.38        |
|140732       |199352.79        |
|131528       |435245.42        |
|44300        |574850.08        |
|4796         |368198.11        |
|5654         |572966.51        |
|96029        |292616.93        |
|1910         |129346.86        |
|17480        |280705.33        |
--------------------------------
```

Figure 10.12 – Customer revenue DataFrame output

6. Now we are going to need a location to save the data to. Create and set a database and schema for the output table.

```
session.sql("CREATE OR REPLACE DATABASE C10_R6").collect()
session.sql("CREATE OR REPLACE SCHEMA C10_R6.PUBLIC").collect()
session.sql("USE DATABASE C10_R6").collect()
session.sql("USE SCHEMA PUBLIC").collect()
```

   Setting the database and schema ensures that Snowflake knows where to create the new table. Without this step, an error may occur indicating that no current database is set.

7. Write the aggregated results to a new database table.

```
customer_revenue_df.write.save_as_table(
    "CUSTOMER_REVENUE",
    mode="overwrite"
)
```

   This creates the `CUSTOMER_REVENUE` table in the active database and schema.

8. Let's confirm that the table was created successfully.

```
session.table("CUSTOMER_REVENUE").show()
```

   This loads and displays the newly created table, as shown in the following figure.

```
------------------------------------
|"O_CUSTKEY"  |"TOTAL_REVENUE"  |
------------------------------------
|4796         |368198.11        |
|141908       |769496.30        |
|87212        |357474.08        |
|52973        |178099.51        |
|138173       |156048.36        |
|145336       |3077365.69       |
|117988       |3194321.85       |
|143809       |4013399.95       |
|11581        |3478401.09       |
|23191        |3520731.85       |
------------------------------------
```

Figure 10.13 – CUSTOMER_REVENUE table output

How it works

Snowpark provides a DataFrame-based programming model that allows data transformations to be defined using familiar programming constructs while executing those operations within Snowflake.

In this recipe, the `ORDERS` table was loaded into a DataFrame, and a series of transformations were applied, including grouping and aggregation. These transformations are not executed immediately. Instead, Snowpark builds a logical plan representing the sequence of operations to be performed.

Execution occurs only when an action is called. In this case, the `show()` function triggered execution and returned results to the notebook, allowing the intermediate and aggregated results to be validated.

When the `save_as_table()` function was invoked, Snowpark translated the DataFrame operations into SQL and executed them within Snowflake's compute engine. The result of this execution persisted as a new table in the specified database and schema.

Setting the database and schema beforehand ensured that Snowflake knew where to create the table. Without a current database and schema, Snowflake cannot determine the target location for the output, which results in an error.

This approach allows data to be read, transformed, and written back to Snowflake entirely within the platform, eliminating the need for external processing frameworks while still enabling flexible and scalable data processing workflows. These steps are done transparently and under the covers, without requiring a Spark developer to worry about the underlying details.

Applying tags to support policy-based governance

Snowflake provides native governance capabilities that allow organizations to classify and manage data using metadata. One of the key features supporting this capability is the use of tags. Tags enable metadata to be associated with objects such as tables and columns, providing a flexible mechanism for organizing, classifying, and managing data.

Tags can be used for a variety of purposes, including data classification, governance, auditing, and automation. In this recipe, tags are created and applied to columns to establish a metadata foundation for policy-based governance. This metadata can then be used to drive governance controls such as dynamic data masking and other policy-driven enforcement mechanisms.

Getting ready

You will need access to a Snowflake environment with privileges to create tags and modify table metadata. The SQL statements in this recipe can be executed using Snowsight or the Snowflake CLI.

How to do it

Tags are created and applied to classify data within a table.

1. Begin by creating a database and schema for this recipe.

   ```
   CREATE OR REPLACE DATABASE C10_GOV_DB;
   CREATE OR REPLACE SCHEMA C10_GOV_DB.CLASSIFICATION;
   ```

   The `CLASSIFICATION` schema should be created successfully

2. Let's create a sample table that contains data to be classified. This table will be used to demonstrate how tags can be applied to classify data.

   ```
   CREATE OR REPLACE TABLE C10_GOV_DB.CLASSIFICATION.CUSTOMER_DATA
   (
     CUSTOMER_ID NUMBER,
     FULL_NAME   STRING,
     EMAIL       STRING,
     REGION      STRING
   );
   ```

Table CUSTOMER_DATA successfully created.

3. Now insert sample data into the table. This will provide you with a dataset for testing classification.

```
INSERT INTO C10_GOV_DB.CLASSIFICATION.CUSTOMER_DATA VALUES
(1, 'John Smith', 'john.smith@email.com', 'US'),
(2, 'Jane Doe', 'jane.doe@email.com', 'EU');
```

The statement should insert two rows.

4. Let's create a tag to represent data sensitivity levels. This creates a Snowflake tag named SENSITIVE_DATA_TAG. Tags are metadata objects that can be applied to database objects, such as tables and columns, to store classification information. The ALLOWED_VALUES clause defines a controlled set of values that can be assigned to the tag. In this case, the tag is used to represent levels of data sensitivity, ensuring that only predefined classifications HIGH, MEDIUM, or LOW can be applied. Defining allowed values helps enforce consistency in how data is classified across the environment.

```
CREATE OR REPLACE TAG SENSITIVE_DATA_TAG
 ALLOWED_VALUES 'HIGH', 'MEDIUM', 'LOW';
```

Tag SENSITIVE_DATA_TAG successfully created.

> **Note**
>
> This structure enables tags to be used reliably in downstream processes such as data masking and policy enforcement.

5. Assign the SENSITIVE_DATA_TAG to the EMAIL column with a value of HIGH. This classification indicates that the data in this column is highly sensitive. Tags are applied at the metadata level, meaning the data itself is not changed. Instead, this classification can be used to drive governance decisions, such as applying masking policies or restricting access.

```
ALTER TABLE C10_GOV_DB.CLASSIFICATION.CUSTOMER_DATA
MODIFY COLUMN EMAIL
SET TAG SENSITIVE_DATA_TAG = 'HIGH';
```

Statement executed successfully.

6. Now apply the same tag to the `FULL_NAME` column but assign it a value of `MEDIUM`. This indicates a lower level of sensitivity compared to the `EMAIL` column. Applying different values of the same tag allows for more granular classification across columns. This enables governance rules to be applied differently depending on the sensitivity level assigned.

```
ALTER TABLE C10_GOV_DB.CLASSIFICATION.CUSTOMER_DATA
MODIFY COLUMN FULL_NAME
SET TAG SENSITIVE_DATA_TAG = 'MEDIUM';
```

   Statement executed successfully.

7. Let's view the tags applied to the table and its columns.

```
SELECT *
FROM TABLE(
  C10_GOV_DB.INFORMATION_SCHEMA.TAG_REFERENCES_ALL_COLUMNS(
    'C10_GOV_DB.CLASSIFICATION.CUSTOMER_DATA',
    'TABLE'
  )
);
```

   The object name is fully qualified to ensure the correct table is referenced, regardless of the current session context. This returns metadata showing the tags applied to each column in the `CUSTOMER_DATA` table. Since the tags in this recipe were applied at the column level, the `TAG_REFERENCES_ALL_COLUMNS` function is used to retrieve the tag assignments.

	TAG_DATABASE	TAG_SCHEMA	TAG_NAME	TAG_VALUE	LEVEL	OBJECT_DATABASE	OBJECT_SCHEMA	OBJEC
1	C10_GOV_DB	CLASSIFICATION	SENSITIVE_DATA_TAG	HIGH	COLUMN	C10_GOV_DB	CLASSIFICATION	CUSTOMI
2	C10_GOV_DB	CLASSIFICATION	SENSITIVE_DATA_TAG	MEDIUM	COLUMN	C10_GOV_DB	CLASSIFICATION	CUSTOMI

Figure 10.14 – Tags applied to table columns

How it works

Tags in Snowflake are metadata objects that can be associated with databases, schemas, tables, and columns. They allow data to be classified without modifying the underlying data itself. In this recipe, a tag was created with predefined allowed values representing levels of sensitivity. The tag was then applied to specific columns in the `CUSTOMER_DATA` table. These assignments create metadata that can be used for governance, auditing, and policy enforcement.

The `INFORMATION_SCHEMA.TAG_REFERENCES_ALL_COLUMNS` function provides visibility into how tags are applied at the column level, enabling organizations to track and manage classifications across their accounts.

There's more...

Tags in Snowflake provide a flexible metadata framework that extends beyond simple data classification.

Common uses of tags include:

- **Data classification**: Categorizing data based on sensitivity, business domain, or regulatory requirements.
- **Policy-driven data protection**: Tags can be referenced by masking and row access policies to dynamically enforce data security rules.
- **Auditing and compliance**: Tags help identify and track sensitive data across databases and schemas.
- **Automation and metadata-driven processes**: Tags can be used to drive automated workflows and governance controls.
- **Standardization across environments**: Tags enable consistent metadata practices across teams and projects.

In the next recipe, tags will be used to dynamically enforce masking policies, demonstrating how classification can directly drive data protection.

Implementing dynamic data masking using tags

Snowflake provides dynamic data masking capabilities that allow sensitive data to be protected at query time without modifying the underlying data. Masking policies can be applied to columns to control how data is displayed based on roles or other conditions.

When combined with tags, masking policies can be applied dynamically based on metadata classifications. This enables a scalable, policy-driven approach to data protection.

In this recipe, a masking policy is created and applied using tags to dynamically protect sensitive data.

Getting ready

You will need access to a Snowflake environment with privileges to create masking policies, tags, and modify table metadata. The SQL statements in this recipe can be executed using Snowsight or the Snowflake CLI.

This recipe builds on the previous recipe, *Applying tags to support policy-based governance*. Ensure that the database, schema, table, and tag created in that recipe already exist before proceeding.

How to do it

A masking policy is created and applied using a tag to dynamically control how sensitive data is displayed.

1. Begin by creating roles to demonstrate masking behavior. These roles will be used to demonstrate how masking behaves differently depending on access.

   ```
   CREATE OR REPLACE ROLE DATA_FULL_ACCESS;
   CREATE OR REPLACE ROLE DATA_LIMITED_ACCESS;
   ```

   Role `DATA_LIMITED_ACCESS` successfully created.

2. Next, create a database and schema that will be used throughout the recipe.

   ```
   CREATE OR REPLACE DATABASE C10_GOV_DB;
   CREATE OR REPLACE SCHEMA C10_GOV_DB.CLASSIFICATION;
   ```

   Statement executed successfully.

3. You will need to assign the roles to your user Snowflake login name. Replace <your_loginname> with your Snowflake login name.

   ```
   GRANT ROLE DATA_FULL_ACCESS TO USER <your_loginname>;
   GRANT ROLE DATA_LIMITED_ACCESS TO USER <your_loginname>;
   ```

   Statement executed successfully.

4. Next, grant the demonstration roles access to the database and schema that contain the table.

   ```
   GRANT USAGE ON DATABASE C10_GOV_DB
   TO ROLE DATA_FULL_ACCESS;

   GRANT USAGE ON SCHEMA C10_GOV_DB.CLASSIFICATION
   TO ROLE DATA_FULL_ACCESS;

   GRANT USAGE ON DATABASE C10_GOV_DB
   TO ROLE DATA_LIMITED_ACCESS;
   ```

```
GRANT USAGE ON SCHEMA C10_GOV_DB.CLASSIFICATION
TO ROLE DATA_LIMITED_ACCESS;
```

Statement executed successfully.

5. Let's grant usage on the database and schema to the roles. This allows both roles to access the objects needed for the demonstration.

```
GRANT SELECT ON TABLE C10_GOV_DB.CLASSIFICATION.CUSTOMER_DATA
TO ROLE DATA_FULL_ACCESS;

GRANT SELECT ON TABLE C10_GOV_DB.CLASSIFICATION.CUSTOMER_DATA
TO ROLE DATA_LIMITED_ACCESS;
```

Statement executed successfully.

6. Now enable both roles to query the table. Grant select access on the table.

```
GRANT SELECT ON TABLE C10_GOV_DB.CLASSIFICATION.CUSTOMER_DATA
TO ROLE DATA_FULL_ACCESS;

GRANT SELECT ON TABLE C10_GOV_DB.CLASSIFICATION.CUSTOMER_DATA
TO ROLE DATA_LIMITED_ACCESS;
```

Statement executed successfully.

7. Let's create a masking policy named `EMAIL_MASKING_POLICY`. Masking policies define how data is displayed at query time without modifying the underlying data. The policy accepts a column value (`val`) as input and returns a value based on the defined logic. In this example, the `CURRENT_ROLE()` function is used to determine which role is executing the query.

    a. If the role is `DATA_FULL_ACCESS`, the original value is returned

    b. For all other roles, the value is replaced with `'***MASKED***'`

This approach allows data visibility to be controlled dynamically based on the user's role.

```
 CREATE OR REPLACE MASKING POLICY EMAIL_MASKING_POLICY
AS (val STRING)
RETURNS STRING ->
```

```
CASE
  WHEN CURRENT_ROLE() = 'DATA_FULL_ACCESS' THEN val
  ELSE '***MASKED***'
END;
```

Masking policy `EMAIL_MASKING_POLICY` successfully created.

8. Associate the masking policy with the tag. You will link the masking policy to the tag, enabling dynamic policy enforcement based on tag assignments. This classification indicates that the data in this column is highly sensitive. Tags are applied at the metadata level, meaning the data itself is not changed. Instead, this classification can be used to drive governance decisions, such as applying masking policies or restricting access.

```
ALTER TAG SENSITIVE_DATA_TAG
SET MASKING POLICY EMAIL_MASKING_POLICY;
```

Statement executed successfully.

9. Now query the table using the full access role.

```
USE ROLE DATA_FULL_ACCESS;

SELECT *
FROM C10_GOV_DB.CLASSIFICATION.CUSTOMER_DATA;
```

The `FULL_NAME` and `EMAIL` columns should display unmasked values.

	# CUSTOMER_ID	A FULL_NAME	A EMAIL	A REGION
1	1	John Smith	john.smith@email.com	US
2	2	Jane Doe	jane.doe@email.com	EU
3	1	John Smith	john.smith@email.com	US
4	2	Jane Doe	jane.doe@email.com	EU

Figure 10.15 – Displays unmasked values

10. Let's query the table using the limited access role.

```
USE ROLE DATA_LIMITED_ACCESS;
```

```
SELECT *
FROM C10_GOV_DB.CLASSIFICATION.CUSTOMER_DATA;
```

The `FULL_NAME` and `EMAIL` columns should now display masked values.

	# CUSTOMER_ID	A FULL_NAME	A EMAIL	A REGION
1	1	***MASKED***	***MASKED***	US
2	2	***MASKED***	***MASKED***	EU
3	1	***MASKED***	***MASKED***	US
4	2	***MASKED***	***MASKED***	EU

Figure 10.16 – Displays masked values

How it works

Dynamic data masking in Snowflake allows policies to be applied to columns so that data is transformed at query time based on defined conditions, without modifying the underlying data.

In this recipe, a masking policy was created to evaluate the role executing the query using the `CURRENT_ROLE()` function. Based on this condition, the policy either returned the original value or a masked value. This demonstrated how data visibility can be controlled dynamically depending on the role.

The masking policy was then associated with a tag rather than directly applied to a column. Because the `SENSITIVE_DATA_TAG` was already assigned to specific columns in the previous recipe, the masking policy was automatically enforced on those columns.

This creates a metadata-driven approach to data protection, where classification (via tags) determines how data is protected (via masking policies). As a result, applying or updating a tag can immediately affect how data is displayed, without requiring changes to the table structure.

This approach enables scalable governance, as policies do not need to be manually applied to each column. Instead, tags act as a central mechanism for enforcing consistent data protection rules across the environment.

There's more...

Tags and masking policies are most effective when managed as part of a centralized governance strategy. A common best practice is to store tags and policies in a dedicated database, separate from the databases that contain business data.

By centralizing tags and policies, they can be consistently applied across multiple databases and schemas, enabling a single source of truth for governance rules.

This approach is particularly beneficial when working with zero-copy cloning. When a database is cloned in Snowflake, the underlying data structures are copied, including any tag assignments on tables and columns. However, by keeping the tags and masking policies themselves in a separate, centralized database, the definitions are not duplicated during the clone.

As a result, cloned environments continue to reference the same centralized tags and policies. This avoids unnecessary duplication, reduces maintenance overhead, and prevents complications that can arise from managing multiple versions of the same governance objects.

Centralizing governance objects also supports better lifecycle management, as updates to tags or policies can be made in one location and immediately take effect across all associated data assets.

11

Introduction to Snowflake Cortex

As organizations continue to expand their use of data, there is an increasing demand to make that data more accessible, actionable, and intelligent. Snowflake Cortex introduces a set of capabilities that bring AI and machine learning directly into the Snowflake Data Cloud, allowing users to interact with data in new ways without moving it outside the platform.

Traditionally, leveraging AI required moving data to external systems, managing infrastructure, and integrating multiple tools. Cortex simplifies this process by embedding AI capabilities directly within Snowflake, enabling users to generate insights, summarize information, and even create SQL using natural language.

In this chapter, we explore how to get started with Snowflake Cortex and how these capabilities can be applied to real-world data scenarios. Rather than covering every feature in depth, this chapter focuses on practical entry points that demonstrate how AI can be integrated into existing Snowflake workflows.

The following topics will be covered in this chapter:

- Using Cortex AI functions to generate and summarize text
- Querying data using natural language with Cortex Analyst
- Creating and querying a Cortex Search service
- Using Snowflake Coco to generate customer insights

Technical requirements

This chapter requires access to a modern internet browser (Chrome, Edge, Firefox, and so on) and access to the internet to connect to your Snowflake account. You will also need access to a Snowflake account with Cortex capabilities granted. Some features may require specific roles or permissions depending on your Snowflake configuration.

You can download the example project and code for this book by following the instructions in the ***Download the example code files*** section in the *Preface* of this book.

Using Cortex AI functions to generate and summarize text

In this recipe, we will explore how Snowflake Cortex AI functions can be used to generate and analyze text directly within SQL queries. Traditionally, tasks such as summarization, classification, and text generation required exporting data to external AI or machine learning platforms. With Cortex AI SQL functions, these capabilities are now embedded directly within Snowflake, allowing users to apply AI to both static text and structured data without moving data outside the platform. This recipe demonstrates how to use these functions to generate text, summarize content, and derive insights from real data scenarios.

Getting ready

You will need to be connected to your Snowflake instance via Snowsight or the CLI client to execute this recipe. You will also need access to a Snowflake account with Cortex AI functions enabled. For information on availability, required privileges, and supported models, refer to the Snowflake Cortex AI SQL documentation: `https://docs.snowflake.com/en/user-guide/snowflake-cortex/aisql`.

How to do it…

In this recipe, we will use Snowflake Cortex AI functions to generate and summarize text directly within SQL. We will start with simple prompts and then apply these functions to structured data.

The steps are as follows:

1. First, you will set the appropriate role and create a database for this recipe. To do so, run the following SQL:

   ```
   USE ROLE SYSADMIN;

   CREATE OR REPLACE DATABASE C11_R1;
   USE DATABASE C11_R1;
   USE SCHEMA PUBLIC;
   ```

   The commands should succeed with a Statement executed successfully.

2. Next, you will use the `COMPLETE` function to generate text based on a prompt. This function sends the provided prompt to a **large language model** (**LLM**) and returns a generated response as part of the query result.
   In this example, you will provide a simple prompt asking for a description of Snowflake. Note that we must specify the model to use as the first argument, followed by the prompt text.

   To do so, run the following SQL:

```
SELECT AI_COMPLETE(
    'llama3.1-8b',
    'Write a short description of Snowflake as a data platform.'
) AS GENERATED_TEXT;
```

   You should see a generated response describing Snowflake. The exact output may vary slightly each time the query is executed.

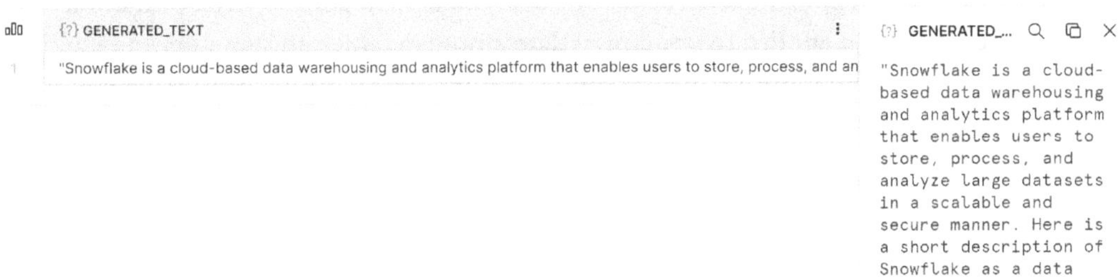

Figure 11.1 – Generated text output

> **Note**
>
> Snowflake provides multiple models that can be used with Cortex functions. The availability of models may vary depending on your account and region.

3. You will now use the `SUMMARIZE` function to reduce a longer piece of text into a shorter, more concise version. This is useful for scenarios such as summarizing reports, feedback, or descriptions. In this example, you will provide a paragraph describing Snowflake and generate a summary from it.
   To do so, run the following SQL:

```
SELECT SNOWFLAKE.CORTEX.SUMMARIZE(
    'Snowflake is a cloud-based data platform that provides data storage,
processing, and analytics solutions. It enables organizations to
```

```
consolidate data into a single source of truth and supports structured and
semi-structured data workloads at scale.'
) AS SUMMARY_TEXT;
```

You should see a shortened version of the provided text returned as the result.

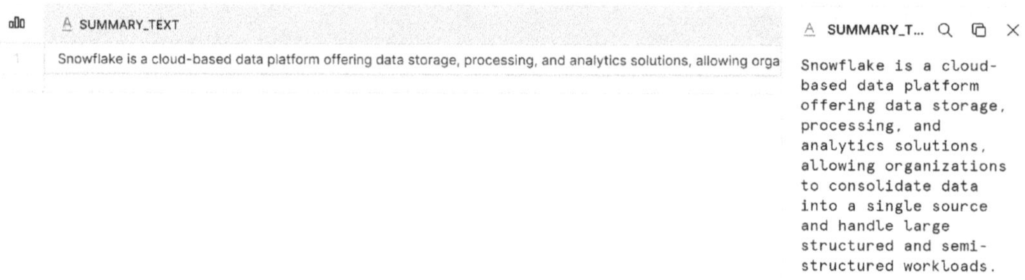

Figure 11.2 – Summarized text output

4. So far, you have applied Cortex functions to static text. In practice, these functions are most useful when applied to structured data stored in tables. In this step, you will create a table containing sample customer feedback and use Cortex functions to analyze that data.
   First, create a table to store feedback data:

   ```
   CREATE OR REPLACE TABLE CUSTOMER_FEEDBACK (
       FEEDBACK_ID NUMBER,
       COMMENTS STRING
   );
   ```

   Next, insert sample data into the table. The comments are intentionally longer than a typical short review so that the summarization results are easier to observe.

   ```
   INSERT INTO CUSTOMER_FEEDBACK VALUES
   (1,
   'I really like the product, and the overall quality has been excellent, but
   the delivery arrived three days later than expected and I did not receive a
   clear update from the shipping team.'),
   (2, 'The customer service team responded quickly, answered my questions
   clearly, and helped resolve my issue without needing multiple follow-up
   emails.'),
   (3, 'The product works as expected, but the packaging was damaged when it
   arrived and the setup instructions could have been easier to understand.'),
   ```

```
(4, 'I am very satisfied with the purchase because the product was easy to
use, arrived on time, and matched the description on the website.');
```

You should see a response that you have inserted 4 rows.

5. Now that you have structured data, you can apply the `SUMMARIZE` function to each row. To do so, run the following SQL:

```
SELECT
    FEEDBACK_ID,
    COMMENTS,
    SNOWFLAKE.CORTEX.SUMMARIZE(COMMENTS) AS SUMMARY
FROM CUSTOMER_FEEDBACK;
```

You should see each comment along with a summarized version generated by the AI function. This demonstrates how AI can be applied directly to table data as part of a standard query.

# FEEDBACK_ID	COMMENTS	SUMMARY
1	I really like the product and the overall quality has been excelle	The product was liked and of good quality, but delivery was lat
2	The customer service team responded quickly, answered my c	The customer service team effectively addressed and resolved
3	The product works as expected, but the packaging was damag	The product functioned correctly but arrived with damaged pac
4	I am very satisfied with the purchase because the product was	The purchase met expectations as it was easy to use, arrived o

Figure 11.3 – Summary or table comments

6. In addition to summarization, Cortex functions can be used for classification tasks by providing a clear prompt. In this example, we will classify each feedback comment as Positive, Neutral, or Negative. This query sends each comment along with a classification instruction to the model.
To do so, run the following SQL:

```
SELECT
    FEEDBACK_ID,
    COMMENTS,
    SNOWFLAKE.CORTEX.COMPLETE(
        'llama3.1-8b',
        CONCAT('Classify the following feedback as Positive, Neutral, or
Negative: ', COMMENTS)
    ) AS SENTIMENT
FROM CUSTOMER_FEEDBACK;
```

You should see a classification returned for each row. The exact wording may vary slightly, but each response should align with the sentiment of the comment

FEEDBAC	COMMENTS	SENTIMENT
1	I really like the product and the overall quality has	I would classify this feedback as: **Mixed** However, if I had to choose
2	The customer service team responded quickly, ar	I would classify this feedback as **Positive**. The customer service tean
3	The product works as expected, but the packagir	Here is the classification of the feedback: * Positive: The product works
4	I am very satisfied with the purchase because the	I would classify the feedback as **Positive**. The customer is expressin

Figure 11.4 – Classification of comments

> **Note**
>
> The quality and consistency of results depend on how the prompt is written. Clear and specific prompts generally produce better results.

How it works...

In this recipe, you used Snowflake Cortex AI functions to generate, summarize, and classify text directly within SQL queries. These functions allow you to apply LLMs to both static text and structured data without moving data outside of Snowflake.

The `COMPLETE` function is used to generate text based on a prompt. In this recipe, you used it to produce descriptive text and to classify customer feedback by providing clear instructions within the prompt. The quality of the output is influenced by how the prompt is written, which means more specific prompts typically produce more consistent and accurate results.

The `SUMMARIZE` function is designed to reduce longer text into a shorter, more concise version. When applied to structured data, such as a table column, the function operates on each row independently and returns a summarized version of the input text. As demonstrated, shorter input text may result in minimal changes, while longer text produces more meaningful summaries.

These functions are executed as part of a standard SQL query, meaning they can be combined with other SQL operations such as filtering, joins, and aggregations. This enables you to integrate AI-generated results directly into your data pipelines and analytical workflows.

Under the hood, Snowflake sends the prompt or input text to a managed model and returns the generated result as part of the query output. The models are hosted and managed by Snowflake, which removes the need to provision infrastructure or move data to external systems.

It is important to note that the results generated by these functions are not guaranteed to be identical across executions. Because the output is generated by an AI model, slight variations may occur. For this reason, results should be reviewed and validated, particularly when used in production scenarios.

By embedding AI capabilities directly into SQL, Snowflake enables a new pattern where data processing and AI-driven insights can be performed within the same platform, simplifying architecture and accelerating development workflows.

There's more...

Snowflake Cortex provides a growing set of AI functions beyond the examples shown in this recipe. These include capabilities for working with different data types and performing more advanced analysis using SQL. To explore the full list of available Cortex AI functions and their usage, refer to the official Snowflake documentation: `https://docs.snowflake.com/en/user-guide/snowflake-cortex/aisql`.

As Cortex continues to evolve, new functions and capabilities are regularly introduced. Reviewing the documentation can help you stay up to date and identify additional use cases for applying AI within your Snowflake account.

Querying data using natural language with Cortex Analyst

In this recipe, you will explore how Snowflake Cortex Analyst enables you to query structured data using natural language. Traditionally, querying data required writing SQL statements with a clear understanding of the underlying schema. Cortex Analyst introduces a new approach by allowing you to describe what you want to retrieve using natural language, which is then translated into SQL and executed against your data.

Cortex Analyst operates on top of a semantic model, which provides context about how data should be interpreted. While the full setup of semantic models is beyond the scope of this recipe, this example demonstrates how natural language queries can be translated into SQL and used to interact with structured data.

Getting ready

You will need to be connected to your Snowflake account via Snowsight to execute this recipe.

You will also need access to a Snowflake account with Cortex Analyst enabled. Cortex Analyst relies on a semantic model to interpret natural language queries, so you will need access to a database and tables that can be used for this purpose.

How to do it...

In this recipe, you will create a simple dataset and demonstrate how natural language can be used to generate SQL queries through Cortex Analyst.

1. First, set the appropriate role and create a database for this recipe. To do so, run the following SQL:

```
USE ROLE SYSADMIN;

CREATE OR REPLACE DATABASE C11_R2;
USE DATABASE C11_R2;
USE SCHEMA PUBLIC;
```

The commands should succeed with a success message.

2. Let's create a sample sales table. To do so, run the following SQL:

```
CREATE OR REPLACE TABLE SALES (
    ORDER_ID NUMBER,
    CUSTOMER_NAME STRING,
    REGION STRING,
    SALES_AMOUNT NUMBER
);
```

The commands should succeed with a success message.

3. Now insert sample data into the table. To do so, run the following SQL:

```
INSERT INTO SALES VALUES
(1, 'John Smith', 'North', 1200),
(2, 'Jane Doe', 'South', 850),
(3, 'Mike Johnson', 'North', 640),
(4, 'Emily Davis', 'West', 1500),
(5, 'Chris Brown', 'South', 920);
```

The result should state 5 rows inserted.

4. Before using natural language, you can validate the dataset using a traditional SQL query. To do so, run the following SQL:

```
SELECT REGION, SUM(SALES_AMOUNT) AS TOTAL_SALES
FROM SALES
GROUP BY REGION;
```

This query aggregates sales by region and returns the results. Make a note of the output, as you will compare it with the results generated through natural language queries.

REGION	TOTAL_SALES
South	1770
North	1840
West	1500

Figure 11.5 – Aggregate sales by region results

Before you can query data using natural language, Cortex Analyst requires a semantic view that provides context about the underlying data. In the next few steps, you will create a semantic view using the Autopilot feature and connect it to the SALES table created earlier. Navigate to Cortex Analyst in Snowsight by selecting **AI & ML** from the left pane, then selecting **Analyst**.

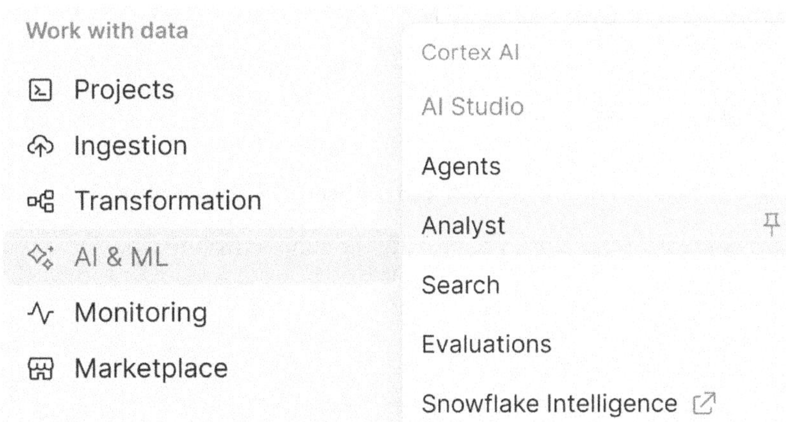

Figure 11.6 – Cortex Analyst menu

5. Within Cortex Analyst, you will locate the **Select database to see semantic views** dropdown and select the `C11_R2` database that you created in the previous steps

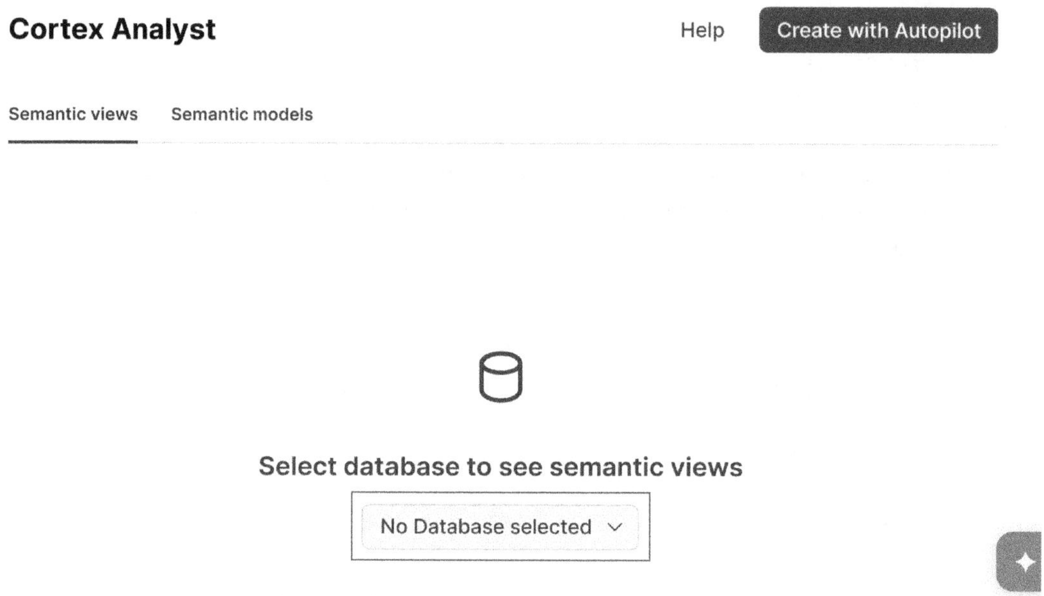

Figure 11.7 – Select database for semantic views

6. Next, click Create with Autopilot to begin configuring the Semantic view.

Figure 11.8 – Select Create with Autopilot

7. You will select SQL queries to provide the context for the view.

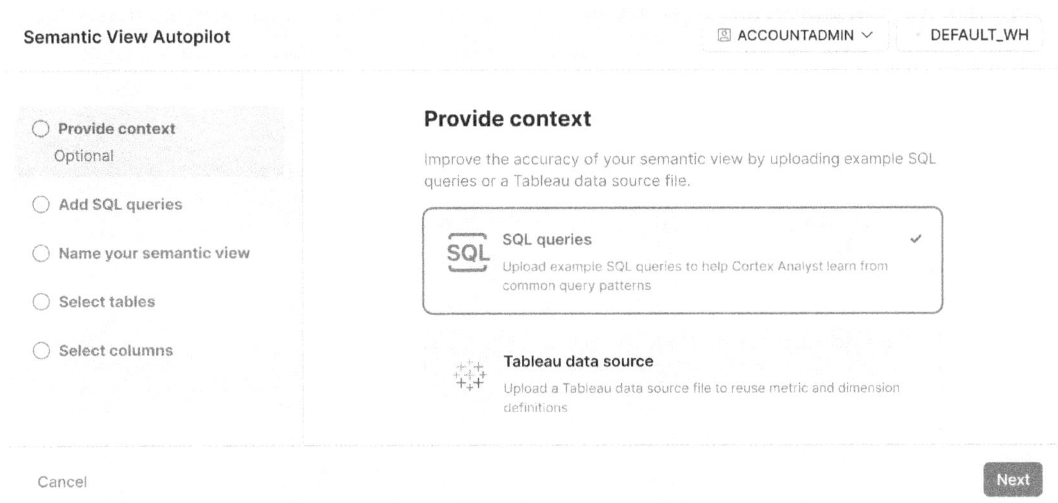

Figure 11.9 – Select SQL queries

8. Click on the **Select from query history** button and then click **Next**.

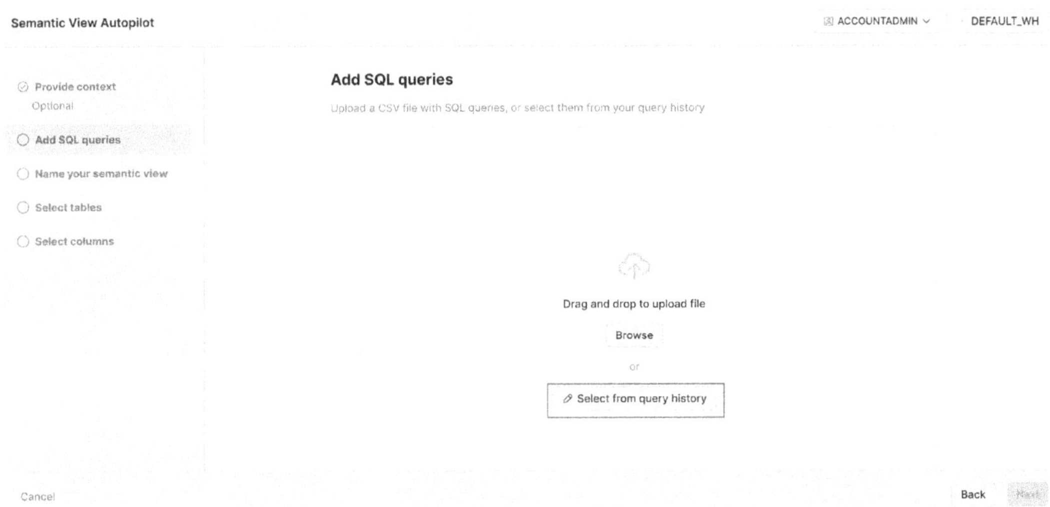

Figure 11.10 – Select from query history

9. Next, provide the following question and SQL query that describe how the data will be used. If the query is available in your query history from the earlier step in this recipe, you can select it directly. Otherwise, you can manually enter the question "`What was the total sales by region?`" and the SQL query shown below.

```
SELECT REGION, SUM(SALES_AMOUNT) AS TOTAL_SALES
FROM C11_R2.PUBLIC.SALES
GROUP BY REGION;
```

Click the **Add (Shift + Enter)** button and then click **Next**.

Figure 11.11 – Add SQL queries

10. Provide a name for the semantic view, such as `C11_SALES`, and click **Next**.

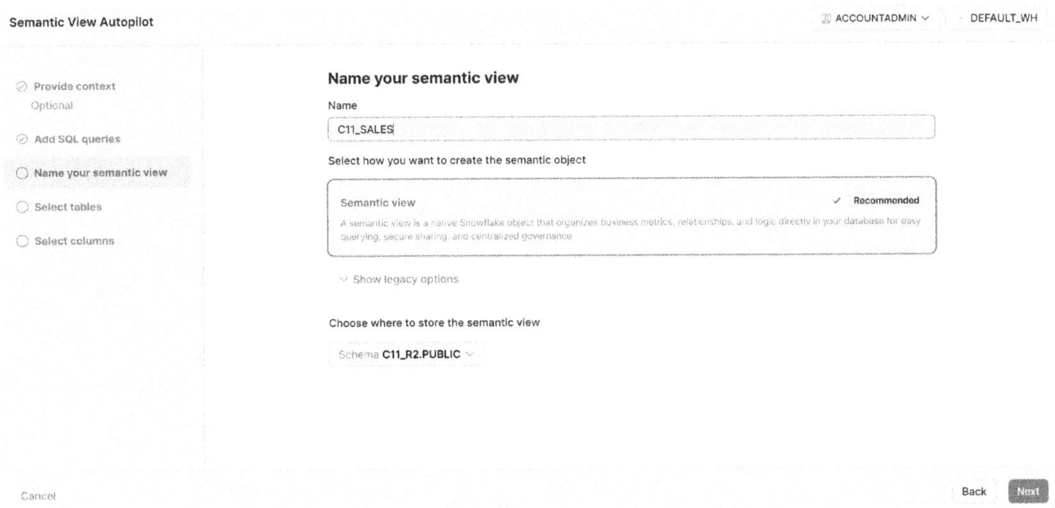

Figure 11.12 – Name semantic view

11. Now ensure that the `SALES` table is selected, then click **Next**

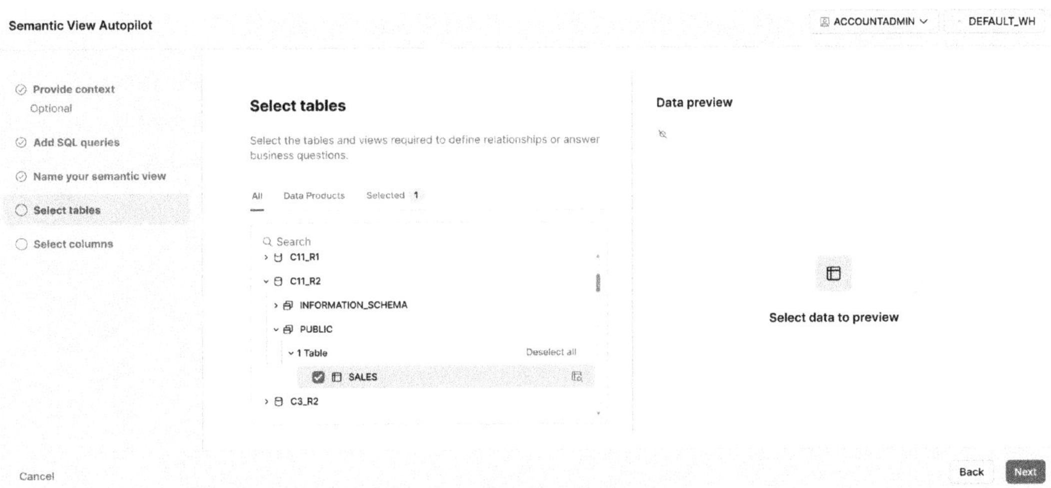

Figure 11.13 – Select tables

12. You will now verify that all columns from the SALES table are selected, then click **Create**.

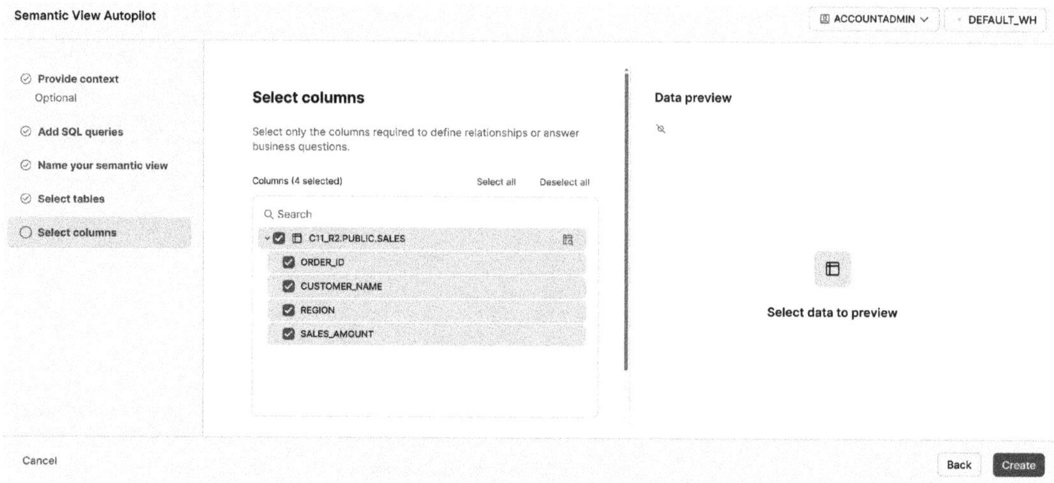

Figure 11.14 – Select columns

This will initiate the generation of the C11_SALES semantic view.

13. You can now use this semantic view to interpret natural language queries against the SALES data. To begin, select the **Playground** option in the upper-right corner. This will open a prompt input area where you can enter natural language questions and execute them against the semantic view.

Figure 11.15 – Completed semantic view

14. In the prompt input area, enter the following natural language question: "`Show total sales by region`" and submit the prompt to execute the query. Cortex Analyst will interpret the request, generate the corresponding SQL query, and return the results. You should see output similar to the results returned in *Step 2*.

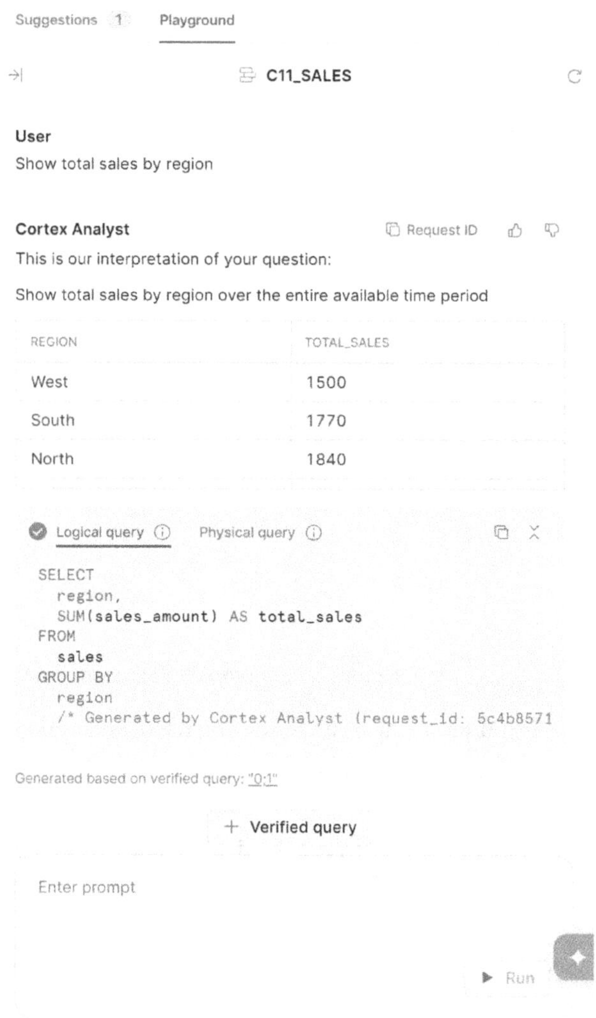

Figure 11.16 – Cortex Analyst prompt response

15. You can refine your query by providing additional instructions using natural language. In the prompt input area, enter the following: "`Show total sales by region where total sales are greater than 900`" and submit the prompt to execute the query. Cortex Analyst will interpret the updated request, generate a new SQL query that includes filtering logic, and return the refined results. You should see that only regions with total sales greater than 900 are included in the output.

How it works...

In this recipe, you used Snowflake Cortex Analyst to translate natural language into SQL queries and execute them against structured data. Cortex Analyst enables this by combining natural language processing with a semantic understanding of the underlying data.

At the core of Cortex Analyst is the semantic view. The semantic view provides context about how data should be interpreted, including table structures, column meanings, and relationships. In this recipe, you created a semantic view using the Autopilot feature, which generated this context based on the `SALES` table and the SQL query you provided.

When you enter a natural language prompt, Cortex Analyst analyzes the request and maps it to the semantic view. For example, phrases such as "`total sales`" and "`by region`" are interpreted and translated into SQL operations such as aggregation and grouping. Based on this interpretation, Cortex Analyst generates a SQL query that reflects the intent of the request.

Once the SQL query is generated, it is executed within Snowflake, and the results are returned to the user. In many cases, the generated SQL can also be reviewed, allowing you to validate how the natural language request was translated into query logic.

As demonstrated in this recipe, you can refine queries by providing additional instructions in natural language. Cortex Analyst uses the updated prompt to generate a new SQL query that incorporates additional logic, such as filtering conditions.

The accuracy of the generated SQL depends on both the clarity of the prompt and the quality of the semantic view. Well-defined schemas and consistent naming conventions improve how effectively natural language can be interpreted.

By enabling natural language interaction with structured data, Cortex Analyst lowers the barrier to querying data while still leveraging the performance, scalability, and governance capabilities of Snowflake.

Creating and querying a Cortex Search service

In this recipe, you will create and query a Cortex Search service in Snowflake. Cortex Search enables semantic and keyword-based search over text data stored in Snowflake, making it useful for scenarios such as support search, document discovery, and **retrieval-augmented generation** (**RAG**) workflows. Rather than manually building embeddings, managing vector indexes, or maintaining separate search infrastructure, Cortex Search allows you to define a searchable service directly over Snowflake data and query it using SQL.

Getting ready

You will need to be connected to your Snowflake instance via Snowsight or the CLI client to execute this recipe.

You will also need access to a Snowflake account with Cortex Search enabled and a role with the required privileges to create and query a Cortex Search service.

How to do it...

In this recipe, you will create a sample table containing support transcript data, create a Cortex Search service over that table, and preview search results using SQL. The steps are as follows:

1. First, you will need to set the appropriate role and create a database, schema, and warehouse for this recipe. To do so, run the following SQL:

```
USE ROLE SYSADMIN;

CREATE OR REPLACE DATABASE C11_R3;

CREATE OR REPLACE SCHEMA C11_R3.PUBLIC;

CREATE OR REPLACE WAREHOUSE CORTEX_SEARCH_WH
WAREHOUSE_SIZE = 'XSMALL'
AUTO_SUSPEND = 60
AUTO_RESUME = TRUE;

USE DATABASE C11_R3;
USE SCHEMA PUBLIC;
```

   The commands should succeed with a success message.

2. Next, create a table to store support transcript data.

```
CREATE OR REPLACE TABLE SUPPORT_TRANSCRIPTS (
 TRANSCRIPT_ID NUMBER,
 TRANSCRIPT_TEXT STRING,
 REGION STRING,
 AGENT_ID STRING
);
```

   You should see a success message stating that the table was created successfully.

3. Next, insert sample data into the table.

```
INSERT INTO SUPPORT_TRANSCRIPTS VALUES
(1, 'My internet has been down since yesterday and I need help restoring
the service.', 'North America', 'AG1001'),
(2, 'I was overcharged on my last bill and need someone to explain the
additional fees.', 'Europe', 'AG1002'),
(3, 'I cannot reset my password because the email link is not working.',
'Asia', 'AG1003'),
(4,
'The router I received appears to be faulty and I would like to request a
replacement.', 'North America', 'AG1004'),
(5, 'The mobile app keeps crashing whenever I try to view my account
balance.', 'Europe', 'AG1005');
```

You should see a success message stating 5 records were inserted.

4. Now create a Cortex Search service over the `TRANSCRIPT_TEXT` column. The `ON` clause identifies the text column that will be searched. The `ATTRIBUTES` clause identifies columns that can be returned with the results or used for filtering. The `WAREHOUSE` clause identifies the warehouse Snowflake will use to build and refresh the service.

```
CREATE OR REPLACE CORTEX SEARCH SERVICE TRANSCRIPT_SEARCH_SERVICE
  ON TRANSCRIPT_TEXT
  ATTRIBUTES REGION, AGENT_ID
  WAREHOUSE = CORTEX_SEARCH_WH
  TARGET_LAG = '1 day'
  EMBEDDING_MODEL = 'snowflake-arctic-embed-l-v2.0'
  AS (
    SELECT
        TRANSCRIPT_TEXT,
        REGION,
        AGENT_ID
    FROM SUPPORT_TRANSCRIPTS
  );
```

This command creates the Cortex Search service and starts building the search index. For small datasets, the process typically completes quickly and returns a success message indicating that the service was created successfully.

5. Now that the search service has been created, you can test it using the `SEARCH_PREVIEW` function. This function accepts the name of the Cortex Search service along with a JSON request that defines the search criteria.
   In this example: The query parameter contains the text you want to search for. The columns parameter identifies which columns should be returned in the results. The limit parameter restricts the number of matching records returned. The following example searches for transcripts related to internet issues and returns up to three matching results. To do so, run the following SQL:

```
SELECT PARSE_JSON(
  SNOWFLAKE.CORTEX.SEARCH_PREVIEW(
    'C11_R3.PUBLIC.TRANSCRIPT_SEARCH_SERVICE',
    '{
      "query": "internet issues",
      "columns": [
        "TRANSCRIPT_TEXT",
        "REGION",
        "AGENT_ID"
      ],
      "limit": 3
    }'
  )
)['results'] AS RESULTS;
```

   You should see the following result.

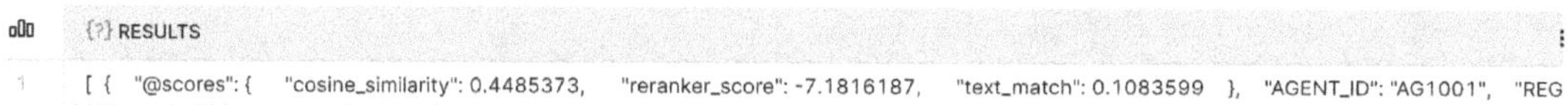

Figure 11.17 – Cortex preview results

6. You can also filter search results by using one of the attributes defined in the search service. In this step, you will search for support issues and return only results from North America.

```
SELECT PARSE_JSON(
  SNOWFLAKE.CORTEX.SEARCH_PREVIEW(
    'C11_R3.PUBLIC.TRANSCRIPT_SEARCH_SERVICE',
    '{
      "query": "service problem",
      "columns": [
```

```
          "TRANSCRIPT_TEXT",
          "REGION",
          "AGENT_ID"
        ],
        "filter": {
          "@eq": {
            "REGION": "North America"
          }
        },
        "limit": 3
      }'
    )
  )['results'] AS RESULTS;
```

You should see search results limited to support transcripts from North America. If you double-click on the result record, the results will appear in a box as shown below.

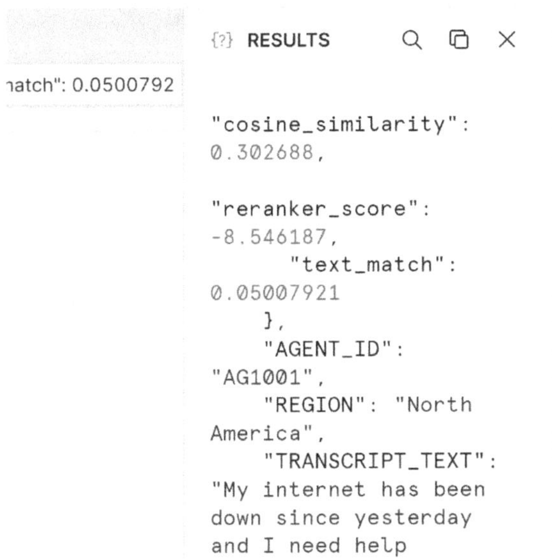

Figure 11.18 – Cortex search limited result set

7. Finally, try a search phrase that does not exactly match the wording in the table. To do so, run the following SQL:

```
SELECT PARSE_JSON(
  SNOWFLAKE.CORTEX.SEARCH_PREVIEW(
    'C11_R3.PUBLIC.TRANSCRIPT_SEARCH_SERVICE',
```

```
      '{
        "query": "billing problem",
        "columns": [
          "TRANSCRIPT_TEXT",
          "REGION",
          "AGENT_ID"
        ],
        "limit": 3
      }'
    )
  )['results'] AS RESULTS;
```

You should see the result related to the customer being overcharged, even though the query text does not exactly match the wording in the transcript. This demonstrates how Cortex Search can identify relevant results using semantic meaning in addition to keyword matching.

```
        "text_match":
0.021752777
      },
      "AGENT_ID":
"AG1002",
      "REGION": "Europe",
      "TRANSCRIPT_TEXT":
"I was overcharged on
my last bill and need
someone to explain the
additional fees."
    },
    {
      "@scores": {
```

Figure 11.19 – Cortex search fuzzy match

How it works...

In this recipe, you created a Cortex Search service over text data stored in a Snowflake table. The service indexed the `TRANSCRIPT_TEXT` column and made it searchable using semantic and keyword-based retrieval.

The `CREATE CORTEX SEARCH SERVICE` statement defines the source data, searchable text column, attributes, warehouse, target lag, and embedding model. Snowflake uses this definition to prepare the data for search and maintain the service over time.

The ON clause identifies the text column that users will search. The ATTRIBUTES clause identifies additional columns that can be returned with search results or used as filters. In this recipe, REGION and AGENT_ID were included as attributes so that the returned results could provide context and support filtering.

The TARGET_LAG setting controls how fresh the Cortex Search service should remain relative to the underlying table. Snowflake uses the specified warehouse to build and refresh the service. For larger datasets, creating or refreshing the service may take longer and may require careful warehouse sizing.

The SEARCH_PREVIEW function allows you to test the service from SQL. It accepts the service name and a JSON request containing the search query, returned columns, filters, and result limit. The function returns JSON, which you parse using PARSE_JSON to display the results.

Cortex Search is useful when users need to retrieve relevant text based on meaning, not only exact keyword matches. This makes it especially useful for enterprise search and retrieval-augmented generation scenarios where the search results provide context for downstream AI workflows.

There's more...

Cortex Search can also be used as part of larger AI application patterns, including RAG, where relevant search results are provided as context to a large language model. To learn more about Cortex Search and available configuration options, refer to the official Snowflake documentation at https://docs.snowflake.com/en/user-guide/snowflake-cortex/cortex-search/cortex-search-overview.

Using Snowflake Coco to generate customer insights

In this recipe, you will explore how Snowflake Coco (formerly known as Cortex Code) can be used to generate a complete Snowflake solution using natural language prompts. Rather than writing SQL step by step, you will describe the desired outcome and allow Snowflake Coco to generate the necessary objects, queries, and logic to implement the solution.

Snowflake Coco enables a more interactive development workflow by helping translate intent into executable SQL. In this example, you will use Snowflake Coco to create a customer insight solution that sources data from Snowflake sample datasets, performs aggregation and ranking, and generates AI-driven insights. This demonstrates how Snowflake Coco can help assemble multiple Snowflake capabilities into a working solution while still requiring you to review and validate the generated logic.

Getting ready

You will need to be connected to your Snowflake instance via Snowsight to execute this recipe.

You will also need access to a Snowflake account with Snowflake Coco enabled. Snowflake Coco is also available through a CLI for integration into local development workflows. In this recipe, you will use the Snowsight interface.

How to do it...

In this recipe, you will use Snowflake Coco to generate a complete Snowflake solution using natural language prompts. Rather than writing SQL manually, you will describe the desired outcome and iteratively refine the generated solution.

1. In Snowsight, open Snowflake Coco by selecting the star-like icon located on the right-hand side of the interface. This opens the Snowflake Coco panel, as shown in the following figure.

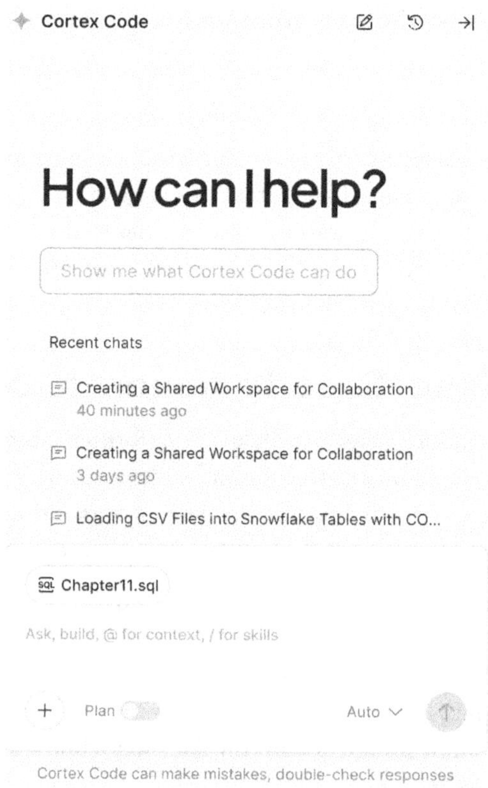

Figure 11.20 – Snowflake Coco panel

Once opened, you can begin interacting with Snowflake Coco using natural language prompts.

> **Note**
>
> Snowflake Coco is an interactive assistant, and the experience may vary between users. During this recipe, Snowflake Coco may prompt you to confirm actions, execute generated SQL, or provide additional input.

If prompted, review the suggestions and proceed by accepting the recommended actions to continue through the recipe.

2. In the Snowflake Coco prompt area, enter the following:

```
"Create the Snowflake SQL needed to set up a database and schema for a
chapter 11 Cortex Code recipe. Use a database named C11_R4 and the PUBLIC
schema."
```

Submit the prompt.

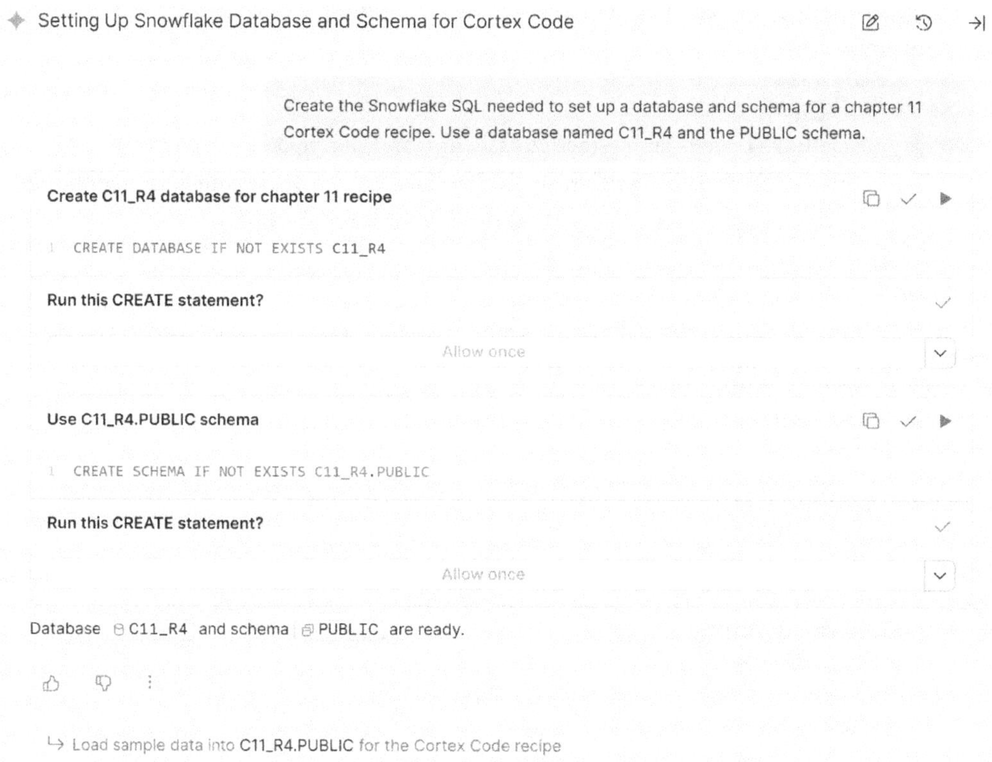

Figure 11.21 – Snowflake Coco create working environment

3. Next, describe the outcome you want to achieve. To keep the query efficient, you will limit the amount of data processed. In the Snowflake Coco prompt area, enter the following:

```
"Create a Snowflake solution that identifies the top 10 customers by total
sales using Snowflake sample data. Use data from
SNOWFLAKE_SAMPLE_DATA.TPCDS_SF10.CUSTOMER and STORE_SALES. Limit the source
dataset to approximately 1000 sales rows so the query runs quickly. Store
the results in a table in the C11_R4.PUBLIC schema. Include customer ID,
customer name, total sales, sales rank, and a short AI-generated business
insight for each customer."
```

In this prompt, you described the desired outcome at a business level rather than specifying the technical implementation. You asked Snowflake Coco to:

- Identify the top 10 customers by total sales across all data

- Use the Snowflake Coco prompt with the Snowflake sample dataset (`TPCDS_SF10`) to ensure efficient query execution
- Limit the dataset to approximately 1,000 rows to keep the query fast and manageable
- Store the results in a table in the `C11_R4.PUBLIC` schema
- Calculate total sales and rank customers globally
- Generate a short AI-based business insight for each customer

By defining the goal in this way, Snowflake Coco determines how to implement the solution using Snowflake features such as joins, aggregation, ranking, and AI functions, while you focus on describing the desired outcome.

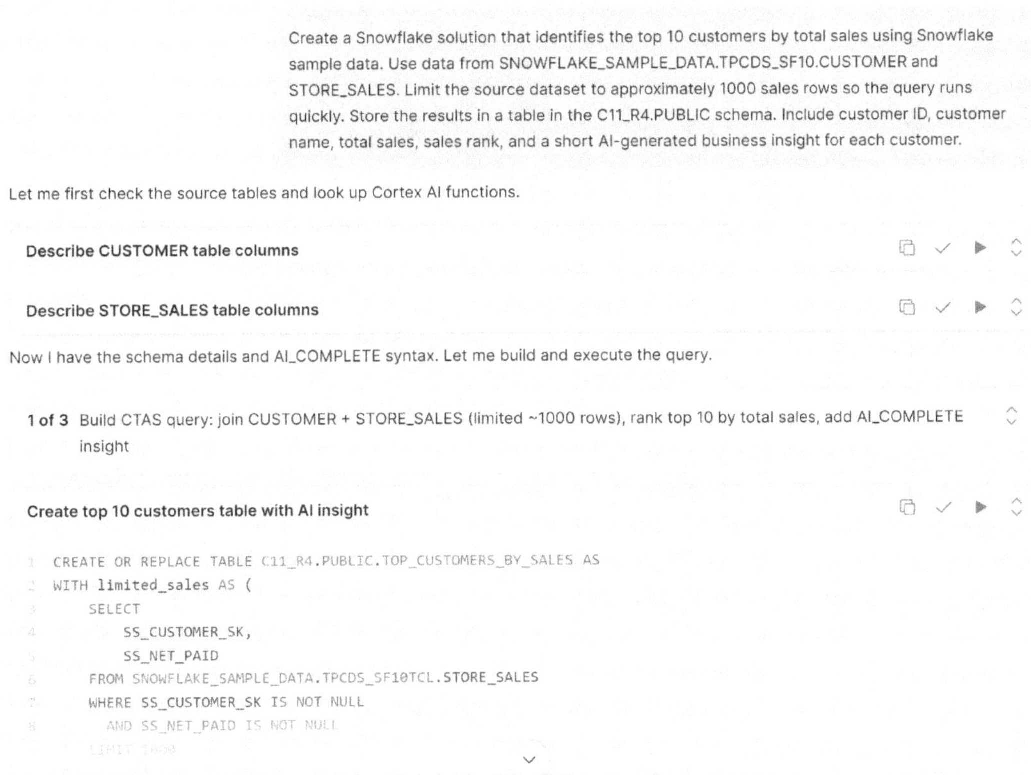

Figure 11.22 – Snowflake Coco generating business solution

4. You can now ask Snowflake Coco to retrieve the results. In the Snowflake Coco prompt area, enter the following and submit the prompt.

```
"Show the results of the table that was just created, ordered by total
sales descending."
```

Snowflake Coco will generate and execute a query to display the results. You should see the top customers by total sales along with ranking and AI-generated insights.

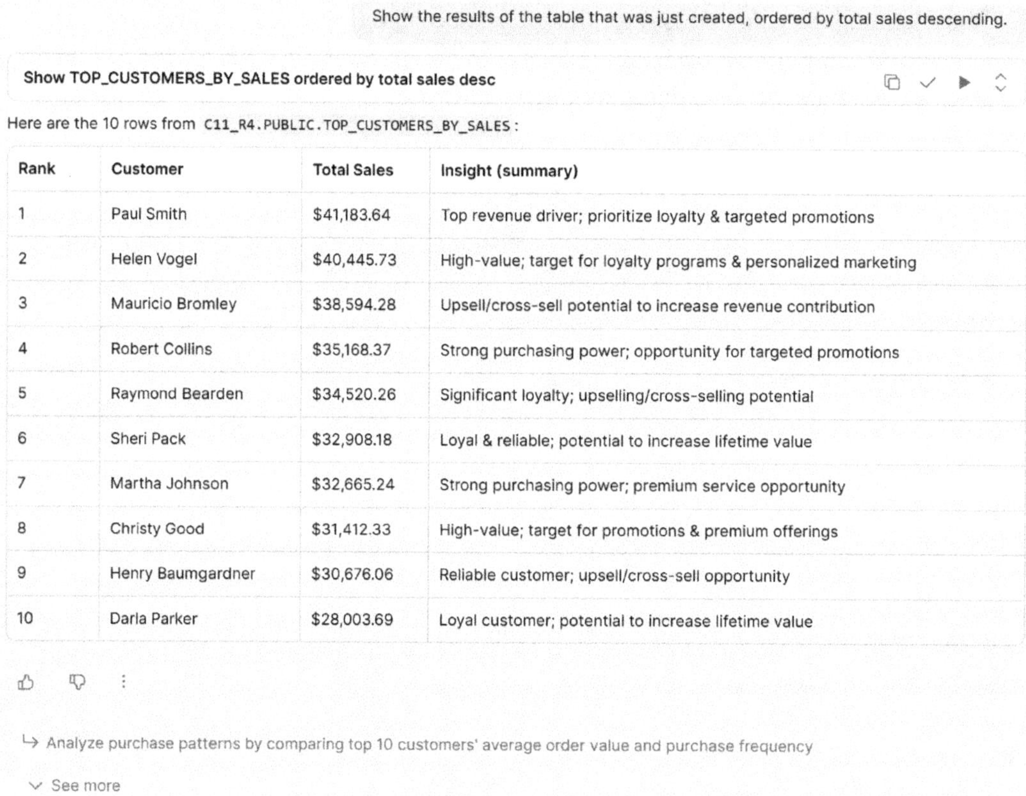

Rank	Customer	Total Sales	Insight (summary)
1	Paul Smith	$41,183.64	Top revenue driver; prioritize loyalty & targeted promotions
2	Helen Vogel	$40,445.73	High-value; target for loyalty programs & personalized marketing
3	Mauricio Bromley	$38,594.28	Upsell/cross-sell potential to increase revenue contribution
4	Robert Collins	$35,168.37	Strong purchasing power; opportunity for targeted promotions
5	Raymond Bearden	$34,520.26	Significant loyalty; upselling/cross-selling potential
6	Sheri Pack	$32,908.18	Loyal & reliable; potential to increase lifetime value
7	Martha Johnson	$32,665.24	Strong purchasing power; premium service opportunity
8	Christy Good	$31,412.33	High-value; target for promotions & premium offerings
9	Henry Baumgardner	$30,676.06	Reliable customer; upsell/cross-sell opportunity
10	Darla Parker	$28,003.69	Loyal customer; potential to increase lifetime value

Figure 11.23 – Snowflake Coco display results

5. Now ask Snowflake Coco to explain the solution it generated. In the Snowflake Coco prompt area, enter the following and submit the prompt:

```
"Explain how this solution works, including how total sales are calculated,
how customers are ranked, and how the AI-generated insight is created."
```

Snowflake Coco will return an explanation of the logic used in the solution.

Figure 11.24 – Snowflake Coco how solution works

In just a few prompts, you created a complete Snowflake solution that combines data sourcing, transformation, ranking, and AI-generated insights.

How it works...

In this recipe, you used Snowflake Coco to generate and execute a complete Snowflake solution using natural language prompts. Rather than manually writing SQL, you described the desired outcome and allowed Snowflake Coco to translate that intent into executable SQL statements.

Snowflake Coco leverages LLMs to interpret your prompts and generate SQL based on the current worksheet context, including the selected database, schema, and available objects. In this example, Snowflake Coco generated SQL to create the working environment, source data from the Snowflake sample dataset, calculate total sales, rank customers, and produce an AI-generated insight column.

The generated solution combines several Snowflake capabilities. It performs joins across multiple tables, aggregates sales data, and uses windowing functions to rank customers. It also incorporates a Cortex AI function to generate a short business insight for each result. These are the same concepts covered throughout the book, but in this case, they were assembled through natural language rather than written manually.

Snowflake Coco operates in an interactive manner. It may prompt for confirmation, suggest refinements, or generate multiple steps to complete a request. Once SQL is generated, it is executed within Snowflake, and the results are returned directly in the worksheet. This allows you to iteratively refine your solution by adjusting prompts and reviewing the output.

It is important to note that while Snowflake Coco can accelerate development, the generated SQL should always be reviewed. Understanding how joins, aggregations, and ranking logic work is essential for validating correctness, performance, and governance.

By combining natural language prompts with SQL generation, Snowflake Coco enables a new development workflow. Instead of focusing solely on writing code, you focus on defining the desired outcome, while Snowflake assists in generating and executing the solution.

There's more...

Snowflake Coco provides a powerful new way to interact with Snowflake by allowing you to describe what you want to accomplish and have the platform assist in generating the solution. As demonstrated in this recipe, you can move from a high-level idea to a working implementation using only a few natural language prompts.

The capabilities of Snowflake—data ingestion, transformation, analytics, governance, and now AI—are all accessible through this approach. Rather than navigating each feature individually, you can leverage Snowflake Coco to help assemble these capabilities into complete solutions more efficiently.

While this recipe focused on a specific use case, Snowflake Coco can be applied to a wide range of scenarios, including building pipelines, creating data models, generating analytical queries, and incorporating AI-driven insights. As Snowflake continues to evolve, these capabilities will expand, making it even easier to develop and refine data solutions.

As a next step, consider revisiting earlier recipes in this book and exploring how Snowflake Coco can be used to generate or enhance those solutions. Try describing the desired outcome using natural language and compare the generated SQL to the manual implementations. This exercise can help reinforce your understanding while demonstrating how Snowflake Coco can accelerate your development workflow.

The more you experiment with Snowflake Coco, the more you will discover how quickly ideas can be translated into working solutions within Snowflake.

Get this book's PDF version and more

Scan the QR code (or go to packtpub.com/unlock). Search for this book by name, confirm the edition, and then follow the steps on the page.

UNLOCK NOW

Note: Keep your invoice handy. Purchases made directly from Packt don't require an invoice.

12

Unlock Access to the Code Bundle and the PDF Version

Your copy of this book includes the following exclusive benefits:

Complete Code Bundle

Download the full source code for this book's examples and projects.

DRM-Free PDF Version

Download DRM-free PDF and ePub copies of this book.

7-Day Packt Library Access

Get 7-day unlimited access to 8,000+ books and videos. No credit card required.

Available for first-time Packt+ trial users only.

Next-Gen Reader Access

Read this book on Packt Reader with progress sync, dark mode and note-taking.

Follow this guide to unlock them. The process takes only a few minutes and only needs to be completed once.

Unlock this book's free benefits in three easy steps

Step 1

Have your purchase invoice ready for *step 3*. If you have a physical copy, scan it using your phone and save it as a PDF, JPG, or PNG.

For more help on finding your invoice, visit `https://www.packtpub.com/unlock-benefits/help`.

> Note
>
> **Note**: If you bought this book directly from the Packt website, no invoice is required. After *step 2*, you can access your exclusive content right away.

Step 2

Scan the QR code or go to `packtpub.com/unlock`.

On the page that opens (similar to *Figure 12.1* on desktop), search for this book by name and select the correct edition.

Figure 12.1: Packt unlock landing page on desktop

Step 3

After selecting the book, sign in to your Packt account or create one for free. Then, upload your invoice (PDF, PNG, or JPG, up to 10 MB). Follow the on-screen instructions to finish the process.

Need help?

If you get stuck and need help, visit `https://www.packtpub.com/unlock-benefits/help` for a detailed FAQ on how to find your invoice and more. This QR code will take you to the help page.

> Note
>
> **Note**: If you are still facing issues, reach out to `customercare@packt.com`.

Other Books You May Enjoy

If you enjoyed this book, you may be interested in these other books by Packt:

Data Modeling with Snowflake

Serge Gershkovich

ISBN: 978-1-83702-803-0

- Master data modeling fundamentals to get your designs right on the first attempt with time-saving benefits
- Discover Snowflake's cloud-native architecture and unique features
- Apply modeling concepts to achieve higher efficiency by leveraging Snowflake architecture
- Get to grips with modeling concepts like normalization and slowly changing dimensions (SCDs)
- Read and transform semi-structured data, including hierarchies, using pre-built recipes and examples
- Explore organizational frameworks like Data Vault and Data Mesh
- Understand the business metrics that drive scalable, cost-effective data projects

Engineering Lakehouses with Open Table Formats

Dipankar Mazumdar, Vinoth Govindarajan

ISBN: 978-1-83620-723-8

- Explore lakehouse fundamentals, such as table formats, file formats, compute engines, and catalogs
- Gain a complete understanding of data lifecycle management in lakehouses
- Learn how to systematically evaluate and choose the right lakehouse table format
- Optimize performance with sorting, clustering, and indexing techniques
- Use the open table format data with ML frameworks like TensorFlow and MLflow
- Interoperate across different table formats with Apache XTable and UniForm
- Secure your lakehouse with access controls and ensure regulatory compliance

Packt is searching for authors like you

If you're interested in becoming an author for Packt, please visit `authors.packt.com` and apply today. We have worked with thousands of developers and tech professionals, just like you, to help them share their insight with the global tech community. You can make a general application, apply for a specific hot topic that we are recruiting an author for, or submit your own idea.

Share your thoughts

Now you've finished *Snowflake Cookbook, Second Edition* we'd love to hear your thoughts! Scan the QR code below to go straight to the Amazon review page for this book and share your feedback or leave a review on the site that you purchased it from.

`https://packt.link/r/1806384779`

Your review is important to us and the tech community and will help us make sure we're delivering excellent quality content.

Index

P

Q

R

S

U

V

W

www.ingramcontent.com/pod-product-compliance
Lightning Source LLC
LaVergne TN
LVHW060018210926
848481LV00013B/3738